First Amendment Rights

—

First Amendment Rights

AN ENCYCLOPEDIA

Volume One
Traditional Issues on the First Amendment

Nancy S. Lind and Erik T. Rankin

ABC-CLIO

Santa Barbara, California • Denver, Colorado • Oxford, England

Library of Congress Cataloging-in-Publication Data

Lind, Nancy S., 1958–
    First Amendment rights : an encyclopedia / Nancy S. Lind and Erik T. Rankin.
       p. cm.
    Includes bibliographical references and index.
    ISBN 978-1-61069-212-0 (hardcopy : alk. paper) — ISBN 978-1-61069-213-7
(ebook)   1. United States. Constitution. 1st Amendment.   2. Freedom of speech—
United States.   3. Freedom of the press—United States.   4. Freedom of religion—
United States.   I. Rankin, Erik.   II. Title.
    KF4770.L56   2013
    342.7308'503—dc23   2012021801

ISBN: 978-1-61069-212-0
EISBN: 978-1-61069-213-7

17   16   15   14   13   1   2   3   4   5

This book is also available on the World Wide Web as an eBook.
Visit www.abc-clio.com for details.

ABC-CLIO, LLC
130 Cremona Drive, P.O. Box 1911
Santa Barbara, California 93116-1911

This book is printed on acid-free paper ∞

Manufactured in the United States of America

Copyright Acknowledgments

VOLUME TWO

Contents

Acknowledgments

We would like to thank the following individuals for their invaluable assistance. First and foremost, we would like to thank Danica Taylor for her strict adherence to deadlines and ability to digest large amounts of materials for us. We would like to thank Jason Hochstatter, who single-handedly prepared the bibliography for the book. Other students who provided assistance include Jonathan Gaeta, Katie Colaric, and Jacqueline Locascio, all of whom we owe a debt of gratitude.

We would be remiss if we did not also thank Denver Compton as our acquisitions editor, who answered innumerable emails and helped move us along through the process. Finally, the authors who graciously allowed reprint of their articles as well as authors who wrote original text for the book must be thanked.

Introduction

The First Amendment states, "Congress shall make no law respecting an establishment of religion, or prohibiting the free exercise thereof; or abridging the freedom of speech, or of the press; or the right of the people peaceably to assemble, and to petition the Government for a redress of grievances." Each of the tenets of the First Amendment has brought considerable controversy. Is the First Amendment "absolute" as some scholars would have us believe, or is the interpretation of it likely to change based on the political climate? Some examples from the past few years will suffice to show how the First Amendment remains in the foreground of the U.S. judicial system.

A 17,000-member-strong interest group, Freedom from Religion Foundation, has filed complaints to school districts in Alabama permitting student-led prayers that use the name of Jesus during high school football games on school property. They contend that religion has no place in public high schools and these prayers violate the students' rights to freedom of religion. Similarly, this foundation has contacted the chief of the U.S. Forest Service and asked to have a Catholic shrine of Jesus sitting on top of Big Mountain in Whitefish, Montana, removed. The foundation sees the statue as a longstanding violation of the First Amendment's prohibition against establishment of a religion.

On October 17, 2011, the U.S. Supreme Court agreed to hear a First Amendment case about whether it is appropriate for Congress to pass laws making it a crime to lie about military decorations. At issue is whether statements known to be false by the speaker are entitled to First Amendment protections. Similarly, during its 2011 term, the Court did not rule on whether the Federal Communications Commission (FCC) violated First Amendment freedom of speech standards when the FCC regulates profanity and nudity on the airwaves.

Another 21st-century issue is whether freedom of the press has been restricted during times of war. In the war in Afghanistan, for example, there are prohibitions placed on the media to prevent them from entering into and reporting from war zones. The question is whether there is a compelling state interest to justify the restriction of the presses' First Amendment rights.

Another critical issue relates to whether allowing citizens with a cell phone or video camera to film law enforcement officers performing their duty in public is protected by the First Amendment. On August 26, 2011, the First Circuit of the U.S. Court of Appeals in Boston ruled in *Glik v. Cunniffe et al.*[1] that allowing this action is a "basic, vital, and well-established liberty safeguarded by the First Amendment. It is firmly established that the First Amendment's aegis extends further than the text's proscription on laws 'abridging the freedom of speech, or of the press,' and encompasses a range of conduct related to the gathering and dissemination of information." The court continued, "The filming of government officials engaged in their duties in a public place, including police officers performing their responsibilities, fits comfortably within these principles. Gathering information about government officials in a form that can readily be disseminated to others serves a cardinal First Amendment interest in protecting and promoting 'the free discussion of governmental affairs.'"

One of the most unusual cases dealing with the First Amendment occurred in 2008, when a large group of people gathered in front of the U.S. Supreme Court building to protest actions in Guantanamo Bay. In question was a federal statute (40 U.S.C. § 6135) that provides: "It is unlawful to parade, stand, or move in processions or assemblages in the Supreme Court Building or grounds, or to display in the Building and grounds a flag, banner, or device designed or adapted to bring into public notice a party, organization, or movement." The protesters started on public sidewalks but spilled over to the Supreme Court plaza. Arrested protesters challenged this statute on the grounds that it violated their First Amendment rights of assembly. Courts, however, have continued to hold that the Supreme Court and its structures have special status when it comes to the First Amendment. Appellants argued that the statute has been unduly interpreted to prohibit nondisruptive forms of expression such as picketing and leafleting in the Supreme Court building or grounds. According to the Washington, D.C., Court of Appeals in 2011, in *Kinane v. United States,* "This court has already resolved the issues raised in appellants' contentions in favor of the government, and we find no reason to deviate from our previous holdings."[2]

In late 2011, members of the various Occupy movements refused to leave public parks when required by statute to do so. They have claimed First Amendment rights to gather and assemble but they have failed to distinguish gathering from squatting. Protesters in the Occupy Trenton movement in October 2011 took their case to court arguing that police requests to remove unattended signs and to refrain from using electricity in public parks is a direct violation of their First Amendment rights of assembly and speech.

The commonality among all these cases is that they involve actions of individuals against actions of the state. This is critical in that the First Amendment only protects individuals from state action, not private.

It is interesting that many media outlets champion the Roberts Court as a defender of free speech. The *New York Times,* for example, proclaimed in 2011 that the First Amendment is a "signature product" of the Roberts Court.[3] Monica Youn of the New York School of Law reports that the data demonstrate otherwise. She notes,

> In its first five years, from 2006 until 2011, the Roberts Court granted certiorari in 29 cases in which a free speech violation was claimed (including the speech, press, assembly, and association guarantees). In these cases, the Court held that that a free speech violation existed in 10 of the cases, and that no free speech violation had been demonstrated in 19 of these cases. Thus, simply looking at the numbers, the Roberts Court has supported a free speech claim in 34.48 percent of argued cases.[4]

Epstein and Segal further note that between 1953 and 2004, the Supreme Court supported free speech claims in over 54 percent of its heard cases.[5]

The purpose of *First Amendment Rights: An Encyclopedia* is to provide a resource that is easily accessible as a reference, yet is more than just a list of names and dates. The chapters' authors were selected on the basis of their research and scholarship within the issue examined and writing for a broad-based audience. In Volume 1, we have reprinted chapters that provide an overview of approaches to the First Amendment as well as chapters that examine key historical controversies. In Volume 2, we update the materials by providing primarily post-2008 cases that examine the application of the First Amendment by the Roberts Court and explicate recent challenges provided by such items as new technology and its impact on the First Amendment. Each volume can be read independent of the other.

Volume 1 highlights the traditional issues embodied within the First Amendment. In Chapter 1, Lenz discusses the role the Court has played in resolving the absolutist language of the Constitution that deals with free expression. Even though absolutist language is used in the Constitution, the courts have rejected the literal meaning of the words and have imposed restrictions. Freedom of religion, speech, and press are all components of the First Amendment that have required Supreme Court rulings to clarify limitations on free expression. The "clear and present danger" test, the harm principle, and the fundamental right analysis are some of the tools that the Court uses when deciding freedom of expression cases.

In Chapter 2, Renstrom provides an overview of a variety of factors contributing to the First Amendment including freedom of religion, freedom of speech, and freedom of the press. The author discusses one critical question that arises when dealing with issues of religion: How much contact is the government allowed to have with religious groups short of designation of a state church? A major factor in deciding freedom of religion cases is the holding that the Free Exercise Clause protects religious belief but not necessarily religious conduct. Regarding freedom of speech, some actions may be regulated if they constitute a "clear and present danger." Actions, such as parades and protests, are viewed as a type of speech. Two major issues that would affect freedom of the press cases would be press that has the potential to threaten national security and libelous press. It is critical that the Court decide when government intervention might be justified in these types of cases.

In Chapter 3, Walker discusses atypical issues regarding the First Amendment, one being the claim by some women that pornography should be censored because it violates the rights of women. A law that would have prohibited pornography on this basis was declared unconstitutional by the Seventh Circuit Court of Appeals because it established an "approved" view of women and female sexuality. Some women argue that prohibiting pornography actually is detrimental to women and that it represents a content-based censorship. Other content-based censorships discussed in the chapter are academic freedom and scientific research, including stem-cell research and cloning.

In Chapter 4, Bresler discusses freedom of association and how the conservative Rehnquist Court worked to more fully protect this right. The main focus of the chapter is the *Boy Scouts of America v. Dale* case, which involved Dale being denied the ability to become a leader within the organization because he was a homosexual. The Boy Scouts of America (BSA) claimed that homosexuality violated their moral code and that they should be protected under freedom of association, while Dale argued that freedom of association did not grant the BSA the right to select leaders in defiance of a state civil rights law. By a 5–4 vote the Court ruled in favor of the BSA. The author notes that the future of the strength of this freedom will depend on whether the Court becomes more egalitarian or libertarian, and that the Court will have to refine its doctrine to match 21st-century societal values.

In Chapter 5, Pollock focuses on freedom of speech and how it provides the foundation for each of the other liberties protected by the First Amendment. The Court's decisions have created and increasingly expansive interpretation of freedom of speech, have worked to advance "truth" in the "marketplace of ideas," and have emphasized the function of free speech in facilitating a representative democracy. The author notes that "speech" protected by the First Amendment has evolved to include symbolic speech, such as nonverbal conduct. Some of the aspects of free speech that this chapter discusses include offensive speech, speech used in campaigns, and freedom of expressive association.

Chapter 6 discusses the regulation of commercial speech, which can be defined as speech by an individual or corporation intended to make a profit, and its role within the First Amendment. Commercial speech was initially excluded from the protections of the First Amendment, but a series of Court decisions beginning in the mid-1970s gave commercial speech limited protection. Many claim that political speech is essential for the workings of a free democratic society, and that the free clash of ideas will lead to the truth. Therefore, political speech is given more protection than commercial speech, which leads to severe limitations on the protection of artistic and scientific speech, generally by the Securities and Exchange Commission (SEC). The chapter highlights the differences and effects of mandatory disclosure requirements and outright prohibitions on speech.

In Chapter 7, Cornwell works toward finding an answer to the question posed after the outburst of media coverage on the Iraq War that the American people witnessed: Did the process of embedding journalists create the illusion of a free press when, in fact, information and images were restricted and manipulated by the government to shape public opinion about the war? The United States is the only nation that provides constitutional protection to the press, although it is not absolute protection. Cornwell discusses First Amendment scholar Thomas Emerson's four values of the freedom of expression: it is central to discovering truth, it is part of the process of self-actualization, it provides a safety valve for a society as it changes over time, and it is crucial for a participatory democracy. The chapter also describes five different theories of the press and notes that the libertarian and social responsibilities models are used in the U.S. media. Cornwell notes that judicial precedent favors the idea that the government will not infringe on the liberty of the press without showing that the restriction serves a more important interest.

In Chapter 8, Cornwell describes the multiple 21st-century issues relating to freedom of the press, with a heavy emphasis on technological innovation and shifts in media regulation. The media have the ability to inflate or deflate the level of public attention an issue receives, thus engaging in agenda setting. Cornwell discusses strategic lawsuits against public participation (SLAPP) that occur when a threat of a lawsuit is enough to stop further criticism of a business, and the role of the courts in allowing or dropping these cases. An increasingly smaller number of large corporations are controlling larger and larger portions of the media, leading to a more widespread use of these lawsuits and other types of corruption.

In Chapter 9, Pollock discusses how the Establishment Clause and the Free Amendment Clause, which are meant to complement each other, sometimes conflict. A governmental action that supports free exercise can also be characterized as aiding religion. These laws were initially intended to create a wall of separation between the church and state. The more recent Court cases dealing with church–state issues have increased the kind of aid that government can give to religious schools, but generally have put more limitations on when religion can be used in school.

In Chapter 10, Pollock details Supreme Court cases related to religious exemptions from the Free Exercise Clause, which are exemptions that the government may choose to grant and exemptions that the government must grant. An example of the former type of exemption would include a tax law, which would give the legislature broad discretion in choosing whether to give exemptions to religious groups, while an example of the latter would be if the exemption was created exclusively for religion. The chapter discusses the state and federal implications of the Religious Freedom Restoration Act and the Religious Land Use and Institutionalized Persons Act. Recent Court cases have dealt with the Free Exercise Clause in conjunction with the Freedom of Speech Clause.

The volume ends with case briefs from the earliest decisions on the First Amendment and ending with cases decided in 2008.

Volume 2 highlights contemporary challenges to the First Amendment. It updates all First Amendment issues since 2008. In Chapter 1, McClure analyzes how the First Amendment has fared during the first six terms of the Roberts Court. Most of the cases decided during this period were centered on free expression with the Court deciding to expand free speech rights in some areas and reject further expansion in others. The Court expanded the rights of free speech in the areas of tort liability, minors' access to offensive material, depictions of animal cruelty, commercial speech, and campaign finance as political speech. At the same time, it allowed state or federal restrictions for speech affecting national security, involving student expression off campus, by public employees, for student recruitment, by unions, for candidate nominations, and for mandated disclosures. Overall, the Roberts Court has become more of a defender of First Amendment rights than many expected, but it has not yet become the most protective First Amendment Court in history, as claimed by others. However, decisions in a couple of key First Amendment cases heard during the seventh term may give a good indication of whether the Court is going to move more to one side than the other.

In Chapter 2, DiMaggio discusses the Julian Assange WikiLeaks controversy and tackles the question of whether the First Amendment covers the disclosure of confidential government information. WikiLeaks—established in 2006—serves the main goal of introducing American citizens to important, political news that they otherwise would not be made aware of; however, with seemingly good intentions in mind, WikiLeaks has faced scrutiny by the U.S. government and citizens for leaking military video footage and government documents that were not meant for citizen viewing because they are a "matter of national security." No court decision has been made yet and it has not yet been determined if the Espionage Act and other efforts to punish WikiLeaks and protect the government from future leaks are currently applicable.

Proving to be a popular form of communication in the 21st century, social media (Web 2.0) has impacted our lives via Facebook, Twitter, and so forth. With the popularity of these sites, questions have emerged about where social media fits in with the First Amendment. This issue has been taken to the courts on multiple occasions and still remains a controversial issue today. These cases have revolved around social networking companies, public employees, students, and much more; therefore, the scope of social media's relationship with First Amendment concerns is vast. In Chapter 3, Kahl discusses how each First Amendment right coincides with social media cases, including questions of the applicability of shield laws, anonymously/pseudonymous sharing of information, and so on.

In Chapter 4, Cannon discusses the issue of "sexting"—the sending of nude, semi-nude, sexual pictures via cell phones—in relation to the First Amendment. Sexting has become a new phenomenon with the emergence of camera phones and is oftentimes a trend among teenagers. An alarming example of the implications of sexting is the existence of what the authors call "sextortion," the blackmailing of minors by predators that is most often used by sexual offenders as a means of getting teens to send explicit photos of themselves via the Internet. As the saying goes, "technology progresses faster than the law." For this reason, the legality of sexting is still a controversial debate in America and as the authors point out, many court cases have risen out of this issue. Cannon conclusively argues that although sexting can have harmful consequences, minors that "sext" should not be faced with the same charges as sexual offenders and should be subject to misdemeanor, as opposed to felony, charges.

In Chapter 5, Goldman addresses the difficult issues raised when students' First Amendment rights clash with schools' operational needs and custodial responsibilities. It is a unique chapter in its focus on student rights.

In Chapter 6, Wenkart discusses some of the important legal provisions bearing on the establishment of religion and its free exercise. While most of his examples are drawn from California, they are similar to the decisions in other states.

Similar to modern television shows, the development of video games in the 21st century has initiated controversy over their use of violence and offensive language. Rousse considers in Chapter 7 whether electronic game companies are protected under the First Amendment.

Historically, the courts have been tough on video game companies in an effort to monitor and regulate video game production, distribution, content, and other relevant issues. As of 2011, however, the Supreme Court ruled that video game companies are protected under the First Amendment like other corporations.

In Chapter 8, McIntosh discusses freedom of speech in the market and within commercial advertising. As we progress as a consumer-oriented society, the impact of commercial advertising on our daily lives continues to increase significantly. Examples of this can be seen in the establishment of radio networks, television networks, and computer networks. With the growing strength and influence of large corporations and marketing firms on society, these groups have utilized freedom of speech and have fought to have the same First Amendment rights as individual citizens.

In Chapter 9, Zompetti et al. explore the dynamic tension between public safety and the collective First Amendment right of assembly. They trace the historical and legal implications of the First Amendment's relevance to social activism, and look at the recent Occupy Wall Street movement as a case study for viewing the safety/

speech dialectic. In the end, they argue that the peaceable assembly protection of the First Amendment is vital for the protection of activist voices, while also providing a legal framework to protect society as a whole.

In Chapter 10, Rotunda summarizes *Citizens United v. Federal Election Commission* and discusses efforts that have been made by citizens to fight this case's ruling. He explains that *Citizens United* came in response to the organization Citizen United's attempt to release *Hillary, The Movie* close to the 2010 election. The organization intended to use this documentary as a means to hinder Clinton's success in the election. Subsequently, this case's primary purpose was to address the issue of whether U.S. corporations and entities should have the same First Amendment rights as American people. If so, then these entities would have the right to contribute to political campaigns. In addition to discussing the facts of this case, Rotunda also discusses its consequences.

In Chapter 11, Ripken discusses corporations' First Amendment rights post-*Citizens United.* In *Citizens United,* the Supreme Court ruled that corporations have the same First Amendment rights as individuals and therefore, have the right to spend their money for campaign purposes. Overall, this ruling resulted in citizen outrage across America. In addition to discussing citizens' responses to *Citizens United,* this chapter also discusses how corporations can legally act as individuals even though the Supreme Court never stated that corporations *are* people.

In Chapter 12, Brownstein and Amar discuss the issue of harassment and freedom of speech at funeral services (most often of military personnel). They address the question of whether freedom of speech can be monitored and regulated at funerals so that freedom of speech still exists for protestors but mourners are not victimized or harassed. The authors attribute the multiple cases to the above research question. They also argue that funerals are a time of vulnerability for mourners and, therefore, these people should not be exposed to hurtful statements that are currently protected under the First Amendment. They conclude by asking the question of whether funeral protestors should be held subject to an intentional infliction of emotional distress tort.

In Chapter 13, Volokh addresses the issue of the applicability of the Religious-Exemption Law to Muslims. The Religious-Exemption Law provides employees with workplace exemptions that support religious beliefs. Volokh mentions Muslim policewomen's desires to wear Muslim headdresses at work as an example of how religious exemption pertains to Muslim workers.

Supporting the Supreme Court's decision that religious exemption is just as pertinent and applicable to Muslims as other religious persons, Volokh argues that those claiming the need for a religious exemption often are and should be supported by the courts if their request is sincere and does not interfere with their ability to work effectively.

The final chapter by Lind and Rankin addresses the highly politicized and controversial issues centered on the relationship between insurance payments for contraceptives and whether those mandated payments violate the religious clauses of the First Amendment.

We hope you learn more about our cherished First Amendment freedoms challenged throughout U.S. history and are inspired to research more on the First Amendment.

Notes

1. *Glik v. Cunniffe et al.,* 10-1764. U.S. Court of Appeals, First Circuit.

2. *Kinane v. United States*, 12 A.3d 23 (2011).

3. Adam Liptak, "A Significant Term, With Bigger Cases Ahead," *New York Times*, June 28, 2011.

4. Monica Youn, "The Roberts Court's Free Speech Double Standard," American Constitution Society Blog, http://www.acslaw.org/acsblog/all/monica-youn (accessed January 15, 2012).

5. Lee Epstein and Jeffrey Segal, "Trumping the First Amendment," *Journal of Law and Policy* 21, no. 81 (2006).

I

First Amendment Approaches

| Timothy O. Lenz

Freedom of expression is an essential element of democracy. The political importance of free expression is reflected in the fact that it is addressed in the first of the ten amendments constituting the Bill of Rights, and it is guaranteed in absolutist language. The First Amendment provides that Congress shall make no law "respecting an establishment of religion, or prohibiting the free exercise thereof; or abridging the freedom of speech, or of the press." The First Amendment's **absolutist language** is unusual compared to freedom of expression in most constitutional democracies, which typically provide for qualified or conditional freedom of expression. In most modern constitutions, the declaration of the right to freedom of religion, speech, and press is accompanied by explicit statements limiting freedom of expression. The absolutist language of the First Amendment is problematic insofar as it is hard to reconcile with the fact that there are restrictions of free expression in the United States. Judges, members of Congress, and other government officials have never read the First Amendment literally to mean there can be no law restricting freedom of expression. In the United States, freedom of expression is actually a complex system of thinking about individual freedom and government control[1] that includes the First Amendment, statutory law, administrative regulations, and an extensive body of case law interpreting the Constitution. Understanding the First Amendment requires examining (1) the different areas of First Amendment jurisprudence (freedom of religion, speech, and press) and (2) the methods, doctrines, and tests that judges have used to determine the meaning of the words in the First Amendment.

The need for judicial interpretation of the text of the Constitution is usually attributed to the fact that someone has to provide concrete meaning for ambiguous phrases such as "unreasonable search and seizure," "cruel and unusual punishment," and "due process of law." The First Amendment requires interpretation not because of ambiguity but because of clarity. The absolutist language prohibiting Congress from making any law restricting freedom of expression is the primary reason why the First Amendment is not read literally to mean what it says. Instead, there are various approaches to determining what kinds of expression are not protected by the First Amendment and therefore can be prohibited, what kinds of expression are protected and therefore cannot be restricted, and what kinds of expression are protected but can nonetheless be regulated.

The Supreme Court rejected the literal or plain meaning of the words approach in its earliest First Amendment cases. In *Reynolds v. United States* (1878),[2] Mormons argued that a federal statute providing that bigamy "shall be punished by a fine of not more than $500, and by imprisonment of not more than five years," was unconstitutional because it restricted their religious freedom to practice polygamy. The Court upheld the law by concluding that the Framers never intended to protect polygamy, which all Western nations considered "odious," and which England considered an offense against society. This case established the principle that Congress could restrict certain religious practices despite the First Amendment language providing that Congress shall make no law restricting the free exercise of religion. The *Reynolds* majority,[3] written by Justice Morrison Waite, provided an approach that continues to be used today in First Amendment cases: "Laws are made for the government of actions, and while they cannot interfere with religious belief and opinions, they may with practices." The distinction between religious beliefs, which cannot be restricted, and religious practices, which can be restricted, became the conceptual framework for determining the boundaries of expression generally. For example, the distinction between thought, which cannot be restricted, and action, which can be restricted, is essential for understanding freedom of speech.

Freedom of Speech

The Court's first important free speech cases arose during the World War I era. In *Schenck v. United States* (1919), Justice Oliver Wendell Holmes, Jr., wrote for a unanimous Court upholding the Espionage Act of 1917 prosecution of individuals who opposed U.S. participation in World War I and urged men eligible for the military draft to oppose conscription. Holmes asserted that not even the strongest advocate of freedom of expression would allow an individual to falsely shout fire in a crowded theater and cause a panic. The fire analogy is still widely used as an argument against reading the First Amendment literally to mean absolute freedom of expression. In his dissenting opinion in the Pentagon Papers case (*New York Times v. United States*, 1971),[4] where the government tried to prevent a newspaper from publishing a study of Vietnam War decision making, Chief Justice Warren E. Burger cited the Holmes fire analogy to support the argument that the government can restrict freedom of the press because the First Amendment does not give newspapers an absolute right to publish. The *Schenck* Court reasoned that the First Amendment does not protect words that create a "**clear and present danger**" that they will bring about "substantive evils" that Congress has a right to prevent, such as harming the war effort. Consequently, the government does not have to wait until political speech actually undermines its policies, creates public disorder, promotes imminent lawlessness, or foments revolution.

The logic of the clear and present danger test allowed the government to act only when there was a cognizable (clear) and proximate (imminent) threat. In *Abrams v. United States* (1919),[5] Holmes dissented from a majority opinion, written by Justice John Hessin Clarke, upholding the Sedition Act of 1918 prosecutions of war critics because he thought the clear and present danger test was being applied to allow the government to punish speech that might be harmful or merely had a "**bad tendency**." Holmes's dissent advocated a more libertarian reading of the First Amendment, one that was based on a free-market model of freedom of expression. The market model assumes that "the ultimate good desired is better reached by free trade in ideas." It also asserts "the best test of truth is the power of the thought to get itself accepted in the competition of the market." The market is a culturally powerful concept in a nation committed to the ideals of democratic capitalism, and the logic of the free marketplace of goods has been applied to the free marketplace of ideas, where it is assumed that individual choice prevails unless the government has a good reason for intervening for or against ideas.

Beginning in the 1920s, on a case-by-case basis, the Court expanded the scope of freedom of expression by nationalizing the First Amendment, applying the First Amendment to state and local government officials as well as Congress. But during the World War II and Cold War eras, the Court used the distinction between thought and action to uphold national and state laws that restricted freedom of speech to maintain public order or protect national security. However, the Court did become more protective of civil liberties by requiring the government to meet the burden of proof to justify laws that restricted freedom of speech, press, or religion. In effect, the Court applied the **harm principle** to civil liberties cases. As articulated by Thomas Jefferson and the English political philosopher John Stuart Mill, the harm principle provides that government power can only be used to protect an individual from being harmed by another person, and laws cannot be legitimately used primarily or exclusively to regulate morality or to protect individuals from harming themselves.

The concept of fighting words illustrates how the harm principle has been applied to cases. In *Chaplinsky v. New Hampshire* (1942),[6] Justice Frank Murphy, writing for the majority, held that a person could be arrested for creating a public disturbance by calling the arresting police officer "a Goddamned racketeer" and a "damned Fascist" because the First Amendment did not protect fighting words. The Court reasoned that some words, including "the lewd and the obscene, the profane, the libelous, and the insulting or 'fighting words,'" have little or no expressive value and "by their very utterance inflict injury or tend to incite an immediate breach of the peace." The government's power to maintain social order justifies laws that prohibit insults, which make the blood boil and provoke immediate physical retaliation.

During the 1950s and 1960s, the liberal justices on the Warren Court used the harm principle as a libertarian doctrine that limited traditional government power to restrict freedom of religion, speech, and press. The harm principle effectively undermined the traditional police power to legislate morality by requiring the government to provide evidence that a law that restricted freedom of expression had a secular legislative purpose such as the prevention of physical or social harm.

Beginning in the 1940s, justices who believed that the clear and present danger test was being used to rationalize government restrictions on free speech began to search for alternative approaches. Justice John M. Harlan II advocated a balancing approach in which an individual's claimed right to free speech was balanced against the government-claimed power to limit it. Although balancing seems like a reasonable, even wise, approach to deciding civil liberties cases, it is controversial because balancing produces rulings that are not based on clearly identified principles or are not generally applicable because they are case-specific decisions. Balancing also is a method that has an important substantive impact on the outcome of civil liberties cases. The practical effect of weighing an (often unpopular) individual's rights against the (usually popular) majority's, community's, society's, or government's interests in decency, morality, national security, or good moral order is that First Amendment rights are tried in the court of popular opinion.

The fear that individual rights would be balanced away produced two alternative approaches to the First Amendment. The first approach was to return to a literal-absolutist reading of the First Amendment. Justice Hugo L. Black, who served from 1937 to 1971, was the Court's foremost advocate of a literal-absolutist reading of the First Amendment as prohibiting any law restricting freedom of speech. But Black achieved this clear, simple rule for reading the First Amendment to mean there could be no laws restricting freedom of speech by narrowly defining speech. Black maintained that the First Amendment protected only political speech, not commercial speech such as advertising, and only pure speech, not symbolic speech or expressive conduct such as demonstrations, nude dancing, flag burning, or campaign contributions. Black's approach has never been accepted by a majority of the Court, which considers expressive conduct protected by the First Amendment but subject to a variety of time, place, and manner restrictions. There is no absolute First Amendment right to demonstrate. In many cases the question is not always whether expression is protected by the First Amendment, but how much protection the Constitution provides.

The second approach, which remains the dominant approach of the Court, is fundamental rights analysis. Fundamental rights analysis is based on the distinction between ordinary interests, which democracies can determine by majoritarian political processes, and basic, preferred, or fundamental rights, which constitutional democracies protect from majoritarian politics. Fundamental rights, such as freedom of expression, can be restricted only if the government demonstrates that it has a compelling interest in doing so and there is no less restrictive means to achieve that compelling end. The fundamental rights approach has generally been libertarian insofar as it has put the burden of proof on the government to provide evidence of the need to restrict fundamental rights.

The widespread acceptance of fundamental rights analysis has not solved the problem of determining the boundaries of free speech. The Court has recognized that advertising is a kind of commercial speech with some First Amendment protection, but there remains controversy about how much protection is provided for advertising for goods (e.g., tobacco or alcohol) or services. And in recent years the Court's acceptance of campaign contributions as a form of political speech has raised questions about the constitutionality of campaign finance laws.

The political correctness movement has also been controversial. The conservatives on the Court have been most skeptical of the constitutionality of speech codes and hate crime laws. In *RAV v. City of St. Paul* (1992),[7] the Court struck down a city ordinance that made it a crime to put on public or private property a burning cross, swastika, or other symbol likely to arouse "anger, alarm, or resentment in others on the basis of race, color, creed, religion, or gender." Justice Antonin Scalia's majority opinion concluded that the hate crime ordinance violated the judicial doctrine of content neutrality, which requires the government to remain neutral toward the ideas it regulates, because the ordinance specifically listed some hate crimes but not others. The Court considers content-based restrictions on speech "presumptively invalid." The government could justify a hate crime law where there was evidence that the ordinary criminal statutes were insufficient. But when the government regulates free speech by requiring demonstrators to obtain permits, for example, it cannot take sides by granting permits to those whose ideas it supports while denying permits to those ideas it opposes. Taking sides constitutes viewpoint discrimination. The content-neutrality doctrine does not require the government to treat all ideas as though they were equally valid, but it does limit the government's ability to regulate the marketplace of ideas by promoting certain ideas and prohibiting others.

With the notable exception of political correctness, the liberals on the Court have been more supportive of content neutrality than the conservatives on the Court, who are more skeptical of a doctrine that treats all political ideas as relatively equal without distinguishing between freedom and fascism or artistic expression and pornography. Conservatives are likely to consider content neutrality akin to value relativism. In a case, *City of Erie v. Pap's A.M.*, 2000,[8] where the majority decision, written by Justice Sandra Day O'Connor, upheld a state law prohibiting totally nude dancing, Justice Scalia's concurring opinion emphasized that the Framers intended the First Amendment to protect political expression, not nude dancing, and therefore the government could regulate nude dancing and other behavior both to protect against harm and to promote traditional moral values. Chief Justice William H. Rehnquist took a similar position in dissent in *Texas v. Johnson* (1989),[9] where the majority decision, written by Justice William J. Brennan, Jr., struck down the Texas flag desecration law that was used to convict Gregory Johnson of burning an American flag at a political demonstration during the 1984 Republican National Convention in Dallas. Rehnquist argued that the government could protect the flag, which is a unique symbol of the nation. This view is articulated even more clearly in conservative interpretations of the Establishment Clause.

Freedom of Religion

The end of the Cold War and the rise of the culture wars are reflected in the Supreme Court's agenda. Radical political speech cases have been replaced by cases raising questions about religion and values. The main freedom of religion issue has been the conflict between the wall of separation and the accommodation understandings of the Establishment Clause of the First Amendment. The liberal Warren Court Justices generally read the Establishment Clause to have created a wall of separation between church and state. The conservative Burger and Rehnquist Court Justices generally read the Establishment Clause to allow government to support religion as long as it does not officially establish a church, support a particular denomination, or inhibit a particular religion. The Court still uses the *Lemon* test, first developed in the 1971 case *Lemon v. Kurtzman*,[10] for determining whether government support violates the Establishment Clause. The *Lemon* test has three parts. First, the law must have a secular legislative purpose; its intent must be secular, not religious. Second, the law must neither advance nor inhibit religion; its results must be neutral. Third, the law cannot foster excessive entanglement of government and religion.

The justices who support the wall of separation approach generally do so because they believe that the Framers desired government neutrality between belief and nonbelief as a way to avoid the historical tendency of religious groups to use political power to establish orthodoxy and use law to compel certain religious beliefs and practices. Justice Tom C. Clark's opinion in *Abington v. Schempp*,[11] the 1963 case where the Court struck down Bible reading and recitation of the Lord's Prayer in public schools, reflects this view of the separation of church and state as a solution to the historical experience with religion as a source of political conflict. Justice Clark described the government's official position between the people and religion as "wholesome neutrality." Justice Stephen G. Breyer's opinions in cases challenging the display of the Ten Commandments on public property are based on his reading of the establishment clause as intended to avoid religious conflict as a political issue.

The Court's reading of the Free Exercise Clause of the First Amendment is informed by the distinction between belief and practice. The former is absolute; the latter is not. Religious conduct is subject to regulation[12] but because the free exercise of religion is a fundamental right, the government must have a compelling interest to restrict it. Historically, state and local governments had wide latitude to use their police powers—traditionally defined as the power to pass laws for the public health, welfare, safety, and morals—to legislate morality. The mid-twentieth-century civil rights revolutions undermined this traditional power by reading the Constitution to require that laws regulating freedom of expression have a secular legislative purpose such as the prevention of harm. There often is no bright line between moral and secular regulatory policy, but the Court does use the distinction to limit government power. The liberal justices are more willing to strike down a law whose primary purpose is the promotion of virtue or the prevention of vice, while the conservative justices have been more willing to allow the political branches of government to determine how much promotion of virtue and prevention of vice is appropriate. Conservatives generally read the Constitution to allow government to enact moral regulatory policies concerning obscenity and indecency, school prayer, abortion, patriotism, and sexual behavior.

Freedom of the Press

The passage of the Alien and Sedition Acts in 1798 is early evidence that Congress did not read the First Amendment literally to mean there could be no law restricting freedom of the press. The Sedition Act made seditious libel, defined broadly to include strong or intemperate criticism of the government, a criminal offense. Although the acts were repealed before the Supreme Court ruled on their constitutionality, the Court's First Amendment rulings allow restrictions on freedom of the press. The general rule concerning freedom of the press is that the Framers intended the First Amendment to prohibit prior restraint (or censorship) but to allow subsequent punishment for publishing certain materials, such as defamatory articles, or broadcasting certain programming, such as indecent broadcasts. The rule against prior restraint does have notable exceptions, including the protection of national security. Furthermore, unlike the print press, the broadcast media are licensed by the government. Congress has delegated to the Federal Communications Commission the authority to consider whether it is in the public interest to grant a broadcast license application or renewal. So the government does have some power to regulate the content of broadcast programming. Some press advocates have claimed that the First Amendment gives the institutional press special status as the "fourth estate," checking the "three official branches" of government (quoting Justice Potter Stewart, dissenting in *Branzburg v. Hayes*, 1972),[13] and shielding reporters from subpoenas, search warrants, and compelled grand juries, but the Court has never accepted the argument. The emergence of new electronic media, particularly the Internet, has challenged established First Amendment law.

Obscenity and Indecency

Obscenity is not protected by the First Amendment, but defining obscenity has been difficult. Until the middle of the twentieth century, the courts upheld the government's broad power to suppress obscene materials by applying an old English common-law test that defined obscenity as materials that tended to corrupt those whose minds were open to such influences. This definition was so broad that it limited adults to reading materials fit for children and the mentally depraved. Consequently, in *Roth v. United States* (1957),[14] the Court, with Justice Brennan writing for the majority, defined obscenity as material in which "the average person, applying contemporary community standards," found that the "dominant theme of the material taken as a whole" appealed to prurient interests. This definition has been modified since then, but it remains the basic framework for identifying obscenity. Indecency has been even harder to define than obscenity, and indecent materials have some First Amendment protection. When deciding whether a law regulating indecency is constitutional, the Court considers the harm that the government is trying to prevent. Congress passed the Communications Decency Act of 1996 to protect minors from harmful material on the Internet. The act, which made it a felony to knowingly transmit obscene or indecent materials to a person under 19 years old, was declared unconstitutional in *Reno v. American Civil Liberties Union* (1997),[15] because (1) the word "indecency" could be defined so broadly that it included protected materials, (2) existing filtering technology did not adequately differentiate between materials that the government could restrict and materials that adults had a right to access, and (3) there were less restrictive ways (i.e., fines rather than felony charges) to achieve the compelling government interest in protecting minors. Congress then passed the Children's Online Protection Act (1998), which addressed some of the Court's concerns by (1) subjecting individuals to fines rather than criminal prosecution and (2) providing that the use of screening devices such as a credit card was an affirmative defense for an individual subject to the act. Nevertheless, the Court struck down the law because its definition of prohibited material was still too broad, and the screening was of questionable effectiveness. Congress responded with the Children's Internet Protection Act of 2001, which required libraries receiving federal funding to use Internet filtering technology, and the Court upheld the act.

These cases illustrate how the modern Court judges laws restricting freedom of expression. The justices generally require the government to provide some empirical evidence of the need to restrict fundamental freedoms, and the justices assess the effectiveness of the means the government has chosen to achieve its ends. Consequently, today's First Amendment cases are not about first principles, such as the role of freedom of expression in a democratic society, as much as they are about the secondary rules that define the boundaries of free expression: the drawing of buffer zones around abortion clinics; Federal Communications Commission investigations of viewer complaints about broadcast indecency; or congressional debates about the effectiveness of Internet filtering technology in an age of globalization. As a result, these essentially administrative approaches to the First Amendment are likely to become even more important in defining freedom of expression.

Glossary

Absolutist language: an interpretation of the First Amendment that allows "no balancing" tests to be used.

Bad tendency test: freedom of speech does not protect any threat to the public order.

Clear and present danger: test to measure whether words have a tendency to incite a dangerous situation.

Harm principle: action can only be banned if it causes harm to another person.

Notes

1. Thomas I. Emerson, *The System of Freedom of Expression* (New York: Vintage Books, 1971).
2. *Reynolds v. United States*, 98 US 145 (1878).
3. *Schenck v. United States*, 249 US 47 (1919).
4. *New York Times Co. v. United States*, 403 US 713 (1971).
5. *Abrams v. United States*, 250 US 616 (1919).
6. *Chaplinsky v. State of New Hampshire*, 315 US 568 (1942).
7. *R.A.V. v. City of St. Paul*, 505 US 377 (1992).
8. *City of Erie v. Pap's A.M.*, 529 US 277 (2000).
9. *Texas v. Johnson*, 491 US 397 (1989).
10. *Lemon v. Kurtzman*, 403 US 602 (1971).
11. *Abington Township School District v. Schempp (consolidated with Murray v. Curlett)*, 374 US 203 (1963).
12. *Cantwell v. Connecticut*, 310 US 296 (1940).
13. *Branzburg v. Hayes*, 408 US 665 (1972).
14. *Roth v. United States*, 354 US 476 (1957).
15. *Reno v. American Civil Liberties Union*, 521 US 844 (1997).

2

Overview of the First Amendment

| Peter Renstrom

Introduction

The several provisions of the First Amendment are designed to protect the sensitive area of personal belief and opinion. The Establishment Clause forbids creation of a state church or direct governmental subsidies to churches. The more troublesome question has been how much contact is permissible short of designation of a state church.

The first significant attempt to develop standards for religious establishment came in *Everson v. Board of Education.*[1] In *Everson*, the Court upheld state legislation authorizing reimbursement of school transportation costs to parents of children attending either public or parochial schools. The Court indicated that the state ought to assume a position of "neutrality" with respect to religion, but concluded that the Establishment Clause should not prevent people from receiving general government services notwithstanding incidental benefit to institutionalized religion. So long as the student or individual citizen is the primary beneficiary of government service, the Establishment Clause is not violated. One criterion of establishment is whether an action of government has a secular purpose. The Court invalidated a state-sponsored prayer exercise for public schools in *Engel v. Vitale,*[2] on secular purpose grounds. The Court modified the establishment standard in *Lemon v. Kurtzman,*[3] as it struck down a state law authorizing public money to be used for nonpublic school expenses, including teacher salaries. The three-prong *Lemon* test held that, in addition to having a secular purpose, a government must not enact policies that advance or hinder religion as a primary effect or consequence. Furthermore, a government policy may not put church and state in an "excessively entangled" relationship. The teacher salary supplement program in *Lemon* failed the "entanglement" element. The *Lemon* test did not prohibit all forms of aid to nonpublic schools, however.

Using the "child benefit" approach, the Court upheld a state income tax deduction for all costs of elementary and secondary level children in *Mueller v. Allen.*[4] The deductions applied to expenses involved for both public and nonpublic schools. The Court ruled in *Agostini v. Felton,*[5] that public school staff could provide remedial services to students on the premises of nonpublic schools. In *Agostini* the

Court abandoned the previously held position that mere presence of public school employees on parochial school grounds created an impermissible "symbolic link between government and religion." Similarly, in *Rosenberger v. University of Virginia*,[6] the Court concluded that providing financial support to a religious student group did not convey an endorsement or indicate a preference for the particular religion. The Court reasoned that if the university provided subsidies to nonreligious groups, it must provide the same kind of support to religious groups. The Court reached a similar conclusion in *Lamb's Chapel v. Center Moriches Union Free School District*,[7] in which it ruled that public school districts could not deny access to religious groups to public school premises if other non-curriculum groups also had access to those facilities. Religious displays on public premises also presented highly sensitive establishment questions. In *Allegheny County v. American Civil Liberties Union*,[8] the Court ruled that use of religious symbols in public displays may be permitted as long as no message of endorsement or preference is communicated. Finally, the Court struck down the use of clergy at public school graduation ceremonies in *Lee v. Weisman*,[9] because school authorities had too great an influence on religious content.

The Free Exercise Clause of the First Amendment prohibits governmental interference with religious practices. Although the clause absolutely protects religious belief, conduct related to the pursuit of belief may be subject to limitation. The *Sunday Closing Law Cases*[10] permit secular regulation to encroach upon religious practice, but only in the absence of alternate means of achieving secular ends. The Warren Court added the "compelling interest" element to the free exercise standard in *Sherbert v. Verner.*[11] The Burger Court retained this standard in *Wisconsin v. Yoder*,[12] but the Rehnquist Court returned to the secular purpose test in *Employment Division v. Smith.*[13]

The Congress attempted to overturn the *Smith* decision and reinstate the more protective *Sherbert/Yoder* free exercise standard by statute. The Religious Freedom Restoration Act of 1993 was found unconstitutional by the Court, however, in *City of Boerne v. Flores*,[14] on Fourteenth Amendment grounds. Two other decisions are included in the free exercise section of this chapter. In *Gillette v. United States*,[15] the Court did not allow an exemption from the military draft process for persons asserting religion-based objection to particular wars as distinct from war generally. Finally, the Court upheld a state sales and use tax levied upon a religious organization's sale of religious materials in *Jimmy Swaggart Ministries v. Board of Equalization.*[16]

The First Amendment prohibits impairment of free speech. The basic principles for free speech cases were first considered in *Schenck v. United States*,[17] in which the Court held that expression may be regulated when the expression creates a "clear and present danger." *Gitlow v. New York*[18] modified the *Schenck* standard by permitting restriction of expression if it tended to lead to an injurious result.

A balancing test for expression was developed in *Dennis v. United States*,[19] in which speech that advocated illegal action was examined. Expression through an action substitute or symbolic gesture is generally protected speech as seen in *Tinker v. Des Moines Independent Community School District*,[20] and the flag desecration case of *Texas v. Johnson*.[21] The nature of speech as communication was examined in *Cohen v. California*,[22] in which a state unsuccessfully sought to regulate "offensive" speech. A "hate speech" ordinance was struck down by the Court in *R.A.V. v. City of St. Paul*,[23] because it was not content neutral. *Schaumburg v. Citizens for a Better Environment*[24] utilized the overbreadth doctrine to strike down a local ordinance. In *Lebron v. National Railroad Passenger Corp.*,[25] the Court ruled that although Amtrak is legally a private entity, it is an agency of government and cannot ban advertising simply because of the political content of an advertisement. Similarly, the Court ruled in *United States v. National Treasury Employees Union*,[26] that the federal government cannot prevent lower-level executive branch employees from receiving compensation for appearances, speeches, articles, or other expressive conduct.

The fundamental ingredient of a free press is the absence of prior restraint or government censorship. *Near v. Minnesota*[27] was the Court's first extensive discussion of prior restraint and its generally suspect character. The prior restraint doctrine provided, at least in part, the basis for the Court's review of the injunction preventing publication of the Pentagon Papers in *New York Times Co. v. United States*.[28] The Court has permitted prior restraint under certain circumstances, however. In *Hazelwood School District v. Kuhlmeier*,[29] for example, a school principal was permitted to remove articles from a high school paper before its publication. The free press protection extends beyond the prohibition on prior restraint. The extent to which libelous statements are protected was examined in *New York Times Co. v. Sullivan*.[30] In *Hustler Magazine v. Falwell*,[31] the Court refused to fashion new standards for public figures subjected to intentionally inflicted emotional distress. The press has claimed that the First Amendment provides special privileges to the press to give full effect to its news-gathering function. The Court gave this claim full consideration in *Branzburg v. Hayes*.[32] The tension between the requirements of fair criminal trials and a free press has prompted numerous Supreme Court decisions. While the press may be kept from accessing pretrial proceedings, the Court ruled in *Richmond Newspapers, Inc. v. Virginia*[33] that trials must remain open to the press even over the contrary wishes of a criminal defendant. Commercial press now receives extensive protection from the First Amendment. The basic standards that apply in commercial speech or press cases were fashioned in *Central Hudson Gas & Electric Co. v. Public Service Commission*.[34] The extent to which commercial press may be protected from government regulation is examined in *Glickman v. Wileman Bros.*[35] Although the broadcast medium falls within the scope of the Free Press Clause, it historically has been treated differently from the print medium. A recent examination of the rationale for that distinction can be found in *Turner*

Broadcasting System, Inc. v. Federal Communications Commission.[36] The advent of Internet communication may provide the basis for a comprehensive reconsideration of broadcast and cable regulation. The first case involving regulation of content on the Internet was *Reno v. American Civil Liberties Union (ACLU),*[37] in which the Court struck down provisions of the Communications Decency Act of 1996.

The Supreme Court has consistently placed obscenity outside the protection of the First Amendment. Having done so, the central problem becomes fashioning definitional standards that allow protected speech to be distinguished from obscenity. The Court's first major effort to develop such standards came in *Roth v. United States.*[38] The Burger Court sought to reestablish clarity in the definition of obscenity in *Miller v. California.*[39] In the wake of *Miller,* many localities attempted to regulate obscenity and adult entertainment. The Court upheld one such attempt through the zoning process in *Young v. American Mini Theatres, Inc.*[40]

The Court has allowed state regulations that prohibit production and distribution of child pornography and in *Osborne v. Ohio,*[41] upheld criminal sanctions for the private possession of such material. Besides criminal sanctions, other techniques have been developed to control distribution of pornography. In *Kingsley Books, Inc. v. Brown,*[42] for example, the Court considered the use of injunctions to prevent sales of materials found to be obscene.

Free expression occasionally involves conduct such as assembling, marching, picketing, or demonstrating. It is an area in which the speech itself is likely to be protected, but the associated conduct may be subject to regulation. The interests of expression must be balanced against the government's interest in maintaining public order. Government may impose restrictions on the time, place, and manner in which expression may occur. In *Adderley v. Florida,*[43] the Court held that jail grounds may be off-limits for a demonstration. More recently the Court upheld the right of persons to access a privately owned shopping center to express political views in *PruneYard Shopping Center v. Robins.*[44] Licensing or permit requirements have generally been viewed with suspicion by the Court, as have ex parte injunctive proceedings used to restrain assembly before it occurs. In *Carroll v. President and Commissioners of Princess Anne County,*[45] the Court struck down an attempt to enjoin a rally of a militant white supremacist organization. The most troublesome assembly question before the Court in the last several years has been protests at abortion clinics. In *Schenck v. Pro-Choice Network,*[46] the Court reviewed judicial restraints placed on antiabortion protesters.

The First Amendment does not explicitly protect the right of association, but it is now understood that group organization is a legitimate means of expression. The freedom to associate is drawn from the several expressed protections of the First Amendment. The character of association as a means of expression is thoroughly developed in *National Association for the Advancement of Colored People (NAACP) v. Alabama,*[47] a case involving an attempt by a state to compel disclosure of an organization's membership list. Although the Court decided the case on Fourteenth Amendment due process grounds, the principal thrust of the decision was to protect associational freedom. The Court also extended associational freedom in *Keyishian v. Board of Regents*,[48] in which it held that mere membership in a particular organization cannot lead to dismissal from public employment. The Court acknowledged the expressive character of parades in *Hurley v. Irish-American Gay, Lesbian & Bisexual Group*,[49] and held that private sponsors of parades could exclude groups from participating. Associational activity as it relates to the electoral process has been examined in several contexts. Portions of the Federal Election Campaign Act were stricken down in *Buckley v. Valeo*,[50] because of impermissible interference with political campaign expenditures. Political parties are also protected associations. The Court held in *Tashjian v. Republican Party*,[51] that parties can determine the rules by which their primary elections are conducted. At the same time, the Court has allowed states to regulate the electoral process as such. The Court upheld, for example, ballot access restrictions in *Munro v. Socialist Workers Party*,[52] and allowed a state to prohibit a political party from nominating a candidate for political office who was already a candidate of one of the two major parties in the state. The Court, however, ruled that a state could not ban anonymous political campaign literature in *McIntyre v. Ohio Elections Commission*.[53] Finally, the Court recently examined the issues of term limits and political patronage. In *U.S. Term Limits, Inc. v. Thornton*,[54] the Court ruled that states could not establish term limits for either the United States Senate or House of Representatives, and in *Wabaunsee County v. Umbehr*,[55] held that a government contract with a private service provider could not be terminated because the contractor expressed criticism of the contracting governmental unit.

The First Amendment addresses four basic freedoms that its authors deemed imperative to a free society functioning within a democratic political system. These include the freedom of religion, speech, the press, and the dual right to assemble peaceably and to petition the government.

The Court did not have occasion to consider the free speech provision until shortly after World War I. The first important free speech case, *Schenck v. United States*, held that the First Amendment does not provide absolute freedom of expression, but rather conditional protection. Justice Holmes emphasized this point by making use of the often quoted example that the First Amendment would not protect a person who falsely shouted "fire" in a crowded theater and thus caused a panic. The authors of the First Amendment, however, were not as concerned with an utterance such as "fire" as they were with political and social expression. The interests of those wishing to express themselves must be weighed against the public interest. That balancing process is complex and has given rise to a typology of expression that distinguishes among speech that requires no additional conduct, called pure speech; speech that does require additional conduct, sometimes referred to as speech "plus"; and speech that occurs through symbolic surrogates.

The Framers of the Constitution believed that liberty could not be maintained without a free press. The reality of a free press means the press must be free from government control, printing what it desires without fear of censorship or prior restraint. There are many related issues the Framers did not anticipate, however. Since radio and television were unknown in the late eighteenth century, the Framers did not anticipate the power of electronic news media. Neither were certain questions of obscenity and commercial speech perceived at the beginning of the American constitutional era. The Supreme Court has had to balance the freedoms mandated in the First Amendment with other individual rights.

The enunciated right of peaceful assembly contains elements of expression found both in the right of free speech and in the right of association. Assembly cases usually involve marching, picketing, demonstrating, petition gathering, and similar activities. While free speech may be protected, associated conduct may be subject to regulation by the state. Not only is government interested in protecting property rights, it is also interested in maintaining public order. The essential rule is that government may impose restrictions on the time, place, and the manner in which an expression may occur through assembly. The First Amendment does not expressly protect the right of association. That right is inferred from the free speech, peaceful assembly, and right to petition clauses of the First Amendment. While free speech focuses on one's right to express his or her views, the association right focuses on one's right to join a group, and be present at group meetings, but not necessarily to express oneself directly.

The First Amendment was conceived as a constraint on the power of central government. With the exception of the Alien and Sedition Acts of 1798, Congress enacted little legislation that found its way to the Supreme Court on First Amendment free speech grounds until *Schenck v. United States,* Soon thereafter the Court was involved in a series of decisions that extended the various components of the First Amendment to the states through the Fourteenth Amendment. Early evidence of this intention was found in *Meyer v. Nebraska*, in which the Court struck down a state statute prohibiting the teaching of German to any student below the ninth-grade level in either public or private school. The Court said in *Meyer* that the term "liberty" included, among other things, the right to "acquire useful knowledge" and engage in "common occupations of life," such as teaching. The free speech protection of the First Amendment was formally linked to the states two years later in *Gitlow v. New York*, when the Court concluded that freedom of speech was "among the fundamental personal rights and 'liberties' protected by the Fourteenth Amendment from impairment by the states." Nationalization of the press and assembly components of the First Amendment followed soon thereafter in *Near v. Minnesota*, and *De Jonge v. Oregon*,[56] respectively.

The religious freedom provisions were incorporated in the 1940s. The Free Exercise Clause was absorbed in *Cantwell v. Connecticut*,[57] and the Establishment

Clause was made applicable to the states in *Everson v. Board of Education*. The result of these decisions is that the safeguards residing within the First Amendment stand against unreasonable actions by both national and state governments in circumscribing personal belief and opinion.

Establishment of Religion: Child Benefit Doctrine

Everson v. Board of Education upheld reimbursement of costs of transporting nonpublic school students. At issue in *Everson* was a New Jersey statute that authorized local school districts to make "rules and contracts for the transportation of children to and from schools." The Ewing Township Board of Education authorized reimbursements to parents covering costs of transporting their children to private schools, including local church-affiliated schools. These church schools gave their students regular religious instruction conforming to the religious tenets of their faith in addition to secular education. The Court upheld the reimbursement program. The Court found the reimbursements were not an aid to religion, but rather an attempt to promote the safe travel of schoolchildren. Crucial to the Court's holding was the proposition that institutional religion was not the recipient of aid. Rather, services (reimbursement in this case) were extended directly to students and their parents. This view has become known as the "child benefit" theory, and has been invoked frequently to place certain aid programs outside the coverage of the Establishment Clause.

Everson placed state policies within reach of the Establishment Clause. At the same time, the Court took an "accommodationist" position in *Everson*. While urging that the wall between church and state be kept "high and impregnable," the Court pursued neutrality through the child benefit concept, an approach that allowed religious institutions to benefit indirectly from government programs that are themselves "neutral" with regard to religion, provided that the institutional church is not the primary or principal beneficiary of government aid. The child benefit approach has been used extensively in school aid cases since. In *Board of Education v. Allen*,[58] a New York program to loan textbooks to nonpublic school students was upheld. The Court concluded that the program's purpose was the "furtherance of the educational opportunities available to the young," and that the law "merely makes available to all children the benefits of a general program to lend school books free of charge."

With comparable limitations, textbook lending practices have consistently been upheld in such cases as *Wolman v. Walter*.[59] *Wolman*, however, examined several other kinds of aid programs for nonpublic elementary and secondary schools including standardized testing services, diagnostic and therapeutic services, instructional materials and equipment, and field trip services. All disbursements authorized under the law had equivalent expenditure categories for public schools. The amount of aid for each program was limited by the amount of per pupil expenditure for public school students. The Court upheld four programs and invalidated two. The two invalidated were those providing instructional materials and equipment and field trip services. *Wolman* provides a useful example of the way the Court has used the three-pronged establishment test from *Lemon v. Kurtzman*. Most of the assistance in question was sufficiently circumscribed to satisfy establishment concerns. The textbooks, for example, were lent upon pupil request and their choices were confined to texts approved for use in public schools. The Court upheld the testing, diagnostic (speech, hearing, and psychological), and therapeutic services because no nonpublic school personnel delivered the services, the services were obtained in "neutral" locations off public school grounds, none of the services advanced ideology, and the activities required no monitoring. These components of the aid package passed the purpose, primary effect, and entanglement tests. The instructional materials and field trip services did not pass Establishment Clause muster. The Court found that because of the sectarian mission of the nonpublic school, "aid to the educational function of such schools necessarily results in aid to the sectarian school enterprise as a whole." Despite limiting materials to those "incapable of diversion to religious use," these materials "inescapably had the primary effect of providing direct and substantial advancement of the sectarian enterprise." The Court also concluded that the child benefit doctrine could not avoid the primary effect problem; loaning the materials to the pupil rather than the nonpublic school directly only "exalts form over substance." The field trips were found defective because the nonpublic schools controlled the timing and, within a certain range, the "frequency and destinations" of the trips. The trips are an "integral part of the educational experience, and where the teacher works within and for a sectarian institution, an unacceptable risk of fostering religion is an inevitable byproduct." The result of the *Wolman* ruling was that services that can be identified as going directly to the nonpublic school student are permitted. Thus, transportation, textbooks, and most off-premises auxiliary services do not violate the Establishment Clause. Failing one or both of these tests are tuition reimbursements, facility maintenance, instructional materials and equipment, and teacher salary supplements.

In 1980 the Court narrowly upheld a reimbursement program for mandated testing in *Committee for Public Education & Religious Liberty v. Regan*.[60] The reimbursement program was similar to one struck down in *Levitt v. Committee for Public Education & Religious Liberty*,[61] but in *Regan*, nonpublic schools had no control over test content and cost-reporting procedures had been tightened. At the conclusion of the majority opinion, Justice White commented on the Court's difficulty in handling the school aid issue.

Establishment Standards

Lemon v. Kurtzman prohibited salary supplements for nonpublic school teachers. *Lemon* involved a Pennsylvania statute that authorized reimbursement to nonpublic schools for expenditures "for teachers, textbooks, and instructional materials." The reimbursement was limited to "courses presented in the curricula of the public schools." A school seeking reimbursement needed to identify the separate costs of the eligible "secular educational service." The contested statute specifically prohibited reimbursement for "any course that contains any subject matter expressing religious teaching, or the morals or forms of worship of any sect." A unanimous Supreme Court struck down the statute on the ground that the statute fostered an "excessive entanglement" of government and religion. In assessing the entanglement question, the Court indicated it must "examine the character and purposes of the institutions which are benefitted, the nature of aid that the state provides, and the resulting relationship between the government and the religious authority."

The Court articulated a three-prong establishment test in *Lemon v. Kurtzman*. The Court's ruling reflected the decisive role of the entanglement criterion in school aid establishment cases. The Court again noted the difference between precollege levels of education and higher education as it had in *Tilton v. Richardson*.[62] Religious indoctrination is only an incidental purpose of education at the college level, while educational objectives at the lower levels have a "substantial religious character." In addition, the college-level student is more discriminating than the younger student, thus less susceptible to religious indoctrination. *Lemon* emphasizes that the Court sees programs at the elementary and secondary levels as inherently susceptible to religious indoctrination. *Lemon* cast serious doubt on purchase-of-service programs. Monitoring personnel, especially teachers, would be an ongoing obligation that would excessively entangle government and the church school. Transportation and books, on the other hand, have no content to be evaluated or they are subject only to a onetime review. Service items are much more difficult to fit into child benefit coverage than are books and transportation.

A year prior to *Lemon*, the Court upheld tax exemptions on church-owned property in *Walz v. Tax Commission [of the City of New York]*.[63] *Walz* addressed the question of whether tax exemptions for religious property are compatible with the Establishment Clause. The exemption authorized by state law included "real or personal property used exclusively for religious, educational, or charitable purposes as defined by law and owned by any corporation or association organized or conducted exclusively for one or more such purposes and not operating for profit." Walz, a property owner and taxpayer, contended that the exemption indirectly compelled him to financially support religious organizations owning exempted properties. The Supreme Court upheld the exemption. Chief Justice Burger said that the First Amendment "will not tolerate either governmentally established religion or governmental interference with religion." The Court introduced the entanglement criterion that would become a decisive factor in many subsequent establishment cases.

Walz provided the Supreme Court a comparatively easy way to handle the establishment issue. Unlike direct aid programs, tax exemption had a long history. Although benefits may be conveyed at least indirectly to religion, such tax exemptions were quite distinct from grant programs. The exemptions were also different politically in that they did not generate the divisive debate often associated with direct grant programs.

The tax exemption issue reappeared in *Texas Monthly, Inc. v. Bullock*,[64] in which the Rehnquist Court considered a state sales and use tax exemption for religious publications. The law exempted periodicals published or distributed by a "religious faith" that consisted entirely of writings either "promulgating the teachings of the faith" or "sacred to a religious faith." The exemption was challenged by the publisher of a "general interest" periodical not entitled to the exemption. The Court struck down the exemption because it had no secular purpose. When exemptions are granted, they must fall to a "wide array of nonsectarian groups as well as religious organizations. The Court noted a second establishment problem. Under the exemption, public officials were to determine whether a message or activity is "consistent with the teachings of the faith." Such a requirement produces a level of entanglement between government and religion greater than would occur through enforcement of the tax laws without the exemption.

The issue in *Hernandez v. Commissioner of Internal Revenue*[65] was whether fees collected by the Church of Scientology for "auditing" and "training" were deductible charitable contributions or nondeductible payments for services. The IRS disallowed the deductions, and the Supreme Court affirmed. The Court held that Congress had tried to distinguish charitable, "unrequited payments" from payments made with "some expectation of a quid pro quo in terms of goods or services." The former are deductible, while the latter are not. The Court found the payments to the church had been quid pro quo in character.

Primary Effects

Mueller v. Allen upheld a state income tax deduction for certain costs associated with the education of elementary and secondary-level students. Deductions applied to expenses incurred by students attending either public or private schools. Justice Rehnquist said that the Establishment Clause does not necessarily prohibit a program that "in some manner aids an institution with a religious affiliation." With that perspective, Rehnquist proceeded to the establishment test set forth in *Lemon v. Kurtzman*. The tax deduction clearly served a secular purpose. The Court found a state's decision to defray educational costs regardless of the type of school to evidence a purpose that is both "secular and understandable."

A "more difficult" question for the Court was whether the Minnesota law had the "primary effect" of advancing religion. Several features of the tax deduction led the Court to conclude the policy met the effects test. First, the educational deduction was but one of many available under Minnesota tax laws. State legislatures ought to have "especially broad latitude" in developing deductions as a means of both equalizing the tax burden of its citizens and encouraging educational expenditures. Second, the educational deduction was available to *all* parents; it did not target only parents of students attending nonpublic schools. Third, any assistance to nonpublic schools was not transmitted directly to the nonpublic schools. Rather, assistance was "channeled" through individual parents and only got to parochial schools as a consequence of "numerous private choices of individual parents of school-age children."

The decision in *Mueller v. Allen* was a departure from the Burger Court's response a decade earlier to similar issues raised in *Committee for Public Education & Religious Liberty v. Nyquist. Nyquist* invalidated three financial aid programs for nonpublic elementary and secondary schools established by the New York legislature. One program provided direct money grants to qualified schools in low-income urban areas for maintenance and repair of school facilities and equipment. A second program created a tuition reimbursement plan for parents with annual taxable income of less than $5,000. The third program provided tax deductions to parents failing to qualify for direct reimbursement. The Court found a secular legislative purpose for all three programs, but noted the "propriety of a legislature's purposes may not immunize from further scrutiny a law which either has a primary effect that advantages religion or which fosters excessive entanglement between church and state." The maintenance and repair grants failed the primary effect criterion because there was no restriction on the grant usage. This program advanced religion "in that it subsidized directly the religious activities of sectarian elementary and secondary schools."

The establishment problem was that the program provided incentive or encouragement to send a child to a nonpublic school. The Court explicitly refused to accept the argument that reimbursements to low-income parents protected their free exercise options. In the Court's view, the reimbursements and tax relief constituted "encouragement and reward" for sending students to nonpublic schools, a prohibited primary effect. The Court said in *Mueller* that Minnesota's tax deduction was "vitally different" from the programs struck down in *Nyquist*. The Court pointed specifically to the broader class of recipients—parents of all schoolchildren—and the channeling of assistance directly to the parents as the decisive differences.

The Court allowed use of federal construction monies for projects at church-affiliated institutions of higher education in *Tilton v. Richardson*, however. *Tilton* upheld Title I of the Higher Education Facilities Act of 1963, which provided construction grants to church-related colleges and universities for buildings and facilities "used exclusively for secular educational purposes." It also prohibited use of funds for any project that may be used for "sectarian instruction, religious worship, or the programs of a divinity school." Applicants for funds were required to "provide assurances that these restrictions will be respected," and enforcement was to be accomplished by government on-site inspections. Key to upholding the Act was the

Court's opinion that "excessive entanglement did not characterize the relationship between government and church under the Act." The Court cited three factors that diminished the extent and the potential danger of the entanglement. First, institutions of higher learning are significantly different from elementary and secondary schools. Second, the aid provided through the building grants was of a "non-ideological character." Third, entanglement was lessened because the aid came in the form of a "one-time, single purpose construction grant." There were "no continuing financial relationships or dependencies." These factors also substantially lessened the potential for divisive religious fragmentation in the political arena.

Tilton had substantial impact on First Amendment standards in two ways. First, the entanglement criterion introduced the year before in *Walz v. Tax Commission*, was decisive in *Tilton*. It marked the first application of the standard in a school aid case. Second, Chief Justice Burger developed the distinction between higher education and the elementary-secondary levels of education as a key element in determining the degree to which entanglement existed. Combined with the nature of the bricks and mortar character of the aid, excessive entanglement was not found in *Tilton*. The Court expanded this view in *Hunt v. McNair*,[66] as it upheld a state financing arrangement that involved making proceeds from the sale of revenue bonds available to finance building projects at institutions of higher education, including nonpublic colleges and universities. The monitoring required during the payback period of the program was more extensive than in *Tilton*, but not yet excessive. Similarly, the Court upheld a broad, noncategorical grant program for private colleges, including religiously affiliated institutions, in *Roemer v. Board of Public Works*.[67] The Court said the Establishment Clause requires "scrupulous neutrality by the State" but not a "hermetic separation."

Title VII of the Civil Rights Act of 1964 prohibits employment discrimination, but contains an exemption for religious organizations. This exemption was challenged on establishment grounds if applied to secular activities in *Church of Jesus Christ of Latter-Day Saints v. Amos*.[68] Amos had been discharged from his job at a church-owned facility that was open to the public and that served no religious purpose. He argued that the church should not be able to discriminate on religious grounds in employment practices for nonreligious jobs. The Court unanimously ruled, however, that the exemption did not violate the Establishment Clause. The Court said that the secular purpose test does not mean the law's purpose "must be unrelated to religion." The purpose requirement is aimed at preventing government from abandoning neutrality and acting to promote a particular point of view on religious matters. It is a permissible legislative purpose to "alleviate significant government interference with the ability of religious organizations to define and carry out their religious missions." For a law to have forbidden effects, it is necessary for the government itself to "advance religion through its own activities and influence."

Public Displays

Allegheny County v. American Civil Liberties Union (ACLU) examined the question of religious displays on public property. The decision actually considered two displays. The first was a display of a creche depicting the Christian nativity scene on the main inside staircase of the Allegheny County Courthouse. With the creche was a banner saying "Glory to God in the Highest." The creche was donated by a Roman Catholic group, a fact indicated on a sign attached to the display. The second display was an 18-foot Hanukkah menorah placed next to a Christmas tree and sign saluting liberty on the steps of the Pittsburgh City Hall. The menorah was owned by a Jewish group, but was stored and placed on display by the city. The ACLU and several local residents sought to permanently enjoin both displays on Establishment Clause grounds. In a five-to-four decision, the Court ruled that the creche display impermissibly advanced religion, but by a six-to-three vote allowed display of the menorah. On the creche display, Justice Blackmun said that the "essential principle" of the Establishment prohibition is that government does not "take a position on questions of religious belief." Government's use of symbolism becomes unconstitutional if it "has the effect of endorsing religious beliefs." The effect of the government's use of symbolism, Blackmun continued, "depends upon its context." In ruling on the creche and menorah displays, the task of the Court is to determine whether, in their "particular physical settings," either has the effect of "endorsing or disapproving religious beliefs." The creche used "words as well as the picture of the nativity scene, to make its religious meaning unmistakably clear." Unlike the nativity scene in *Lynch v. Donnelly*,[69] there is nothing in the context of the courthouse display that "detracts from the creche's religious message."

The menorah display brought a different result and a different alignment of justices. Although the menorah is a "religious symbol," its "message is not exclusively religious." Setting was again the key. At city hall, the menorah stood "next to a Christmas tree and a sign saluting liberty." This display was not an endorsement of religion, but "simply a recognition of cultural diversity." Thus, for Establishment Clause purposes, the city's "overall display" must be seen as conveying a "secular recognition of different traditions for celebrating the winter holiday season."

Allegheny County was not the Court's first encounter with nativity scenes. The first came five years earlier in *Lynch v. Donnelly*. There a municipality had included a creche in its Christmas celebration display. When the creche was challenged as a violation of the Establishment Clause, the Court allowed the display. The Court said that it had consistently rejected a "rigid, absolutist view" of the Establishment Clause. In addition, the Court said the "wall of separation" metaphor inaccurately represented the relationship of church and state. "Our society cannot have segments or institutions which exist in a vacuum or in total isolation from all other parts, much less from government." The Court maintained that history shows unbroken acknowledgment of the role of religion in American life, and the creche scene merely depicted the historical origins of Christmas. The Court concluded that the city's motives for including the creche were secular, that religion was not impermissibly advanced, and that excessive entanglement of religion was not created.

The related question of whether a state violates the Establishment Clause when a private party is permitted to display an unattended religious symbol in a public forum was examined in *Capitol Square Review & Advisory Board v. Pinette*.[70] Vincent Pinette, on behalf of the Ku Klux Klan, sought a permit from the Capitol Square Review and Advisory Board to place a cross in Capitol Square in Columbus, Ohio. The state capitol building is located on the Square, and the Square qualifies as a "public forum" for First Amendment purposes. Already located on the site was a Christmas tree displayed by the state, and a Hanukkah menorah displayed by a private group. Although Pinette proposed to display a disclaimer with the cross indicating that the government neither sponsored nor endorsed its presence on the site, the Board denied his application. The Supreme Court ruled in favor of Pinette, but the seven-justice majority was unable to agree on the establishment standard to be used in this case. Justice Scalia spoke for the plurality of himself, Chief Justice Rehnquist, and Justices Kennedy and Thomas, and concluded that the Klan's religious display in Capitol Square was private expression. The plurality saw no endorsement in permitting the display. Scalia drew heavily on *Lamb's Chapel v. Center Moriches Union Free School District*, in which the Court had held that public school facilities, already open to a wide variety of uses, must be open to religious groups as well. The equal access factors that the Court found in *Lamb's Chapel* were also present here—the state did not sponsor the Klan's expression, the expression took place on public property already open to the public for expressive activity, and permission was requested on the same terms as applied to other groups. The Court saw no promotion of religion in this situation. Scalia found it "peculiar" to say that the government "promotes" or "favors" a religious display by giving it the "same access to a public forum that all other displays enjoy." The Board had contended that any distinction between private speech and government speech disappears when the private speech is conducted too closely to the "symbols of government"; when private speech can be mistaken for government speech. The Court disagreed, at least when the "government has not fostered or encouraged the mistake." Ohio may require all private displays in Capitol Square to be identified as such. Such a regulation would be a content-neutral "manner" restriction, which is "assuredly constitutional." The state may not, however, based on a misperception of official endorsement, ban all private religious speech or "discriminate against it requiring religious speech alone to disclaim public sponsorship."

Aid to Nonpublic Education

Agostini v. Felton saw the Supreme Court review and overturn its previous decision in an earlier case. Title I of the Elementary and Secondary Act of 1965 was intended to provide remedial instruction to educationally deprived students. The remedial instruction supported by Title I funding could not cover religious content and was typically confined to such subjects as mathematics and reading. The Supreme Court held in *Aguilar v. Felton*[71] that services funded under Title I could not be provided to students on religious school premises. It was the Court's conclusion in *Aguilar* that offering such services in religious school facilities excessively entangled church and state in a way that violates the establishment of religion prohibition of the First Amendment. As a result of *Aguilar*, services to students at religious schools were provided on public school premises. The School Board of New York City and parents of religious school students eligible for Title I were of the view that implementation of the program under the conditions set forth in *Aguilar* created problems relating to both quality and cost. The Supreme Court agreed. In *Agostini*, Justice O'Connor indicated that the Court's rulings following *Aguilar* "modified in two significant respects the approach we use to assess indoctrination." First, the Court has "abandoned the presumption" that the placement of public school employees on parochial school grounds "invariably results in the impermissible effect of state-sponsored indoctrination or constitutes a symbolic union between government and religion." Second, O'Connor said that the Court had departed from the rule relied on in *Aguilar* that "all government aid that directly aids the educational function of religious schools is invalid." O'Connor concluded that it was evident from the Court's current position that New York City's Title I program first reviewed in *Aguilar* would "not be deemed to have the effect of advancing religion through indoctrination."

The Court reaffirmed the establishment standards from *Lemon v. Kurtzman* in two shared-time cases in 1985. In *Grand Rapids School District v. Ball*[72] and *Aguilar v. Felton*, it struck down programs in public school systems that sent teachers into nonpublic schools to provide remedial instruction. These programs were seen as advancing religion and fostering an excessively entangled relationship between government and religion. The Court said that state-paid teachers, "influenced by the pervasively sectarian nature of the religious schools in which they work," may subtly or overtly indoctrinate students with particular religious views at public expense. The symbolic union of church and state inherent in the provision of secular, state-provided instruction in religious school buildings "threatens to convey a message of state support for religion." The "conveying a message" criterion was coupled with the "student benefit" doctrine in *Witters v. Washington Department of Services for the Blind*.[73] Witters suffered from a condition that made him eligible for state vocational rehabilitation assistance for blind persons. He sought the assistance to cover the costs of his studies at a Christian college where he was engaged in a program leading to a religious vocation. The aid was denied on the ground that public money could not be used to obtain religious instruction. The Court ruled that such aid did not advance religion because the aid was given directly to Witters. Any money that eventually got to religious institutions came as a result of the "genuinely independent and private choices of the aid recipients."

The Court reiterated the *Witters* rationale in *Zobrest v. Catalina Foothills School District*,[74] ruling that a public school district could place a sign-language interpreter for a deaf child in a parochial school without violating the Establishment Clause. Chief Justice Rehnquist said that the First Amendment has never "disabled" religious institutions from participating in publicly sponsored social welfare programs. To the contrary, the Court has "consistently held that government programs that neutrally provide benefits to a broad class of citizens defined without reference to religion are not readily subject to an Establishment Clause challenge just because sectarian institutions also receive an attenuated financial benefit." Rehnquist observed that if religious groups were precluded from receiving general governmental benefits, a church could not, for example, be protected by police or fire departments.

Finally, the Court held that the Establishment Clause does not categorically prohibit the placement of a public school employee in a sectarian school. The Court saw nothing in the record to suggest that a sign-language interpreter "would do more than accurately interpret whatever material is presented to the class as a whole." In other words, the interpreter was seen as an entirely content-neutral medium who neither added to nor subtracted from the substantive discussions taking place at school.

The Village of Joel is a community in southeast New York populated exclusively by Satmar Hasidic Jews. The village was incorporated in 1977 out of what was formerly a portion of the town of Monroe. The Satmars are an extremely conservative Jewish sect, and wish to prevent interactions with nonresidents of the village as much as possible. Virtually all of the school-age children of the village attend private religious schools. There are a number of village children, however, who are handicapped or disabled in some way and require special attention. At the time the village was incorporated, these students received state and federally funded special services at the religious schools from teachers and other staff of the Monroe-Woodbury School District at the religious schools. Several years later, the Supreme Court ruled in *Aguilar v. Felton* that public school staff could not deliver services at religious school sites. The arrangement between the Monroe-Woodbury School District and the Satmar village fell within the reach of the ruling and subsequently was terminated. Hasidic parents then had to choose whether to send their children to public schools to receive the special services or have their children go without those services. Most chose the latter, fearing that their children would be ridiculed because of their language (the students spoke only Yiddish), dress, and manner.

In 1989 New York enacted a law establishing a separate public school district, Kiryas Joel Village School District (KJVSD), for the village. The sole function of the new district was to provide special education services to the special-needs children of the village and other Hasidic communities located nearby. The law was challenged on establishment grounds by Louis Grumet and Albert Hawk as individual taxpayers and on behalf of the New York State School Boards Association. The Supreme Court held the law unconstitutional in *Board of Education v. Grumet.*[75] Justice Souter said that the Constitution "allows the state to accommodate religious needs by alleviating special burdens." Accommodation, however, is not a "principle without limits." Souter suggested a number of alternatives for providing bilingual and bicultural education to the Satmar children. The problem with the New York statute was that it was "tantamount to an allocation of political power on a religious criterion." Accommodation is possible as long as it is "implemented through generally applicable legislation," but the line chosen for drawing the Kiryas Joel Village School District was one "purposely drawn to separate Satmars from non-Satmars."

The Rehnquist Court reviewed a different kind of initiative in *Bowen v. Kendrick.*[76] Congress passed the Adolescent Family Life Act in 1981 in response to the "severe adverse health, social and economic consequences" that frequently come after pregnancy and childbirth among unwed adolescents. The Act authorized federal grants to public or nonprofit private organizations for "services and research in the area of premarital adolescent sexual relations and pregnancy." Recipients of a grant were required to provide certain services, such as counseling and education relating to family life. Various individuals and organizations challenged the program on Establishment Clause grounds because funding under the Act had gone to religious institutions whose counsel emphasized abstention and rejection of abortion as a pregnancy option. The Court ruled that the Act was not facially defective. The Act was aimed at the legitimate and secular objective of "eliminating or reducing social and economic problems caused by teenage sexuality, pregnancy and parenthood." The Act did not require that grantees have religious affiliation, and the services provided were "not religious in character." While the approach chosen to deal with adolescent sexuality and pregnancy may "coincide" with those of religious denominations, the approach was not "inherently religious."

Endorsement

In *Rosenberger v. University of Virginia*, the University of Virginia collected fees from all its students for a Student Activities Fund (SAF) that was used to support student activities and organizations on campus. Policy governing distribution of the funds did not permit subsidizing religious activities. The line separating "religious activities" from nonreligious activities, however, was not altogether clear. Some organizations that were "religious" could be subsidized if they were engaged in "cultural" rather than "religious" activities. There were also categories of non-religious groups that could not be subsidized under the allocation policy. Ronald Rosenberger and several other students began publishing a magazine entitled *Wide Awake*. The magazine was intended to provide a "Christian perspective on both personal and community issues" and was distributed without charge on the campus. Rosenberger's organization, which was able to access University facilities, applied for funding to underwrite the publication costs for *Wide Awake*. Production of the magazine was seen as a religious activity, however, and the application was rejected. Rosenberger, the editor in chief of *Wide Awake*, and two other students brought suit in federal court. The Supreme Court ruled for Rosenberger in a five-to-four decision. Justice Kennedy said that it is "axiomatic" that the government may not regulate speech based on the message it conveys. Once the state opens a limited forum, however, it may not exclude speech "where its distinction is not reasonable in light of the purpose served by the forum, nor may it discriminate against speech on the basis of its viewpoint." The Court determined that the University's objection to *Wide Awake* constituted viewpoint discrimination.

Issues involving religious content and its place in public educational institutions had been to the Court many times prior to the *Rosenberger* case. In *Zorach v. Clauson*,[77] for example, the Court upheld off-campus "released time" for religious education. *Zorach* explored the extent to which the Establishment Clause requires strict separation of church and state with regard to such religious instruction. The case dispelled some of the criticism generated by the invalidation of a slightly different program four years earlier in *Illinois ex rel. McCollum v. Board of Education*.[78] In the New York program reviewed in *Zorach*, students were released from regular classes to receive religious instruction. The religion classes were taught by nonschool personnel and were conducted off the school grounds, a point of difference from *McCollum*. Release from school in *Zorach* was voluntary and was initiated by a written request from the student's parents. Students not attending religious instruction remained in their regular classrooms. Verification of attendance at religion classes had to be submitted to public school authorities. The Court in *Zorach* found this released-time approach to be satisfactory in that the program involved "neither religious instruction in public school classrooms nor the expenditure of public funds." Justice Douglas observed in his majority opinion that "[w]e are a religious people whose institutions presume a Supreme Being." As a result, when government "cooperates with religious activities by adjusting the schedule of public events to sectarian needs, it follows the best of our traditions." Although government may not aid or favor religion or any religious sect, there is "no constitutional requirement which makes it necessary for government to be hostile to religion. The dissenters, stated that *McCollum* had found an on-premises released-time program to be a governmentally assisted religious activity, and had come closer to the strict separationist language of *Everson* than the *Everson* decision itself.

A somewhat different question was raised in *Edwards v. Aguillard*,[79] in which the Court struck down Louisiana's creation science law. The state's Balanced Treatment for Creation-Science and Evolution-Science in Public School Instruction Act reviewed in *Aquillard* prohibited the teaching of the theory of evolution in public schools unless accompanied by instruction in the theory of creation science. No school was required to teach evolution or creation science, but if either theory was taught, the other must be taught as well. The Court found the law constitutionally defective. Determination of whether challenged legislation comports with the Establishment Clause is based on the three-pronged test first defined in *Lemon v. Kurtzman*. The Court concluded that the Louisiana law failed the secular purpose test. While noting that the stated purpose of the law was the protection of academic freedom, the Court said it was clear from the law's legislative history and sponsor comments that the Act was not designed to further that goal.

In addition, the Act failed to ensure instruction in creation science. Rather than protecting academic freedom, the Court concluded that the Act had the "distinctly different purpose of discrediting evolution by counter-balancing its teaching at every turn with the teaching of creation science." Brennan said the Court "need not be blind to the legislature's preeminent religious purpose," which was "to advance the religious viewpoint that a supernatural being created humankind." The Act's legislative history documented the fact that the proposed change in the science curriculum was done "to provide persuasive advantage to a particular religious doctrine that rejects the factual basis of evolution in its entirety." As a result, the Court concluded that the primary purpose of the Act was to endorse particular religious doctrine through use of the symbolic and financial support of government and therefore violated the Establishment Clause.

The Court's ruling in *Aquillard* closely paralleled *Epperson v. Arkansas*,[80] a case decided two decades earlier. *Epperson* invalidated a state law that prohibited a teacher in a state-supported school from teaching "the theory or doctrine that mankind ascended or descended from a lower order of animals." Epperson's school district adopted a biology text that contained a chapter on evolution. Epperson was faced with the "literal dilemma" of using the adopted text and simultaneously committing an offense that could subject her to dismissal. The Court said that the First Amendment does not "permit the State to require that teaching and learning must be tailored to the principles or prohibitions of any religious sect or dogma." The Arkansas statute did not satisfy that condition. To the contrary, the Arkansas law "selects from the body of knowledge a particular segment which it proscribes for the sole reason that it is deemed to conflict with a particular religious doctrine." *Epperson* reflected a strict separation position much like that found in *Engel v. Vitale* and *Abington v. Schempp*.[81] The problem in *Epperson*, however, involved embracing a particular religious perspective or doctrine rather than the broader issue of religion versus nonreligion. *Epperson* required that government refuse to favor any particular religious doctrine or any attempt to disadvantage religious belief that may be distasteful to other religious views. In maintaining its neutral posture, a state may not avoid establishment problems by simply stating a secular purpose or disclaiming religious preference. A Kentucky statute, for example, required the posting of a copy of the Ten Commandments in every public school classroom in the state. Each posted copy had a small disclaimer saying that "secular application of the ten commandments is clearly seen in its adoption as the fundamental legal code of western civilization and the common law of the United States." A notation was also made that all posted copies were purchased with funds other than public funds. The Supreme Court nonetheless struck down the statute in *Stone v. Graham*,[82] calling the declaration of secular purpose "self-serving." The Ten Commandments is "undeniably a sacred text" and "no legislative recitation of a supposed secular purpose can blind us to that fact," said the Court. While the state may integrate the Commandments into the school curriculum used in the study of history or comparative religions, the "posting of religious texts on the wall serves no such educational purpose." Thus the enactment failed the secular purpose test, and, despite private funding, the Establishment Clause was violated by the "mere posting of the copies under auspices of the legislature."

School Prayer

Engel v. Vitale decided that the Establishment Clause prohibited daily recitation of the New York Regents' Prayer. *Engel* generated a great deal of controversy because the spiritual exercise at issue was a prayer composed by a public body. The New York State Board of Regents, an agency with broad supervisory authority over the public schools in New York, recommended to school districts that the school day begin with a prayer they specified, although no pupil was to be compelled to join in the recitation of it.

The Supreme Court held that by "using its public school system to encourage recitation of the prayer, the State of New York has adopted a practice wholly inconsistent with the Establishment Clause." Justice Black wrote that the Establishment Clause must "at least mean that in this country it is no part of the business of government to compose official prayers for any group of the American people to recite as part of a religious program carried on by government." The exercise "officially establishes the religious beliefs embodied in the Regents' prayer." That the prayer was not overtly denominational or that participation was voluntary could not save the prayer from a fatal establishment defect, argued Black. The establishment prohibitions go beyond just keeping governmental power and influence from coercing religious minorities to conform to the prevailing officially approved religion. The

Establishment Clause rests on the belief that "a union of government and religion tends to destroy government and to degrade religion." The Court said its decision did not indicate a hostility toward religion or prayer. Rather, the problem was the state's role in a spiritual exercise.

Engel v. Vitale took a decidedly different direction from previous establishment decisions such as *Everson v. Board of Education* and *Zorach v. Clauson*. These cases suggested that the Establishment Clause allowed a limited interaction between church and state. Under such a view, religious practitioners could benefit from general secular purpose enactments. *Engel*, however, held that strict separation is required when governmental interaction involves actual spiritual practices. The *Engel* case prompted a wave of criticism. The Court held firm, however, and in the following year struck down other school practices in *School District v. Schempp*[83] and *Murray v. Curlett*.[84] At issue in these cases were legislative enactments that designated recitation of the Lord's Prayer and the reading of Bible passages as spiritual activities to begin each public school day. As in *Engel*, the Court found the states' involvement with such practices to be incompatible with the establishment prohibition. The Court said in *Abington* that separation of church and state was based on a recognition of the teachings of history that powerful sects or groups might bring about a fusion of governmental and religious institutions. The other prohibited possibility would be to "convert a dependence of one upon the other to the end that official support of the State or Federal Government would be placed behind the tenets of one or of all orthodoxies." The Court further noted that such establishment limitations do not interfere with free exercise protections. Although a state may not use its power to prevent someone from religious exercise, the Free Exercise Clause "has never meant that a majority could use the machinery of the State to practice its beliefs." The reactions to the school prayer and Bible-reading decisions led to various attempts formally to amend the Constitution to permit voluntary prayer. Given the politically volatile nature of the issue, the Court has generally steered clear of further establishment cases involving school prayer. Instead it has concentrated in recent years on cases related to financial assistance programs.

Closely related to school prayer is the so-called moment of silence. The Court struck down a state statute authorizing a moment of silence to be used for meditation or voluntary prayer in public schools in *Wallace v. Jaffree*.[85] The case began as a challenge to three statutes in Alabama. The first was enacted in 1978 and authorized a one-minute period of silence in all public schools "for meditation." The second was passed in 1981 and provided for a period of silence "for meditation or voluntary prayer." In 1982 Alabama adopted yet another statute allowing teachers to lead "willing students" in prayer at the beginning of class. The 1982 statute prescribed that the prayer be to "Almighty God the Creator and Supreme Judge of the World." The Supreme Court held the statute to be unconstitutional. Justice Stevens said the right to speech and the right to refrain from speaking are "complementary components of a broader concept of individual freedom of mind." The right to "choose his own creed" is the counterpart of one's right to "refrain from accepting the creed established by the majority." Stevens said the Court historically had unambiguously conceded that the freedom of conscience protected by the First Amendment "embraces the right to select any religious faith or none at all." This conclusion derives support not only from protection of the interest of freedom of conscience but also from the view that "religious beliefs worthy of respect are the product of free and voluntary choice by the faithful." Addition of the words "or voluntary prayer" indicated that the state "intended to characterize prayer as a favored practice." Such an endorsement was not consistent with the principle that government must pursue a course of complete neutrality toward religion. Justice O'Connor offered a concurring opinion that distinguished the defective Alabama law from those laws that simply call for a moment of silence. The latter do not deal with an exercise that is "inherently religious," she said, and the participating student "need not compromise his or her beliefs." O'Connor argued that when a state mandates a moment of silence, it does not necessarily "endorse any activity that might occur during the period."

At the conclusion of the 1982 term, the Court upheld the practice of opening legislative sessions with a prayer offered by a state-paid chaplain in *Marsh v. Chambers*.[86] The Court distinguished legislative prayer from school prayer by citing the unique history of the former. The Court noted the practice was first begun with the writing of the Bill of Rights, a clear indication, it said, that the Framers of the Constitution did not view legislative prayer as prohibited activity.

Public Access

New York law allows local public school districts to establish policies permitting use of school property after school hours. Under terms of this law the Center Moriches School District fashioned rules allowing, among other things, use of its school facilities for social, civic, and recreational purposes, but categorically prohibited use by any group for religious purposes. A local church unsuccessfully sought access to school property to show a film series on family values and child rearing. A unanimous Supreme Court ruled in *Lamb's Chapel v. Center Moriches Union Free School District* that denying the church group access to the school facilities was unconstitutional on free speech grounds. The First Amendment forbids the government from regulating speech in ways that "favor some viewpoints or ideas at the expense of others." The District's categorical denial of access to all religious groups did not make the policy viewpoint neutral. Justice White said the film the religious group wished to exhibit dealt with otherwise permissible subject matter and that denial of access for its presentation was "solely because the film dealt with the subject from a religious standpoint." The denial of access was thus discrimination on the basis of viewpoint. White linked the free speech rationale to the establishment standards from *Lemon v. Kurtzman*. The District had asserted that the refusal of access to all religious groups was necessary to avoid establishment of religion problems. The Court disagreed. When school property was widely used by a variety of private organizations, there was "no realistic danger than the community would think that the District was endorsing religion or any particular creed." Further, any benefit to religion or to the church would be, said White, "no more than incidental."

The access issue raised in *Lamb's Chapel* was not new to the Court. In *Board of Education v. Mergens*,[87] the Court reviewed provisions of the Equal Access Act of 1984, a federal law that requires public secondary schools receiving federal educational funds to allow political or religious student groups to meet on school premises, provided other non-curriculum-related groups are allowed to do so. Under the Act, a school need not permit any student group to use facilities beyond those related to the curriculum. If at least one group unrelated to the school curriculum has access, however, the school becomes a "limited open forum," and religious or political groups must be able to access the same facilities as well. The Court upheld the Act against an Establishment Clause challenge in *Mergens*. The school district had a formal policy recognizing that student clubs are a "vital part of the education program," and about 30 non-curriculum student clubs met on school premises at the time Mergens sought access for a Christian Bible club, which triggered the Act's equal access requirements. The question then was whether the Act violated the Establishment Clause. It was argued by the school district that if it permitted religious groups to use school facilities, that action would constitute an official recognition or endorsement of religion. The Court disagreed.

The Court had previously ruled that an equal access policy was constitutional at the university level in *Widmar v. Vincent*.[88] In *Widmar* a state university denied use of its facilities to a group wishing to use those facilities for religious worship and religious discussion. The Court held that the denial of access was unjustified. The Court found the university had "discriminated against student groups and speakers based on their desire to use a generally open forum to engage in religious worship and discussion." Although religious groups may benefit from use of the university facilities, "enjoyment of merely 'incidental' benefits does not violate the prohibition against the 'primary advancement' of religion." Furthermore, the facilities were available to a "broad class of non-religious as well as religious speakers." The provision of benefits to "so broad a spectrum of groups is an important index of secular effect."

The Court applied the three-pronged test articulated in *Lemon v. Kurtzman* and concluded that the "logic of *Widmar* applies with equal force to the Equal Access Act." Congress's reason for enacting the law was to "prevent discrimination against religious and other types of speech." Such a purpose, said Justice O'Connor, "is undeniably secular." Access to facilities did not advance religion either. There is a "crucial difference between *government* speech endorsing religion, . . . and *private* speech endorsing religion." The Court concluded that high school students were "mature enough" to understand that a school does not endorse religion or support student speech that it merely permits on a nondiscriminatory basis." The proposition, O'Connor continued, that "schools do not endorse everything they fail to censor is not complicated." Indeed, Congress specifically rejected the contention that high school students are "likely to confuse an equal access policy with state sponsorship of religion." Furthermore, the Act limits participation of school officials at meetings of student religious organizations and requires that meetings occur during non-instructional time. As a result, the Act "avoids the problems of the students' emulation of teachers as role models' and 'mandatory attendance requirements.'" The Court acknowledged that the possibility of student peer pressure remained, but concluded that a school can make it clear that permitting a religious club to use facilities is not an endorsement of the club members' views.

Content-based limitations on expression are particularly suspect. As the Court held in *Carey v. Brown*,[89] a case involving selective regulation of labor picketing, "government may not grant the use of a forum to people whose views it finds acceptable, but deny use to those wishing to express less favored or more controversial views." The Court concluded that "selective exclusion from a public forum may not be based on content alone, and may not be justified by reference to content alone." Nevertheless, a state may be able to justify time, place, and manner restrictions on expression so long as they are not selective. In *Heffron v. International Society for Krishna Consciousness, Inc.*,[90] the Court upheld a state fair regulation that required the sale, exhibition, or distribution of printed material only from assigned locations. The Court found the regulation reasonable and applicable to all groups, not merely religious organizations.

Public Ceremonies

Lee v. Weisman struck down prayers at public school graduation ceremonies. Justice Kennedy wrote for a five-justice majority. The Court saw the state's involvement with religious content as "pervasive" in this case. Kennedy focused on the choices attributable to the state in this case. First, the school principal had authority to decide whether to have clergy-led prayers. Second, the principal had the choice of which community clergy would participate. Finally, the principal provided the clergy with guidance as to the content of the prayers. It was the Court's conclusion that such state involvement with these prayers violated "central principles" of the Establishment Clause. Kennedy said, "One timeless lesson [of the First Amendment] is that if citizens are subjected to state-sponsored religious exercises, the State disavows its duty to guard and respect that sphere of inviolable conscience and belief which is the mark of a free people." If the prayers are allowed at these ceremonies, objectors would face the dilemma of "participating, with all that implies, or protesting." Primary and secondary-level students ought not be forced to make such a choice. Voluntary attendance at these ceremonies was seen as insufficient to save them. High school graduation is "one of life's most important occasions." It is for this reason that the school district argued that prayer ought to be included, but the Court saw this as a fatal establishment defect. The state is not allowed "to exact religious conformity from a student as the price of attending her own high school graduation."

It was anticipated that *Lee v. Weisman* could provide the Court with an opportunity to reconsider the three-pronged test fashioned more than two decades earlier in *Lemon v. Kurtzman*. The school district argued that the proper establishment test should hinge on whether the government coerces people toward some "official" view of religion. This coercion of the religious belief test was seen as providing the appropriate balance between keeping government away from matters of conscience, but at the same time protecting a right of public expression of religious beliefs. Because the state's involvement with religious content was so "pervasive" in this case, the Court found it possible to make a decision "without reconsidering the general constitutional framework" by which establishment issues are examined.

Free Exercise of Religion: Compelling Interest Test

Sherbert v. Verner held that a state may not disqualify a person from unemployment compensation because she refused to work on Saturdays for religious reasons. *Sherbert* said the protection of free exercise interests may produce a religion-based exemption from secular regulation. Sherbert was a Seventh-Day Adventist who was discharged from her job because she would not work on Saturday. Failing to find other employment because of her "conscientious scruples not to take Saturday work," Sherbert filed for unemployment compensation benefits under provisions of South Carolina law. The law required that any claimant is ineligible for benefits if he or she has failed, without good cause, to accept suitable work when offered. Through appropriate administrative proceedings, Sherbert's unwillingness to work on Saturdays was determined to disqualify her from benefits. The Supreme Court held for Sherbert in a seven-to-two decision. The Court saw the burdens imposed on her in this case as too great. She was forced to choose between "following the precepts of her religion and forfeiting benefits" or "abandoning one of the precepts of her religion to accept work." Facing such a choice "puts the same kind of burden upon the free exercise of religion as would a fine imposed against appellant for her Saturday worship." The Court failed to find that protection of the unemployment compensation fund from fraudulent claims by unscrupulous claimants feigning religious objections to Saturday work was a sufficiently compelling state interest.

Even if the fund were threatened by spurious claims, South Carolina would need to demonstrate that no alternative forms of regulation would combat such abuses. In requiring the religion-based exemption for Sherbert, the Court imposed a requirement of possible differential treatment for those seeking unemployment benefits for refusal to work on Saturdays. The Court suggested, however, that such classification was not the establishment of religion. The decision "reflects nothing more than the governmental obligation of neutrality in the face of religious differences."

Sherbert v. Verner, was something of a replay of the free exercise issues seen in two of the *Sunday Closing Law Cases*, *Braunfeld v. Brown* and *Gallagher v. Crown Kosher Super Market, Inc.*[91] Sherbert was subjected to economic hardship, like the merchants in *Braunfeld* and *Gallagher*, but the burden in the *Sunday Closing Law Cases* was less extensive and less direct. The merchants claiming a religious freedom violation had to close their businesses on Sunday under the law, but also had to be closed on Saturday to adhere to the tenets of their faith. While this resulted in some economic hardship, they could be open for business on the five weekdays. The choice of these merchants thus was not between practicing their religion and having to close their businesses altogether, but choosing between their religious obligations or a sixth day of commercial activity. Sherbert's choice was more categorical—if she chose her religion, she had neither job nor unemployment benefits. It was the Court's judgment that government could not require of someone the kind of choice Sherbert faced, but could require the kind of choice the merchants had to make under the Sunday commercial restrictions. The compelling interest criterion is far more demanding than merely showing secular purpose. Coupled with the alternate means requirement carried over from the *Sunday Closing Law Cases*, *Sherbert* substantially expanded the protection afforded by the Free Exercise Clause.

At the same time, the broadened protection for free exercise raised serious establishment questions. They can be seen clearly in *Thomas v. Review Board of Indiana Employment Security Division*.[92] Thomas was denied unemployment compensation after voluntarily quitting his job for religious reasons. The Court held the denial of benefits a violation of Thomas's free exercise rights. Only Justice Rehnquist dissented. In his view, the Court took a step back from *Thomas* and *Sherbert* in *Estate of Thornton v. Caldor, Inc.*,[93] invalidating a state law that gave any employee the absolute right to refuse to work on his or her Sabbath. The Court said the statute failed the primary effect test of *Lemon v. Kurtzman*, in that it required religious concerns automatically to control all secular interests in the workplace.

The *Sherbert* and *Thomas* decisions had essentially said that a state imposes an unacceptable burden on religion when it denies an important benefit because of conduct mandated by religious belief. *Hobbie v. Unemployment Appeals Commission*[94] extended that reasoning. *Hobbie* differed from *Sherbert* and *Thomas* in that Hobbie had been employed some two and one-half years before undergoing the religious conversion that produced the employment conflict. Indeed, Florida attempted to distinguish Hobbie's situation from the other two cases by arguing that she was the agent of change herself and was responsible for the consequences of the conflict between her job and her religious beliefs because her conversion came subsequent to her employment. The Court rejected this position by saying that Florida had asked the Court "to single out the religious convert for different, less favorable treatment than that given an individual whose adherence to his or her faith precedes employment." The timing of Hobbie's conversion was characterized as immaterial to the issue of a free exercise burden. Justice Brennan said that the First Amendment protects the free exercise rights of those who "adopt religious beliefs or convert from one faith to another after they are hired." The Court concluded that *Sherbert*, *Thomas*, and *Hobbie* presented a situation in which the employee was forced to choose between fidelity to religious belief and continued employment. The forfeiture of benefits for choosing fidelity brings "unlawful coercion to bear on the employee's choice."

In *Frazee v. Illinois Department of Employment Security*,[95] the Court considered the case of a claimant who called himself a Christian but was not a member of an established religious sect. He did not contend that his refusal to work rested on a tenet or teaching of an established religious body, but rather that as a Christian, he could not work on "the Lord's day." The Court ruled for Frazee saying that none of the previous decisions "turned" on the matter of sect membership. Neither did they require that a tenet of an established sect prohibited the kind of work the claimant refused to perform. Rather, the prior cases "rested on the fact that each of the claimants had a sincere belief that religion required him or her to refrain from the work in question." Membership in an organized religion, especially one with a specific tenet forbidding Sunday work, "undoubtedly" would "simplify the problem of identifying sincerely held religious beliefs," but the Court rejected the notion that to claim free exercise protection, "one must be responding to the commands of a particularly religious organization." Finally, the Court responded to the state court's reference to America's "weekend way of life," one which requires many to work. If all Americans were to abstain from Sunday work, said the Illinois Appellate Court, "chaos would result." The Supreme Court, however, was "unpersuaded that there will be a mass movement away from Sunday employ if William Frazee succeeds in his claim."

Compulsory Education

Wisconsin v. Yoder created a free exercise exemption to a state compulsory school attendance law. Jonas Yoder did not contest the attendance law as discriminatory against religion, nor was the legitimacy of the state's interest in advancing education challenged per se. The respondents were members of the Old Order Amish and the Conservative Amish Mennonite Church. They had sent their children to public schools through the eighth grade, but they refused to keep their children in public schools until age 16 as required by law. The respondents argued that attendance of Amish children in high school was contrary to their religious beliefs and way of life, might endanger their salvation, and possibly threaten the ongoing existence of the sect by drawing teenagers away from their beliefs. The Court unanimously found for the Amish. The Court acknowledged the state's paramount responsibility for education, but held that even a fundamental function such as education was not "totally free from the balancing process when it impinges on other fundamental rights and interests." In this instance, the "impact of the compulsory attendance law on respondents' practice of the Amish religion is not only severe, but inescapable." The effective choice left to the Amish was to "abandon belief and be assimilated into society or be forced to migrate to some other and more tolerant region." The Court attempted to confine the holding by emphasizing that the Amish were disputing only one or possibly two years of high school–level education. It was training that would be of little value in the agrarian Amish community. Further, the Court noted the character of the Amish, specifically mentioning such characteristics as their self-reliance, their peaceful and law-abiding lifestyle, and their unique history. The Amish history and tradition were crucial in connecting their religious beliefs to their unusual way of life, which in turn created a unique free exercise injury when the compulsory attendance law was enforced against them.

Wisconsin v. Yoder illustrates the extent to which secular regulation has been modified by the Supreme Court. Wisconsin's compulsory education law was clearly a statute of general application with nothing to suggest ill intent with respect to religion or any religious group. The state's substantial interest in educating its young was not questioned, but when the state's interest in requiring Amish children to attend a year or two of high school was weighed against the Amish religious freedom interest, the state's interest was found to be subordinate. *Yoder* expanded *Sherbert v. Verner*, by requiring a religion-based exemption from an enactment established pursuant to a substantial state interest.

Despite the Court's use of the compelling interest standard into the 1980s, it became evident in the cases of *United States v. Lee*[96] and *Goldman v. Weinberger*[97] that the Court was considering a change in this standard. In *Lee* the Court examined a challenge brought by a member of the Old Order Amish who refused to withhold social security taxes from his employees or pay the employer's portion of these taxes. Lee argued that payment of these taxes as well as the receipt of any benefits under the program would violate tenets of the Amish religion. The Court acknowledged the conflict between the Amish faith and the obligation of employers under the social security system, but concluded that not all "burdens on religion are unconstitutional." Chief Justice Burger indicated that the government may limit religious liberty if it can show that its action is "essential to accomplish an overriding governmental interest." The Court's seeming revision of the compelling interest standard in *Lee* became more apparent in *Goldman*. Goldman, an Orthodox Jew and ordained rabbi, was serving in the air force as a psychologist at a military hospital. Throughout his service, Goldman complied with the requirement of his religion to keep his head covered by wearing a yarmulke at all times. He was told that wearing the yarmulke violated a regulation contained in the air force dress code. Goldman challenged the dress regulation arguing that his conduct interfered with no one and could be readily accommodated, and that there was no governmental interest that justified interference with his religious practice. The Court concluded that different standards apply when military regulations are involved. Justice Rehnquist suggested that the military "by necessity" is a "specialized society separate from civilian society." The "essence" of military service, Rehnquist continued, is the "subordination of the desires and interests of the individual to the needs of the service." Accordingly, the courts must "give great deference" to the judgment of military authorities. Soon after the *Goldman* ruling, Congress enacted legislation to overturn the decision. The law allowed members of the armed forces to wear items of religious apparel, even while in uniform, as long as the religious item is "neat and conservative" and does not interfere with the performance of assigned military duties. Notwithstanding the congressional override of *Goldman*, the Court's decisions in *Lee* and *Goldman* suggested that the Court was withdrawing from the compelling interest standard of *Sherbert* and *Yoder*.

Alternative and Least Restrictive Means

The *Sunday Closing Law Cases* upheld Sunday restrictions on commercial activity. Four cases (called the *Sunday Closing Law Cases* in aggregate) challenging state and local prohibitions on Sunday business activities came to the Supreme Court in 1961. Two of the four cases were decided essentially on establishment and equal protection grounds. *McGowan v. Maryland*[98] and *Two Guys from Harrison— Allentown, Inc. v. McGinley*,[99] upheld the retail restrictions. In the other two cases, *Gallagher v. Crown Kosher Super Market, Inc.* and *Braunfeld v. Brown* the petitioners, both Orthodox Jews, added free exercise allegations to their establishment and equal protection claims. This tactic weakened their constitutional position, because only Justices Douglas, Brennan, and Stewart found the Sunday closing laws defective by free exercise standards. The Court said the commercial restrictions in *Gallagher* and *Braunfeld* were legitimate secular regulations, the purpose of which was the designation of a uniform day of rest. The Court held that while the regulation may impose some free exercise burden on the litigants, they were not denied the opportunity for free exercise. They merely had to forego a day's work. Free exercise only made the practice of their religious beliefs more expensive. The Free Exercise Clause cannot, except in rare circumstances, be used to strike down legislation "which imposes only an indirect burden on the exercise of religion." The

Court said the Free Exercise Clause does not require that "legislators enact no law regulating conduct that may in some way result in an economic disadvantage of some religious sects and not to others because of the special practices of the various religions." The Court did offer one important qualification, however. A state may enact a general law the purpose of which is to advance the state's secular goals and that may impose an indirect burden on religious observance. But it may do so only if the state may not "accomplish its purpose by means which do not impose such a burden."

The *Sunday Closing Law Cases* modified the secular regulation rule, although the Court rejected free exercise arguments in each of the four cases. The secular regulation doctrine was an attractive approach for the Court because of its simplicity. As applied, however, the doctrine proved undesirably "rigid," and produced results deemed "harsh" by many. The Warren Court began modification of the doctrine in the *Sunday Closing Law Cases*. The Court resolved the free exercise issue in the four Sunday closing cases by weighing the burdens on religious practice flowing from the secular rule. After assessing the competing interests, the Court concluded the burden borne by the sabbatarians was indirect. If the state had required Saturday work, the burden would have been direct and prohibited. What the state did, instead, was deny a person closing a business on Saturday the opportunity to be open on Sunday. The Court's use of the direct-indirect burden approach clearly suggested that at least certain kinds of secular regulations would require exemptions if they survived First Amendment scrutiny at all. The secular regulation rule was altered further by the addition of the alternate means provision. This placed an affirmative obligation on the state to show the lack of alternatives that could accomplish the secular end without imposing a burden on religious exercise. The real impact of this change became apparent in *Sherbert v. Verner*.

General Secular Regulation Test

Employment Division v. Smith ruled that a state could withhold benefits from employees terminated from their jobs for ceremonial use of peyote. Oregon had refused to pay benefits because use of a controlled hallucinogen was a crime in the state, and was "misconduct" for which an employee could be dismissed and rendered ineligible for unemployment benefits. The employees in this case had used the peyote in the sacramental rituals of the Native American Church and sought exemption on free exercise grounds. The Court ruled that although the state legislature could have established such an exemption, the Free Exercise Clause did not require it. "We have never held," said Justice Scalia, that an "individual's beliefs excuse him from compliance with an otherwise valid law prohibiting conduct that the State is free to regulate." As long as religion is not itself the object of the regulation, and any burden is "merely the incidental effect of a generally applicable and otherwise valid provision, the First Amendment has not been offended." To permit individuals to exempt themselves from such regulations would make "professed doctrines of religious belief superior to the law of the land," and in effect "permit every citizen to become a law unto himself." The *Sherbert* test, said the Court, was "developed in a context that lent itself to individualized governmental assessment of the reasons for the relevant conduct," and was seen as inappropriate for a challenge of an "across-the-board criminal prohibition on a particular form of conduct." The government's ability to enact and enforce generally applicable regulations of "socially harmful conduct cannot depend on measuring the effects of a governmental action on a religious objector's spiritual development." To make an individual's obligation to comply with a law "contingent on the law's coincidence with his religious beliefs, except where the State's interest is 'compelling,' contradicts both constitutional tradition and common sense." Justices Blackmun, Brennan, and Marshall applied the *Sherbert* test and concluded that the failure of Oregon to make an exception for religious uses of peyote did not outweigh Smith's free exercise interests.

The secular regulation rule to which the Court returned in *Employment Division v. Smith* was first applied in *Reynolds v. United States*.[100] Congress had made the practice of polygamy illegal. The Mormons challenged the law, arguing that polygamy was required by their religion and that enforcement of the law would violate their right to free exercise. The Court disagreed in *Reynolds*, upholding the law as a generally applicable secular regulation, and as such, a constitutional exercise of congressional power to regulate the territories of the United States. Similarly, the Court upheld compulsory smallpox vaccinations over religious objections in *Jacobson v. Massachusetts*.[101] In doing so, the Court indicated the presence of a strong presumption that attaches to legislation enacted for public health purposes.

The Court struck down compulsory flag salute requirements for public school students in *West Virginia State Board of Education v. Barnette*.[102] *Barnette* invalidated a compulsory flag salute, but it did not exempt religion from secular laws. Three years prior to *Barnette*, in *Minersville School District v. Gobitis*,[103] the Court had upheld a flag salute requirement. Both cases raised the question of whether public school pupils could be compelled, under threat of expulsion and fine, to salute the flag. The Barnette and Gobitis children, members of the Jehovah's Witnesses sect, refused to participate because to do so would have put them in conflict with their religious beliefs, which forbade oaths to "images" such as flags. Through Justice Jackson, the six-justice majority in *Barnette* sought to resolve the case on free expression grounds. As an expression issue, the Jehovah's Witnesses' behavior could be evaluated by using the "clear and present danger" test, a criterion established in *Schenck v. United States*. Justice Jackson concluded that the children's silence was a form of expression that did not create a clear and present danger. Neither did their refusal to salute the flag "interfere with or deny rights of others to do so." Clear and present danger could justify restriction of expression, but "it would seem that involuntary affirmation could be commanded on even more immediate and urgent grounds than silence."

The Court judged that the First Amendment permitted no authority to impose participation in a ceremony "so touching matters of opinion and political attitude." To the contrary, "if there be any fixed star in our constitutional constellation, it is that no official, high or petty, can prescribe what shall be orthodox in politics, nationalism, religion, or other matters of opinion." *Barnette* reversed the heavily criticized *Gobitis* decision, but it did so without dismantling the secular regulation rule or encouraging religious preference. The Court opted instead to view free exercise interests as largely contained within expression protections. The compulsory flag salute was offensive because it dealt with matters of belief and opinion, a transgression the First Amendment cannot tolerate regardless of religion. Because the state could not require any child to salute the flag, the Court avoided carving out an exception for Jehovah's Witnesses. The implications of the broader basis for the decision can readily be seen by comparing the *Barnette* outcome to the outcome of the earlier flag salute case. *Gobitis* was an example of the secular regulation approach in its purest form. Justice Frankfurter's majority opinion argued that protection of religion does not preclude legislation of a general scope as long as the legislation is not directed against the doctrinal loyalties of particular sects. Even "conscientious scruples" cannot relieve the individual from obedience to general law not aimed at the promotion or restriction of religious beliefs. The secular interest being promoted by flag ceremonies is a preeminent interest. What it seeks is cohesion and national unity, an interest "inferior to none."

Church of the Lukumi Babalu Aye, Inc. v. City of Hialeah[104] involved the practices of the Santeria religion. The faith originated in the nineteenth century as many Yorubas from Africa were brought to Cuba as slaves. Santeria was the result of a combination of traditional Yoruba religion with elements of Roman Catholicism. A basic tenet of the religion is the development of personal relationships with spirits (orishas). These spirits, while possessing substantial power, are not immortal. Rather, they are sustained by periodic ritual sacrifice of animals. In April 1987 the Church of the Lukumi Babalu Aye leased land in Hialeah, Florida, and announced its intention to establish a Santeria church in the community. The prospect of a Santeria church in the area was "distressing" to many members of the Hialeah community. In September 1987 the City of Hialeah adopted ordinances that increased the penalty for animal cruelty, prohibited "possession, sacrifice or slaughter" of certain animals within the city (licensed slaughterhouses were excepted), and enlarged the authority of local officials to prosecute those involved in the sacrifice of animals. Sacrifice was defined as to "unnecessarily kill, torment, torture, or mutilate an animal in a public or private ritual or ceremony not for the primary purpose of food consumption." The ordinances were challenged by the Church on free exercise grounds. A unanimous Supreme Court ruled for the Church.

Justice Kennedy delivered the opinion of the Court, which was joined by Chief Justice Rehnquist, and Justices White, Stevens, Scalia, and Thomas. Their review of the ordinances "confirm[ed] that the laws in question were enacted by officials who did not understand, failed to perceive, or chose to ignore the fact that their official actions violated the nation's essential commitment to religious freedom." There was no doubt that Santeria is a "religion" entitled to First Amendment protection. Kennedy said that in this case, the record "compels the conclusion that suppression of the central element of the Santeria worship service was the object of the ordinances." The inquiry into the neutrality of the ordinances led the Court to conclude that they "had as their object the suppression of religion." Essential to the protection of free exercise rights is the principle that government cannot "in a selective manner impose burdens only to conduct motivated by religious belief."

Without precisely defining a general applicability standard, it was the Court's judgment that Hialeah's ordinances "fall well below the minimum standard" necessary to protect First Amendment rights. The ordinances pursued the city's interests "only against conduct motivated by religious belief." Kennedy said the ordinances "had every appearance" of restrictions that society was willing to impose on the Santeria worshippers, "but not upon itself." In his view, this is the "precise evil" the general applicability requirement is intended to avoid.

Religion and Taxation

Jimmy Swaggart Ministries v. Board of Equalization upheld a state sales and use tax imposed on a religious organization's sale of religious materials. The California law required retail sellers to register with the state. In addition, the law levied a six percent tax on in-state sales and a six percent use tax on materials purchased outside the state. The Swaggart Ministries, incorporated in Louisiana, offered materials for sale in California over a period of years. In 1981 the Board of Equalization conducted an audit and advised the Ministries that it needed to pay accumulated taxes on articles sold at its "evangelical crusades" dating back to 1974. The tax was challenged by the Ministries as a violation of both religion clauses. A unanimous Supreme Court rejected the challenge. The Swaggart Ministries based its Free Exercise Clause challenge on cases such as the license tax ruling in *Murdock v. Pennsylvania*.[105] The Court, however, distinguished the flat license taxes that operated as a "prior restraint on the exercise of religious liberty" in *Murdock* from the sales tax in this case. In *Murdock*, the license tax acted as a precondition to free exercise. That defect was "simply not present where a tax applies to all sales and uses of tangible personal property in a State." The California tax was not a tax on the right to "disseminate religious information, ideas, or beliefs per se." Rather, the tax was on the "privilege of making retail sales of tangible personal property," and was owed regardless of the motivation of the sale. The sale of a Bible by a religious organization is treated like the sale of a Bible by a bookstore. Consequently, the Court saw "no danger" that religious activity was being "singled out for special and burdensome treatment." The Ministries also contended that an impermissible burden was produced by diminishing their income and thereby decreasing the resources it could devote to religious pursuits. The Court recognized that the Ministries incurred some economic cost, but the tax was no different from other generally applicable laws and regulations such as health and safety regulations to which the Ministries must adhere. The Establishment Clause challenge focused on whether administration of the tax produced an unacceptable degree of entanglement between government and religion. The Court ruled that the administration and record-keeping burdens involved in collection and payment of the California tax did not "rise to a constitutionally significant level." The contact required only "routine regulatory interaction," a level that was not seen as violating the nonentanglement command. Imposition of the tax, said O'Connor, did not "require the State to inquire into the religious content of the items sold or the religious motivation for selling or purchasing the items, because the materials are subject to the tax regardless of content or motive."

The Jimmy Swaggart Ministries attempted to base its challenge of the California sales and use tax on *Murdock*. *Murdock* involved a municipal license tax that was imposed on all persons selling or canvassing door-to-door. The tax was challenged by Jehovah's Witnesses as an infringement of their ability freely to exercise their religious beliefs. Justice Douglas observed that the distribution of religious tracts is "an age old form of missionary evangelism." Such distribution is "as evangelical as the revival meeting," and is a form of religious activity as protected as "worship in the churches and preaching from the pulpit." The Court did not find the nondiscriminatory character of the tax sufficient to save it. The tax "does not acquire constitutional validity because it classifies the privileges protected by the First Amendment along with the wares and merchandise of hucksters and peddlers and treats them all alike." Free exercise holdings had established previous to *Murdock* that freedom of religious exercise was not absolute and that religious beliefs would not free an individual from the demands of general secular regulation. Just a year prior to *Murdock*, for example, the Court upheld a similar license tax in *Jones v. Opelika*.[106] It said the tax imposed only an incidental burden upon free exercise while allowing a state to "insure orderly living." *Murdock*, however, suggests that injury created by a secular regulation may be too great. In this case, the license tax was imposed on the religious exercise of evangelism, a protected religious practice. Certain regulations, despite their secular purpose and nondiscriminatory administration, simply cannot be applied in some situations. This is especially true when a particular secular regulation has the potential of interfering with the ability of a sect to perpetuate itself.

Conscientious Objection: Selective Service

Gillette v. United States held that religion-based objections to a particular war, as distinct from wars generally, does not entitle a person to exemption from the military draft. *Gillette* examined the language of the Selective Service Act, which exempts registrants who are "conscientiously opposed to participation in war in any form." Gillette had attempted to limit his objection to participation in the Vietnam War, but the Supreme Court held he was not entitled to such a free exercise exemption. The Court determined that Congress could provide exemptions to the draft for those having religion-based objections to wars generally without violating establishment prohibitions. While conscription of those with "conscientious scruples" against all wars would violate the free exercise proscription, there are governmental interests of "sufficient kind and weight" to justify drafting people who object to particular wars. The Court determined that the draft laws were not "designed to interfere with any religious ritual or practice, and do not work a penalty against any theological position." In addition, the burdens imposed are incidental when compared to the substantial government interest in creating and administering an equitable exemption policy. The Court also noted the interest of the government in "procuring the manpower necessary for military purposes," an interest of sufficient weight to permit burdening Gillette's free exercise rights. The establishment claim was based on the argument that allowing exemption only to those with objection to all wars discriminated against faiths that "distinguish between personal participation in 'just' and 'unjust' wars." The Court held that congressional objectives in requiring objection to all wars were neutral, secular, and did not reflect a religious preference.

Gillette was unique in singling out a particular war for religion-based conscientious objection to an American draft law. The claim of exemption required only "theistic religious beliefs" and training, and not a "merely personal moral code." The Court addressed this language in *United States v. Seeger*,[107] holding that a conscientious objector claimant need not declare a belief in a Supreme Being as long as the claimant had beliefs that served in the place of an orthodox belief in God. The term "Supreme Being" was said to mean a broader view of something to which everything else is subordinate. In *Welsh v. United States*,[108] the Court required exemption for a claimant without the basis of his objections resting on religious training or belief as long as the claimant genuinely believed in pacifism. A selective conscientious objector such as Gillette, on the other hand, created problems of implementation "so wrought with establishment defects" as to outweigh the free exercise interest served by the exemption.

More recent considerations were offered on this issue in *Rostker v. Goldberg*,[109] *Selective Service System v. Minnesota Public Interest Research Group*,[110] and

Wayte v. United States.[111] *Rostker* upheld a 1980 presidential proclamation issued pursuant to the Military Selective Service Act requiring every male citizen and resident alien to register for potential conscription. In the *Minnesota Public Interest Research Group* case, the Court permitted denial of federal student aid to persons failing to register for the draft, saying the policy had been aimed at securing compliance rather than seeking punishment of nonregistrants. The policy had been challenged on bill of attainder, self-incrimination, and equal protection grounds. In *Wayte*, the Court allowed the temporary use of a passive enforcement of the draft registration law whereby initial prosecutions were undertaken only against those nonregistrants who publicized their own resistance to the policy or were reported by others to be in violation. The Court said such an approach would be impermissible only if discriminating motive and effect could be shown.

Religious Freedom Restoration Act

In response to the Court's free exercise ruling in *Employment Division v. Smith*, Congress enacted the Religious Freedom Restoration Act (RFRA), which provided that government at any level may not "substantially burden" religious exercise without demonstrating a compelling governmental interest pursued in the least restrictive way. Congressional authority to adopt such a law was based on Section 5 of the Fourteenth Amendment. The RFRA was intended to replace the free exercise standards articulated by the Court in *Smith* with the more protective standards that had been in place prior to *Smith*. The Court had an opportunity to determine whether the Fourteenth Amendment enabled Congress to take such action in *City of Boerne v. Flores*. The membership of St. Peter's Catholic Church, located in Boerne, Texas, had outgrown the capacity of its church building. The Church unsuccessfully sought permission from the city to raze the building and then construct a larger structure on the same spot. The city denied the building permit because the area in which St. Peter's was located had been zoned for historic preservation. The Church brought suit in federal court claiming a violation of the RFRA, but the case was dismissed on the grounds that the RFRA was unconstitutional. The Supreme Court agreed. The case was resolved on federalism rather than religious freedom grounds.

The Court was unconvinced that the examples of burdensome regulations offered in support of the RFRA were enacted or enforced "due to animus or hostility to the burdened religious practices or that they indicate some widespread pattern of religious discrimination in this country." In the Court's view, the RFRA could not be considered "remedial, preventive legislation, if those terms are to have any meaning." The Court saw the RFRA as an attempt to effect "substantive change in constitutional protections." Furthermore, its "sweeping coverage ensures its intrusion at every level of government, displacing laws prohibiting official actions of almost every description and regardless of subject matter."

City of Boerne v. Flores was not decided on free exercise grounds even though the Religious Freedom Restoration Act was enacted by Congress in an attempt to overturn the Court's decision in *Employment Division v. Smith*. Congressional attempts to reverse Supreme Court decisions by statute is not novel, but reflective of normal legislative-judicial interaction. Two recent examples serve to illustrate. The Court ruled in *Goldman v. Weinberger* that a military dress regulation could be used to prevent an Orthodox Jew from wearing a yarmulke while in military uniform and performing his duties as a clinical psychologist at a military hospital. The ruling generated extensive debate in Congress, which eventually produced legislation enabling armed forces members to wear religious apparel while in uniform as long as the apparel was "neat and conservative" and did not "interfere with the performance" of any military duties. Three years after *Goldman*, the Court decided several cases involving federal civil-rights laws. Among them were *Wards Cove Packing Co. v. Atonio*,[112] *Martin v. Wilks*,[113] and *Lorance v. AT&T Technologies, Inc.*[114] These decisions made it more difficult for plaintiffs in employment discrimination cases to access federal courts, and elevated evidentiary standards for claims that did access federal courts, thus making it harder to actually demonstrate illegal conduct by employers. The Civil Rights Act of 1991 was enacted by Congress to reverse the effect of these Court decisions. These two examples reflect the conflict that often occurs when the Court makes statutory interpretations. In such instances, if the Congress disagrees with the Court's interpretation of a statute, it may respond to the ruling by statute. The *Boerne* case involved congressional response to the Court's interpretation of the Constitution, not federal statute. Here, the Court ruled that Congress may not use the Fourteenth Amendment to "correct" or change a substantive judicial interpretation of the Constitution. Rather, federal remedial power must be limited to actual enforcement of constitutional protections.

Freedom of Speech: Clear and Present Danger Standard

Schenck v. United States established the clear and present danger test for evaluating restrictions of expression. *Schenck* was the first significant free speech case to come before the Supreme Court. At issue was the constraint on speech imposed by the Espionage Act of 1917. The Act made it a crime to interfere with recruitment of persons into the armed services. Schenck was convicted of obstructing the draft by printing and distributing materials that urged draft-eligible men to resist conscription. The Court unanimously upheld the conviction with Justice Holmes speaking for the Court. He said the right of expression is not absolute, but rather is conditional and has boundaries set by the circumstances in which it is undertaken. Even the most "stringent protection of free speech would not protect a man in falsely shouting fire in a theater and causing a panic." Having established a situational context for evaluating expression, Justice Holmes then described a "clear and present danger" standard by which expression can be assessed. The issue in every case involving expression is "whether the words used are used in such circumstances and are of such a nature as to create a clear and present danger that they will bring about the substantive evil that Congress has a right to prevent." If speech is linked closely enough to illegal action, it is speech that can be restricted. As Justice Holmes put it, "it is a question of proximity and degree." Schenck's expression was intended to have an effect on persons subject to the draft, a point conceded by Schenck. Under certain circumstances such as peacetime, Schenck's expression would not have been dangerous enough to warrant prosecution. But his words were disseminated while the nation was at war, and the war context gave quite a different effect to his expression. The clear and present danger test allowed certain speech to be regulated through prosecution as long as the government could show that the expression endangered legitimate governmental functions and societal interests. The test required that the danger be both recognizable and immediate.

Significance

Several cases immediately following *Schenck* provided the Court an opportunity to refine further the clear and present danger criterion. In *Frohwerk v. United States*,[115] a unanimous Court upheld the conviction of an author of several newspaper articles that were highly critical of American involvement in World War I. The Court felt the language of the articles was effectively comparable to Schenck's leaflets. The Court also upheld the conspiracy conviction of Eugene Debs for a speech critical of the war effort in *Debs v. United States*.[116] The speech focused on socialism, "its growth and a prophecy of its success." The Court had no objection to the content of the speech, but made it clear that if the "manifest intent" of a speech encourages those hearing it to obstruct the recruiting service, the "immunity of the general theme may not be enough to protect the speech." In *Abrams v. United States*,[117] the Court upheld Abrams's conviction for distribution of materials critical of the government's commitment of forces to Russia in the wake of the Russian Revolution.

Bad Tendency Standard

Gitlow v. New York, created the "bad tendency" standard for evaluating freedom of expression issues. *Gitlow* modified the clear and present danger test to allow suppression of speech that might tend to produce "substantive evil." *Gitlow* also formally linked the provisions of the Free Speech Clause of the First Amendment to state enactments through the Due Process Clause of the Fourteenth Amendment. Gitlow, a member of the Left Wing Section of the Socialist Party, was convicted under provisions of New York's criminal anarchy statutes for his advocacy of the "overthrow of the government by force, violence, and unlawful means." The criminal advocacy was demonstrated in two published tracts entitled "The Left Wing Manifesto" and "The Revolutionary Age." The Court held the statute did not deprive Gitlow of his "liberty of expression," nor did it "penalize the utterance or publication of abstract 'doctrine' or academic discussion having no quality of incitement to any concrete action." Rather, the statute aimed at "language advocating, advising, or teaching the overthrow of organized government by unlawful means." The Court felt the statute was properly focused on advocacy of action directed toward the accomplishment of an illegal purpose, i.e., overthrowing the government. The Court said the police power of the state is appropriately used to "punish those who abuse freedom of expression by utterances inimical to the public welfare." Judgment as to what utterances might be so inimical to the general welfare and "involve such danger of substantive evil" essentially rests with the state's legislative body, and "every presumption is to be indulged in favoring the validity of the statute." Utterances that incite to overthrow the government were found to be "within the range of legislative discretion." A state cannot be said to have acted arbitrarily or unreasonably when it "seeks to extinguish the spark without waiting until it has enkindled the flame or blazed into the conflagration." A state may, in the exercise of its judgment, "suppress the threatened danger in its incipiency."

Gitlow v. New York had the practical effect of permitting legislatures to restrict expression that might lead to unlawful ends. The unlawful consequences need not be immediate. *Gitlow* permitted the government to take preventive action to keep expression from jeopardizing public safety. The ruling was characterized as allowing the government to "kill the serpent while it is still in the egg." In the years following *Gitlow*, however, the Court began to suggest it would be more demanding in cases involving the First Amendment. As distinct from enactments involving economic regulation, legislation touching First Amendment protections would be viewed with suspicion because the Constitution elevates First Amendment freedoms to a "preferred position." The preferred position doctrine had its origin in Justice Stone's celebrated Footnote 4 in *United States v. Carolene Products Co.*[118] The burden of demonstrating the need for impairment of First Amendment freedoms falls directly on the government in "preferred position" cases. The footnote was frequently cited in the 1940s, especially in labor picketing and free exercise of religion situations. An intermediate position between the preferred position and the *Gitlow* bad tendency doctrine began to evolve after World War II with the balancing test articulated in *Dennis v. United States*.

Political Association

Dennis v. United States upheld Sections 2 and 3 of the Alien Registration Act of 1940, the first federal attempt to restrict political expression and association since the Alien and Sedition Acts of 1798. *Dennis* examined the constitutionality of the

Act, particularly the sections that prohibited advocacy of overthrowing the government by force and organizing groups with that objective. Dennis was a leader of the Communist Party of the United States. The criminal charges brought against him and others were confined to illegal advocacy and conspiracy. The Court upheld the Alien Registration Act, which was also known as the Smith Act. The Vinson Court could have developed a rationale along the lines of *Gitlow v. New York*, which permitted the government to declare that even advocacy of governmental overthrow is unprotected expression. Instead, it utilized the clear and present danger test to determine if the Communist Party members posed a sufficient threat to warrant restriction. The Court opted for the latter approach although Chief Justice Vinson reshaped the clear and present danger standard in doing so. Vinson said the severity of the threat involved was heavier than the immediacy or probability of the danger. The likelihood of the threat actually materializing is not required either. An attempt to overthrow the government by force, even though "doomed from the outset, is a sufficient evil for Congress to prevent it."

The first test of associational rights came in *Whitney v. California*,[119] in which the Court upheld a state criminal syndicalism statute that prohibited organizing and being a member of a group advocating unlawful force as a political weapon. Whitney had participated in a convention of the Communist Labor Party of California, which had passed resolutions advocating various revolutionary acts. Whitney claimed she had neither supported the resolutions nor wished the party to urge violation of California's laws. She was convicted nonetheless because she had remained at the convention and had not disassociated herself from the party and its adopted resolutions. The Supreme Court upheld her conviction. The Court refused to reexamine the jury's fact determination that Whitney had not sufficiently detached herself from the party's objectives. The Court concluded that remaining in attendance until the close of the convention and maintaining membership "manifested her acquiescence." The justices said that California's law did not impermissibly restrain free speech or assembly. The "essence of the offense denounced by the Act is the combining with others in an association for the accomplishment of the desired ends through the advocacy and use of criminal and unlawful methods." Because such united and joint action constituted an even greater threat to public peace and security, a state may reasonably exercise its police power to prevent groups from "menacing the peace and welfare of the State." The *Whitney* ruling seemed to provide license for convicting political radicals because of their association alone, but the Court began to disengage from *Whitney* almost immediately. In *DeJonge v. Oregon* and *Herndon v. Lowry*,[120] the Court reversed convictions of admitted members of the Communist Party because, as individuals, neither defendant had violated a criminal law. While an organization may have criminal objectives, simply attending a peaceful meeting called by such an organization cannot transfer criminal liability to individual members. The formal end to *Whitney* came in *Brandenburg v. Ohio*,[121] in which the Court unanimously struck down a state syndicalism statute. The defendant in *Brandenburg* was the leader of a Ku Klux Klan group who had spoken at a Klan rally. The Court said "the mere abstract teaching of the moral propriety or even moral necessity for a resort to force and violence is not the same as preparing a group for violent action and steeling it for such action." Accordingly, a statute that fails to draw this distinction impermissibly intrudes on First Amendment freedoms.

The Smith Act imposed significant restraints on political speech and association. *Dennis v. United States* cleared the way for numerous conspiracy convictions under the Smith Act between 1951 and 1957. In *Yates v. United States*,[122] however, the Court set evidentiary requirements that substantially diminished the likelihood of securing convictions under the Smith Act. The Court said the *Dennis* distinction between advocacy of illegal acts and abstract doctrinal advocacy had been ignored by trial courts subsequent to *Dennis*. Whether *Dennis* had really made this distinction is debatable, but the key result of *Yates* was that the government was now required to demonstrate specific illegal acts by party members to convict under the Smith Act. Abstract advocacy and mere membership were insufficient bases for a Smith Act conviction. This clarification limited the impact of *Dennis*, but four years later the Court upheld the section of the Smith Act making it a crime to be a member of a group advocating forcible overthrow in *Scales v. United States*.[123] In *Scales* the Court did require evidence comparable to that required in *Yates*, saying, for example, that in order to gain a conviction under the membership provision, a person's membership had to be both knowing and active, and that the person had to have shown "specific intent to bring about violent overthrow" of the government. Prosecutions under the Smith Act were essentially abandoned soon thereafter.

The Internal Security Act of 1950 traveled a parallel course. The Act required Communist organizations to register with the federal government, and created a Subversive Activities Control Board to determine which organizations needed to register. The government had little success in implementing provisions of the Act, and in *Albertson v. Subversive Activities Control Board*,[124] the Court unanimously held that individual members of the Communist Party could not be compelled to register on self-incrimination grounds.

Symbolic Speech

Tinker v. Des Moines Independent Community School District upheld the wearing of armbands as a protected substitute for speech. *Tinker* involved three public school students in Des Moines, Iowa, who were suspended from school for their symbolic protest of the government's policy in Vietnam, which involved the wearing of black armbands. They brought suit to enjoin the school district from enforcing its regulation against the wearing of armbands. The Supreme Court ruled in favor of the students. The Court found the "silent, passive expression of opinion, unaccompanied by any disorder or disturbance" to be "closely akin" to pure speech. Although the wearing of the armbands used a symbolic action instead of speech as such, the action warranted First Amendment protection. The state may not prohibit expression of opinion without evidence that the rule is necessary to avoid interference with school discipline or the rights of others. Anticipation of a disturbance cannot provide the basis for regulating speech. The Court also found the ban defective in that it selectively singled out the symbol representing opposition to the Vietnam War while ignoring other political symbols.

Tinker affirmed the principle that symbolic expression may be protected by the Free Speech Clause of the First Amendment. A year later, the Court upheld a conviction for the burning of a draft card in protest of the Vietnam War in *United States v. O'Brien*.[125] The Court agreed that O'Brien's gesture was communicative, but it also found the act of destroying the draft card impaired a legitimate function of the government. Although certain symbolic acts may be protected, Chief Justice Warren said that the Court "cannot accept the view that an apparently limitless variety of conduct can be labelled 'speech' whenever the person engaging in the conduct intends thereby to express an idea." In *California v. La Rue*,[126] the Court upheld a liquor control regulation forbidding establishments with liquor licenses from having nude entertainment. The Court did not find performances with sexual overtones protected as symbolic speech.

Texas v. Johnson upheld the right of persons to express their political views by burning the American flag. Johnson was part of a group that gathered in Dallas to demonstrate at the 1984 Republican National Convention. The group marched through downtown Dallas to city hall where Johnson set fire to the flag. He was arrested and subsequently convicted for violation of the Texas law prohibiting flag desecration. The Supreme Court overturned the conviction and struck down the law. Texas' principal interest advanced in support of its conviction of Johnson was preservation of the flag as a "symbol of national unity." Justice Brennan pointed to prior decisions "recognizing the communicative nature of conduct relating to flags." He said that while government generally has a "freer hand in restricting expressive conduct" than the written or spoken word, it may not "proscribe particular conduct because it has expressive elements." Preservation of the flag as a symbol, on the other hand, relates to "suppression of expression." If there is a "bedrock principle underlying the First Amendment," said Brennan, it is that government may not "prohibit expression of an idea simply because society finds the idea itself offensive or disagreeable." Prior cases have not recognized an exception where the flag is involved nor have they allowed government to "insure that a symbol be used to express only one view of that symbol.

The flag desecration case of *Texas v. Johnson* was among the more controversial decisions in recent years, but was not the first case involving flags. The Court has recognized since the 1930s that flags have symbolic value as expression. In

1931 the Court struck down a state law in *Stromberg v. California*[127] that outlawed the display of a red flag because it symbolized "opposition to organized government." The Court felt that if such symbolic expression as this could be restricted, more general political debate would be seriously jeopardized. Although it has recognized the government's authority to punish certain improper conduct regarding the flag, the Court has generally permitted its symbolic use. *Street v. New York*,[128] for example, struck down a state law prohibiting flag mutilation. This case involved flag burning, but the Court focused on the overbroad character of the restriction. In *Smith v. Goguen*,[129] the Court reversed a conviction for the "contemptuous" conduct of a person who had sewn a small flag to the seat of his pants. That same year, the Court ruled in *Spence v. Washington*[130] that superimposing a peace symbol on the flag and flying it upside down was protected. These decisions notwithstanding, symbolic expression may be subject to regulation. The line is drawn by examining the action or conduct through which the message is conveyed.

Following the Court's decision in *Texas v. Johnson*, Congress enacted the Flag Protection Act of 1989. The Act made it a crime to "knowingly mutilate, deface, physically defile, burn, maintain on the floor or ground, or trample upon any flag of the United States." Upon passage of the federal law, flags were burned in a number of political demonstrations. *United States v. Eichman* and *United States v. Haggerty*[131] arose out of prosecutions for flag-burning incidents in Seattle and Washington, D.C., respectively. The cases were combined for review by the Supreme Court. The Court held that the federal law, like the state law in *Johnson*, violated the free speech protection of the First Amendment. Justice Brennan spoke for the same five-justice majority from *Johnson*, and his opinion substantially reiterated the rationale from that case. While conceding that flag burning is "expressive conduct," the government sought to have the Court declare flag burning a kind of expression that falls outside the full protection of the First Amendment. In drafting the federal law, an effort had been made to avoid the defect identified in *Johnson*—that is, regulating conduct on the basis of content. Although the Flag Protection Act contained no explicit content-based limitation on prohibited conduct, Justice Brennan said it was "nevertheless clear that the Government's asserted interest is related to the suppression of free expression, and is concerned with the content of such expression." The government's interest in "protecting the physical integrity of a privately owned flag" is based on the "perceived need to preserve the flag's status as a symbol of our nation and certain national ideals." The destruction of a flag, by itself, however, "does not diminish or otherwise affect the symbol." The government's desire to "preserve the flag as a symbol for certain national ideals is implicated only when a person's treatment of the flag communicates a message to others that is inconsistent with those ideals." The language of the Act "confirms" congressional intent to prevent the "communicative impact of flag destruction." Each of the terms chosen to define the criminal conduct "unmistakably connotes disrespectful treatment of the flag and suggests a focus on those acts likely to damage the flag's symbolic value." Allowing the government to prohibit flag burning when it endangers the flag's symbolic role would permit the state to "prescribe what shall be orthodoxy by saying that one may burn the flag to convey one's attitude toward it . . . only if one does not endanger the flag's representation of nationhood and national unity." Notwithstanding congressional effort to approach flag desecration differently from Texas, the Court still found the same fundamental flaw—"it suppresses expression out of concern for its likely communicative impact." Finally, the Court refused to reassess the *Johnson* ruling in light of Congress's asserted recognition of a "national consensus" favoring a prohibition on flag burning. Even presuming such a consensus exists, "any suggestion that the Government's interest in suppressing speech becomes more weighty as popular opposition to that speech grows is foreign to the First Amendment."

Offensive Speech

Cohen v. California held that even "offensive" expression is entitled to First Amendment protection. Cohen was arrested in the Los Angeles County Courthouse for wearing a jacket upon which were the words "Fuck the Draft." At his trial Cohen testified that the jacket was his means of stating his intensely held feelings about the draft and American involvement in Vietnam. Cohen was convicted of violating a statute prohibiting "malicious and willful disturbing of the peace" by conduct that is "offensive." The Supreme Court set aside Cohen's conviction. The Court ruled that the words were the issue rather than Cohen's conduct; it was his "speech" that was prohibited by enforcement of the law. The Court also held that the words on Cohen's jacket were not directed at anyone. Furthermore, a state cannot excise arguably offensive epithets by functioning as a guardian of public morality. Justice Harlan said the First Amendment is "designed and intended to remove governmental restraints from the arena of public discussion." A consequence of free speech "may often appear to be only verbal tumult, discord, and even offensive utterance," but that is the "price of the freedom."

　　Cohen v. California involved an attempt to regulate offensive speech through criminal prosecution for breach of the peace. The Court has ruled that obscene or libelous utterances are not protected by the First Amendment because they are of such minimal communicative value that any possible benefit is clearly outweighed by the social interest in order and morality. The Court included so-called fighting words in the category of unprotected speech in *Chaplinsky v. New Hampshire*.[132] In *Terminiello v. Chicago*,[133] however, the Court reversed the breach of the peace conviction of a highly provocative speaker, holding that a municipal ordinance was inappropriately applied to limit speech that "invites dispute." Two years later, however, the Court upheld the disorderly conduct conviction of a street-corner speaker in *Feiner v. New York*.[134] The Court said that when "clear and present danger of riot, disorder, interference with traffic upon the public street, or other immediate threat to public safety, peace, or order appears, the power of the State to prevent or punish is obvious." The case of *Rankin v. McPherson*,[135] involved the right of a public employee to engage in "offensive" speech. McPherson, an employee of a county constable, was fired from her job for saying to a coworker following the assassination attempt on President Reagan that "if they go for him again, I hope they get him." The Court ruled that McPherson's remarks should not have caused her to be fired because her remarks were made in the course of discussion of a matter of public concern. While a threat to kill the president would not be protected expression, McPherson's statement was not itself a threat and could not be criminalized. The inappropriate or controversial character of a remark is irrelevant to the question of whether it deals with a matter of public concern. Debate on such matters must be given "breathing space" to allow discussion to remain "uninhibited, robust, and wide-open." A different kind of offensive expression problem was examined in *Federal Communications Commission (FCC) v. Pacifica Foundation*.[136] Upon receipt of a listener's complaint, the FCC found that a radio station had aired an indecent program. The FCC issued an order to the station threatening subsequent sanction if such broadcasting reoccurred. The Supreme Court upheld the FCC's authority to issue such an order.

Hate Speech

The City of St. Paul, Minnesota, made it a crime to engage in "hate speech." An ordinance made it a misdemeanor to engage in speech or conduct likely to "arouse anger, alarm, or resentment in others on the basis of race, color, creed, religion or gender." The ordinance was challenged by a juvenile charged with violating the law by burning a cross on a black family's lawn. All nine members of the Court agreed in *R.A.V. v. City of St. Paul* that the ordinance violated the First Amendment, but the Court was deeply split on its reasons for that conclusion. Justice Scalia's opinion regarded the regulation as facially unconstitutional because it prohibited speech solely on the basis of its content. Under the ordinance, expression containing "abusive invective" is permissible unless it "addressed one of the specified disfavored topics." The First Amendment, said Scalia, does not permit St. Paul to "impose special prohibitions" on speakers who express views on subjects public officials place out-of-bounds. The question for those five justices joining Scalia's opinion was whether "content discrimination is reasonably necessary" to achieve a compelling interest. Their answer was "plainly not." The only interest served by the content limitations was the city council's "special hostility towards the particular biases thus singled out."

The Supreme Court returned to the hate crimes issue a year after *R.A.V.* in *Wisconsin v. Mitchell*.[137] The Wisconsin approach to hate speech was to authorize longer sentences for those criminal offenders who select their victims on the basis of "race, religion, color, disability, sexual orientation, national origin or ancestry." Todd Mitchell was convicted of aggravated battery, an offense that typically carries a two year maximum sentence in Wisconsin. Mitchell was sentenced to four years, however, because the jury determined that he intentionally had chosen his victim on the basis of race. The Wisconsin Supreme Court, citing *R.A.V.*, ruled for Mitchell. According to the state court, the Wisconsin legislature criminalized "bigoted thought with which it disagree[d]." A unanimous U.S. Supreme Court upheld the Wisconsin law, however, finding the argument that the enhanced sentence punishes only conduct to be persuasive. A physical assault "is not by any stretch of the imagination expressive conduct protected by the First Amendment." At the same time, the threshold condition for triggering the enhanced sentence is discriminatory motive in the selection of a particular victim. In other words, the Wisconsin law punishes someone more severely for conduct "motivated by a discriminatory point of view" than for the same conduct "engaged in for some other reason or for no reason at all." The Court resolved the problem in the state's favor in two ways. State legislatures possess "primary responsibility for fixing criminal penalties." As a result, state legislatures may reasonably decide that bias-motivated offenses warrant more substantial penalties. Motive plays the "same role" in Wisconsin's statute as it plays in federal and state antidiscrimination laws. Furthermore, judges who are about to sentence criminal offenders have traditionally been able to consider a "wide variety of factors" beyond the evidence directly bearing on guilt in determining an appropriate sentence. One such important factor is the defendant's motive for committing the crime. The Court saw the definition of aggravating circumstances for capital crimes as analogous. The Court also distinguished the Wisconsin law from the ordinance struck down in *R.A.V. v. City of St. Paul*. In *R.A.V.*, the ordinance had selectively targeted speech deemed offensive and, thus, violated the prohibition against "content-based discrimination." The Wisconsin law, on the other hand, aimed at "conduct unprotected by the First Amendment." In addition, the Wisconsin statute selected bias-motivated crimes for enhanced penalty because this kind of conduct is "thought to inflict greater individual and societal harm." The Court concluded that a state's "desire to redress these perceived harms provides an adequate explanation for its penalty-enhancement provisions over and above mere disagreement with offenders' beliefs or biases."

Overbreadth Doctrine

Schaumburg v. Citizens for a Better Environment struck down a local ordinance on the basis of the overbreadth doctrine. The Supreme Court examined a local ordinance that prohibited door-to-door solicitations for contributions by organizations not using at least 75 percent of their receipts for charitable purposes. A charitable purpose excluded such items as salaries, overhead, solicitation costs, and other administrative expenses. An environmental group was denied permission to solicit because it could not demonstrate compliance with the 75 percent requirement. The organization challenged the ordinance on First Amendment grounds, and the Court struck it down over the single dissent of Justice Rehnquist. The Court's primary objection was that the ordinance covered too much. The Court noted that a class of organizations existed to which the 75 percent rule could not constitutionally be applied. These were organizations "whose primary purpose is not to provide money or services to the poor, the needy, or other worthy objects of charity, but to gather and disseminate information about and advocate positions on matters of public concern."

Schaumburg v. Citizens for a Better Environment is important because it produced a requirement that statutes distinguish sufficiently between lawful and unlawful expression or behavior. In *Coates v. Cincinnati*,[138] the Court struck down a city ordinance that prohibited three or more persons from assembling on public sidewalks and conducting themselves in such a way as to "annoy any police officer or other persons who should happen to pass by." The Court found the ordinance "makes a crime out of what under the Constitution cannot be a crime." It was also impermissibly vague. It conveyed no standard of conduct and "men of common intelligence must necessarily guess at its meaning." Although the overbreadth and vagueness doctrines have often been invoked to invalidate enactments as in *Schaumburg* and *Coates*, some ordinances survive such challenges.

In *Grayned v. Rockford*,[139] the Court allowed an anti-noise ordinance prohibiting disturbances in the proximity of schools in session. The specific school context separated the restriction from the typically vague and general breach of the peace ordinance. The enactment was seen as a reasonable time, place, and manner restriction. It was narrowly tailored to further Rockford's compelling interest in having undisrupted school sessions and was not an impermissibly broad prophylactic.

In *Hoffman Estates v. Flipside, Inc.*,[140] the Court upheld an ordinance requiring a license to sell items designed or marketed for use with illegal drugs against claims that the ordinance was both vague and overbroad. The Court ruled that the ordinance merely sought to regulate the commercial marketing of illegal drug paraphernalia and did not reach other than commercial speech. The only potential limit on Flipside's conveying of information was confined to the commercial activity related to illegal drug use. The Court also found the vagueness claim unpersuasive. The "designed for use" provision of the ordinance covered at least some of the items sold at Flipside. The "marketed for use" language provided ample warning to the retailer about licensure and the display practices that could result in violation of the ordinance.

The *Schaumburg* reasoning was later applied to a state limitation on charity fund-raising expenses in *Secretary of State v. Joseph H. Munson Company*.[141]

Maryland had enacted a statute designed to prevent abusive and fraudulent fund raising by prohibiting a charity from spending more than 25 percent of its gross income for expenses. The Court invalidated the law, saying fund raising for charities was so intertwined with speech that it required First Amendment protection. The Maryland statute was based on the "fundamentally mistaken premise" that fund-raising costs that exceed 25 percent are fraudulent. In another case closely resembling *Munson*, the Court struck down a North Carolina "charitable solicitation" law that regulated the practices of professional fund raisers. The law divided fees charged by fund raisers into three categories. A fee up to 20 percent of receipts was deemed "reasonable." A fee between 20 and 35 percent was "unreasonable" if it could be shown that the solicitation did not involve certain activities, such as advocacy on a public issue as directed by the recipient of the solicitation proceeds. A fee of greater than 35 percent was presumed "unreasonable" but was rebuttable by the fundraiser. The law also required fundraisers to disclose the amounts of money actually turned over to charities during the past 12 months. This information was to be made available to potential donors before the solicitation campaign began. In addition, licensure of all fundraisers was mandated. A coalition of fundraisers and charitable organizations successfully challenged the provisions on free speech grounds. The Supreme Court found the provisions unconstitutional in *Riley v. National Federation for the Blind*.[142]

The Court also used the overbreadth doctrine to invalidate a local ordinance in *Board of Airport Commissioners v. Jews for Jesus*.[143] This case involved an ordinance banning "all First Amendment activities within the Central Terminal area of Los Angeles International Airport." The defect in the regulation was the policy went further than regulating expressive activity that might create problems, such as congestion or disruption in the airport. Such a regulation might be a permissible time, place, and manner restriction. Instead, this ordinance banned all expression in an effort to create a "virtual First Amendment Free Zone." Not only were groups such as Jews for Jesus reached by the regulation, but the ban extended "even to talking and reading, or the wearing of campaign buttons or symbolic clothing." Under such a sweeping ban virtually everyone entering the airport could be found in violation of the ordinance.

Regulation of Political Advertising

Michael Lebron sought to display a political advertisement on a large electronic billboard, known as the Spectacular, located in Penn Station, a facility owned by the National Railway Passenger Corporation (Amtrak). At the time Lebron signed a contract to lease space on the Spectacular, he indicated his ad would be political. He subsequently submitted a photograph of his ad and was informed that Amtrak did not allow political advertising on the Spectacular. Lebron filed suit in federal court claiming that refusal to display his advertisement was content-based censorship by a government agency. The district court ruled for Lebron, but the Court of Appeals for the Second Circuit reversed, concluding that Amtrak is not a government agency but a private entity. As a result, the Second Circuit ruled that Amtrak and its advertising policies were outside the reach of the First Amendment. The Supreme Court disagreed in *Lebron v. National Railroad Passenger Corp.*

Neither state nor federal government is "able to evade the most solemn obligations imposed in the Constitution by simply resorting to the corporate form." If such a thesis were true, *Plessy v. Ferguson*,[144] which allowed railroads to segregate passengers by race, could be "resurrected by the simple device of having the State of Louisiana operate segregated trains through a state-owned Amtrak." Scalia concluded that when the government creates a corporation "by special law, for the furtherance of governmental objectives, and retains for itself permanent authority to appoint a majority of the directors of the corporation, the corporation is part of the Government for purposes of the First Amendment."

The Bill of Rights is intended to protect individuals from unlawful actions of government. A plaintiff like Michael Lebron must demonstrate, among other things, that a rights violation was committed by an agency (or agent) of government. State action has been a centrally important issue in equal protection cases, but in *Lebron* the Second Circuit held that First Amendment claims require meeting a more stringent state action standard. The *Lebron* case provided the Supreme Court with an opportunity to clarify the standard by which state action is defined in First Amendment cases. Lebron argued that Amtrak was a governmental entity because, among other things, it was established by federal law, wholly owned by the federal government, subsidized by federal funds, and managed by a board of directors appointed by the federal government. Amtrak's contention that it was a private entity was based on the proposition that its function was commercial rather than governmental. It was further contended that language in the federal law creating Amtrak expressly declared that it was not a federal agency or instrumentality. The Court concluded that where the government creates a corporation by special law for the "furtherance of governmental objectives" and retains permanent authority to appoint the corporation's board of directors, the corporation is "part of the Government for purposes of the First Amendment." The Court also concluded that it was not for Congress to determine by statute the status of an entity such as Amtrak for the purposes of determining the applicability of constitutional rights.

Government Employee Expression

The Federal Ethics in Government Act of 1978 was amended in 1989 to prohibit federal officials and employees from receiving compensation for any appearance or expressive activity, even if the subject matter was unrelated to their work responsibilities. The honorarium ban included members of Congress, federal judges, certain executive branch employees above the salary grade of GS-15, and virtually all remaining federal employees up through the GS-15 grade level. The Act did not prohibit appearances or expressive activity on the part of covered officials and employees, but prohibited compensation for that activity. Violators were subject to civil penalty of up to $10,000 or the amount of compensation received. Several individual employees and unions representing them filed suit in federal court asserting that the ban on compensation violated the First Amendment. The Supreme Court found the ban to be unconstitutional and enjoined enforcement of the Act in *United States v. National Treasury Employees Union.*

Previous rulings such as *Pickering v. Board of Education*[145] had recognized, Justice Stevens suggested, that Congress may impose restraints on job-related speech of public employees that would be "plainly unconstitutional if applied to the public at large." Here, however, the government asked the Court to apply *Pickering* as a "wholesale deterrent to a broad category of expression by a massive number of potential speakers." The honoraria ban as applied to these employees "burdens speech" because the ban "deters an enormous quantity of speech before it is uttered, based only on speculation that the speech might threaten the Government's interests." Stevens pointed to the "significant contributions to the marketplace of ideas" made by federal employees such as Nathaniel Hawthorne, Walt Whitman, and Herman Melville. While the employees involved in this case had yet to make "comparable contributions to American culture," they share "important characteristics" with those artists. Even though these employees work for the government, said Stevens, they have not relinquished the First Amendment rights "they would otherwise enjoy as citizens to comment on matters of public interest." With few exceptions, the content of the employees' messages has "nothing to do with their jobs and does not even arguably have any adverse effect on their efficiency of the offices in which they work." The government's concern in enacting the honoraria ban was that federal employees not misuse or appear to misuse power by accepting compensation for their unofficial and nonpolitical expressive activities. The Court judged this interest "undeniably powerful," but noted the absence of any evidence of misconduct related to honoraria. Instead of a concern about the "cumulative effect of a widespread practice" that Congress deemed to "menace the integrity and the competency of service," the government relied on "limited evidence of actual or apparent impropriety." The Court concluded that the "speculative benefits the honoraria ban may provide the Government are not sufficient to justify this crudely crafted burden on [the employee's] freedom to engage in expressive activities." The Court found the lower courts' injunction "overinclusive," however, to the extent it reached senior executives not party to this case and to those situations in which an "obvious nexus" existed between the employee's job and either the subject matter of his or her expression or the interest of the person paying an honorarium.

Federal employees are subject to regulations that affect their free expression rights. The Hatch Act, for example, prohibits federal employees from participating in various political activities. The Hatch Act was upheld in *United Public Workers v. Mitchell*,[146] in which the Court concluded that such regulation does not violate the First Amendment if Congress reasonably believes it will interfere with the efficient performance of public service. The restriction at issue in *National Treasury Employees Union* was prompted by ethics concerns. Notwithstanding the importance of setting high ethical standards for those in government, most strong ethics reform proposals have the potential to impinge on free speech rights. The government argued in this case that expression was not prohibited under the regulation, only compensation for that expression. It also was asserted that the purpose of the ban on honoraria was to preserve the integrity of the federal workforce. The government contended that the controlling precedent in this case was *Pickering*. In that case, a public school teacher was dismissed because of his extensive criticism of both the school board and the school superintendent. The dismissal was based on the school board's determination that the teacher's views were "detrimental to the efficient operation and administration of the schools in the district." The Court ruled that Pickering's dismissal was not justified in this instance, but also recognized that government may restrict expression of its employees under some circumstances. *Pickering* requires courts to weigh an employee's interest in commenting on matters of "public concern" against the government's interest in having its employees perform effectively. Using the *Pickering* standard, the government argued in *National Treasury Employees Union* that the ban on compensation imposed only a minimal burden on expressive activity, a burden that was outweighed by the governmental interest in preserving the integrity of the federal workforce.

Freedom of the Press: Prior Restraint

Near v. Minnesota struck down a state law that imposed an unconstitutional prior restraint. Prior restraint is governmental censorship, and typically takes one of two forms. Prior restraint occurs when government must approve all content, or categorically bans particular content before publication.

The Court emphasized that the core of the free press protection is freedom from governmental censorship. The doctrine of prior restraint is built on the proposition that restraint of expression *before* it can occur constitutes a grave threat to free speech. Near published a weekly newspaper that engaged in vicious attacks on various public officials in Minneapolis. He was subsequently enjoined from publication under provisions of a Minnesota statute authorizing the abatement of any "malicious, scandalous and defamatory newspaper, magazine or periodical" as a "public nuisance." The Court found the statute unconstitutional. Before addressing the prior restraint question, the Court first determined that the free press provision fell within the liberty safeguarded by the Due Process Clause of the Fourteenth Amendment and applies to the states. The Court found the Minnesota statute defective because it was "not aimed at the redress of individual or private wrongs." Rather, it was aimed at distribution of material "for the protection of the public welfare." Although prosecution might occur against such publications after the fact, the state had insufficient interest to warrant a prior restraint. Chief Justice Hughes argued that the "object of the statute is not punishment, in the ordinary sense, but suppression." The suppression is "accomplished by enjoining publication, and that restraint is the object and effect of the statute." In short, the objectives and means embodied in the statute were the essence of censorship. The Court also pointed out that the statute too seriously limited what might be said about public officials. References to public corruption, malfeasance, or neglect of duty create a public scandal by their very nature. Under the statute, such content is scandalous and defamatory by definition. The Court said, "the recognition of authority to impose previous restraint upon publication in order to protect the community against the circulation of charges of misconduct, and especially of official misconduct necessarily would carry with it the admission of the authority of the censor against which the constitutional barrier was erected." While "charges of reprehensible conduct, and in particular official malfeasance, unquestionably create a public scandal, the theory of the constitutional guaranty is that even a more serious public evil would be caused by authority to prevent publication."

Near v. Minnesota was the Court's first significant censorship decision and provided the baseline standard in the critical matter of defining prior restraint. *Near* holds such restraint to be heavily suspect, but possibly justifiable in the instance of threats to national security, obscenity, incitements to governmental overthrow or other violence, or interference with private interests. The prior restraint exceptions set forth in *Near* have remained largely undisturbed. The Court struck down a "gag order" intended to safeguard jury selection in a criminal trial in *Nebraska Press Association v. Stuart*,[147] and freed the publication of the so-called Pentagon Papers in *New York Times Co. v. United States*, The "papers" were classified Defense Department documents that were illegally taken from the Pentagon and given to the *New York Times* and *Washington Post*. The documents contained a detailed and somewhat embarrassing historical account of American involvement in Vietnam. The Court also held that a group wishing to criticize the way a businessman conducted his business could circulate leaflets near the businessman's home and church in *Organization for Better Austin v. Keefe*.[148] Prior restraints have been allowed, however, within the exceptions stated in *Near*. In *Snepp v. United States*,[149] the Court required an ex-Central Intelligence Agency agent to obtain clearance from the agency prior to publication of any material relating to his former employment with the CIA, a regulation in place because agents have "frequent access to classified information, including information regarding intelligence sources and methods." The authority of school officials to exclude certain content from student publications was upheld in *Hazelwood School District v. Kuhlmeier.*

New York Times Co. v. United States (The Pentagon Papers Cases) dissolved an injunction against the *New York Times* restraining publication of the Pentagon Papers. The *Pentagon Papers Cases* examined the question of whether a prior restraint upon publication may be warranted if national security is threatened. The *New York Times* and the *Washington Post* came into possession of copies of Defense Department documents detailing the history of American involvement in the Vietnam War. After failing to prevent publication by direct request to the newspapers, injunctions were sought in federal court by the Nixon administration against the two papers to stop publication of the documents on national security grounds. An injunction was obtained against the *Times*, but not against the *Post*. The Supreme Court determined that injunctive restraints against either paper were unwarranted. In a brief per curiam opinion, the Court said there is a "heavy presumption" against prior restraint and that the "heavy burden" had not been carried in these cases.

The *Pentagon Papers Cases* represented an important free press challenge. The Supreme Court decision was expected to provide a definitive statement on when prior restraint might constitutionally be imposed, but the decision did not produce such a ruling. The Court's judgment actually hinged on the fairly narrow issue of whether the government had sufficiently demonstrated that immediate and irreparable harm would result from publication of the documents. Although the *Times* prevailed, the various opinions did not constitute a strong ruling for press freedom. The criminal prosecution of Daniel Ellsberg, who had furnished copies of the documents to the *Times* and the *Post* in the first place, was ultimately dismissed. Thus the Court was precluded from another opportunity to consider the free press issues contained in the Pentagon Papers imbroglio. Similarly, an attempt to prevent publication of an article in *The Progressive* about the manufacture of a hydrogen bomb was resolved prior to the matter reaching the Supreme Court.

Almost all the states have laws designed to prevent criminals from profiting from their crimes by selling their stories to book publishers or filmmakers. The Court's ruling in *Simon & Schuster, Inc. v. Members of the New York State Crime Victims Board*,[150] declared such laws unconstitutional. New York enacted such a law in 1977 soon after the arrest of David Berkowitz, an alleged serial killer. Berkowitz was popularly known as "Son of Sam," and New York's law became known as the "Son of Sam" law. Under terms of the law, any money earned by persons who admit to criminal conduct through their expressive works is placed in escrow and held for distribution to eligible victims for a five-year period. Initially, the New York law applied only to those convicted of a crime. Ironically, because Berkowitz was found incompetent to stand trial, the law was never applied to him. This case arose out of a contractual agreement between Simon & Schuster and an organized crime figure, Henry Hill. Hill and an author had produced a book, entitled *Wiseguy,* about his criminal life. The book was a commercial success, selling more than a million copies. The book was subsequently made into a film entitled, "Goodfellas," which enjoyed both critical and commercial success. The Crime Victims Board determined the book to be covered by the Son of Sam law. The Board ordered Hill to turn over payments already received, and ordered Simon & Schuster to turn over all future money payable to Hill. Simon & Schuster brought suit seeking declaration that the law was incompatible with the First Amendment. A unanimous Supreme Court agreed. Justice O'Connor said that a statute is "presumptively inconsistent" with the First Amendment if it "imposes a financial burden on speakers because of the content of their speech." The Court found the Son of Sam law to be such a content-based statute. The law "singles out income derived from expressive activity for a burden the State places on no other income, and it is directed only at works with a specified content." The financial disincentive of the law, said O'Connor, was placed "only on speech of a particular content." Furthermore, the Court concluded that the law was fatally "overinclusive," because it applied to works on "any subject, provided that they express the author's thoughts or recollections about his crime, however tangentially or incidentally." The Court concluded that such a law reached too "wide a range of literature" to pass First Amendment scrutiny.

Hazelwood School District v. Kuhlmeier upheld the broad authority of school officials to monitor and censor content thought to be objectionable for student publications. Former staff members of a high school newspaper brought suit claiming Hazelwood School District violated their First Amendment rights by deleting articles from a particular issue of the newspaper. The articles described student pregnancy experiences and the effect on students of parental divorce. The newspaper was produced by a journalism class as a part of the high school curriculum. The procedure established by the school district was that the principal reviewed all page proofs prior to publication. In this case, the principal objected to the article on pregnancy as inappropriate for some of the school's younger students. The article on divorce was found objectionable because it actually identified a parent by name and included accusations of abusive conduct. With publication imminent, the principal ordered the pages on which the two articles appeared to be withheld from the paper even though these pages contained other, unobjectionable material. The Supreme Court ruled that there was no First Amendment violation. While acknowledging that students do not "shed their constitutional rights to freedom of speech or expression at the schoolhouse gate," the Court said that the rights of students in public schools are not "automatically coextensive with the rights of adults in other settings." Rather, they must be applied in light of the "special characteristics of the school environment." A school "need not tolerate" student speech that is "inconsistent" with its "basic educational mission, even though the government could not censor similar speech outside the school." The Court rejected the assertion that the paper was a forum for public expression. School facilities are public forums only if they are open for "indiscriminate use" by the "general public" or a portion of the general public. On the other hand, if facilities have been "reserved for other intended purposes," no public forum exists and school authorities may impose "reasonable restrictions." In this case, the school district merely adhered to its policy that publication of the newspaper was part of the educational process and an activity subject to the control of the school staff. Because there was no intent to open the paper to "indiscriminate use" by the student body or even the newspaper's student staff, the Court ruled that the school officials were entitled to reasonably regulate the content of the paper. Educators may exercise greater control over certain expression to assure that participants "learn whatever lessons the activity is designed to teach," that readers or listeners are not exposed to material that may be "inappropriate for their level of maturity," and that the positions taken are not "erroneously attributed to the school." Educators, said the Court, do not violate the First Amendment by "exercising editorial control over the style and content of student speech in school-sponsored expressive activities" so long as their actions are "reasonably related to legitimate pedagogical concerns."

Hazelwood School District v. Kuhlmeier contained the central free press issue of censorship. Some distinctions can be drawn within the general prohibition against government censorship. Florida law, for example, prohibited publication of identifying information about the victim of a sex crime. The newspaper had been ordered to pay damages for publishing a victim's name although lawfully obtained from police records. The information had been included in a police report left in a law enforcement agency press room. Access to the room or documents located there was not restricted. The police report in which an individual was identified had been discovered by a reporter-trainee who copied the entire report. The information was subsequently published in a story appearing in the *Florida Star*. B.J.F., the identified victim, filed suit against the newspaper claiming negligent violation of the statute and was awarded both compensatory and punitive damages. The Supreme Court reversed in *Florida Star v. B.J.F.*[151] The Court chose not to establish the "broad" principle that damages for encroachment on privacy rights could never prevail over truthful publication. Instead, the Court resolved the issue on "limited principles" that "sweep no more broadly" than the "appropriate context" of this particular case. The Court drew heavily on *Smith v. Daily Mail Publishing Co.*,[152] which held that if a newspaper "lawfully obtains truthful information," it may not be punished for publication of that information "absent a need to further a state interest of the highest order." In this case the newspaper had accurately reported information lawfully obtained from a government agency. The Court saw "ample" and "less drastic means" open to the state to safeguard information than limiting publication. While acknowledging that protecting the privacy of sexual assault victims was "highly significant," imposing liability under these circumstances is "too precipitous a means" of protecting those interests.

Another state law permanently prohibited a grand jury witness from disclosing his or her testimony. To the extent the prohibition applied to a person's own testimony after the grand jury term ended, a unanimous Supreme Court struck down the regulation in *Butterworth v. Smith.*[153] The Court recognized the "tradition of secrecy" that has evolved as one of the ways to ensure grand jury impartiality and protect against "overreaching" by the state. At the same time, mere "invocation of grand jury interests is not 'some talisman that dissolves all constitutional protections.'" In this case the state sought to prevent Smith, a reporter, from "publication of information relating to alleged government misconduct—speech which has traditionally been recognized as lying at the core of the First Amendment."

New York Times Co. v. Sullivan held that publications may not be subjected to libel damages for criticism of public officials and their official conduct unless deliberate malice could be shown. *Sullivan* attached stringent conditions to certain kinds of libel actions involving speech attacking public officials. A state libel action was brought by a police commissioner in an Alabama court against the *New York Times* for its publication of a paid advertisement that charged police mistreatment of black students protesting racial segregation. It was stipulated that the advertisement contained errors of fact. The trial judge found the statements in the advertisement to be libelous and instructed the jury that injury occurred through publication, and that both compensatory and punitive damages could be presumed. Substantial damages were awarded by the jury, which also found malice on the part of the *Times*. The Supreme Court reversed the judgments in a unanimous decision. The Court's position was that libel law must provide free speech safeguards. To allow unrestricted libel actions "would discourage newspapers from carrying 'editorial advertisements' of this type, and so might shut off an important outlet for the promulgation of information and ideas." Such laws would shackle the First Amendment in its attempt to secure the widest possible dissemination of information from diverse and antagonistic sources. Even the factual errors did not jeopardize the advertisement's protected status. The protection of the advertisement, clearly "an expression of grievance and protest on one of the major public issues of our time," is not contingent on the truth, popularity, or social utility of the ideas and beliefs that are offered. Mistakes or errors of fact are inevitable in free debate and must be protected if freedom of expression is to have the "breathing space" it needs. Neither does injury to the reputation of a public official itself justify limiting expression. "Criticism of their official conduct does not lose its constitutional protection merely because it is effective criticism and hence diminishes their official reputations." Any rule "compelling the critic of official conduct to guarantee the truth of all his factual assertions—and to do so on pain of libel judgments virtually unlimited in amount—leads to a comparable self-censorship." Such a rule severely dampens the vigor and limits the variety of public debate. The Court did allow for recovery of damages when it can be proved that statements were made with actual malice, that is, with knowledge that statements were false, or with reckless disregard of whether they were false or not.

New York Times Co. v. Sullivan expanded the Court's experience with seditious libel, a special category of libel that involves defamation of government and its officials. The Alien and Sedition Acts of 1798 would have provided a basic test of seditious libel, but they never reached the Court. The Court has generally included libel in the category of unprotected speech. *Sullivan* provided the Court an opportunity to refine that classification. Libel laws cannot inhibit debate on public issues even if the debate includes strong and unpleasant attacks on the government and its officials. *Sullivan* held that public officials could protect themselves through libel actions in situations in which false statements were made with "actual malice" or with "reckless disregard of their falsity." The *Sullivan* decision approached an almost unconditional free press position relative to public officials. The Court soon extended *Sullivan* to criminal libel prosecutions in *Garrison v. Louisiana*.[154] In *Garrison* the Court said that regardless of limitations in other contexts, "where the criticism is of public officials and their conduct of public business, the interest in private reputation is overborne by the larger public interest, secured by the Constitution in the dissemination of the truth." Yet in *McDonald v. Smith*,[155] the Court held that communications to governmental officials influencing reputation are not immune from libel suits. McDonald had written to President Reagan urging the president not to nominate Smith to the position of United States attorney. Smith did not receive the nomination and subsequently filed a libel action against McDonald, claiming his letters to be malicious and knowingly false. McDonald argued that he was immune from such suit under his First Amendment right to petition the government. In a unanimous decision, the Court said that while the right to petition is guaranteed, "the right to commit libel with impunity is not."

The question of whether groups may be protected from defamatory statements was addressed in *Beauharnais v. Illinois*.[156] The Court upheld an Illinois statute prohibiting derogatory comment about any racial or religious group. The Court said that "we are precluded from saying that speech concededly punishable when directed at individuals cannot be outlawed if directed at groups with whose position and esteem in society the affiliated individual may be inextricably involved."

The Court reinforced the "deliberate malice" standard in *Bose Corp. v. Consumers Union of United States, Inc.*[157] The Court held that determination of malice in defamation suits is subject to full and thorough review on appeal. *Bose* called for appellate courts to exercise independent judgment and to make their own determination as to whether actual malice had been established with "convincing clarity." This is a more rigorous standard than is normally utilized at appellate levels, and it offers greater protection to publishers defending libel actions by creating a two-tiered system for finding actual malice. *Sullivan* protected publications from libel suits when critical comment had been made about governmental officials.

Soon thereafter the category of government official was expanded to include public figures, private citizens who are in the midst of public events, or persons who attract wide public attention. In *Rosenbloom v. Metromedia, Inc.*,[158] the Court went so far as to require reckless falsity in all actions, whether the plaintiff was a public official, a public figure, or a private individual. Rosenbloom, a distributor of nudist magazines, had been charged with possession of obscene materials. The Court ruled that Rosenbloom could not collect damages for radio broadcasts that referred to him as a "smut peddler" even after he was acquitted on the obscenity charges. *Gertz v. Robert Welsh, Inc.*[159] held that an individual did not become a public figure simply because the public was interested in a particular event with which he was associated. After a police officer had been convicted of murder, the attorney who represented the victim's family in a civil action against the officer was characterized in a magazine article as the "architect of a frame-up" of the officer, as having a criminal record, and as a Communist. The Court concluded the attorney was not a public figure, and thus did not need to show reckless falsity as a public figure must. Similarly, a federally funded researcher's media response to receipt of a senator's award for wasting public funds was held insufficient to establish public figure status in *Hutchinson v. Proxmire*.[160] U.S. Senator William Proxmire regularly conferred "Golden Fleece" awards to federal agencies he believed had engaged in "egregiously wasteful spending." The agency funding Hutchinson's research on various behavior patterns of animals received an award, and Hutchinson sought damages for defamation.

Yet another aspect of libel was addressed in 1984. In *Keeton v. Hustler Magazine, Inc.*[161] and *Calder v. Jones*[162] the Court found that courts have jurisdiction over out-of-state magazines and newspapers if the publications are regularly circulated in the state in which the court is located. Thus plaintiffs are afforded greater discretion in choosing which court will hear their libel actions. The Court maintained that the First Amendment had no direct bearing on the matter of jurisdiction and that the potential for danger to activities protected by the First Amendment is well integrated into the substantive law governing libel actions.

In 1985 the Court added a content criterion for private libel cases in *Dun & Bradstreet, Inc. v. Greenmoss Builders, Inc.*[163] It ruled that no finding of actual malice need occur unless the case involves a matter of public concern. Greenmoss had sued Dun & Bradstreet for damages based on the circulation of an erroneous credit report. Dun & Bradstreet claimed that Greenmoss must show the erroneous report was published with actual malice. The Court responded that purely private matters are of less First Amendment concern than public matters, thus underscoring the difference between private cases and cases involving public figures. *Greenmoss* increased the likelihood that private parties will collect damages in libel actions by eliminating the focus on actual malice. In *Philadelphia Newspapers, Inc. v. Hepps*,[164] however, the Court opined that a private figure suing a newspaper for defamation carries the burden of proving that defamatory statements of public concern are false. This is the converse of traditional libel law in which the defense must prove the statements true in order to prevail and that this switch in the burden of proof makes it more difficult for plaintiffs to win, especially because proving a negative is already very difficult. Soon after *Hepps*, the Court added the detail in *Anderson v. Liberty Lobby, Inc.*,[165] that trial judges should summarily dismiss, before a trial begins, public figure libel suits unless there is clear and convincing evidence of actual malice. This is the standard of proof any public figure plaintiff must demonstrate in order to succeed in a libel trial. The *Anderson* ruling enhances the probability that defendants will win pretrial dismissals in libel actions brought by public figures.

Libel: Parodies and Misquotes

Hustler Magazine v. Falwell held that a public figure cannot be awarded damages for the "intentional infliction of emotional distress" caused by the publication of a parody. Campari Liqueur conducted an advertising campaign in which celebrities discussed their first experiences with the liqueur—their "first times." *Hustler* published an advertisement parody, so labeled in small print at the bottom of the page, in which Falwell, a prominent religious and political personality, was represented as recalling his "first time" as a drunken and incestuous affair with his mother in an outhouse. Falwell brought suit against *Hustler*, claiming that publication of the parody entitled him to damages for libel and intentional infliction of emotional distress. The jury found that the parody could not reasonably be understood as representing actual facts, and it ruled for the magazine on the libel claim. The jury awarded Falwell damages on the emotional distress claim, however. The U.S. Court of Appeals for the Fourth Circuit affirmed, saying that in an emotional stress action brought by public figures, actual malice need not be shown. The Supreme Court unanimously reversed the lower courts and ruled for *Hustler*. The case presented the Court with a "novel" First Amendment question: whether a public figure may recover damages for "emotional harm" caused by publication of material "offensive to him, and doubtless gross and repugnant in the eyes of most." Falwell asked the Court to find that a state's interest in protecting public figures from emotional distress is "sufficient to deny First Amendment protection to speech that is patently offensive and is intended to inflict emotional injury," even when that speech could not "reasonably have been interpreted as stating actual facts about the public figure involved." This, said Rehnquist, "we decline to do." The sort of "robust" political debate encouraged by the First Amendment will necessarily produce expression that is "critical" of public figures who are "intimately involved in the resolution of important public issues." Such criticism will not always be "reasoned or moderate," and public figures will be subjected to "vehement, caustic, and sometimes unpleasantly sharp attacks." Only defamatory falsehoods uttered with knowledge that they are false or with "reckless disregard" for the truth provide a public figure with an opportunity to hold a speaker liable for damage to reputation. Falwell argued that as long as the utterance was "intended to inflict emotional distress, was outrageous, and did in fact inflict serious emotional distress," it did not matter whether the statement was fact or opinion or whether it was true or false. The Court rejected this contention. Rehnquist said that while the law does not regard the intent to inflict emotional distress as one that should "receive much solicitude," many things done with motives that are "less than admirable are protected by the First Amendment." Although bad motives may be "deemed controlling for purposes of tort liability" in other areas of the law, the First Amendment prohibits such a result in the "area of public debate about public figures." Were the Court to hold otherwise, said Rehnquist, there can be "little doubt" that political cartoonists and satirists "would be subject to damages awards without any showing that their work falsely defamed its subject." Rehnquist examined the history of political cartoons and caricatures. He concluded that despite their "sometimes caustic nature, . . . graphic depictions and satirical cartoons have played a prominent role in public and political debate." From a historical perspective, it is "clear that our political discourse would have been considerably poorer without them." He then rejected Falwell's contention that the *Hustler* parody was "so outrageous as to distinguish it from more traditional political cartoons." Rehnquist acknowledged that the *Hustler* caricature of Falwell was "at best a distant cousin" of the traditional political cartoon. If it were possible, he said, to lay down a "principled standard" to separate them, "public discourse would probably suffer little or no harm." Rehnquist doubted, however, that such a standard existed and "was certain" that the "pejorative description 'outrageous' does not supply one." "Outrageousness" in the field of political and social discourse has "an inherent subjectiveness" that would allow a jury to "impose liability on the basis of the jurors' tastes or views, or perhaps on the basis of their dislike of a particular expression." An "outrageousness" standard thus "runs afoul" of the "long-standing refusal" to permit damages to be awarded because expression may have an "adverse emotional impact on the audience."

The Court's decision in *Hustler Magazine v. Falwell* was important for two reasons. First, the decision indicated that the Court was not interested in making it easier for public figures to collect damages when subjected to criticism and satire. On the contrary, the decision discouraged plaintiffs who felt offended by media treatment from resorting to litigation as a means of recovery. Second, the decision dispelled speculation that the Court was on the verge of abandoning the "actual malice" rule established in *New York Times Co. v. Sullivan*. The so-called *Sullivan* rule has served as the basis for publications defending themselves in libel actions. During the past decade, the Court seemed to be in doubt as to whether the *Sullivan* rule provided public figures with enough room to protect themselves. The Court's decision in the *Hustler* case was squarely founded on *Sullivan*, and it was apparent that the Court was satisfied with the *Sullivan* rule as the basis for evaluating "public figure" libel actions. Since *Sullivan*, statements of opinion about public figures, as opposed to statements of "fact," have enjoyed virtual protection from libel actions. In addition to *Sullivan*, further support for a privilege for "comment" can be found in *Gertz v. Robert Welch, Inc.*, in which the Court said that under the First Amendment, "there is no such thing as a false idea. However pernicious an opinion may seem, we depend for its correction not on the conscience of judges and juries, but on the competition of other ideas." In *Milkovich v. Lorain Journal*,[166] the Court clarified this point and ruled that opinions are not categorically insulated from being found defamatory. Chief Justice Rehnquist said that the Court did not think that "this passage from *Gertz* was intended to create a wholesale defamation exception for anything that might be labeled opinion." Such an interpretation is not only contradictory to the "tenor and context" of the *Gertz* opinion, but would "ignore the fact that expressions of opinion may often imply an assertion of objective fact." The Court was satisfied that the "breathing space" needed for free expression was "adequately secured without the creation of an artificial dichotomy between 'opinion' and 'fact.'" A statement as a matter of public concern "must be provable as false before there can be liability under state defamation law." The key in these cases is separating "pure" opinion from opinion that "contains actionable assertions of fact."

The question in *Masson v. New Yorker Magazine, Inc.*[167] was whether fabricated quotations attributed to a public figure constituted sufficient cause to go to trial in a libel action. Masson, a psychoanalyst, was the subject of an unfavorable article by Janet Malcolm that appeared in *The New Yorker*. Before writing the article, Malcolm interviewed Masson extensively. Most of the interview sessions were taped. There were, however, several statements attributed to Masson for which there was no recording. Masson filed a libel action claiming that several statements enclosed in quotation marks were fabricated or deliberately misquoted. A U.S. district court granted summary judgment for *The New Yorker*, concluding that while Malcolm had deliberately altered the quotations, the inaccuracies did not raise a question of actual malice to put to a jury. The Supreme Court disagreed. According to Justice Kennedy, the constitutional question was whether the evidence was sufficient to show that a publisher "acted with the requisite knowledge of falsity or reckless disregard as to truth or falsity." Key to the Court's inquiry was the concept of falsity—whether the "requisite falsity inheres in the attribution of words to the petitioner [Masson] which he did not speak." Kennedy acknowledged that any "alteration of a verbatim quotation is false," but this falsity is only technical. Some alterations may make only minor changes to correct grammar or syntax. This kind of alteration clearly does not show actual malice. If an author, said Kennedy, changes a speaker's words, but "effects no material change in meaning, including any meaning conveyed by the manner or fact of expression, the speaker suffers no injury to reputation that is compensable as defamation." The Court refused to make determination of the falsity of quotations as a special kind of libel inquiry. Rather, the Court applied its longstanding definition of actual malice. A deliberate alteration of a speaker's words does not constitute knowledge of falsity, Kennedy concluded, "unless the alteration results in a material change in the meaning of the statement." Using quotation marks to attribute words not in fact spoken "bears in a most important way on the inquiry, but it is not dispositive in every case."

Newsperson's Privilege

Branzburg v. Hayes held that newspersons must disclose sources of information to a grand jury. After having published reports about drug use and manufacture, Hayes was subpoenaed to appear before a state grand jury and identify those persons he had seen using and making illegal narcotics. Hayes refused to testify and was cited for contempt. Through Justice White, the Supreme Court found that the First Amendment "does not invalidate every incidental burdening of the press that may result from the enforcement of civil or criminal statutes of general applicability." In balancing the interests of protecting the criminal process and the news-gathering function of the press, the former must prevail. The burden on the press was seen as too uncertain to justify treating newspersons differently from ordinary citizens. Journalists must respond to relevant questions put to them in the course of a valid grand jury investigation or criminal trial. The press burden in *Branzburg* was not prior restraint, a tax, a penalty on content, or a compulsion to publish. The Court suggested, however, that the impact of its holding would be limited. "Only where news sources themselves are implicated in crime or possess information relevant to the grand jury's task need they or the reporter be concerned about grand jury subpoenas. Nothing before us indicates that a large number or percentage of all confidential news sources fall into either category." Finally, the Court argued that abuse or harassment of the press would be subject to judicial scrutiny and possible intervention.

Branzburg rejected the argument of newspersons that they possess a privileged relationship with their sources, and had the effect of leaving information gathering largely unprotected. *Branzburg* said that even an unconditional freedom to publish would be of limited value if information gathering was unprotected. To protect the news-gathering function, several states have adopted shield laws designed to protect the confidentiality of sources. No such legislation exists at the federal level, although *Branzburg* did prompt introduction of such proposals.

The Burger Court rejected other claims of the press regarding its rights in the gathering of information. In *Saxbe v. Washington Post Co.*[168] the Court upheld federal prison regulations that prohibited press interviews with particular inmates. The

Court said that the Constitution does not impose upon government the "affirmative duty to make available to journalists sources of information not available to members of the public generally." Four years later, in *Houchins v. KQED, Inc.*[169] the Court upheld a refusal to allow media access to a county jail that had been the site of a prisoner's suicide and other alleged violent incidents, as well as charges of inhumane conditions. The majority saw the case as one involving a "special privilege of access" such as that denied in *Saxbe*. This is "a right which is not essential to guarantee the freedom to communicate or publish."

The Court refused to defer to editorial privilege in the libel case of *Herbert v. Lando*.[170] Herbert was a retired army officer with extended service in Vietnam. He received widespread media attention when he accused his superior officers of covering up reports of atrocities and other war crimes. Some three years after Herbert's disclosures, the Columbia Broadcasting System broadcast a report on Herbert and his charges on the television program *60 Minutes*. Lando produced and edited the program. He also published an article on Herbert in the *Atlantic Monthly*. Herbert's suit alleged that the "program and article falsely and maliciously portrayed him as a liar and a person who had made war crime charges to explain his relief from command." In attempting to develop proofs for his case, Herbert tried to obtain the testimony of Lando before trial, but Lando refused, claiming that the First Amendment protected against "inquiry into the state of mind of those who edit, produce, or publish, and into the editorial process." The Supreme Court found against Lando, holding that the First Amendment does not restrict the sources from which a plaintiff can obtain evidence. Indeed, "it is essential to proving liability that plaintiffs focus on the conduct and state of mind of the defendants." If demonstration of liability is potentially possible, "the thoughts and editorial processes of the alleged defamer would be open to examination." Such examination includes being able to inquire directly from the defendants whether they knew or had reason to suspect that their damaging publication was in error. The editorial privilege sought by Lando would constitute substantial interference with the ability of a defamation plaintiff to establish the ingredients of malice.

The Court ruled in *Cohen v. Cowles Media Co.*[171] that the news media is not protected from damage suits if the promise of confidentiality is breached. Cohen was closely associated with a gubernatorial campaign. He offered to render certain information about the opposing candidate for lieutenant governor, but only if the media promised not to disclose him as the source. The promise was given, and the information was exchanged. Over the objection of the reporters who had promised confidentiality, the editorial staff of two newspapers decided to reveal Cohen's name. It was their editorial judgment that readers were entitled to know the source and his interest in the outcome of the gubernatorial election. Cohen subsequently lost his job. He brought suit in state court alleging, among other things, breach of contract. The Minnesota Supreme Court ruled that the First Amendment prevented enforcement of such civil claims against the newspapers. The U.S. Supreme Court disagreed. The newspapers relied on previous decisions holding that states could not "punish" publication of lawfully obtained information. The Court, however, did not see that line of cases as governing here. Rather, the Court drew upon decisions rejecting special privilege for the press. Justice White said for the majority that it is "beyond dispute" that a newspaper has "no special immunity from the application of general laws." Generally applicable laws such as Minnesota's do not offend the First Amendment "simply because their enforcement against the press has incidental effects on its ability to gather and report the news." Further, the Court rejected the argument that the law punished publication of truthful information.

Coverage of Criminal Trials

Richmond Newspapers, Inc. v. Virginia determined that the press has a constitutional right of access to criminal trials. In *Richmond Newspapers* the defendant's counsel requested that a murder trial be closed to the public. The prosecutor expressed no objection, and the trial judge ordered the courtroom cleared. Under Virginia law, a trial judge has the discretion to exclude from a trial any person whose "presence would impair the conduct of a fair trial." The Supreme Court held the closure order was a violation of the right of access, a press right protected by the First Amendment. Chief Justice Burger traced the history of open trials and concluded "that a presumption of openness inheres in the very nature of a criminal trial under our system of justice." The Court said the open trial serves a therapeutic purpose for the community, especially in the instance of shocking crimes. Open trials offer protection against abusive or arbitrary behavior, and allow criminal processes "to satisfy the appearance of justice." Although access to trials is not specifically provided in the First Amendment, it is implicit. Without the freedom to attend trials, important aspects of free speech and a free press could be diminished. The closure order was defective because the trial judge made no finding of fact that an order was required. Alternatives to closure were not explored, there was no recognition of any constitutional right for the press or the public to attend the proceeding, and there was no indication that witness problems could not have been handled otherwise.

    Richmond Newspapers, Inc. v. Virginia rested on a distinction between the trial itself and pretrial proceedings, and elevated the press interest to prevailing weight in the former. In most instances, the Supreme Court has found that a criminal defendant needed to be shielded from media coverage in pretrial hearings as a basic requirement of due process.

    Consistent with the objective of minimizing adverse pretrial publicity, the Court allowed closure of pretrial proceedings in *Gannett Co. v. De Pasquale*.[172] The Court held in *Nebraska Press Association v. Stuart* that material from a public proceeding or record could not be kept from the public through a court gag order.

Nebraska Press Association also said the press cannot be restrained from reporting what it observes.

A balance of press and criminal defendant interests was struck in *Chandler v. Florida*,[173] in which the Court upheld a policy whereby trials might be broadcast as long as broadcast coverage was not disruptive, intrusive, or prejudicial to the outcome of the trial.

In *Press-Enterprise Co. v. Superior Court* (I),[174] the Court added the detail that the voir dire examination must also be open to the public and the press. The presumption of openness can only be overcome by an "overriding interest" that needs protection through narrowly tailored closure. Two years later the Court softened the distinction between trials and pretrial criminal proceedings in *Press-Enterprise Co. v. Superior Court* (II),[175] It narrowed the scope of *Gannett* by saying that closure of pretrial proceedings can only occur when such action is "essential to preserve higher values and is narrowly tailored to serve the interest," a standard that will likely make the closure of pretrial proceedings more difficult.

Commercial Press

Central Hudson Gas & Electric Co. v. Public Service Commission established standards by which commercial content in speech may be evaluated. The United States experienced fuel shortages in the early 1970s, and New York's Public Service Commission ordered all electric utilities in the state to stop promoting the use of electricity. Even after the fuel shortage eased, however, the Commission sought to continue the ban on promotional advertising. Central Hudson Gas & Electric Co. unsuccessfully challenged the advertising ban in the state courts on First Amendment grounds. The Supreme Court found the categorical elimination of promotional advertising by electric utilities to violate the First Amendment. Commercial speech is expression exclusively related to the "economic interests of the speaker and its audience." What First Amendment protection is afforded commercial speech is "based on the informational function of advertising." Although government may regulate commercial messages that inaccurately inform the public about lawful activity, the government's power is "more circumscribed" if the communication is neither "misleading nor related to unlawful activity."

The state's interest in energy conservation was, in contrast, "directly advanced" by the advertising ban. The final consideration was whether the Commission's "complete suppression of speech ordinarily protected by the First Amendment is no more extensive than necessary to further the State's interest in energy conservation." The order applied to all advertising "regardless of the impact of the touted service on overall energy use." The Court concluded that as important as the energy conservation rationale was, it could not justify suppression of information about, for example, "electric devices or services that would cause no net increase in total energy use." In the absence of a showing that more limited speech regulation would be ineffective, the Court could not "approve the complete suppression of Central Hudson's advertising."

The Burger Court was responsible for expanding the protections afforded commercial content. *Central Hudson* established the currently used criteria for reviewing commercial expression. *Pittsburgh Press Co. v. Pittsburgh Commission on Human Relations*[176] demonstrated several years earlier that particular kinds of commercial speech may be regulated. Restrictions such as that in *Pittsburgh Press* were not altered by *Central Hudson*. The Pittsburgh Press Company was found to be in violation of a Human Relations Commission ordinance because it placed help-wanted advertisements in sex-designated columns. The Commission ordered the newspaper to end the gender-referenced layout of the advertisements, and the Supreme Court ruled that the order was not prior restraint. The Court first determined that the advertisements were commercial speech, not merely because they were advertisements but because of their commercial content. They were, in fact, "classic examples of commercial speech" because of the proposal of possible employment. They were therefore unlike the political advertisement in *New York Times Co. v. Sullivan*. The Pittsburgh Press Company argued that editorial judgment about where to place an advertisement should control, rather than its commercial content. The Court answered that "a newspaper's editorial judgments in connection with an advertisement take on the character of the advertisement and, in those cases, the scope of the newspaper's First Amendment protection may be affected by the content of the advertisement." The kind of editorial judgment involved in this case did not strip commercial advertising of its commercial character. Even more crucial was the fact that the commercial activity involved was illegal employment discrimination. In the Court's view, advertisements could be forbidden in this instance just as advertisements "proposing a sale of narcotics or soliciting prostitution" could be forbidden. The justices concluded that any First Amendment interest that applies to an ordinary commercial proposal is "altogether absent when the commercial activity itself is illegal and the restriction on advertising is incidental to a valid limitation on economic activity."

The commercial speech holding in *Central Hudson* had its origin in *Valentine v. Chrestensen*.[177] The latter decision clearly put commercial speech outside First Amendment coverage. *New York Times Co. v. Sullivan* substantially narrowed the *Chrestensen* concept of commercial speech, and following *Pittsburgh Press*, the Burger Court narrowed the definition even further. In *Bigelow v. Virginia*,[178] the Court protected the publication of an advertisement by an organization offering services related to legal abortions in another state. The Court held the advertisement "conveyed information of potential interest and value to a diverse audience," not merely a commercial promotion of services. The next year, in *Virginia State Board of Pharmacy v. Virginia Citizens Consumer Council, Inc.*,[179] the Court struck down a

statute that made advertising of prescription drugs a form of conduct possibly leading to a suspension of license. The Court argued that even if the advertiser's interest
is a purely economic one, such speech is not necessarily disqualified from protection. The consumer and society in general have a "strong interest in the free flow
of commercial information." Such a free flow is indispensable in a predominantly
free enterprise economy that requires many private economic decisions.

Under terms of the Agricultural Marketing Agreement Act, the Secretary of
Agriculture may assess a fee from those engaged in the "handling" of agricultural
commodities to help underwrite the costs of advertising initiatives designed to promote particular products. A number of California handlers of peaches, plums, and
nectarines including Wileman Brothers and Elliott, Inc. challenged on First Amendment grounds the secretary's authority to issue such "marketing orders." The Supreme Court rejected the free speech challenge in *Glickman v. Wileman Bros.*[180]

Instead, Justice Stevens set a context from which the Court approached this
case. The claimed disagreement with the content of the generic advertising and
the effectiveness of the advertising had "no bearing on the validity of the entire
program." Furthermore, the businesses required to pay for the generic advertising
"do so as part of a broader collective enterprise in which their freedom to act independently is already constrained by the regulatory scheme." Justice Stevens suggested that three characteristics of this regulatory scheme distinguish it from laws
the Court has struck down in the past. The marketing orders "impose no restraint
on the freedom of any producer to communicate any message to any audience,"
do not compel anyone to "engage in any actual or symbolic speech," and do not
compel the producers to "endorse or to finance any political or ideological view."
Because Wileman Brothers engaged in the business of marketing California nectarines, plums, and peaches, "it is fair to presume that they agree with the central message" of the generic advertising. Accordingly, the Court saw no reason to subject the
regulations to closer scrutiny than that applicable to the other anticompetitiveness
features of the marketing orders. The First Amendment has never been construed,
said Justice Stevens, "to require heightened scrutiny of any financial burden that
has the incidental effect of constraining the size of a firm's advertising budget."
The "compelled speech" case law was seen as inapplicable here because the use of
assessments to pay for the generic advertising did not require Wileman Brothers to
"repeat an objectionable message" or "engender any crisis of conscience."

Wileman Brothers' preference to foster an independent message that might
better promote its own products did not, in the Court's view, make this case "comparable to those in which objection rested on political or ideological disagreement
with the content of the message."

Regulation of commercial content by professional associations was at issue
in *Shapero v. Kentucky Bar Association.*[181] Lawyers are able to advertise, but are
not permitted by rules of the profession to directly solicit legal business. Shapero

wished to send a letter to potential clients threatened with foreclosure, but approval was withheld by the state bar association on the ground that the letter violated a state court rule barring targeted advertising. The court rule was grounded on the American Bar Association's Model Rules of Professional Conduct, which prohibit such solicitation. The Supreme Court held that the comprehensive ban on targeted, direct-mail solicitation violated the First Amendment. The Court saw the sending of "truthful and nondeceptive" letters to potential clients as protected commercial speech. Such speech, said the Court, can only be restricted in order to pursue "substantial governmental interests" and only in ways that "directly advance" such interests. The "possibility of improper conduct and the improbability of effective regulation" are diminished in the direct-mail situation. The direct-mail approach, said the Court, is less "coercive" than in-person solicitation and can be scrutinized as are other forms of advertising.

The Florida Bar Association sought to change a number of its regulations for attorney advertising. Among the proposed changes was a categorical prohibition on direct-mail advertising by lawyers or lawyer-referral services to accident victims who had potential wrongful death or personal injury claims. The Florida Supreme Court did not approve a total ban on direct-mail advertising, but fashioned a rule that prohibited direct-mail contact to accident victims for 30 days from the date of an accident. The Supreme Court ruled that the modified rule did not violate the First Amendment in *Florida Bar v. Went For It, Inc.*[182] Attorney advertising is commercial speech, a category of communication entitled to limited First Amendment protection. The analytic framework for commercial speech cases comes from *Central Hudson Gas & Electric Co. v. Public Service Commission*. Provided that the advertising is not misleading nor involves illegal activity, *Central Hudson* allows regulation of commercial speech if the government can demonstrate that a narrowly drawn regulation materially advances a substantial governmental interest.

The Florida Bar Association contended that the regulation protected the privacy of personal injury victims and their families from "intrusive" unsolicited contact by attorneys, and protected the reputation of the legal profession by keeping its members from engaging in inappropriate conduct. Justice O'Connor said the Court had "little trouble" finding the interest of protecting potential clients' privacy to be substantial. Indeed, the state's interest in protecting the "well-being, tranquility, and privacy of the home is certainly of the highest order." The Court also found the regulation to advance the state's interest in a "direct and material" way. The regulation attempted to forestall irritation with the state-licensed legal profession that direct solicitation engenders, and throwing the letter away does not abate the irritation that comes from simply receiving such a targeted solicitation. Those challenging the direct-mail regulation argued that the rule prohibited targeted mailing even to those with relatively minor injuries. The Court was not convinced that a regulation distinguishing potential recipients of direct mail by degree of pain or grief could be developed.

Ladue, Missouri had an ordinance banning all residential signs except those falling within ten specified exemptions. Among the exemptions were "residence identification" signs, "for sale" signs, and signs warning of safety hazards. Commercial establishments, churches, and nonprofit organizations were allowed to place certain signs that were not allowed at residential sites. Margaret Gilleo placed a two-foot by three-foot sign in her yard expressing her opposition to the Persian Gulf War. She was informed that she was in violation of the sign ordinance. She first sought a variance from the ordinance from the city council. When she failed to obtain the variance, she obtained a temporary injunction against enforcement of the ordinance. The city council amended the ordinance by eliminating the language allowing for variances and grandfathering signs already exempted under the original ordinance. Gilleo then amended her complaint and pursued a permanent injunction against the modified ordinance. In late 1991 a federal district court granted a permanent injunction against enforcement of the more recent version of the ordinance, and the Supreme Court unanimously agreed in *City of Ladue v. Gilleo*.[183] Justice Stevens acknowledged that signs are a "form of expression" protected by the Free Speech Clause. Unlike oral speech, however, signs pose a variety of problems that "legitimately call for regulation." Stevens suggested that there are two "analytically distinct" grounds for challenging municipal regulation of signs. One is that the regulation "restricts too little" because its exemptions discriminate on the basis of the signs' content. An impermissibly underinclusive regulation may either attempt to give one side of a "debatable public question an advantage" or place government in a position to "select the permissible subjects for public debate." The second ground on which sign regulations might be attacked is that they "simply prohibit too much protected speech." The Ladue ordinance covered "even such absolutely pivotal speech as a sign protesting an imminent government decision to go to war." The ordinance left residents of Ladue with virtually no way to display any sign on their property. Indeed, Ladue had "almost completely foreclosed a venerable means of communication that is unique and important." Signs that "react to a local happening or express a view on a controversial issue both reflect and animate change in the life of a community." The Court also was unpersuaded that Ladue's ordinance was nothing more than a "time, place or manner" regulation that left residents with sufficient alternate means to express themselves. Displaying a sign from one's own residence, said Stevens, "often carries a message quite distinct from placing the same sign somewhere else, or conveying the same text or picture by other means." The location of signs provides information about the identity of the speaker, an "important component of many attempts to persuade." Although government may need to "mediate among various competing uses, including expressive ones," for public streets and facilities, its "need to regulate temperate speech from the home is surely much less pressing." In conclusion, Stevens observed homeowners have strong incentives for preventing "visual clutter" in their own yards. Such self-interest "diminishes the danger of unlimited proliferation of residential signs." The

Court was convinced that "more temperate measures" could satisfy Ladue's stated regulatory needs without harm to the First Amendment interests of its residents.

The Federal Alcohol Administration Act was passed in 1935 and imposed various regulations on the marketing of alcoholic beverages. The Act prohibits, among other things, statements about the alcohol content of beer and other malt beverages on container labels or in product advertising. Coors Brewing Company sought approval of proposed labels and advertising that included alcohol content statements for its beer. The applications were denied by the Bureau of Alcohol, Tobacco, and Firearms, the federal agency that administers the Act. The regulation covering advertising was upheld, and Coors did not appeal. The labeling regulation, however, was struck down by a federal district court, a decision affirmed by the Supreme Court in *Rubin v. Coors Brewing Co.*[184] Both the government and Coors agreed that the labels bore only "truthful, verifiable, and nonmisleading factual information," thus the Court's inquiry focused on the two asserted governmental interests for the beer label regulation. The government claimed that the label restriction "facilitated" efforts to effectively regulate alcohol, but the Court was unpersuaded that the government's interest in facilitating state regulatory initiatives was substantial enough. The second interest advanced by the government was to curb "strength wars"—that is, to deter competition for customers on the basis of the alcohol content of beer. The Court agreed that deterring strength wars was a substantial interest. Justice Thomas turned to the closeness of "fit" between the government's objective in deterring strength wars and the means chosen to achieve that end. The government, he said, carries the burden of showing that the label ban advances the government's interest in a "direct and material way," and that burden is not met by "mere speculation and conjecture." The Court concluded that the label regulation could not directly and materially advance the government's asserted interest because of the "overall irrationality of [its] regulatory scheme." Although the federal label restriction prohibited disclosure of alcohol content on labels unless required by state law, federal law applied a contrary policy to advertising. The federal restriction on statements about alcohol content in advertising applied only in states that prohibited such statements. Because only 18 states had such advertising limitations, brewers remained "free to disclose alcohol content in advertisements, but not on labels, in much of the country." Thomas suggested that advertising seemed to be a "more influential weapon" in strength wars than labels, thus the failure to prohibit disclosure of alcohol content in advertising made "no rational sense" if the true governmental objective was suppression of strength wars. Thomas also noted that brewers were able to "signal" higher alcohol content through use of terms such as "malt liquor." One would think, he continued, that if the government sought to suppress strength wars by prohibiting use of numbers reflecting alcohol content, it would also preclude brewers from "indicating higher alcohol beverages by using descriptive terms." Although the government's interest in combating strengths wars "remains a valid goal," Thomas continued, the "irrationality of this unique and puzzling regulatory framework ensures that the labeling ban will fail to achieve that end."

The state of Rhode Island prohibited the advertising of liquor prices as part of a more comprehensive set of regulations applying to alcoholic beverages. All media within the state were prohibited from carrying any such advertising, and all retail liquor outlets were prohibited from posting advertising visible from outside their premises. These restrictions applied to all such price advertising, including ads that were truthful and did not mislead. Two retail liquor outlets successfully sought to enjoin enforcement of the price advertising regulation. The Supreme Court struck down the ban in *44 Liquormart, Inc. v. Rhode Island*.[185] Although several opinions were issued, there was consensus on that part of the ruling stemming from the Twenty-First Amendment, which repealed Prohibition, and delegated to the states the authority to regulate alcohol, including its transport. Justice Stevens said that the amendment "does not qualify" the prohibition against laws abridging free speech; it does not "license the States to ignore their obligations under other constitutional provisions." There was less consensus on the commercial speech aspects of the case. Stevens attempted to differentiate between commercial messages. Regulation of commercial messages undertaken to protect consumers from misleading or untruthful sales practices "justifies less than strict review." On the other hand, when a state imposes a categorical ban on truthful, nonmisleading commercial messages for purposes unrelated to the preservation of a fair bargaining process, there is "far less reason to depart from the rigorous review that the First Amendment generally demands." There are, Stevens noted, "special dangers that attend complete bans on truthful, nonmisleading commercial speech" that cannot be explained away by reference to "commonsense" differences between commercial and noncommercial speech. Bans that target truthful and nonmisleading commercial messages rarely protect consumers from "commercial harms." Rather, they often serve only to "obscure an 'underlying governmental policy' that could be implemented without regulating speech." Indeed, bans against truthful, nonmisleading commercial speech usually are based on the "offensive assumption that the public will respond irrationally to the truth." The First Amendment, Stevens concluded, requires the Court to be especially skeptical of restrictions that seek to "keep people in the dark for what government perceives to be their own good." That skepticism "applies equally" to attempts to "deprive consumers of accurate information about their chosen products." This decision suggests that proposed regulation of cigarette advertising will face stringent examination by the Court. Justice Thomas categorically rejected that the government can keep "legal users of a product or service ignorant in order to manipulate their choices in the marketplace." Because the proposed restrictions on cigarette advertising are aimed at advertising to minors—that is, to nonlegal users of cigarettes—it might be possible for the Court to uphold the restrictions notwithstanding the ruling in *44 Liquormart*.

The Discovery Network is a private company that broadcasts educational and social programs. In addition, it publishes a magazine promoting its programming, but also containing information about current events. The magazines were distributed from freestanding newsracks, 62 of which were located by permit on public property in Cincinnati, Ohio. In March 1990 the city revoked the Discovery Network's permit to place news racks on public property. The revocation notice said the magazines were "commercial handbills" within the meaning of a city ordinance that prohibited the distribution of that class of material on public property. The Supreme Court ruled against the prohibition in *Cincinnati v. Discovery Network, Inc.*[186] The Court concluded that Cincinnati had not "carefully calculated the costs and benefits associated with the burden on speech associated with the prohibition." Justice Stevens focused on the city's contention that the restriction could be justified because commercial speech, as distinct from noncommercial speech such as the reporting of news, "has only a low value." In his view, the argument "seriously underestimates the value of commercial speech," and provides insufficient justification for the "selective and categorical ban on news racks dispensing commercial handbills." Even though the city had not acted with animus toward the content of the Discovery Network's publication, whether a news rack was subject to the regulation was determined by the "commercial" content of the magazines in any news rack. Cincinnati did not regulate newsracks generally. Rather, it sought only to eliminate news racks containing commercial publications. The Court found no justification for such a prohibition other than the city's "naked assertion that commercial speech has low value." The absence of a neutral justification for the "selective ban" on news racks precluded Cincinnati from "defending its news rack policy as content-neutral."

Broadcast and Cable Regulation

The Cable Television Consumer Protection Act of 1992 included "must carry" provisions that required cable television operators to carry programming of certain local and public broadcast stations. This requirement was immediately challenged. The Court ruled in *Turner Broadcasting System, Inc v. FCC (Turner I)* that review of the FCC's "must carry" regulations should be conducted at the intermediate scrutiny level. Applying that standard, the Court placed the burden on the FCC of demonstrating that the requirement advanced important governmental interests in the least restrictive way. The Court then remanded the case for further consideration of whether the "must carry" requirement actually met this test. On remand, a three-judge district court upheld the provisions by a two-to-one vote. The cable industry pursued direct appeal to the Supreme Court in *Turner Broadcasting System, Inc. v. Federal Communications Commission (FCC) (Turner II)* but was unsuccessful in persuading the High Court that the regulation was unconstitutional.

Three interrelated interests were identified in *Turner I* as being served by the "must carry" requirements: (1) preservation of local broadcast television carried over the air; (2) promotion of multiple-source information dissemination; and (3) promotion of fair market competition for television programming. The Court reaffirmed in *Turner II* that each constituted an important government interest. Congress was reasonably concerned that without the "must carry" regulations, significant numbers of broadcast stations would be refused carriage on cable systems, and that those stations not carried on cable would "deteriorate to a substantial degree or fail altogether." Further, Congress was concerned that without regulatory action, there would be a reduced number of "media voices available to consumers." Employing an approach that extended deference to legislative judgments, the Court concluded that Congress had a substantial basis for believing that a "real threat" to the broadcast industry justified enactment of the "must carry" provisions. Among the evidence supporting the congressional conclusions were: (1) the "considerable and growing market power" that cable operators had over local programming markets; (2) the local "monopoly" that cable operators possess over cable households; (3) the increasing capacity and inclination of cable operators to reposition local broadcast stations to less-viewed channels or drop those stations from their systems altogether; and (4) the growing number of stations that had lost operating revenue as a result of "adverse carriage decisions" of the cable systems. Taken together, the Court was satisfied that Congress had sufficient basis to conclude that local broadcast stations were "endangered" in the absence of regulation, and that the "must carry" approach served the government's interests in a "direct and effective way." Finally, the Court examined the "fit" between the asserted interests and the means chosen to advance them. The "must carry" regulations potentially interfered with protected speech in two ways: restraint of editorial discretion of those operating cable systems, and the greater difficulty cable operators might have in competing for programming on the channels remaining available to them after meeting the "must carry" requirements. The Court concluded that the "must-carry" requirement was "narrowly tailored to preserve a multiplicity of broadcast stations for the 40 percent of American households without cable."

Regulation of the cable industry was preceded by extensive regulation of the broadcast medium. In *Red Lion Broadcasting Co. v. FCC*,[187] for example, the Court upheld a Federal Communications Commission regulation known as the fairness doctrine. Red Lion broadcast a particular program during which the honesty and character of a third party were impugned. The third party demanded free time for a response, but was refused. The FCC then held that Red Lion had failed to satisfy a requirement of equity and equal access. The Supreme Court unanimously upheld the constitutionality of the FCC position. The Court acknowledged that broadcasting is clearly a medium affected by First Amendment interests, but it emphasized some critical differences from the print medium. Among these are the limited number of channels available and the incomparably greater reach of the radio signal. Scarcity of access means Congress "unquestionably has the power to grant and deny licenses," a power vested by Congress in the Federal Communications Commission. The license permits broadcasting, but the licensee "has no constitutional right to be the one who holds the license or to monopolize a radio frequency to the exclusion of his fellow citizens." The Court said the First Amendment does not prevent the government from requiring a licensee to share a frequency with others and to "conduct himself as a proxy" with obligations to present views that are representative of his or her community and that would otherwise be barred from the airwaves. Government has an obligation to preserve access for divergent views because of the unique character of the broadcast medium. Justice White said the people retain their interest in free speech through broadcast and have a collective right to the medium functioning consistently with the ends and purposes of the First Amendment. It is the "right of the viewers and listeners, not the right of broadcasters, which is paramount." Without regulations such as the fairness doctrine, station owners and a few networks would have "unfettered power to make time available only to the highest bidders, to communicate only their own views on public issues, people and candidates, and to permit on the air only those with whom they agreed." The Court concluded that there is no sanctuary in the First Amendment for unlimited private censorship operating in a medium not open to all. The thrust of *Red Lion* is that a balance must be struck between the First Amendment interests of the broadcast medium and the need to regulate governmentally granted channel monopolies. The fairness doctrine at issue in *Red Lion* had not kept the station from expressing its own views. It had only required that reply time be provided when a station carries a broadcast that attacks an individual personally.

The print media may not be required to do the same thing, however. In *Miami Herald Publishing Co. v. Tornillo*,[188] the Court struck down a Florida right-to-reply statute that required reply space in a newspaper for any political candidate who was attacked. Such required space was found to be a constitutionally impermissible prior restraint. Such a law authorizes governmental "intrusion into the function of editors in choosing what material goes into a newspaper."

Similarly, the Court typically has held that the airwaves need not become a common carrier with access guaranteed to any private citizen or group. *Columbia Broadcasting System, Inc. v. Democratic National Committee*[189] determined that a broadcaster policy of refusing to sell editorial advertisements was an acceptable practice and not incompatible with the fairness doctrine, but upheld a right of reasonable access for candidates for federal office in *Columbia Broadcasting System, Inc. v. Federal Communications Commission*.[190]

The power of Congress to prohibit editorials on stations receiving funds from the Corporation for Public Broadcasting was disallowed in *FCC v. League of Women Voters*.[191] Congressionally imposed editorial restrictions affect "precisely that form of speech the Framers were most anxious to protect." Content-defined discussion of public issues is the purest example of discourse that must be allowed to proceed unfettered.

A 1988 amendment to the Federal Communications Act made it a crime to use a telephone to send an "indecent" as well as an "obscene" message for commercial purposes. Although the objective of earlier regulations had been to protect minors from such communications, the 1988 amendment banned "obscene and indecent" communications to any recipient. Challenge to the amendment was considered by the Supreme Court in *Sable Communications of California, Inc. v. FCC*.[192] The Court ruled for Sable Communications with respect to the regulation of "indecent" messages, but upheld the authority of Congress to impose a total ban on "obscene" messages. It had been argued by Sable Communications that the law created a "national standard of obscenity" in a manner incompatible with *Miller v. California*. Although *Miller* allowed localities to enforce their own "communities' standards," it did not preclude Congress from prohibiting "communications that are obscene in some communities under local standards even though they are not obscene in others." The sender, while obligated to comply with the ban, said the Court, is free to "tailor its messages, on a selective basis, to the communities it chooses to serve." The Court was unanimous in striking down the regulation of "indecent" content as an overly broad restriction. The amendment was designed to protect minors from the messages, an interest the Court acknowledged to be "compelling." The ban, however, denied adult access to messages that are "indecent but not obscene," a policy that "far exceeds that which is necessary to limit the access of minors to such messages." The Court distinguished regulation of "indecent" radio broadcasts from the "dial-it medium" because the latter requires the listener to take "affirmative steps to receive the communications." The government's contention that only a total ban could protect against access by minors was, accordingly, seen as "unpersuasive" by the Court.

Among other things, the Cable Television Consumer Protection and Competition Act of 1992 required (in Sections 4 and 5) that most cable systems use a third of their cable capacity to retransmit local broadcast channels. These provisions are referred to as the "must carry" rules. The cable industry argued that the Act prevented it from carrying the content it wished, and thus violated the First Amendment. Broadcasters, on the other hand, contended that cable systems are essentially local monopolies, and as such, are subject to regulations designed to protect broadcasters from unfair competition.

Passage of the Act brought immediate challenge from Turner Broadcasting System and a number of cable programmers. The Supreme Court held in *Turner Broadcasting System, Inc. v. FCC (Turner I)* that the First Amendment does not broadly insulate the cable industry from federal regulations, and that the "must carry" provisions are content neutral. Justice Kennedy said that the "must carry" provisions must be evaluated using a heightened or intermediate level of First Amendment scrutiny. Cable technology has virtually none of the characteristics of broadcast, such as a finite number of frequencies, that provide the rationale for extensive regulation of broadcasters. At the same time, the Court found the "must carry" provisions justified by the "special characteristics of the cable medium: the bottleneck monopoly power" exercised by cable operators and the "danger this power poses to the viability of broadcast television." Cable's position as a "bottleneck" was controlling in the Court's thinking. By virtue of its "ownership of the essential pathway for cable speech," said Kennedy, a cable operator can "prevent its subscribers from obtaining programming it chooses to exclude." The "potential for abuse," he continued, of this private power "over a central avenue of communication cannot be overlooked." The First Amendment prohibits governmental interference with free speech, but it does not "disable the Government from taking steps to insure that private interests not restrict, through physical control of a critical pathway of communication, the free flow of information and ideas." The Court also rejected the contention of the cable industry that the "must carry" regulations were not content neutral, and as a result, required compelling justification by the government. The "overriding objective" of Congress in enacting the "must carry" requirement was "not to favor programming of a particular subject matter, viewpoint or format," but rather, said Kennedy, to "preserve access to free television programming" for those Americans without cable service. The case was remanded to the three-judge court to enable further fact finding on the government's contention that without the "must carry" requirements, cable systems would bring about the failure of broadcast stations. The Court reviewed the findings of the three-judge court in *Turner II*.

Internet Regulation

Congress sought to protect minors from objectionable content available on the Internet by enacting the Communications Decency Act of 1996 (CDA). Among other provisions, the Act prohibited the knowing transmission of "indecent communications" to minors. More generally, the Act prohibited the transmission or display of obscene material. This case presented two questions for the Supreme Court. The first focused on the manner in which the government might protect minors from indecent communications—that is, how were adults and minors to be effectively separated? The Act suggested that Internet users who made a "good faith" effort to prevent access by minors would not violate the Act. Access is most commonly restricted through such devices as access codes or identification numbers. The issue was whether the Act was narrowly tailored enough to pass First Amendment scrutiny. The second issue was whether such terms as "indecency" and "patently offensive" were defined clearly enough in the Act. Upon passage of the Act, actions were filed in federal district court to prevent implementation of the law. One suit was commenced by a wide range of groups including the American Civil Liberties Union, groups of online users, service providers, and nonprofit organizations. A second suit was filed by such groups as the American Library Association, American Booksellers Association, and a number of major Internet access providers such as America Online and Microsoft. These two cases were consolidated as *Reno v. American Civil Liberties Union (ACLU)*.

A three-judge district court found the Act unconstitutional on its face because the language of the statute was vague, and because age verification is too expensive and technologically unfeasible. The Supreme Court agreed. The Court's focus was on the terms "indecent" and "patently offensive." Notwithstanding the "legitimacy and importance" of protecting minors from harmful materials, the Court concluded that the terms were sufficiently vague and ambiguous to render the CDA "problematic" for First Amendment purposes.

Justice Stevens suggested that the vagueness of the CDA was of "special concern" for two reasons. First, the Act is "content-based regulation of speech." The vagueness of such a regulation has an "obvious chilling effect on free speech." Secondly, the CDA is a criminal statute. The "severity of criminal sanctions may well cause speakers to remain silent rather than communicate even arguably unlawful words, ideas, and images." The objective of denying access of minors to potentially harmful material "effectively suppresses a large amount of speech that adults have a constitutional right to receive and address to one another." This burden on adult expression is unacceptable if "less restrictive alternatives would be at least as effective in achieving the legitimate purpose the statute was enacted to serve."

The Cable Communications Policy Act of 1984 prohibited cable television operators from interfering with programming on channels leased to commercial programmers or channels designated for public, educational, or governmental programming. Congress became concerned with the levels of sexually explicit programming permitted under the 1984 Act and sought to enable cable operators to restrict access to such programming. Section 10 of the Cable Television Consumer Protection and Competition Act of 1992 required certain cable operators either to ban "indecent programming" or to block access except to adult subscribers who requested that channels be unblocked. The Federal Communications Commission (FCC) was charged with implementing Section 10 of the Act and issued regulations that enabled a cable system operator to ban any programming the operator determined to be indecent. Cable programmers, including the Denver Area Educational Telecommunications Consortium, challenged the FCC regulations on free speech grounds. In a fragmented ruling, the Supreme Court upheld parts of the Act, but struck down others in *Denver Area Educational Telecommunications Consortium, Inc. v. FCC*.[193] The Court upheld the provision permitting cable operators to ban "patently offensive" material from leased channels, but struck down the provision enabling cable operators to impose similar bans on the public access channels. The

Court also struck down the requirement that cable operators segregate and block offensive content. The permission to ban offensive material from leased channels was upheld for two reasons—a "compelling" need to protect children from sexual material, and a "balance[d] flexibility" of implementation. Broadcasting is "uniquely accessible" to children, said Justice Breyer, and he called the child protection justification for the regulation "extremely important." In addition, the provision is permissive in character, which creates a flexibility that gives cable operators options short of banning programs altogether, such as rescheduling broadcast times to minimize the risk of reaching a young audience. The existence of this "complex balance of interests" persuaded the Court that the permissive nature of the provision, "coupled with its viewpoint neutral application," is a constitutional way to "protect children from the kind of sexual material that concerned Congress while also accommodating First Amendment interests." The Court struck down the language permitting cable operators to restrict programming on public access channels, concluding that there was a history of neither indecent programming on these channels nor a record of cable operator interference with public access channel programming. Allowing cable operators the same authority with respect to public access channels would "greatly increase the risk that certain categories of programming will not appear." Finally, the separation and blocking provisions were found unconstitutional. Although protecting children remained a "compelling interest," the Court did not find that speech restrictions "properly accommodate[d] . . . the legitimate objective they seek to attain." The delays encountered by a subscriber in unscrambling segregated channels would be substantial (up to 30 days) and would prevent viewers who select programs on a day-by-day basis from viewing programming on those channels. Given the availability of less-intrusive alternatives, it was the Court's conclusion that this provision was not "narrowly or reasonably tailored . . . to protect children."

Obscenity Regulation

Roth v. United States established definitional standards for obscenity. *Roth* and its companion case, *Alberts v. California*, addressed the issue of whether "obscenity is utterance within the area of protected speech and press." Roth had been convicted of violating the federal obscenity statute by using the mail to distribute "obscene, lewd, lascivious, filthy, or indecent" material. The Supreme Court upheld both convictions. The Court indicated that the First Amendment was not intended to protect every utterance. Obscenity is not protected because it is "utterly without redeeming social importance." If obscenity falls outside the reach of the First Amendment, it is imperative to develop a precise definition of obscenity that permits distinguishing between protected and unprotected speech. Key to the identification of obscenity is its appeal to prurient interests. Treatment of sex per se "is not itself sufficient reason to deny material the constitutional protection of speech and press." Justice Brennan sought to establish a standard sufficiently proscribed as not to encroach on material legitimately treating sex. The standard chosen was "whether to the average person, applying contemporary community standards, the dominant theme of the material taken as a whole appeals to prurient interest." Prurient interest is referred to in *Roth* and subsequent cases as a "shameful, excessive, obsessive," or "unnatural" interest in nudity or sex. Using this standard, the Court concluded that the two statutes under consideration did not offend the First Amendment.

Roth clearly established that obscenity is not protected speech and upheld a federal attempt to regulate obscenity. The more troublesome issue was differentiating protected speech from unprotected obscenity. The leading definition prior to *Roth* had come from an English case, *Queen v. Hicklin*,[194] The *Hicklin* test allowed "material to be judged merely by the effect of an isolated excerpt upon particularly susceptible persons." Although *Roth* represented progress from the highly restrictive *Hicklin* standard, many questions remained. As the Warren Court struggled with these questions, it lost consensus on standards, and its definition became even less restrictive. In *Jacobellis v. Ohio*,[195] for example, the Court essentially held that material need be pornographic to be restricted, but no more than two justices could agree on a rationale for the policy. *A Book Named "John Cleland's Memoirs of a Woman of Pleasure" v. Attorney General of Massachusetts*[196] was the most permissive of the Warren Court pronouncements on obscenity. It held that the three previously established obscenity criteria—prurient interest, social value, and patent offensiveness—were separate and independent. This was especially important for the social value criterion. If any redeeming social value could be detected, material could not be adjudged obscene, despite its appeal to prurient interest and its patently offensive character. Although the Court was badly divided in *Memoirs*, it could be inferred from the case that only hard-core pornography remained as an unprotected class of material. *Memoirs* also marked the Warren Court's last real effort to grapple with definitional standards for obscenity.

In *Redrup v. New York*,[197] the Court declared it would uphold obscenity statutes only to prohibit distribution of obscene materials to juveniles or in cases in which such materials were obtrusively thrust upon an unwilling audience. *Redrup* allowed the Court to by-pass its stalemate on standards and handle the obscenity matter pragmatically. Earlier the Court had upheld a state prohibition on sale of indecent material to minors in *Ginsberg v. New York*, and later it upheld federal prosecution of firms sending a second mailing to persons in *Rowan v. Post Office*.[198] The only case producing a more restrictive outcome was *Ginzburg v. United States*.[199] The Court upheld Ginzburg's conviction because he commercially exploited the sexual content of the materials he offered for sale. He engaged in pandering, purviewing material that appeals to the prurient interest of prospective customers. Ginzburg's materials were viewed "against a background of commercial exploitation of erotica solely for the sake of their prurient appeal." In situations in which the "purveyor's sole emphasis is on the sexually provocative aspects of his publications, that fact may be decisive in the determination of obscenity." *Ginzburg* modified *Roth* in that materials may pass the initial *Roth* test and yet still be found obscene. Although the materials themselves may not be obscene, they can become illicit merchandise through the "sordid business of pandering."

In *Brockett v. Spokane Arcades, Inc.*,[200] the Court held that a state obscenity law could not ban "lustful" material. Just because sexual response is aroused, expression may not therefore be automatically regulated. The Court said that material that does no more than "arouse 'good, old fashioned, healthy' interest in sex" is constitutionally protected.

The Protection of Children Against Sexual Exploitation Act of 1977 prohibits "knowingly" transporting, receiving, distributing, or reproducing any materials that depict minors engaged in sexually explicit acts. The issue in *United States v. X-Citement Video, Inc.*[201] was whether the knowledge requirement meant that prosecutors must demonstrate that the defendant was aware that performers were actually minors. A number of the videotapes sold by Rubin Gottesman, the owner of X-Citement Video, Inc., featured a performer who was not yet 18 at the time the videos were produced. The U.S. Court of Appeals for the Ninth Circuit ruled that the Act was unconstitutional because it did not clearly require proof that the defendant had knowledge that any of the performers was a minor. The Supreme Court concluded that the Act was properly read as containing a knowledge requirement on the element of performer age. Chief Justice Rehnquist suggested that a statute should be interpreted "where fairly possible" so as to avoid substantial constitutional questions, and that some form of *scienter* (knowledge) is to be implied in a criminal statute even if not expressed. The prosecution is required to demonstrate that the accused had knowledge of each of the essential components of any other crime. From this perspective, the Court concluded that knowledge of the age of performers was implicit in the federal child pornography law. The critical element in separating wrongful conduct from lawful or protected conduct is the age of the performers. Knowledge that at least one performer in sexually explicit material is under age thus must be seen as an essential component for the offenses of transporting and distributing child pornography because neither transporting nor distributing sexually explicit material involving only adult performers is criminal.

The U.S. Supreme Court upheld the "decency and respect for diverse values" provisions in *National Endowment for the Arts v. Finley*.[202] Justice O'Connor indicated that Finley had to demonstrate a "substantial risk" that application of the "decency and respect" provisions will "lead to the suppression of speech." Finley argued that the provision is a "paradigmatic example of viewpoint discrimination" because it rejects artistic speech that either "fails to respect mainstream values or offends standards of decency." The NEA disputed the contention and characterized the provisions as "merely hortatory." The NEA argued that it did not implement the provision in a way that discriminated against particular viewpoints—that the provision "stops well short of an absolute restriction." The Court found it "clear" that the language of the decency provision "imposes no categorical requirement." The advisory language of the statute "stands in sharp contrast to congressional efforts to prohibit the funding of certain classes of speech." In addition, the Court found the political context existing at the time the "decency and respect" language was adopted was "inconsistent with [Finley's] assertion that the provision compels the NEA to deny funding on the basis of viewpoint discriminatory criteria." The language of the law merely admonished the NEA to "take 'decency and respect' into consideration." This "undercut" the argument that the provision "inevitably will be utilized as a tool for invidious viewpoint discrimination." The Court did not perceive a "realistic danger" that the provision would compromise First Amendment values. In other words, the Court concluded that the "decency and respect" criteria would not, in practice, "effectively preclude or punish" the expression of particular views. O'Connor suggested that any "content-based considerations" that may be evaluated in the grant-making process "are a consequence of the nature of arts funding." It would be impossible, she said, "to have a highly selective grant program without denying money to a large amount of constitutionally protected expression." O'Connor suggested that although the First Amendment applies in the subsidy context, the government may "allocate competitive funding according to criteria that would be impermissible were direct regulation of speech or a criminal penalty at stake." As long as legislation does not infringe on any other protected rights, Congress has "wide latitude to set spending priorities." Finally, the Court rejected the contention that the "decency and respect" language was unconstitutionally vague. Although the language was "undeniably opaque," and could raise vagueness concerns if it appeared in a criminal statute or regulatory scheme, the Court found it unlikely that speakers "will be compelled to steer too far clearly of any forbidden area in the context of grants of this nature." When government is acting as "patron rather than as sovereign, the consequences of imprecision are not constitutionally severe."

Obscenity and Zoning

Young v. American Mini Theatres, Inc. upheld zoning ordinances regulating locations of adult theaters. *Young* approved amendments to Detroit zoning ordinances providing that adult theaters be licensed. They could not be located within 1,000 feet of any two other "regulated uses" or within 500 feet of any residential area. The other "regulated uses" included some ten categories of adult entertainment enterprises. An adult theater was defined as one that presented material characterized by emphasis on "specified sexual activities" or "specified anatomical areas." The Court rejected several lines of challenge in *Young*. First, the Court rejected assertions of vagueness in the ordinance because "any element of vagueness in these ordinances has not affected the respondents." The application of the ordinances to the American Mini Theatres "is plain." As for the licensure requirement, the Court noted that the general zoning laws in Detroit imposed requirements on all motion picture theaters. The Court said: "We have no doubt that the municipality may control the location of theaters as well as the location of other commercial establishments." Establishment of such restrictions in themselves is not prohibited as prior restraint. The "mere fact that the commercial exploitation of material protected by the First Amendment is subject to zoning and other licensing requirements is not sufficient reason for invalidating these ordinances." The Court also considered whether the 1,000-foot restriction constituted an improper content-based classification. The Court said that "even within the area of protected speech, a difference in content may require a different governmental response." Citing the public figure category in libel law and prohibitions on exhibition of obscenity to juveniles and unconsenting adults, the Court held that the First Amendment did not foreclose content distinctions. They "rest squarely on an appraisal of the content of the material otherwise within a constitutionally protected area." Even though the First Amendment does not allow total suppression, the Court held that a state may legitimately use the content of mini-theater materials as the basis for placing them in a different classification from other motion pictures. Finally, the Court upheld the regulated-use classification on the basis of the city's interest in preserving the character of its neighborhoods. Detroit has a legitimate interest in attempting to preserve the quality of urban life. It is an interest that "must be accorded high respect," and the city must be allowed "a reasonable opportunity to experiment with solutions to an admittedly serious problem."

Young v. American Mini Theatres, Inc. represents a new wave of cases raising issues about the local regulation of "adult entertainment." The Court has generally supported local regulation as long as expression is not completely prohibited and as long as a compelling interest can be demonstrated. Meeting these conditions is not always easy, however. In *Erznoznik v. Jacksonville*,[203] the Court struck down an ordinance that prohibited the exhibition of films containing nudity, if the screen could be seen from a public street. The Court cited the limited privacy interest of persons on the streets, but it also stressed the overly broad sweep of the ordinance. In *Schad v. Borough of Mt. Ephraim*,[204] the Court invalidated a zoning ordinance that banned live entertainment in a borough establishment. Convictions under the ordinance had been secured against an adult bookstore operator for having live nude dancers performing in the establishment. The borough argued that permitting such entertainment would conflict with its plan to create a commercial area catering only to the "immediate needs of residents." The Court considered such justification "patently insufficient." The ordinance prohibited a "wide range of expression that has long been held to be within the protection of the First and Fourteenth Amendments."

Ten years after *Young*, the Court once again reviewed a local attempt to regulate the location of adult theaters in *City of Renton v. Playtime Theatres, Inc.*[205] Using the rationale from *Young*, the Court upheld a municipality's authority to require dispersal of such establishments. Because the municipal ordinance did not bar adult theaters entirely, it was reviewed as a time, place, and manner regulation. Such regulations are acceptable as long as they serve a substantial interest and do not unreasonably limit avenues of communication. Justice Rehnquist said that the First Amendment requires only that a local unit refrain from denying individuals a "reasonable opportunity to open and operate an adult theater within the city." He said the City of Renton easily met that requirement in the ordinance under review.

FW/PBS, Inc. v. City of Dallas[206] reviewed a comprehensive city ordinance regulating "sexually oriented" businesses, including bookstores. Dallas sought to regulate such businesses through a variety of licensing and zoning requirements. All owners of sexually oriented businesses were required to obtain a license from the city as well as pay an annual fee. The ordinance contained civil disability provisions that prohibited people convicted of certain crimes from obtaining a license. Licenses could also be revoked, or not renewed, if the owner (or his or her spouse) was convicted of certain specified offenses. The ordinance defined "adult motels" as establishments renting rooms for periods under ten hours.

"Adult" motels were a "sexually oriented" business subject to the licensure provisions of the ordinance, and had to be more than 1,000 feet from parks, churches, and residential or business structures. The Court struck down the licensing provision as a prior restraint. Any system of prior restraint, said the Court, carries a "heavy presumption against its constitutional validity" for two reasons. First, such schemes give government "unbridled discretion" that may result in censorship. Second, prior restraint systems seldom impose stringent time limits on the decision maker. The Dallas ordinance not only created the possibility that protected speech could be censored through the licensing requirements, but that the city had "unlimited time within which to issue a license" as well. This created the "risk of indefinitely suppressing permissible speech." The Court found the legislative judgment that short rental periods are likely to "foster prostitution" to be reasonable and unanimously upheld the 10-hour restriction. It was contended that this ordinance provision violated privacy rights by impinging on the right to intimate association. The Court rejected this contention by saying that limiting motel room rentals will not have any "discernable effect on the sorts of traditional personal bonds" referred to in previous right of association cases. Such "personal bonds" that are formed through the use of a motel room for less than ten hours are not those that have "played a critical role in the culture and traditions of the Nation by cultivating and transmitting shared ideals and beliefs."

The Court rejected in *Barnes v. Glen Theater*[207] the argument that the First Amendment precludes a state from enforcing a public decency law to prohibit nude dancing. The parties had agreed that the nude performances were not obscene. As a result, the five-justice majority used symbolic expression standards to resolve the constitutional question. A regulation can withstand First Amendment scrutiny only if it furthers a substantial governmental interest. That interest must be unrelated to the suppression of expression, may only incidentally affect expression, and is to be only as extensive as is required to further the substantial interest. Chief Justice Rehnquist noted the state's "traditional interest in protecting societal order and morality." This interest was seen as both substantial and not directed at expression. Indecency statutes, said Rehnquist, "reflect moral disapproval of people appearing in the nude among strangers in public places." Although nude dancing is expressive conduct within the "outer perimeters" of the First Amendment, it is only "marginally so." In Rehnquist's view, the state was not attempting to regulate nudity because of any erotic message, but because the nudity was public. It is the public nudity that is the targeted "evil the state seeks to prevent, whether or not it is combined with expressive activity."

Private Obscenity

Osborne v. Ohio held that states can outlaw the private possession of pornographic materials featuring minors. Crucial to the decision was the choice of *New York v. Ferber*[208] rather than *Stanley v. Georgia*[209] as the controlling precedent. The law struck down in *Stanley* was intended to prevent "poison[ing] the minds" of those who observed such material. In this case, however, the state did not "rely on a paternalistic interest in Osborne's mind." Rather, Ohio enacted the law in an attempt to "protect the victims of child pornography; it hopes to destroy a market for the exploitive use of children." The Ohio legislature made the judgment that using children as subjects in pornographic materials is "harmful to the physiological, emotional, and mental health of the child." That judgment, said the Court, "easily passes muster" under the First Amendment. Furthermore, it is "surely reasonable" for Ohio to conclude that it will "decrease the production of child pornography if it penalizes those who possess and view the product, thereby decreasing demand." Given the importance of Ohio's interest in protecting the child victims, "we cannot fault Ohio for attempting to stamp out this vice at all levels in the distribution chain." The Court also rejected Osborne's overbreadth contention finding that the state supreme court had interpreted the law in such a way as to sufficiently focus or confine the materials that could be reached under the regulation.

    Stanley v. Georgia held that a state could not prohibit private possession of obscene materials. Stanley was convicted of possessing obscene films. The films were discovered while federal and state agents searched Stanley's home under authority of a warrant issued in connection with an investigation of Stanley's alleged involvement in bookmaking. The Supreme Court unanimously reversed Stanley's conviction. Stanley's First Amendment claim was based on his "right to read or observe what he pleases—the right to satisfy his intellectual and emotional needs in the privacy of his own home and the right to be free from state inquiry into the contents of his library." Georgia's statute was based on the view that there are "certain types of materials that the individual may not read or even possess." The Court was not persuaded, saying that "mere categorization of these films as 'obscene' is insufficient justification for such drastic invasion of personal liberties." Although privacy was a key consideration, the Court stressed the First Amendment aspects of *Stanley*. Justifications for regulation of obscenity "do not reach into the privacy of one's own home." If the First Amendment means anything, it means that a state "has no business telling a man, sitting alone in his own house, what books he may read or what films he may watch." Our whole constitutional heritage "rebels at the thought of giving government the power to control men's minds." Neither may the state justify the prohibition of privately held obscene materials as a means of forestalling antisocial conduct. The state "may no more prohibit mere possession of obscenity on the ground that it may lead to anti-social conduct than it may prohibit possession of chemistry books on the ground they may lead to the manufacture of homemade spirits."

In *United States v. Thirty-Seven Photographs*,[210] the Court allowed a prohibition on the importation of obscenity from abroad even if it were intended for private use. The following year, in *United States v. Twelve 200-Ft. Reels of Super 8 mm. Film*,[211] the Court allowed seizure of materials coming into the country from Mexico. The justices declared that the right privately to possess obscene materials did not afford "a correlative right to acquire, sell, or import such material even for private use only."

Censorship

Kingsley Books, Inc. v. Brown upheld restrictions on the sale of obscene materials through court order. A section of the New York Code of Criminal Procedure authorized enforcement officials in municipalities to invoke injunctive remedies against the "sale and distribution of written and printed matter found after due trial to be obscene," and to obtain an order for "the seizure, in default of surrender, of the condemned publications." The section entitled the person subject to the injunction to have a trial within one day and a decision within two days of the trial. Certain items found in the Kingsley Books establishment were determined obscene, their further distribution enjoined, and their destruction ordered. Kingsley Books did not challenge New York's authority to prohibit the distribution of obscenity. The appeal focused on the remedial technique that included the power to enjoin during the course of the litigation. Kingsley Books asserted that such use of the injunctive remedy amounted to an unconstitutional prior restraint, but the Supreme Court upheld the method. In approving the approach, the Court compared it to imposing criminal sanctions on booksellers. Rather than requiring the seller "to dread that the offer for sale of a book may without prior warning subject him to criminal prosecution with the hazard of imprisonment," the section of the Code at issue "assures him that such consequences cannot follow unless he ignores a court order specifically directed to him for a prompt and carefully circumscribed determination of the issue of obscenity." The Court concluded that the Code "moves after publication" by enjoining from display or sale "particular booklets theretofore published and adjudged to be obscene." When compared with criminal penalties, the "restraint upon appellants as merchants in obscenity was narrower." The restriction imposed under the Code was altogether different from the injunctive restraint disallowed in *Near v. Minnesota.* Unlike *Near*, the New York Code provision "is concerned solely with obscenity," and it "studiously withholds restraints upon matters not already published and not yet found to be offensive."

Kingsley Books held that techniques of censoring written materials, especially books, must contain extensive procedural safeguards. In *Smith v. California*,[212] the Court required in addition that a defendant in an obscenity proceeding must be shown to have knowledge of the material's contents. Without such knowledge, the bookseller will "restrict the books he sells to those he inspected," and this will constitute a state-imposed "restriction upon the distribution of constitutionally protected as well as obscene literature." Neither can material be prohibited from distribution until it has been subjected to a formal hearing as in *Kingsley Books*. In *Bantam Books, Inc. v. Sullivan*,[213] the Court struck down a statute that established a commission to convey to booksellers the potential for prosecution if objectionable material was sold. The Court felt these informal sanctions were effective censorship wholly lacking in necessary safeguards.

Censorship of films occurred from the time films were first produced, and Supreme Court decisions extended virtually no free press protections for them. As motion pictures evolved, however, their unprotected status changed and censorship techniques such as those in *Freedman v. Maryland*,[214] demanded Court attention. A key case in elevating films to partial coverage by the First Amendment was *Joseph Burstyn, Inc. v. Wilson*.[215] The Court found that it "cannot be doubted that motion pictures are a significant medium for the communication of ideas." Although films may possess a "greater capacity for evil," such potential "does not authorize substantially unbridled censorship." The Court was asked in *Freedman* to prohibit film censorship altogether. Although it refused to do so, the Court established procedures for the licensing of films that closely parallel the procedures outlined in *Kingsley Books*. Freedman had refused to submit a film to the State Board of Censors prior to showing it. Maryland stipulated that the film would have been licensed had it been submitted. The Court said a prior restraint mechanism bears a "heavy presumption against its constitutional validity." Specifically, the "administration of a censorship proceeding puts the initial burden on the exhibitor or distributor." The justices went on to outline procedural safeguards "designed to obviate the dangers of the censorship system." First, the "burden of proving that the film is unprotected expression must rest with the censor." Second, although advance submissions may be required, no film may be banned through means "which would lend an effect of finality to the censor's determination." Third, a film cannot be banned unless the process permits judicial determination of the restraint. Fourth, various steps in the process must not take too long. "The exhibitor must be assured that the censor will within a specified brief period, either issue a license or go to court to restrain the showing of the film." Any restraints imposed prior to final judicial determination must be "limited to preservation of the status quo for the shortest fixed period." In *Roaden v. Kentucky*,[216] the Court unanimously determined that a warrantless seizure by a county sheriff of a film during its showing was a prior restraint. Similarly, in *Southeastern Promotions, Ltd. v. Conrad*,[217] the Court held that a city's refusal to rent a city facility for a performance of *Hair* was a prior restraint. The Court said city officials may deny a forum to an obscene production, but such a decision must be made through a properly safeguarded process. In *Heller v. New York*,[218] the Court upheld the seizure of a film under authority of a warrant from a judge who had viewed it prior to signing the warrant. Finally, in *New York v. P.J. Video, Inc.*,[219] the Court reviewed a lower court ruling that established a higher probable cause standard for issuing warrants to seize suspect books or films as opposed to other contraband, such as weapons. The Burger Court ruled that the First Amendment required no higher standard. Such warrant applications should be reviewed with the same standards used for warrant applications generally: that there is a fair probability evidence of a crime will be found in the location to be searched.

Freedom of Assembly and Protest: Public Premises

Adderley v. Florida held that demonstrators may be barred from assembling on the grounds of a county jail. *Adderley* considered whether certain public locations might be put off-limits to demonstrations or assemblies. Adderley and a number of others were convicted of trespass for gathering at a county jail to protest the arrest of several students the day before, as well as local policies of racial segregation at the jail itself. When the demonstrators would not leave the jail grounds when asked, they were warned of possible arrest for trespass. Adderley and others remained on the premises, were arrested, subsequently tried, and convicted. The Court upheld the convictions. The Court concluded that "nothing in the Constitution of the United States prevented Florida from even-handed enforcement of its general trespass statute against those refusing to obey the sheriff's order to remove themselves from what amounted to the curtilage of the jailhouse." The fact that the jail was a public building did not automatically entitle the protesters to unconditional assembly. The state, no less than a private owner of property, has power to preserve the property under its control for the use to which it is lawfully dedicated. The security purpose for which the jail was dedicated outweighed the expression interests of the protesters. Justice Black said that to find for Adderley would be to endorse "the assumption that people who want to propagandize protests or views have a constitutional right to do so whenever and wherever they please." The Court categorically rejected that premise and concluded by saying the Constitution does not forbid a state to "control the use of its own property for its own lawful nondiscriminatory purposes."

Adderley illustrates the "speech plus" concept. In certain situations speech involves accompanying conduct beyond verbal utterances. The conduct may be regulated even if the regulation impairs expression. In *Cox v. Louisiana*,[220] the Court upheld a state statute that prohibited picketing near a courthouse. It said that a state could legitimately insulate its judicial proceedings from demonstrations.

While restrictions were said to be warranted in *Adderley* and *Cox*, breach of the peace convictions of persons demonstrating on the grounds of a state capitol were reversed in *Edwards v. South Carolina*.[221] Similarly, a peaceful sit-in at a public library was protected in *Brown v. Louisiana*.[222] The Court also struck down an ordinance that prohibited picketing in the proximity of school buildings when classes were in session in *Chicago Police Department v. Mosley*.[223] The ordinance was invalidated largely because it excepted labor picketing from the ban. The Court noted the city had a legitimate interest in preventing school disruption, however. Time, place, and manner restrictions have generally been recognized by the Court, provided that significant governmental interests can be demonstrated. Trespass on private property was subject to punishment for many years, although civil-rights sit-ins forced a legislative reevaluation of that policy. A Washington, D.C., regulation prohibiting display of signs conveying criticism of foreign governments within 500 feet of embassies was struck down in *Boos v. Barry*.[224] While recognizing the need to shield foreign governments from criticism, the Court found the display prohibition to be content-based regulation of particular expression. Parallel language banning assembly within 500 feet of embassies was upheld, however, because its application had been confined to security-threatening situations.

The question in *United States v. Kokinda*[225] was whether a Postal Service regulation banning solicitation on sidewalks located entirely on Postal Service property violated the First Amendment. The Court upheld the regulation. Sidewalks have generally been regarded as a forum traditionally open to the public for expressive activity. Regulation of speech on government property that has been traditionally open to the public for expressive activity, such as public streets or parks, is examined under strict scrutiny. On the other hand, expressive activity where the government has not dedicated its property to First Amendment activity is examined only for reasonableness. The Court rejected the argument that all sidewalks be regarded as a traditional public forum. The "location and purpose" of a public sidewalk "is critical to determining whether such a sidewalk constitutes a public forum." The sidewalk subject to regulation in this case did not have the "characteristics of public sidewalks traditionally open to expressive activity." Rather, this postal sidewalk was constructed "solely to provide for the passage of individuals engaged in postal business," thus it was not a traditional public forum sidewalk.

The public forum concept was also the critical consideration in *International Society for Krishna Consciousness, Inc. v. Lee*.[226] Members of Krishna Consciousness are required by their faith to go to public places and engage in activities that include literature distribution and solicitation of donations. The Port Authority of New York and New Jersey operates the three major airports in and near New York City. The Port Authority permitted the Krishnas to engage in various activities in the common areas of the airport grounds, but prohibited the same conduct in those airport locations that had been leased to private airlines. Much of the terminal space fell into the latter category. The Krishnas sought to extend their access to all airport locations and challenged the restrictions on First Amendment grounds. The Supreme Court agreed that the Krishnas were engaged in activities generally protected by the First Amendment, but upheld the ban on solicitations for money. At the same time, the restriction on distribution of literature was held to be unconstitutional. The Court's rulings hinged on whether the air terminals were historically dedicated to expressive activities. The "tradition of airport activity," said Chief Justice Rehnquist, "does not demonstrate that airports have historically been available for speech activity." Rather, the Court saw airline terminals as designed to serve airline passengers and personnel and not the public at large. The ban on direct solicitation was found to be a reasonable way to avoid excessive congestion and disruption to passengers as they moved through the terminals.

A city's authority to regulate concerts held in a municipal park was before the Court in *Ward v. Rock Against Racism*.[227] The city issued a set of use guidelines governing all band shell concerts that, among other things, specified that the city would furnish the amplification equipment and employ an experienced sound technician to operate it. The Supreme Court ruled the guidelines to be a valid place and manner regulation. The city had two objectives in instituting the guidelines: controlling noise and ensuring sound quality. Neither of these purposes, concluded the Court, had anything to do with content.

Private Property

PruneYard Shopping Center v. Robins declared that demonstrators can access privately owned shopping malls to circulate petitions and distribute political pamphlets. *PruneYard* involved a group of high school students who sought to express their opposition to a United Nations Resolution against Zionism. They set up a table near the central courtyard of the shopping center, began distributing pamphlets, and asked patrons of the shopping center to sign a petition. The students were orderly and no objection to their presence was registered by any shopping center customer. The students were informed by a shopping center security guard that their activity was in violation of a center policy that prohibited all such conduct. The group subsequently filed suit, seeking access to the center through a court order. The trial court refused to issue such an order, but the California Supreme Court held that the state constitution entitled the students access to the mall. The United States Supreme Court unanimously upheld the California Supreme Court. The crucial issue for the Court was whether state-protected rights of expression infringed upon the property rights of PruneYard's owners. Citing the state court opinion, Justice Rehnquist said that "a handful of additional orderly persons soliciting signatures and distributing handbills do not interfere with normal business operations." They "would not markedly dilute defendant's property rights." Three other arguments were developed to support the judgment of the California Supreme Court. First, PruneYard "by the choice of its owner is not limited to the personal use of the appellants." PruneYard is rather a "business establishment that is open to the public." Any views expressed by center patrons "thus will not likely be identified with those of the owner." Second, the state's insistence that PruneYard's private property be made available was content neutral in that there was "no danger of governmental discrimination for or against a particular message." Finally, PruneYard and its constituent shop owners could easily disclaim any connection to the expression of the demonstrators. They could explain that the "persons are communicating their own messages by virtue of state law."

PruneYard Shopping Center v. Robins treated the troublesome issue of demonstrator access to private property. The Burger Court position in *PruneYard* represents a compromise between several of its own previous decisions and those of the Warren Court. The Warren Court view is best illustrated by *Amalgamated Food Employees Union v. Logan Valley Plaza, Inc.*[228] In *Logan Valley* the Court upheld the picketing of a business located in a privately owned shopping center. The Burger Court reconsidered *Logan Valley* in *Lloyd Corp. v. Tanner*,[229] and upheld a restriction on handbilling. Although the shopping center invites patrons, the Burger Court said, it is not an invitation of unlimited scope. The invitation is to do business with the tenants of the center. There is "no open-ended invitation to the public to use the center for any and all purposes, however incompatible with the interests of both the stores and the shoppers whom they serve." In addition, the restriction did not deprive the persons from distributing their handbills on the public sidewalks surrounding the center.

The Burger Court abandoned *Logan Valley* altogether in *Hudgens v. National Labor Relations Board (NLRB)*.[230] In *Hudgens*, union members attempted to picket the retail store of their employer, which was located in a privately owned mall. Citing *Lloyd Corp.*, the Court held that the First Amendment "has no part to play in such a case as this." Thus, the Burger Court divorced privately owned shopping centers from First Amendment reach. Through the *PruneYard* decision, however, it did allow protection of expression to flow from state constitutional provisions.

Enjoining Assembly

Carroll v. President and Commissioners of Princess Anne County struck down an ex parte injunction prohibiting a rally of a militant white supremacist organization. An ex parte proceeding is one in which only one party participates or appears. Injunctions are frequently, but not always, used in situations in which permits or licenses to march or demonstrate have been denied. Carroll, a member of a white supremacist organization known as the National States Rights Party, participated in a rally at which aggressively and militantly racist and anti-Semitic speeches were made. At the conclusion of the speeches, it was announced that the rally would be resumed the next night. Local government officials obtained a restraining order in the meantime in an ex parte proceeding. The injunction restrained Carroll and others from holding public meetings for ten days. The Supreme Court unanimously struck down the order. The Court's primary objection was to the ex parte procedure. The order was issued "without notice to petitioners and without any effort, however informal, to invite or permit their participation in the proceedings." The Court recognized that ex parte orders may be appropriate in some situations, "but there is no place within the area of basic freedoms guaranteed by the First Amendment for such orders."

Carroll v. President of Princess Anne established procedural guidelines through which court orders might be obtained against demonstrators. The permit-injunction approach had often been used against civil-rights demonstrators. In *Walker v. Birmingham*,[231] the Court upheld an injunction issued following denial of a parade permit. Walker, Martin Luther King Jr., and others involved in the proposed parade disobeyed the injunction without seeking appellate review of either the injunction or the permit denial that precipitated the court order. The Court found the potentially persuasive objections to the Birmingham permit system to be subordinate to the failure of the demonstrators to obey the court order. The dissenters in *Walker* would have voided the injunction on the grounds that the permit system was unconstitutionally discriminatory. Permits are satisfactory as long as they are confined to reasonable time, place, and manner limitations. Permit or license requirements that are not content neutral or that allow too much discretion to permit-granting officials are unacceptable to the Court.

Another injunction episode involved attempts by the Village of Skokie, Illinois, to prevent an assembly of the National Socialist Party of America, a self-proclaimed Nazi organization. More than half of Skokie's residents are Jewish and a sizeable number were survivors of German concentration camps. Prior to the assembly, an injunction was secured from a state court enjoining the National Socialist Party from a uniformed march, display of swastikas, and distribution of materials that might "promote hatred against persons of the Jewish faith or ancestry." The Illinois Supreme Court refused to stay the injunction. The United States Supreme Court, in *National Socialist Party v. Skokie*,[232] reversed because the denial of the stay at the state level deprived the party of its right to demonstrate for the period until an appellate review could occur, a period estimated to be a year or more. The Court said that if a state seeks to impose a restraint of this kind, "it must provide strict procedural safeguards including appellate review." Absent such review, the state must instead allow the stay." The party never assembled in Skokie, choosing instead to hold a rally in a Chicago park.

The Court dealt with a different kind of permit requirement in *Forsyth County v. Nationalist Movement*.[233] In 1987 Forsyth County, Georgia, was the site of a number of civil-rights demonstrations and counterdemonstrations. In response Forsyth County adopted a permit ordinance that imposed a fee as a condition for obtaining permission to use public property for expressive activity. The county administrator had authority to set the amount of the fee up to a maximum of $1,000 for each day the public properties were used. The Supreme Court found the ordinance unconstitutional. The central objection was that the ordinance gave the local government, in the person of the county administrator, "unbridled discretion," and "created the possibility that assessments might be influenced by the content of the expression." Justice Blackmun said, "Speech cannot be financially burdened, any more than it can be punished or banned, simply because it might offend a hostile mob."

Abortion Clinic Protest

Schenck v. Pro-Choice Network reviewed a federal district court restraining order that prohibited antiabortion protesters from coming within 15 feet of entrances and driveways to an abortion clinic. The order also created "floating" zones of 15 feet around all persons entering the clinic. Two protesters were permitted to engage in "sidewalk counseling" within the zones, but were required to approach patients or staff in a non-confrontational manner and "cease and desist" from any interaction if the person receiving the "counseling" objected to it. Sidewalk counseling typically involves talking with and distributing literature to people entering abortion clinics. The Pro-Choice Network filed motions with a federal court alleging violations of the restraining order by protesters led by Reverend Paul Schenck. The U.S. Supreme Court upheld parts of the injunction, but struck down the "floating buffer zone" component. The Court concluded that the governmental interests of ensuring public safety and order, maintaining free traffic flow, property protection, and protecting a woman's "freedom to seek pregnancy-related services" were present. Those interests, considered "in combination, are certainly significant enough to justify an appropriately tailored injunction to secure unimpeded physical access to the clinics." The fixed buffer zone was upheld because the issuing court could have reasonably concluded that the only way to ensure access was to move the demonstrators away from the driveways and parking lot entrances. The protesters argued that a 15-foot fixed zone constituted a ban on "peaceful, non-obstructive demonstrations." Chief Justice Rehnquist suggested that such an argument ignored the history of this case. The court that had issued the restraining order initially was "entitled to conclude" that some of the protesters "aggressively follow and crowd individuals" seeking entry to the clinics "right up to the clinic door" and then "refuse to move . . . in an effort to impede or block" clinic staff and patients. In addition, protester harassment of police limited the capability of law enforcement to function effectively, making a "prophylactic measure even more appropriate." The protesters also argued that the "cease and desist" provision of the injunction was too restrictive. The Court disagreed, saying that the exception for the two sidewalk counselors was a good faith effort of the trial court to "enhance" the speech rights of the protesters, and the limitation "must be assessed in that light." The "floating zones," however, were found defective because they "burden more speech than is necessary to serve the relevant governmental interests."

One of the tactics used by abortion opponents is to demonstrate near abortion clinics. The clinics have responded by seeking judicial intervention. Two cases decided by the Rehnquist Court prior to *Schenck* examined the statutory bases for possible intervention. The first was *Bray v. Alexandria Women's Health Clinic.*[234] The issue in *Bray* was whether federal judges have authority under an 1871 statute to enjoin antiabortion protesters from obstructing entry to abortion clinics. The law bans conspiracies to deprive persons, or classes of persons, of equal protection under the law. In order to prove a conspiracy in violation of the law, plaintiffs need to show that the conspirators were motivated, at least in part, by a "class-based invidiously discriminatory animus." A plaintiff would further need to show that the conspiracy was designed to interfere with rights protected against encroachment by private parties. It was asserted by the clinics that because only women can have abortions, the demonstrators discriminated against women as a class by interfering with access to legal abortions. The Supreme Court ruled that the plaintiffs did not prove a private conspiracy in violation of the statute. Absent such a finding, the federal courts are without power to restrict demonstrations such as the one involved here. The Court did not see in the record any indications that the abortion protesters were motivated by a purpose directed at women as a class. Opposition to voluntary abortion, said Justice Scalia, "cannot possibly be considered an irrational surrogate for opposition to (or paternalism toward) women." Regardless of one's position on abortion, it "cannot be denied that there are common and respectable reasons for opposing it, other than hatred of or condescension toward (or indeed any view at all concerning) women as a class."

The Rehnquist Court reviewed a restraining order in *Madsen v. Women's Health Center*,[235] which closely paralleled the injunction at issue in *Schenck*. A number of abortion clinics in Florida secured an injunction from a state court restraining such activities as trespassing on clinic property, blocking access to clinic entrances, and harassing persons associated with the clinics as staff or patients. The following year, a more extensive injunction created "buffer zones" of 36 and 300 feet from the clinics. The abortion protesters were forbidden from approaching persons seeking clinic services inside the 300-foot zone. An exception was allowed for potential clinic patients who consented to talk with protesters. Nonthreatening communication and the distribution of literature could occur within the 300-foot zone until the 36-foot perimeter was reached, at which point all interaction between the prospective patients and protesters was prohibited. The amended injunction also prohibited making sounds that could be heard inside the clinics, and prohibited the exhibiting of "images" observable to patients of the clinic. The Supreme Court upheld the 36-foot buffer zone, but struck down the restrictions within the 300-foot zone. The Court rejected the protesters' contention that because the injunction prohibits only the speech of the protesters, it is necessarily viewpoint or content based. To accept their claim, said Chief Justice Rehnquist, would be to classify "virtually every" injunction as content based because, by its nature, it applies only to particular individuals and perhaps their speech. Content neutrality hinges on the purpose of the regulation—a purpose chosen without interference to the content of the regulated speech. The injunction was issued here because the protesters "repeatedly violated" the original restraining order. That protesters all shared the same view on abortion did not in itself demonstrate a viewpoint-based purpose. Rather, the order reflected that the persons "whose *conduct* violated the court's order happen to share the same opinion regarding abortions being performed at the clinic." The Court concluded that the state had "few other options to protect access given the narrow confines around the clinic." The Court also noted that an "even narrower order was issued originally, and that it had failed to protect clinic access." The Court also upheld the noise restriction. The First Amendment, said Rehnquist, "does not demand that patients at a medical facility undertake Herculean efforts to escape the cacophony of political protests." If overamplified loudspeakers "assault the citizenry, government may turn them down." Here the Court distinguished the sound restrictions from the restrictions on observable "images." The latter restriction was too broad—it was more burdensome than necessary to achieve the purpose of limiting threats to clinic patients or their families. Similarly, the Court concluded that there was insufficient justification for creating the 300-foot buffer zone—the desired result could have been accomplished with less burdensome restrictions.

Freedom of Association

National Association for the Advancement of Colored People (NAACP) v. Alabama established a constitutional protection for the freedom of association. This case involved an attempt by the state of Alabama to compel disclosure of the NAACP's membership list as a means of inhibiting the operation of the organization. Alabama sought to enjoin NAACP activities within the state because the NAACP had failed to comply with a statutory requirement that all out-of-state corporations file certain information. Among the documents the NAACP was ordered to produce was a list of all names and addresses of members and agents in Alabama. The Association refused to disclose such a list and was cited for contempt and fined. The Supreme Court unanimously reversed the contempt judgment and determined that the First Amendment included a right of association. The Court first had to resolve the matter of standing. Alabama argued that the NAACP could not "assert constitutional rights pertaining to the members," but the Court found the Association's "nexus with them is sufficient to permit that it act as their representative." Indeed, the Court concluded that the NAACP was the "appropriate party to assert these rights, because it and its members are in every practical sense identical." The Court turned to the associational rights threatened by the compulsory disclosure of NAACP members. Justice Harlan suggested that "effective advocacy of both public and private points of view, particularly controversial ones, is undeniably enhanced by group association." The compelled disclosure was viewed as affecting "adversely the ability of the petitioner and its members to pursue their collective effort to foster beliefs which they admittedly have a right to advocate." The Court saw disclosure as impairing the NAACP in two ways. First, the Association would likely suffer diminished financial support and fewer membership applications. Second, disclosure of the identity of members might prompt "economic reprisal, loss of employment, threat of physical coercion, and other manifestations of public hostility." The Court found that Alabama had not shown a "controlling justification for the deterrent effect on the free enjoyment of the right to associate which disclosure of membership lists is likely to have."

A number of associational rights questions reached the Court soon after. *NAACP v. Alabama* marked the beginning of a new era for associational rights. In *Shelton v. Tucker*[236] the Court struck down a state statute requiring every public school teacher to disclose annually every organization supported by his or her membership or contribution. The Court determined that even a legitimate inquiry into a teacher's fitness and competence "cannot be pursued by means that broadly stifle fundamental personal liberties when the end can be more narrowly achieved." Associational ties have also been an issue with respect to admission to the bar. In *Baird v. State Bar of Arizona*,[237] the Court held that applicants to the bar cannot be compelled to disclose organizational memberships. "Views and beliefs are immune from bar association inquisitions designed to lay a foundation for barring an applicant from the practice of law." In *Law Students Civil Rights Research Council, Inc. v. Wadmond*,[238] however, the Court upheld bar admission inquiries into character and fitness, including questions probing membership in associations advocating unlawful overthrow of the government.

The NAACP was able to affirm another dimension of associational freedom in *NAACP v. Button*.[239] *Button* upheld the NAACP's strategy of representing membership interests through litigation. Many states had enacted anti-solicitation laws prohibiting the "stirring up" of lawsuits. The Court recognized such activity as a means for achieving lawful objectives and a form of political expression for organizations like the NAACP. Indeed, "for such a group, association for litigation may be the most effective form of political association." The Court distinguished litigation seeking vindication of constitutional rights from "avaricious use" of the legal process purely for personal gain.

Political Association

Keyishian v. Board of Regents[240] required that more than "mere membership" in organizations be demonstrated before the imposition of restrictions on associational rights. *Keyishian* examined provisions of New York's Feinberg Law, which authorized the State Board of Regents to monitor organizational memberships of state employees. The Board was required to generate a list of subversive organizations. Membership in any one of them was prima facie evidence of disqualification from public employment, including appointments to academic positions. Although the person being terminated could have a hearing, the hearing could not address the matter of the state's classification of an organization as "subversive." Keyishian and several other faculty members in the state university system were dismissed because of their membership in the Communist Party. The Supreme Court struck down the Feinberg Law. The Court rejected the premise that "public employment, including academic employment, may be conditioned upon the surrender of constitutional rights which could not be abridged by direct government action." The Court found "mere membership" to be an insufficient basis for exclusion. The Court said the statute "sweeps overbroadly in association which may not be proscribed." The regulations "seek to bar employment both for association which legitimately may be proscribed and for association which may not be sanctioned."

The right of association is not explicitly provided in the First Amendment, yet there is a recognized relationship between voluntary association with groups and the protected freedoms of expression and assembly. Decisions such as *Keyishian* reaffirm the notion that the First Amendment extends to associational activity. That was not always the view, however. The first serious test of associational rights came in *Whitney v. California* in which the Court upheld California's Criminal Syndicalism Act, which prohibited organizing and being a member of a group advocating unlawful force as a political weapon. Whitney had participated in a convention of the Communist Labor Party of California, which had passed resolutions advocating various revolutionary acts. Whitney asserted that she had not supported the resolutions nor had she wished the party to urge violation of California's laws. She was convicted nonetheless because she had remained at the convention and had not disassociated herself from the party after the resolutions were adopted. The Supreme Court upheld her conviction. The Court refused to reexamine the jury's finding that Whitney had not sufficiently detached herself from the party. The Court noted that remaining in attendance until the close of the convention and maintaining her membership "manifested her acquiescence." The justices said that California's approach did not restrain free speech or assembly. The "essence of the offense denounced by the Act is the combining with others in an association for the accomplishment of the desired ends through the advocacy and use of criminal and unlawful methods." Because such united and joint action constituted an even greater threat to public peace and security, a state may reasonably exercise its police power to prevent groups from "menacing the peace and welfare of the State."

Whitney seemed to provide license for convicting political radicals because of their association alone, but the Court began to disengage from *Whitney* almost immediately. In *DeJonge v. Oregon* and *Herndon v. Lowry*, the Court reversed convictions of admitted members of the Communist Party, because as individuals neither defendant had violated a criminal law. While an organization may have criminal objectives, simply attending a peaceful meeting called by such an organization cannot transfer criminal liability to an individual. The formal end to *Whitney* came in *Brandenburg v. Ohio*[241] in which the Court unanimously struck down a state syndicalism statute. The defendant in this case was the leader of a Ku Klux Klan group who had spoken at a Klan rally. The Court said "the mere abstract teaching of the moral propriety or even moral necessity for a resort to force and violence is not the same as preparing a group for violent action and steeling it for such action." Accordingly, a statute that fails to draw this distinction impermissibly intrudes on First Amendment freedoms. *Keyishian* specifically overturned *Adler v. Board of Education*,[242] decided 15 years earlier. *Adler* had found the Feinberg Law constitutional, deciding that teachers "have no right to work for the State in the school system on their own terms." The state may inquire into the fitness and suitability of a person for public service, and past conduct may well relate to present fitness. In addition, one's associates, past and present, may properly be considered in determining fitness and loyalty. "From time immemorial, one's reputation has been determined in part by the company he keeps."

Shortly after *Keyishian*, in *United States v. Robel*,[243] the Court voided a McCarron Act provision that prohibited any member of a Communist-action organization from working in a defense facility. As in *Keyishian*, the Court found the statute "casts its net across a broad range of associational activities, indiscriminately trapping membership that can be constitutionally punished and membership that cannot be so proscribed."

In a decision predating *Keyishian* and *Robel* by a year, but using a similar rationale, the Court struck down a loyalty oath provision that imposed penalties upon anyone taking the oath who might later become a member of a subversive organization. The case was *Elfbrandt v. Russell*.[244] The Burger Court upheld a loyalty oath in *Cole v. Richardson*.[245] The oath required public employees to uphold and defend the federal and state constitutions and to oppose the overthrow of federal or state governments by illegal means. *Cole* found the oath permissible in that it did not impose specific action obligations on persons taking it. It required only a general commitment to abide by constitutional processes.

Associational Privacy

Each year, the city of Boston simultaneously celebrates St. Patrick's Day and Evacuation Day (the day the British troops evacuated Boston during the War of Independence) with a parade. The South Boston Allied War Veterans Council has organized the annual parade since 1947. The parade typically includes thousands of participants and historically has been open for the participation of local groups. An organization known as the Irish-American Gay, Lesbian, and Bisexual Group of Boston was formed in 1992. One of its objectives was to march in the parade. The Group's applications to participate were denied by the Council in 1992 and 1993, and the Group obtained a court order enabling its members to march in the parade. The state court ruled for the Group because historically the Council had allowed virtually all other groups to participate in the parade, thus the parade was not seen as an expressive associational activity falling within the reach of the First Amendment, and exclusion of the Group violated the state public accommodations law that prohibits, among other things, discrimination on the basis of sexual preference. Rather than permit Group members from marching in the 1994 parade under court order, the Council canceled the parade and then fashioned written criteria for selecting parade participants. The standards declared that the purpose of the parade was to commemorate "traditional values" and the role of "traditional families." The Council contended that as sponsors of a private parade, it could not be required to include any messages with which it disagreed. The Group contended that state antidiscrimination laws continued to protect their participation, but argued that carrying a banner identifying marchers as gay Irish Americans did not convey a message that could justify their exclusion from participation in the parade. The Court unanimously ruled in *Hurley v. Irish-American Gay, Lesbian & Bisexual Group*[246] that private sponsors could exclude the Group from marching in the parade. The ruling rested on three conclusions: The parade was a private event, a parade is an expressive activity, and the Group's self-identifying presence in the parade was viewed by the Court as "equally expressive." The expression that "inheres" in a parade need not be precisely defined; a "narrow, succinctly articulable message is not a condition of constitutional protection." So even though the Council let many community groups participate in the parade, it did not forfeit constitutional protection "simply by combining multifarious voices, or by failing to edit their themes to isolate an exact message as the exclusive subject matter of the speech." The Court rejected the notion that the state, even for the "enlightened purpose" of discouraging discrimination, could interfere with the expressive rights of a private organization. The state court order compelling participation of the Group required the Council to "alter the expressive content" of their parade. Such use of state power violates the "fundamental rule" of First Amendment protection that a speaker has the "autonomy to choose the content of his own message." All speech, Souter continued, "inherently involves choices of what to say and what to leave unsaid"; one important manifestation of free speech is that "one who chooses to speak may also decide 'what not to say.'" The free speech tradition requires that a speaker should be free from state interference based on the content of his or her expression.

Several associational rights cases have involved the use of fees collected from members for political purposes. Two rulings illustrate the point. In *Communications Workers v. Beck*,[247] the Court ruled that unions cannot compel nonmembers to pay "agency fees" if these fees are used for political or other purposes that are not directly related to collective bargaining. Prior to this decision, unions were free to use agency fees for noncollective-bargaining activities. A number of nonmember employees challenged the Communication Workers of America's (CWA's) use of agency fees to support endorsed political candidates, organize employees at other companies, and to conduct various lobbying activities. They contended that use of fees for such purposes violated the CWA's "duty of fair representation." The issue in this case was whether the collection of agency fees allows a union to financially support "union activities beyond those germane to collective bargaining, contract administration, and grievance adjustment." The Court ruled that it did not.

A similar decision was rendered in a case involving a state bar association. The state bar association of California is "integrated," which means those who wish to practice law in California are statutorily required to become dues-paying members. Virtually all state bar activities are financed by the membership dues, including those that could be characterized as political or ideological. An action was brought by Keller and other state bar association members who wished to prevent use of the mandatory dues for those political activities with which they disagreed. A unanimous Court ruled in *Keller v. State Bar of California*[248] that the state bar's use of compulsory dues for political purposes violated the free speech rights of members who might disagree. The decision effectively limited bar association expenditures to those activities required for the effective regulation of the profession and the improvement of the quality of legal services.

Electoral Process: Campaign Finance

Buckley v. Valeo examined the constitutionality of the Federal Election Campaign Act of 1974. The Federal Election Campaign Act sought to protect the electoral process by limiting political campaign contributions, establishing ceilings on several categories of campaign expenditures, requiring extensive and regular disclosure of campaign contributors and expenditures, providing public financing for presidential campaigns, and creating a Federal Election Commission (FEC) to administer the Act. Suit was filed by a diverse collection of individuals and groups including United States Senator James Buckley, the Eugene McCarthy presidential campaign, the Libertarian Party, the American Conservative Union, and the New York Civil Liberties Union. By differing majorities, the Court upheld those portions of the Act that provided for campaign contribution limits, disclosure, public financing, and the creation of the FEC. The section imposing limits on expenditures was invalidated. In a per curiam opinion, the Court said the Act's contribution and expenditure ceiling "reduces the quantity of expression because virtually every means of communicating ideas in today's society requires the expenditure of money." The Court distinguished, however, between limits on contributions and limits on expenditures—in other words, on those things for which the contributions might be spent. While the latter represents substantial restraint on the quantity and diversity of political speech, limits on contributions involve "little direct restraint." The Court also upheld the Act's public financing provisions by rejecting a claim that a differential funding formula for major and minor parties was unconstitutional.

Buckley generated important follow-up questions regarding regulation of the electoral process. In *First National Bank v. Bellotti*,[249] the Court struck down a state statute prohibiting the use of corporate funds for the purpose of influencing a referendum question. Without a showing that the corporation's advocacy "threatened imminently to undermine democratic processes," the state has no interest sufficient to limit a corporation's expression of views on a public issue. *In Citizens Against Rent Control v. Berkeley*,[250] the Court struck down a municipal ordinance limiting contributions to organizations formed to support or oppose ballot issues. With only Justice White dissenting, the Court drew heavily on *Buckley* and concluded that the ordinance went too far in restraining individual and associational rights of expression. The Court extended the *Buckley* reasoning in *Federal Election Commission v. National Conservative Political Action Committee*,[251] saying the Federal Election Campaign Act could not limit political action committees to an expenditure of $1,000 for promoting the candidacies of publicly funded presidential aspirants. Such an expenditure limit impermissibly infringed on First Amendment speech and association rights.

The Federal Election Campaign Act came under further review in *Federal Election Commission v. Massachusetts Citizens for Life*.[252] Under challenge was the section prohibiting corporations from using general funds to make expenditures related to an election to any public office. Massachusetts Citizens for Life (MCFL), a nonprofit, nonstock corporation, was formed to promote pro-life causes. MCFL used its general treasury to prepare and distribute a special election edition of its newsletter. This publication categorized all candidates for state and federal offices in terms of their support or opposition to MCFL's views. The Supreme Court unanimously ruled that the special edition of the newsletter fell within the scope of the prohibition of the law, but that the provision created unacceptable First Amendment violations for corporations such as MCFL. Most of the rationale supporting regulations of this kind stems from the special characteristics of the corporate structure. The "integrity of the marketplace of political ideas" must be protected from the "corrosive influence of corporate wealth." The availability of resources may make a corporation a "formidable political presence, even though the power of the corporation may be no reflection of the power of its ideas." The Court held that such groups as MCFL simply do not pose that danger of corruption. MCFL was formed for the expressed purpose of promoting political ideas, and its activities cannot be considered as business activities.

The Court upheld, however, the power of the federal and state governments to regulate the campaign expenditures of business corporations in *Austin v. Michigan Chamber of Commerce*.[253] The Michigan Campaign Finance Act prohibited corporations from using general treasury funds for independent expenditures for state political candidates. Rather, corporations were required to use funds specifically segregated for political purposes. The state regulation did allow business corporations to establish political action committees to make such independent expenditures. The Michigan Chamber of Commerce wished to use general treasury funds on behalf of a specific candidate for state office, and it sought to enjoin enforcement of the restriction. The Chamber claimed that, like Massachusetts Citizens for Life, it, too, was a nonprofit ideological corporation. The Court disagreed, citing the organizational characteristics developed in the MCFL decision. MCFL was formed for the "express purpose of promoting political ideas, and cannot engage in business activities." Its "narrow political focus" ensured that its political funding "reflects its political support." The Chamber, on the other hand, had "more varied purposes." Second, MCFL was "independen[t] from the influence of business corporations." Indeed, it was on this basis that the Court found the Chamber to differ "most greatly from the Massachusetts organization." MCFL did not accept contributions from business corporations. Thus, it could not serve as a "conduit for the type of direct spending that creates a threat to the political marketplace." In "striking contrast," the Chamber's members are largely business corporations, whose "political contributions and expenditures can be constitutionally regulated by the State." Business corporations therefore could "circumvent the Act's restrictions by funneling money through the Chamber's general treasury."

The Colorado Republican Party spent in excess of $15,000 for some radio spots and printed material challenging claims made by an incumbent Democratic member of Congress. The question in *Colorado Republican Federal Campaign Committee v. Federal Election Commission*[254] was whether this ad campaign was an independent or a coordinated expenditure. An independent expenditure is beyond the reach of federal limits, while a coordinated expenditure—an expenditure made "in connection" with a candidate's campaign—is subject to federal spending limits. The Colorado Democrats filed a complaint with the FEC contending that the ads constituted a coordinated expenditure and that the cost of the ads exceeded the limit for such spending. The FEC agreed and proposed to settle the matter with a minimal civil penalty. The Colorado Republicans declined, and the FEC brought suit. The Supreme Court ruled that party expenditures can not be restricted unless there is direct evidence that the spending was coordinated with an individual candidate's campaign. Justice Breyer reviewed prior decisions involving federal regulation of campaign financing and identified two relevant propositions: that restrictions on independent expenditures neither impair political advocacy nor relate directly to preventing political corruption. It was Breyer's view that limits on a party's independent expenditures cannot "escape the controlling effect" of these prior rulings. Indeed, the independent expression of a party's views is "core First Amendment activity no less than is the independent expression of individuals, candidates, or other political committees." The Court, said Breyer, was not aware of any "special dangers of corruption associated with a political party's independent expenditures to tip the constitutional balance in another direction." The absence of "prearrangement" and "coordination" do not eliminate but help diminish any danger that a candidate will understand the spending as an "effort to obtain a *quid pro quo*." The diminished risk of corruption, in other words, could not justify the "burden on basic freedoms" produced by the party expenditure restriction. Finally, Justice Breyer rejected the "conclusive presumption" of the FEC that all party expenditures are "coordinated"—that is, that the party and its candidates are "identical." While noting that a party's coordinated expenditures share some "constitutionally relevant features" with its independent expenditures, the Court remanded the question for further examination. The Court also chose not to respond to the contentions of the two major parties that any regulation of party expenditures, independent or otherwise, is barred by the First Amendment.

The question in *Federal Election Commission v. Akins*[255] was whether lobbying organizations that engage in only minimal electioneering activity must comply with the disclosure requirements of the Federal Election Campaign Act (FECA). The American Israel Public Affairs Committee (AIPAC) is a tax-exempt organization that attempts to improve the relationship between the United States and Israel. AIPAC has an annual budget of about $10 million, the bulk of which is used to lobby Congress and the executive branch. The Federal Election Commission (FEC) has taken the position that unless campaign spending is the principal objective of an organization, the campaign finance law disclosure requirements do not apply. The plaintiffs in this case, including James Akins, former Ambassador to Saudi Arabia, were critical of American support for Israel. The plaintiffs filed a complaint with the FEC in 1989 contending that the AIPAC was sufficiently engaged in electoral activity to qualify as a political committee under the terms of the FECA. Specifically, the plaintiffs alleged that AIPAC was violating provisions of federal campaign finance law by making unreported contributions and direct expenditures on behalf of candidates for federal office, and expending funds that were not from a designated and separated political expenditure fund. The FEC dismissed the complaint, concluding that the campaign involvement of AIPAC was not its major objective and involved only a fraction of its overall expenditures. Akins then challenged the FEC dismissal of the complaint in the U.S. District Court for the District of Columbia. The district court eventually upheld the FEC decision to dismiss, but the U.S. Court of Appeals for the District of Columbia Circuit, sitting en banc, reversed, concluding that AIPAC was a political committee subject to all provisions of the FECA. The FEC, on the other hand, argued that the plaintiffs did not have standing to bring the suit. The U.S. Supreme Court ruled that Akins and the others had standing to bring suit against the FEC for its failure to enforce disclosure requirements against AIPAC. At the same time, the Court remanded the case back to the FEC for it to apply its new definition of a political committee. The new definition would expand the scope of a "membership organization," which, in turn, would categorize expenditures like those of AIPAC as "membership communications" rather than political expenditures. The latter would be subject to disclosure, but the former would not.

Electoral Process: Political Parties

Tashjian v. Republican Party ruled that states can not require political parties to hold primary elections open only to registered party members. Connecticut law required that voters in a party primary must be registered members of that party. In an effort to broaden its own electoral base, the Republican Party of Connecticut changed its rules of participation in primaries for federal and state offices to allow registered voters not affiliated with any political party to vote in Republican primaries. The Supreme Court ruled for the Party on associational grounds. Justice Marshall said courts must first consider the character and magnitude of the asserted injury to protected rights, and then evaluate the precise interests offered by the state as justification for any burden. The Party's First Amendment interest was clearly evident to the Court; the freedom to engage in association is an inseparable aspect of the liberty embraced by freedom of speech. Associational freedom extends to partisan political organizations, and the right to associate with the party of one's choice was viewed as an integral part of this basic constitutional freedom. Accordingly, the Party's attempt to broaden its base is conduct "undeniably central to the exercise of the right to association." The statute in this case limited whom the Party could invite to participate in the basic function of selecting the Party's candidates. The law thus limited the Party's "associational opportunities at the crucial juncture at which the appeal to common principle may be translated into concerted actions, and hence to political power in the community." Connecticut attempted to defend the regulation on several grounds, but the Court found each unpersuasive. First, the state claimed the administration of primaries under the Party's rule would cost too much. Even if the state were accurate in its projections, the Court said that the possibility of future cost increases in administering the election policy is not a sufficient basis in this case for interfering with the Party's associational rights. Second, Connecticut contended that the law prevented raiding, a practice whereby voters sympathetic to one party participate in another party's primary in hope of influencing the result. While acknowledging a legitimate state interest in preventing raiding and thereby protecting the integrity of the electoral process, the Court felt a raid on the Republican primary by independents was seen as substantially different from a raid by members of opposing parties. The Court also rejected Connecticut's contention that the law prevented voter confusion. The state argued that the public might not understand what a candidate stands for when he or she is nominated by an "unknown, amorphous body outside the party, while nevertheless using the party name." The Court deferred, however, to the ability of voters to remain sufficiently informed without the state's assistance. Finally, Connecticut contended that its law protected the integrity of the two-party system and the responsibility of party government. Here the Court refused to consider the wisdom of open versus closed primaries and was unwilling to let the state substitute its own judgment for that of the Party, even if the latter's course of conduct was destructive of its own interests.

The Court's ruling in *Tashjian* permitted a political party to determine the rules by which it conducted its own state primaries. A similar ruling was made in *Eu v. San Francisco County Democratic Central Committee*.[256] California election law contained a provision forbidding governing bodies of political parties from endorsing or opposing candidates in primary elections. Another provision made it a misdemeanor for a primary candidate to claim official party endorsement. The Court invalidated these provisions on associational grounds. The ban on primary endorsements keeps a party from "stating whether a candidate adheres to the tenets of the party or whether party officials believe that the candidate is qualified" for office. The law "directly burdens" the party's capacity to "spread its message," said the Court, and it "hamstrings" voters as they attempt to inform themselves about issues and candidates. The party's associational rights allow it to "identify the people who constitute the association," and select candidates who best represent the party's "ideologies and preferences." Interfering with the party's power to endorse "suffocates this right."

The Court has generally steered clear of intervention in partisan political processes. In *O'Brien v. Brown*,[257] for example, the Court invoked the "political question" doctrine when it held that federal courts did not possess the authority to interject themselves into the deliberative processes of a presidential nominating convention. A decade later the Court ruled in *Democratic Party v. LaFollette*[258] that a state could not require national party convention delegates to support the candidacy of the winner of the state's presidential primary.

Notwithstanding this generally noninterventionist tendency, the Court has found state interest in some restrictions on the electoral process to be compelling. In *Rosario v. Rockefeller*,[259] it upheld a requirement that voters register in a party at least 30 days prior to a general election to participate in the next primary. In *Burson v. Freeman*,[260] the Court permitted a state to ban political activities, including the distribution of political campaign materials, within 100 feet of a polling place on election day. Upon examination of the history of election regulation, the Court found a "wide-spread and time-tested consensus that some restricted zone is necessary to serve the States' compelling interest in preventing voter intimidation and election fraud." The law was challenged on the grounds that it was content based—it only regulated political expression around polling places. Justice Blackmun said that failure to regulate all speech does not "render the statute fatally underinclusive." Blackmun also focused on the secret ballot as an integral effort to curb electoral abuses. The only way to preserve the secrecy of the ballot, he argued, "is to limit access to the area around the voter."

In *Burdick v. Takushi*,[261] the Court ruled that a state ban on write-in voting imposed only a "very limited burden" on the right to vote. Noting several different ways party or independent candidates may appear on Hawaii's primary ballot, the Court concluded that the restriction on write-in voting did not unreasonably "interfere with the right of voters to associate and have candidates of their choice placed on the ballot." The Court also rejected the contention that a voter is entitled both to cast and have counted a "protest vote." The function of the election process, said Justice White, is to " 'winnow out and finally reject all but the chosen,' not to provide means of giving vent to 'short-range political goals, pique, or personal quarrels.' "

Most states prohibit candidates for public office from appearing on the ballot as the nominee of more than one political party. Minnesota has such an "antifusion" candidacy law, and it prevented the Twin Cities Area New Party from nominating a state legislative candidate who was already the candidate of one of the two major parties in the state. The fusion or cross-nomination strategy is often important to the viability of minor parties that would otherwise have no chance of electing candidates on their own. The Twin Cities Area New Party brought suit in *Timmons v. Twin Cities Area New Party*[262] asserting that the law violated New Party members' First Amendment right to associational expression. The Supreme Court disagreed. Chief Justice Rehnquist said that the First Amendment protects the right of citizens to "associate and to form political parties for the advancement of common political goals and ideas." At the same time, "it is also clear that States may, and inevitably must, enact reasonable regulations of parties, elections, and ballots to reduce election and campaign related disorder." The states have been granted "broad power" to prescribe the time, place, and manner of elections for federal offices, a power "matched by state control over the election process for state offices." When deciding whether a state election law violates associational rights, the Court must "weigh the 'character and magnitude' of the burden the State's rule imposes on those rights against the interests the State contends justify that burden." Regulations that impose "severe burdens" must advance a compelling interest and be narrowly tailored. The Court was not persuaded by the Party's claim that it had a right to use the ballot itself to "send a particularized message" to its candidates or voters. Ballots serve "primarily to elect candidates, not as fora for political expression." Even with the ban, the Party retained "great latitude" to communicate ideas to voters through its participation in the campaign. In short, the Court concluded that the Minnesota ban did not restrict the ability of the Party and its members to "endorse support, and vote for anyone they like." The Constitution, said Rehnquist, does not require that Minnesota "compromise the policy choices embodied in its ballot-access requirements to accommodate the New Party's fusion strategy."

States typically have been permitted to condition ballot access on some level of support from the electorate. The access requirements may impinge on third parties and independents, however. The Court upheld a California law that denied ballot access to independents who had been registered party members within 17 months prior to an election in *Storer v. Brown*.[263] This case was explicitly distinguished from the Connecticut law in *Tashjian v. Republican Party*. Justice Marshall said the regulations upheld in *Storer* were designed to protect parties from the "disorganizing effect of independent candidacies launched by unsuccessful putative nominees." This action was undertaken to protect the disruption of the political parties from without, and not to prevent parties from taking internal steps affecting their own process for the selection of candidates. Marshall was careful to point out, however, that *Tashjian* should not be read as blanket support for open primaries, or that no state regulation of primary voting qualifications could be sustained.

The Court addressed the issue of ballot access by a third party in *Norman v. Reed*.[264] Illinois law required that new political parties wishing to run candidates for offices within a political subdivision must obtain signatures of five percent of the voters from the last election in the subdivision, or 25,000 voters, whichever was less. Another provision of the statute required the same minimum number of signatures to qualify a candidate running for statewide office. If the political unit was divided into separate districts, the signature requirement had to be met in each of the districts. Yet another statute prohibited new parties from using the same name as an established party. The Harold Washington Party (HWP), named after the former mayor of Chicago, was established in 1989. Its candidate in the 1989 mayoral election in the City of Chicago received more than 40 percent of the vote. The 40 percent support level established the party for ballot access purposes in the city. The following year, a group of people sought to expand the party throughout Cook County. The Cook County Board elects members from two districts, a city district and a suburban district. As an established party within the city, the HWP was able to run candidates in Chicago for countywide office and the city district seats. The party was not permitted, however, to run candidates for the suburban district seats because it had not met the 25,000-signature requirement in the district outside the city. The Supreme Court ruled that the signature requirement for the suburban district was not unduly burdensome under the specific facts of the case. Justice Souter said that citizens have a constitutional right to "create and develop" new political parties. As a result, a state must demonstrate a "sufficiently weighty" interest to justify an access limitation for new parties. The state has an interest in preventing misrepresentation caused by unaffiliated groups using the name of an established party, but the Court saw the categorical bar preventing candidates from one political subdivision from using the name of a party established only in another as broader than necessary to protect against misrepresentation. The 25,000-signature-per-district requirement was viewed as excessive because the same number of signatures would qualify a candidate to run statewide; organizers of a new party could access the statewide ballot with 25,000 signatures from the City of Chicago, but fail to qualify for the Cook County ballot in the suburban district. Souter concluded that if the state "deems it unimportant" to require new statewide parties to demonstrate any distribution of support, it requires "elusive logic" to demonstrate a serious state interest in demanding such a distribution for new local parties.

The Arkansas Educational Television Commission, a public agency of the state of Arkansas, operates a five-station noncommercial network (AETN). Although the Commission's members were political appointees and AETN received state funding, AETN exercised editorial judgment about the content broadcast over its stations. The AETN broadcast a number of debates involving congressional candidates in 1992. Two months after the Democratic and Republican Party candidates for Arkansas' Third Congressional District were invited to participate in a debate, Ralph Forbes, an independent candidate for the congressional seat, asked to be included in the debate. AETN concluded that Forbes was not a viable candidate for the office and declined his request. Forbes sought an injunction directing that AETN allow him to participate in the debate. He asserted that AETN's refusal to allow him to participate violated his First Amendment right of free speech. He was unable to obtain the injunction, however, and the debate took place without his participation. Forbes also was unsuccessful in his suit for damages. A jury was instructed that Forbes was required to show that AETN had excluded him because it either disagreed with his viewpoint or had been subjected to political pressure to exclude him. The jury concluded that Forbes had not demonstrated either circumstance and ruled in favor of AETN. The Court of Appeals for the Eighth Circuit reversed the judgment, however. The Supreme Court ruled in *Arkansas Education Television Commission v. Forbes*[265] that stations have sufficient editorial discretion to exclude nonviable candidates from debates as long as the decision is not based on the candidate's issue positions. The Court first rejected the contention that "public forum" principles applied to this case. The public forum doctrine, said Justice Kennedy, should not be "extended in a mechanical way to the very different context of public television broadcasting." Broad rights of access for outside speakers would be "antithetical . . . to the discretion that stations and their editorial staff must exercise to fulfill their journalistic purpose and statutory obligations." Public and private broadcasters both are required to exercise "substantial editorial discretion in the selection and presentation of their programming." If the courts were to define and require "pre-established criteria for access, it would risk implicating the courts in judgments that should be left to the exercise of journalistic discretion." Candidate debates, Kennedy acknowledged, present a "narrow exception" to the rule that public broadcasting does not lend itself to forum analysis. A candidate debate is different from other programming in that it is designed to be a forum for political speech, and debates have "exceptional significance" in the electoral process. Government does not create a "designated public forum," however, when it "does no more than reserve eligibility for access to the forum to a particular class of speakers, whose members must then, as individuals, obtain permission to use it."

The AETN debate did not have an "open-microphone" format. Rather, the AETN made candidate-by-candidate determinations of which candidates would participate. Kennedy said that the Eighth Circuit's ruling that the debate was a public forum open to all candidates would place a "severe burden" on public broadcasters who air candidates' views. A public television editor might decide that the inclusion of all ballot-qualified candidates would "actually undermine the educational value and quality of debates." Were it faced with the prospect of "cacophony," on the one hand, and "First Amendment liability," on the other, a public television broadcaster might "choose not to air candidates' views at all." A broadcaster might decide instead that the "safe course" is to avoid controversy, and by doing so, "diminish the free flow of information and ideas." The debate's status as a "nonpublic forum," however, did not give AETN "unfettered power to exclude any candidate it wished." Exclusion must not be based on the speaker's viewpoint and must be "otherwise reasonable in light of the purpose of the property." In this case, it was "beyond dispute" that Forbes was excluded not because of his views but because he had "generated no appreciable public interest." His own "objective lack of support, not his platform," was the basis of his exclusion. Thus, AETN's decision to exclude Forbes was a "reasonable, viewpoint-neutral exercise of journalistic discretion consistent with the First Amendment."

Electoral Process: Ballot Access

Munro v. Socialist Workers Party upheld a state law limiting general election ballot access to those candidates receiving at least one percent of the primary vote total. The state of Washington established a two-step process for minor party candidates seeking to get on the general election ballot. Each candidate had first to secure the convention nomination of his or her party. As the nominee, the candidate would appear on the primary election ballot. To access the general election ballot, the candidate needed to receive at least one percent of all votes cast for that office in the primary election. Candidate Dean Peoples was placed on the primary election ballot as the nominee of the Socialist Workers Party. Peoples received only 596 of the 681,690 votes cast in the primary, or .09 percent. Accordingly his name was not placed on the general election ballot. An action was brought in federal court by Peoples, the Party, and two registered voters claiming abridgment of rights secured by the First Amendment. The Supreme Court upheld the restrictions on ballot access. The Court noted that restrictions on ballot access for political parties impinge both on the rights of individuals to associate for political purposes and the rights of qualified voters to cast their votes efficaciously. Such rights are not absolute, however, and are necessarily subject to qualification if elections are to be run fairly and effectively.

The ballot access issue examined in *Munro v. Socialist Workers Party* is not new. For years the Court refrained from engaging in direct supervision of state electoral processes. That policy began to change with the Warren Court's decision to address the issue of legislative apportionment. Regulations that made it difficult for new or minor parties to get on the ballot began to be scrutinized more carefully. In *Williams v. Rhodes*,[266] for example, the Court voided an Ohio statute that required new parties to file a substantial number of petition signatures to access the ballot. Established parties were exempt from the requirement, and the Court ruled that the policy unfairly burdened new parties.

Similarly, the Court struck down an early filing date for candidates other than those nominated by the two major parties in *Anderson v. Celebrezze*.[267] But as Justice White said in *Munro*, there were cases decided during this same period that established with unmistakable clarity that states may, as a manifestation of their interest in preserving the integrity of the election process, require candidates to make a preliminary showing of support to qualify for ballot access. In *Jenness v. Fortsen*,[268] the Court sustained a Georgia requirement that independent and minor party candidates submit petitions signed by at least five percent of those eligible to vote in the election for the office involved. Likewise, the Court upheld a state requirement in *American Party of Texas v. White*[269] minor party candidates demonstrate support through signatures of voters numbering at least one percent of the total votes cast in the most recent gubernatorial election. What is clearly reflected in such cases as *Jenness*, *White*, and *Munro* is that the Court will permit states significant latitude in restricting ballot access as long as access conditions are not excessive.

Campaign Regulations

An Ohio statute required the name and address of the person(s) or organization(s) that distributes literature designed to influence the outcome of an election. The

Ohio Elections Commission (OEC) found that Margaret McIntyre had violated the law by distributing unsigned campaign literature opposing a local tax initiative and fined her $100. In *McIntyre v. Ohio Elections Commission*,[270] the U.S. Supreme Court declared the Ohio law unconstitutional, concluding that an author's decision to remain anonymous, like other decisions concerning publication content, is "an aspect of the freedom of speech protected by the First Amendment." Ohio sought to justify the regulation as a means of preventing dissemination of fraudulent, false, or libelous statements. The Court was not persuaded, however, noting that the Ohio statute contained no language so limiting its application to such statements. Instead, the category of speech regulated by Ohio, said Stevens, "occupies the core of the protection afforded by the First Amendment." Discussion of political issues must be afforded the broadest constitutional protection in order to ensure the fullest possible debate. Stevens continued that "[n]o form of speech is entitled to greater constitutional protection." Although deterrence of misleading or false statements was regarded as a legitimate state interest, the Court was satisfied that Ohio had other means of protecting that interest without the "extremely broad" prohibition on anonymous expression. The state's interest in informing the public was also seen as insufficient to justify the ban on anonymous speech. The identity of a speaker is "no different from other components of [a] document's content that the author is free to include or exclude." The simple interest in providing voters with additional relevant information "does not justify a state requirement that a writer make statements or disclosures she would otherwise omit." Anonymous pamphleteering is "not a pernicious, fraudulent practice, but an honorable tradition of advocacy and of dissent," and anonymity is a "shield from the tyranny of the majority." The right to remain anonymous "may be abused when it shields fraudulent conduct," but political speech will inherently have "unpalatable consequences."

Anonymous pamphleteering and leafletting have been recognized as legitimate forms of expression since the beginning of our constitutional history. Indeed, the *Federalist* was authored by James Madison, Alexander Hamilton, and John Jay under the pseudonym of "Publius." The Court has typically found regulations such as found in *McIntyre* to be suspect. The Burger Court, however, upheld a ban on the posting of political campaign signs on utility poles in *Members of City Council v. Taxpayers for Vincent*.[271] The ban was seen to be content neutral and directed toward a legitimate aesthetic interest. The purpose of the regulation was "unrelated to the suppression of ideas," and interfered with expression only to the extent necessary to eliminate visual clutter. The Court noted that the ban on posting signs did not impinge on any alternative modes of communication.

The Rehnquist Court recognized the value of speaker identity in *Ladue v. Gilleo*. Ladue, Missouri banned residential signs except for a number of exempted categories of signs; for example, signs that identified property, indicated property was for sale, or conveyed safety warnings, among others. Margaret Gilleo placed a sign in her yard indicating her opposition to the Persian Gulf War and was cited for violating the sign ordinance. The Supreme Court unanimously struck down the sign ban as affording residents of Ladue insufficient alternative means to express themselves. Displaying a sign from one's own residence, said Justice Stevens, "often carries a message quite distinct from placing the same sign somewhere else, or conveying the same text or picture by other means." Unlike in *McIntyre*, the Court assigned value to the identity of the speaker in *Ladue*. The location of signs provides important information about the identity of the speaker, often an "important component of many attempts to persuade."

Term Limits

Twenty-three states have adopted some form of term limits on members of Congress. The voters of Arkansas adopted a constitutional amendment (Amendment 73) in 1992 effectively limiting membership in the U.S. House of Representatives to three terms (6 years), and U.S. Senate membership to two terms (12 years). Specifically, Amendment 73 prohibited placing on the ballot the name of an otherwise qualified candidate for Congress if that candidate had already served three terms in the U.S. House or two terms in the U.S. Senate. The amendment permitted incumbents who reached the term limits to run and be reelected by write-in campaigns. Suits were filed in an Arkansas court challenging the constitutionality of Amendment 73. There were a number of plaintiffs, including Congressman Ray Thornton. Various organizations supporting term limits, including U.S. Term Limits, Inc., intervened as defendants. The U.S. Supreme Court in *U.S. Term Limits, Inc. v. Thornton*[272] ruled against Amendment 73. Constitutionality of Amendment 73 "depends critically" on the resolution of two issues, said Justice Stevens. The first is whether the Constitution prohibits states from adding to or altering the qualifications "specifically enumerated" in Article I. Second, if the Constitution does forbid such change, the issue of whether Amendment 73 is a ballot access restriction rather than an "outright disqualification" of otherwise qualified incumbents must be resolved. The majority was guided by the Court's ruling in *Powell v. McCormack*.[273] The issue in *Powell* was whether Congress's power to judge the qualifications of its own members included the power to impose qualifications other than those enumerated in Article I. The Court concluded that it did not.

Powell, however, did not reach the question of whether the Constitution prohibits additional qualifications imposed by states. The supporters of term limits argued that in the absence of an explicit constitutional prohibition, the reserved powers in the Tenth Amendment should allow states to add such qualifications. The Court was not persuaded for two reasons. First, historical materials showed that the Framers drew a basic distinction between the powers of the newly created national government and the powers retained by the preexisting sovereign states. Contrary to the assertions of those supporting Amendment 73, the power to add qualifications is not part of the sovereignty the Tenth Amendment reserved to the states. Petitioners' Tenth Amendment argument, said Stevens, "misconceives the nature of the right at issue because that amendment could only 'reserve' that which existed before." Second, even if states had some original power on this subject, the Court concluded that the Framers intended the Constitution to be "the exclusive source of qualifications for members of Congress," and that the Framers thereby "divested" states of any power to add qualifications.

States typically have wide-ranging authority to regulate elections. Occasionally, the Court invalidates provisions of state election law because they conflict with specific provisions of the U.S. Constitution. The term limit ruling is an example of such a conflict. A similar ruling came in the Louisiana primary case. Since 1978 Louisiana has conducted an "open" primary for congressional offices in October of federal election years. All candidates, regardless of party affiliation, are listed on the same ballot, and all voters are entitled to vote. If a candidate for a particular office receives a majority at the primary, the person is elected to the office without any voting necessary on the federal election day in November. Since this system went into effect, over 80 percent of the state's contested congressional elections have ended with the October open primary. G. Scott Love and other Louisiana voters challenged the primary on the grounds that it violated a federal law that establishes a uniform date in November for congressional elections. A federal district court upheld the Louisiana process, but the U.S. Court of Appeals for the Fifth Circuit reversed that ruling. The Supreme Court ruled in *Foster v. Love*[274] that the process conflicts with federal law in that it allows potentially final election of U.S. senators and representatives before the designated federal election day. The Elections Clause of Article I permits states to determine the "times, places, and manner" of congressional elections, but also permits Congress to "alter such regulations" at any time. The Clause, said Justice Souter, is a "default provision; it invests the States with responsibility for the mechanics of congressional elections, but only so far as Congress declines to pre-empt state legislative choices." The Elections Clause thus gives Congress the power to "override state regulations" by establishing uniform rules for federal elections that are binding on the states. Without "paring the term 'election' in [the federal law] down to the constitutional bone," it is sufficient to resolve this case that a "contested selection of candidates for a congressional office that is concluded as a matter of law before the federal election day, with no act in law or in fact to take place on the date chosen by Congress, clearly violates [the federal law]." Louisiana sought to save the election process by suggesting that there was provision for a "general" election on the federal election day, and that the Louisiana open primary concerns only the manner for electing federal representatives and not the time of the election. Justice Souter characterized this argument as "mere wordplay." After a candidate receives a majority of votes in the open primary,

Louisiana law requires no further act by anyone to "seal the election; the election has already occurred." When Congress established the uniform election day, it was concerned with the "distortion" of the voting process threatened when the results of an early federal election in one state can "influence later voting in other States, with the burden on citizens forced to turn out on two different election days to make final selections of federal officers in presidential election years." The Louisiana open primary process has tended to "foster both evils," said Souter. It has had the effect of "conclusively electing more than 80% of the state's Senators and Representatives before the election day elsewhere," and, in presidential election years, having "forced voters to turn out for two potentially conclusive federal elections."

Government Contractors and Patronage

Wabaunsee County v. Umbehr examined the political speech rights of an independent government contractor. Umbehr was under contract to provide trash collection for Wabaunsee County, Kansas. He was also openly critical of the performance of the Wabaunsee County Commission. Umbehr filed suit in federal court when his contract was terminated by the Commission, contending that the action was prompted by his expressed criticism of county government. The Supreme Court ruled that a private contractor was entitled to the same free speech protections as a government employee. Justice O'Connor acknowledged that the Court had never examined whether the First Amendment limits the capacity of the government to terminate relationships with independent contractors because of the contractors' speech. She noted, however, the "obvious" similarities between government employees and government contractors, and the government employment precedents were seen as controlling this case.

In choosing the government employee precedents, especially the balancing test from *Pickering v. Board of Education*,[275] the Court rejected a "bright line" distinction between government employees and independent contractors. The "bright line" approach advocated by the Board would give the government "carte blanche to terminate independent contractors for exercising First Amendment rights." Furthermore, such an approach would leave First Amendment rights, said O'Connor, "unduly dependent" on whether state law defines a contract for provision of government services as a contract of employment or a contract for services, a "distinction that is at best a very poor proxy for the interests at stake." The case was remanded for further proceedings, and O'Connor described how the proper balancing approach would apply in this case. On remand, Umbehr would have to demonstrate that the termination of his contract was "motivated by his speech on a public concern," a showing that would require him to prove "more than the mere fact he criticized the Board members before they terminated him." If Umbehr could make such a showing, the Board would have a "valid defense" if it could show that "in light of their knowledge, perceptions, and policies at the time of termination, the Board members would have terminated the contract regardless of his speech."

The Burger Court extensively dealt with political appointments. In *Elrod v. Burns*,[276] the Court held that an incoming county official could not fire department employees because they belonged to the wrong party. *Branti v. Finkel*[277] involved assistant public defenders also terminated on the basis of partisanship. The rationale shared by these two cases was that firings based on party affiliation penalized political thought.

This principle was broadened by the Rehnquist Court in *Rutan v. Republican Party*.[278] In *Rutan*, the Court ruled that hiring decisions for public positions could not be based on party affiliation. Justice Brennan said that political victors are entitled to "only those spoils that may be constitutionally obtained." Unless party affiliation is an "appropriate requirement" for a position, the First Amendment precludes use of party affiliation in hiring, promotion, recall, and transfer decisions. Employees who do "not compromise their beliefs" stand to lose in a variety of ways if party affiliation may be used in making job decisions. For example, an employee may lose "increases in pay or job satisfaction attendant to promotion." These are "significant penalties . . . imposed for the exercise of rights guaranteed by the First Amendment." Unless use of patronage is "narrowly tailored" to further a "vital" governmental interest, it encroaches on the First Amendment. Illinois asserted that patronage both produced a more effective workforce and protected political parties. The Court disagreed. Justice Brennan said that government can secure "effective" employees by sanctioning workers whose work is "deficient." Party affiliation is not a proxy for deficient performance as such. Neither is the democratic process furthered by patronage. Parties are "nurtured by other, less intrusive and equally effective methods." To the contrary, patronage "decidedly impairs the elective process by discouraging free political expression by public employees." Justice Scalia said in dissent that a legislature could determine that patronage "stabilizes political parties and prevents excessive political fragmentation—both of which are results in which states have a strong governmental interest."

The Rehnquist Court decided another case with *Umbehr* in 1995 that focused even more tightly on the question of whether patronage-based awarding of government contracts violates the First Amendment. A towing company was among those included on a police dispatch list in Northlake, Illinois. Each company was called "in rotation" with other companies whenever police needed vehicles moved. The company owner openly supported the incumbent mayor's opponent in an election. The incumbent mayor was reelected, and the towing company was removed from the dispatch list. The company's owner claimed that the city's action was in retaliation for his support of the mayor's opponent. The case of *O'Hare Trucking Services, Inc. v. Northlake*[279] differed from *Umbehr* in that it focused more extensively on the patronage issue, and the Court's reasoning drew more extensively from patronage precedents such as *Elrod*, *Branti*, and *Rutan*. These cases had established that public employees can not be discharged for failure to support a political party or its candidates unless political affiliation is a reasonably appropriate requirement for the job. The question in *O'Hare* was whether the same protection extends to an independent contractor. The Supreme Court ruled that it did. There is "no doubt," said Justice Kennedy, that the towing company's owner could not have been removed from the list for refusing to contribute to the mayor's campaign if he had been a public employee. Northlake contended that the protective rulings of *Elrod*, *Branti*, and *Rutan* did not apply here—that unlike a public employee, an independent contractor's First Amendment rights "must yield to the government's asserted countervailing interest in sustaining a patronage system." Kennedy said, however, that the Court could not accept the contention that those who "perform the government's work outside the formal employment relationship" are subject to the "direct and specific" abridgment of First Amendment rights.

Notes

1. *Everson v. Board of Education*, 330 US 1 (1947).
2. *Engel v. Vitale*, 370 US 421 (1962).
3. *Lemon v. Kurtzman*, 403 US 602 (1971).
4. *Mueller v. Allen*, 463 US 388 (1983).
5. *Agostini v. Felton*, 501 US 203 (1997).
6. *Rosenberger v. University of Virginia*, 515 US 819 (1995).
7. *Lamb's Chapel v. Center Morisches Union Free School District*, 508 US 384 (1993).
8. *Allegheny County v. ACLU*, 492 US 573 (1989).
9. *Lee v. Weisman*, 505 US 577 (1992).
10. *Sunday Closing Law Cases*, 366 US 421 (1961).
11. *Sherbert v. Verner*, 374 US 398 (1963).
12. *Wisconsin v. Yoder*, 406 US 205 (1972).
13. *Employment Division v. Smith*, 494 US 872 (1990).
14. *City of Boerne v. Flores*, 521 US 507 (1997).
15. *Gillette v. United States*, 401 US 437 (1971).
16. *Jimmy Swaggert Ministries v. Board of Equalization*, 403 US 378 (1990).
17. *Schenck v. United States*, 249 US 47 (1919).
18. *Gitlow v. New York*, 268 US 652 (1925).
19. *Dennis v. United States*, 341 US 494 (1951).
20. *Tinker v. Des Moines Independent Community School District*, 393 US 503 (1969).
21. *Texas v. Johnson*, 491 US 397 (1989).
22. *Cohen v. California*, 403 US 15 (1971).

23. *R. A. V. v. City of St. Paul*, 505 US 377 (1992).

24. *Schaumburg v.Citizens for a Better Environment*, 444 US 620 (1980).

25. *Lebron v. National Railroad Passenger Corp.*, 513 US 374 (1995).

26. *United States v. National Treasury Employees Union*, 513 US 454 (1995).

27. *Near v. Minnesota*, 283 US 597 (1931).

28. *New York Times Co. v. United States*, 403 US 713 (1971).

29. *Hazelwood School District v. Kuhlmeier*, 484 US 260 (1988).

30. *New YorkTimes v. Sullivan*, 376 US 254 (1964).

31. *Hustler Magazine v. Falwell*, 485 US 46 (1988).

32. *Branzburg v. Hayes*, 408 US 665 (1972).

33. *Richmond Newspapers Inc. v. Virginia*, 448 US 555 (1980).

34. *Central Hudson Gas & Electric Co. v. Public Service Commission*, 447 US 557 (1980).

35. *Glickman v. Wileman Bros.*, 521 US 457 (1997).

36. *Turner Broadcasting v. FCC (II)*, 520 US 180 (1997).

37. *Reno v. ACLU*, 521 US 844 (1997).

38. *Roth v. United States*, 354 US 476 (1957).

39. *Miller v. California*, 413 US 15 (1973).

40. *Young v. American MiniTheatres*, 427 US 50 (1976).

41. *Osborne v. Ohio*, 495 US 103 (1990).

42. *Kingsley Books v. Brown*, 354 US 436 (1957).

43. *Adderley v. Florida*, 385 US 39 (1966).

44. *Prune Yard Shopping Center v. Robins*, 447 US 74 (1980).

45. *Carroll v. President and Commissioners of Princess Anne County*, 393 US 175 (1968).

46. *Schenck v. Pro-Choice Network*, 519 US 357 (1997).

47. *NAACP v. Alabama*, 357 US 449 (1958).

48. *Keyishian v. Board of Regents*, 385 US 589 (1967).

49. *Hurley v. Irish-American Gay, Lesbian & Bisexual Group*, 515 US 557 (1995).

50. *Buckley v. Valeo*, 424 US 1 (1976).

51. *Tashjian v. Republican Party*, 479 US 208 (1986).

52. *Munro v. Socialist Workers Party*, 479 US 189 (1986).

53. *McIntyre v. Ohio Elections Commission*, 514 US 334 (1995).

54. *U.S. Term Limits, Inc. v. Thornton*, 514 US 779 (1995).

55. *Wabaunsee County v. Umbehr*, 518 US 668 (1996).

56. *De Jonge v. Oregon*, 239 US 353 (1937).

57. *Cantwell v. Connecticut*, 310 US 296 (1940).

58. *Board of Education v. Allen*, 392 US 236 (1968).

59. *Wolman v. Walter*, 433 US 229 (1977).

60. *Committee for Public Education and Religious Liberty v. Regan*, 444 US 646 (1980).

61. *Levitt v. Committee for Public Education and Religious Liberty*, 413 US 472 (1973).

62. *Tilton v. Richardson*, 403 US 672 (1971).

63. *Walz v. Tax Commission [of the City of New York]*, 397 US 664 (1970).

64. *Texas Monthly v. Bullock*, 489 US 1 (1989).

65. *Hernandez v. Commissioner of Internal Revenue*, 490 US 680 (1989).

66. *Hunt v. McNair*, 413 US 734 (1973).

67. *Roemer v. Board of Public Works*, 426 US 736 (1976).

68. *Church of Jesus Christ of Latter Day Saints v. Amos*, 483 US 327 (1987).

69. *Lynch v. Donnelly*. 465 US 668 (1984).

70. *Capitol Square Review and Advisory Board v. Pinette*, 515 US 753 (1995).

71. *Aguilar v. Felton*, 473 US 402 (1985).

72. *Grand Rapids School District v. Ball*, 473 US 363 (1985).

73. *Witters v. Washington Department of Services for the Blind*, 474 US 481 (1986).

74. *Zobrest v. Catalina Foothills School District*, 509 US 1 (1993).

75. *Board of Education v. Grumet*, 512 US 687 (1994).

76. *Bowen v. Kendrick*, 487 US 589 (1987).

77. *Zorach v. Clauson*, 343 US 306 (1952).

78. *Illinois ex rel. McCollum v. Board of Education*, 333 US 203 (1948).

79. *Edwards v. Aguillard*, 482 US 578 (1987).

80. *Epperson v. Arkansas*, 393 US 97 (1968).

81. *Abington v. Schempp*, 375 US 203 (1956).

82. *Stone v. Graham*, 449 US 39 (1980).

83. *School District v. Schempp*, 374 US 203 (1963).

84. *Murray v. Curlett*, 472 US 38 (1985).

85. *Wallace v. Jaffree*, 472 US 38 (1985).

86. *Marsh v. Chambers*, 463 US 783 (1983).

87. *Board of Education v. Mergens*, 496 US 226 (1990).

88. *Widmar v. Vincent*, 454 US 263 (1981).

89. *Carey v. Brown*, 445 US 914 (1980).

90. *Heffron v. International Society for Krishna Consciousness*, 449 US 1109 (1981).

91. *Gallagher v. Crown Kosher Super Market, Inc.*, 366 US 617 (1961).

92. *Thomas v. Review Board of Indiana Employment Security Division*, 450 US 717 (1981).

93. *Estate of Thornton v. Caldor, Inc.*, 472 US 7093 (1985).

94. *Hobbie v. Unemployment Appeals Commission*, 480 US 136 (1987).

95. *Frazee v. Illinois Department of Employment Security*, 489 US 829 (1989).

96. *United States v. Lee*, 435 US 252 (1982).

97. *Goldman v. Weinberger*, 475 US 503 (1986).

98. *McGowan v. Maryland*, 366 US 420 (1961).

99. *Two Guys from Harrison—Allentown, Inc. v. McGinley*, 366 US 599 (1961).

100. *Reynolds v. United States*, 98 US 145 (1878).

101. *Jacobson v. Massachusetts*, 197 US 11 (1905).

102. *West Virginia Board of Education v. Barrette*, 319 US 624 (1943).

103. *Minersville SchoolDistrict v. Gibitis*, 310 US 586 (1940).

104. *Church of the Lukumi Babalu Aye, Inc. v. City of Hileah*, 508 US 520 (1993).

105. *Murdock v. Pennsylvania*, 319 US 105 (1943).

106. *Jones v. Opelika*, 316 US 584 (1942).

107. *United States v. Seeger*, 380 US 163 (1965).

108. *Welsh v. United States*, 398 US 333 (1970).

109. *Rostker v. Goldberg*, 453 US 57 (1981).

110. *Selective Service System v. Minnesota Public Interest Research Group*, 468 US 841 (1984).

111. *Wayte v. United States*, 4709 US 5998 (1985).

112. *Wards Cove Packing Co. v. Atonio*, 490 US 642 (1989).

113. *Martin v. Wilks*, 490 US 755 (1985).

114. *Lorance v. AT&T Technologies, Inc.*, 490 v. 900 (1989).

115. *Frowerk v. United States*, 249 US 204 (1919).

116. *Debs v. United States*, 249 US 211 (1916).

117. *Abrams v. United States*, 250 US 616 (1919).

118. *United States v. Carolene Products Co.*, 304 US 144 (1938).

119. *Whitney v. California*, 274 US 357 (1927).

120. *Herndon v. Lowry*, 301 US 242 (1937).

121. *Brandenburg v. Ohio*, 395 US 444 (1969).

122. *Yates v. United States*, 354 US 298 (1957.

123. *Scales v. United States*, 367 US 203 (1961).

124. *Albertson v. Subversive Activities Control Board*, 383 US 70 (1965).

125. *United States v. O'Brien*, 391 US 367 (1968).

126. *California v. La Rue*, 409 US 109 (1972).

127. *Stromberg v. California*, 283 US 359 (1931).

128. *Street v. New York*, 394 US 576 (1969).

129. *Smith v. Goguen*, 415 US 566 (1974).

130. *Spence v. Washington*, 418 US 405 (1974).

131. *United States v. Eichman* and *United States v. Haggerty*, 496 US 310 (1990).

132. *Chaplinsky v. New Hampshire*, 315 US 568 (1942).

133. *Terminello v. Chicago*, 377 US 1 (1949).

134. *Feiner v. New York*, 340 US 315 (1951).

135. *Rankin v. McPherson*, 483 US 378 (1987).

136. *Federal Communications Commission (FCC) v. Pacifica Foundation*, 438 US 728 (1978).

137. *Wisconsin v. Mitchell*, 509 US 476 (1993).

138. *Coates v. Cincinnati*, 402 US 611 (1971).

139. *Grayned v. Rockford*, 404 US 104 (1972).

140. *Hoffman Estates v. Flipside*, 456 US 950 (1982).

141. *Secretary of State v. Joseph H. Munson Company*, 467 US 947 (1984).

142. *Riley v. National Federation for the Blind*, 487 US 781 (1988).

143. *Board of Airport Commissioners v. Jews for Jesus*, 482 US 589 (1995).

144. *Plessy v. Fergusson*, 163 US 537 (1896).

145. *Pickering v. Board of Education*, 391 US 563 (1968).

146. *United Public Workers v. Mitchell*, 330 US 75 (1947).

147. *Nebraska Press Association v. Stuart*, 427 US 539 (1976).

148. *Organization for Better Austin v. Keefe*, 402 US 415 (1971).

149. *Snepp v. United States*, 444 US 507 (1980).

150. *Simon & Schuster, Inc. v. Members of the New York State Crime Victims Board*, 502 US 105 (1991).

151. *Florida Star v. B. J. F.*, 491 US 524 (1989).

152. *Smith v. Daily Mail Publishing Co.*, 443 US 61 (1979).

153. *Butterworth v. Smith*, 494 US 624 (1990).

154. *Garrison v. Louisiana*, 379 US 64 (1964).

155. *McDonald v. Smith*, 472 US 479 (1985).

156. *Beauharnais v. Illinois*, 334 US 250 (1952).

157. *Bose Corp. v. Consumers Union of the United States, Inc.*, 466 US 485 (1984).

158. *Rosenbloom v. Metromedia, Inc.*, 403 US 29 (1971).

159. *Gertz v. Robert Walsh, Inc.*, 418 US 323 (1974).

160. *Hutchinson v. Proxmire*, 443 US 111 (1979).

161. *Keeton v. Hustler Magazine, Inc.*, 465 US 7709 (1984).

162. *Calder v. Jones*, 465 US 783 (1984).

163. *Dun & Bradstreet, Inc. v. Greenmoss Builders, Inc.*, 472 US 749 (1985).

164. *Philadelphia Newspapers v. Hepps*, 475 US 767 (1985).

165. *Anderson v. Liberty Lobby*, 477 US 242 (1986).

166. *Milkovich v. Lorain Journal*, 497 US 1 (1990).

167. *Masson v. New Yorker Magazine, Inc.*, 501 US 493 (1991).

168. *Saxbe v. Washington Post*, 417 US 843 (1974).

169. *Houchins v. KQED, Inc.*, 438 US 1 (1978).

170. *Herbert v. Lando*, 441 US 153 (19979).

171. *Cohen v. Cowels Media Company*, 501 US 663 (1991).

172. *Gannett Co. v. De Pasquale*, 443 US 368 (1979).

173. *Chandler v. Florida*, 449 US 560 (1980).

174. *Press Enterprise Co. v. Superior Court (I)*, 464 US 501 (1984).

175. *Press Enterprise Co. v. Superior Court (II)*, 478 US 1 (1986).

176. *Pittsburgh Press Co. v. Pittsburgh Commission on Human Relations*, 413 US 376 (1973).

177. *Valentine v. Chrestensen*, 316 US 52 (1942).

178. *Bigelow v. Virginia*, 421 US 809 (1975).

179. *Virginia State Board of Pharmacy v. Virginia Citizens Consumer Council, Inc.*, 425 US 748 (1976).

180. *Glickman v. Wileman Bros.*, 521 US 457 (1997).

181. Shapero v. *Kentucky Bar Association*, 486 US 466 (1988).

182. *Florida Bar v. Went For It*, Inc., 515 US 618 (1995).

183. *City of Ladue v. Gilleo*, 512 US 43 (1994).

184. *Rubin v. Coors Brewing Co.*, 514 US 476 (1995).

185. *Liquormart, Inc. v. Rhode Island*, 517 US 484 (1996).

186. *Cincinnati v. Discovery Network*, 507 US 410 (1993).

187. *Red Lion Broadcasting Co. v. FCC*, 395 US 367 (1969).

188. *Miami Herald Publishing Co. v. Tornillo*, 418 US 241 (1974).

189. *Columbia Broadcasting System, Inc. v. Democratic National Committee*, 412 US 94 (1973).

190. *Columbia Broadcasting System, Inc. v. Federal Communications Committee*, 449 US 950 (1980).

191. *FCC v. League of Women Voters*, 468 US 364 (1984).

192. *Sable Communications of California, Inc. v. FCC*, 492 US 115 (1989).

193. *Denver Area Educational Telecommunications Consortium, Inc. v. FCC*, 518 US 727 (1996).

194. *Queen v. Hicklin*, 3 QB 360 (1868).

195. *Jacobellis v. Ohio*, 378 US 184 (1964).

196. *A Book Named "John Cleland's Memoirs of a Woman of Pleasure" v. Attorney General of Massachusetts*, 383 US 413 (1966).

197. *Redrup v. New York*, 386 US 767 (1967).

198. *Rowan v. Post Office*, 397 US 728 (1970).

199. *Ginzburg v. United States*, 383 US 463 (1966).

200. *Brockett v. Spokane Arcades, Inc.*, 472 US 491 (1985).

201. *United States v. X-Citement Video, Inc.*, 513 US 64 (1994).

202. *National Endowment for the Arts v.Finley*, 118 SCt 2168 (1998).

203. *Erznoznik v. Jacksonville*, 422 US 205 (1975).

204. *Schad v. Borough of St. Ephriam*, 452 US 61 (1981).

205. *City of Renton v. Playtime Theaters, Inc.*, 475 US 41 (1986).

206. *FW/PBS, Inc. v. City of Dallas*, 493 US 215 (1990).

207. *Barnes v. Glen Theater*, 501 US 560 (1991).

208. *New York v. Ferber*.

209. *Stanly v. Georgia.*

210. *United States v. Thirty-Seven Photographs*, 402 US 352 (1971).

211. *United States v. Twelve 200-Ft. Reels of Super 8 mm. Film*, 413 US 123 (1973).

212. *Smith v. California*, 361 US 147 (1959).

213. *Bantam Books, Inc. v. Sullivan*, 372 US 58 (1963).

214. *Freedman v. Maryland*, 380 US 51 (1965).

215. *Joseph Burstyn, Inc. v. Wilson*, 343 US 495 (1952).

216. *Roaden v. Kentucky*, 413 US 496 (1973).

217. *Southeastern Productions Limited v. Conrad*, 419 US 892 (1974).

218. *Heller v. New York*, 413 US 483 (1973).

219. *New York v. P. J. Video, Inc.*, 475 US 868 (1986).

220. *Cox v. Louisiana*, 379 US 536 (1965).

221. *Edwards v. South Carolina*, 372 US 229 (1963).

222. *Brown v. Louisiana*, 383 US 13 (19966).

223. *Chicago Police Department v. Mosley*, 408 US 92 (1972).

224. *Boos v. Barry*, 485 US 312 (1988).

225. *United States v. Kokinda*, 479 US 720 (1930).

226. *International Society for Krishna Consciousness v. Lee*, 505 US 672 (1999).

227. *Ward v. Rock Against Racism*, 491 US 781 (1980).

228. *Amalgamated Food Employees Union v. Logan Valley Plaza, Inc.*, 391 US 308 (1968).

229. *Logan Valley in Lloyd Corp. v. Tanner*, 407 US 551 (1972).

230. *Hudgens v. National Labor Relations Board (NLRB)*, 424 US 507.

231. *Walker v. Birmingham*, 388 US 307 (1967).

232. *National Socialist Party v. Skokie*, 432 US 43 (1977).

233. *Forsyth County v. Nationalist Movement*, 432 US 43 (1977).

234. *Bray v. Alexandria Women's Health Clinic*, 506 US 263 (1933).

235. *Madsen v. Women's Health Clinic*, 512 US 753 (1994).

236. *Shelton v. Tucker*, 364 US 479 (1960).

237. *Baird v. State Bar of Arizona*, 401 US 1 (1971).

238. *Law Students Civil Rights Research Council, Inc. v. Wadmond*, 401 US 154 (1971).

239. *NAACP v. Button*, 371 US 415 (1963).

240. *Keyishian v. Board of Regents*, 385 US 589 (1967).

241. *Brandenburg v. Ohio*, 395 US 444 (1969).

242. *Adler v. Board of Education*, 342 US 485 (1952).

243. *United States v. Robel*, 389 US 258 (1967).

244. *Elfbrandy v. Russell*, 384 US 11 (1966).

245. *Cole v. Richardson*, 405 US 679 (1972).

246. *Hurley v. Irish-American Gay, Lesbian & Bisexual Group.*

247. *Communications Workers v. Beck*, 487 US 735 (1988).

248. *Keller v. State Bar of California*, 496 US 1 (1976).

249. *First National Bank v. Bellotti*, 435 US 765 (1978).

250. *Citizens Against Rent Control v. Berkeley*, 454 US 290 (1981).

251. *Federal Election Commission v. National Conservative Political Action Committee*, 470 US 480 (1985).

252. *Federal Election Commission v. Massachusetts Citizens for Life*, 479 US 238 (1986).

253. *Austin v. Michigan Chamber of Commerce*, 494 US 652 (1990).

254. *Colorado Republican Federal Campaign Committee v. Federal Election Commission*, 518 US 604 (1996).

255. *Federal Election Commission v. Akins*, 118 SCt 1777 (1998).

256. *Eu v. San Francisco County Democratic Committee*, 489 US 214 (1989).

257. *O'Brien v. Brown*, 409 US 1 (1972).

258. *Democratic Party v. Lafollette*, 450 US 107 (1981).

259. *Rosario v. Rockefeller*, 410 US 752 (1973).

260. *Burson v. Freeman*, 410 US 752 (1993).

261. *Burdick v. Takushi*, 504 US 245 (1992).

262. *Timmons v. Twin Cities Area New Party*, 520 US 352 (1997).

263. *Storer v. Brown*, 415 US 724 (1974).

264. *Norman v. Reed*, 502 US 279 (1992).

265. *Arkansas Educational Television Commission v. Forbes*, 118 SCt 1633 (1998).

266. *Williams v. Rhodes*, 393 US 23 (1968).

267. *Anderson v. Celebrezze*, 460 US 78 (1983).

268. *Jenness v. Fortsen*, 403 US 431 (1971).

269. *American Party of Texas v. White*, 415 US 767 (1974).

270. *McIntyre v. Ohio Elections Commission*, 514 US 334 (1995).

271. *Members of City Council v. Taxpayers for Vincent*, 466 US 789 (1984).

272. *U.S. Term Limits v. Thornton,* 574 US 779 (1995).

273. *Powell v. McCormack*, 395 US 485 (1969).

274. *Foster v. Love*, 118 SCt 464 (1988).

275. *Pickering v. Board of Education.*

276. *Elrod v. Burns*, 427 US 347 (1976).

277. *Branti v. Finkel*, 445 US 507 (1980).

278. *Rutan v. Republican Party*, 497 US 62 (1990).

279. *O'Hare Trucking Services, Inc. v. Northlake*, 518 US 712 (1996).

3

Issues and Controversies in the First Amendment

| Samuel Walker

Pornography and Women

Some feminists argue that pornography should be censored because it violates the rights of women.[1] Catharine MacKinnon and Andrea Dworkin proposed a law that would give women a right to sue the producers of pornography for violating their civil rights on the grounds that pornography "subordinates" women and causes them actual harm. The city of Indianapolis enacted such an ordinance in the early 1980s, and it was immediately challenged as a violation of the First Amendment.[2] The Seventh Circuit Court of Appeals declared the law unconstitutional in the 1985 case of *American Booksellers Association v. Hudnut,*[3] holding that the law establishes an "approved" view of women and of female sexuality. This represents a content-based form of censorship that the First Amendment prohibits. Or, as the court put it bluntly, "This is thought control." The Supreme Court declined to hear the case and let the lower court decision stand.

Nadine Strossen,[4] president of the ACLU, argues that censoring pornography and other forms of sexually explicit expression would actually harm women. She points out that historically censorship has been a weapon to limit women's freedom. The most important example of this application was the old federal Comstock Law that banned material about birth control from the U.S. mails.[5] Measures such as the Indianapolis anti-pornography ordinance embody a particular view of women and of women and sexuality, and thus represent content-based censorship. Also, censorship measures view women as weak and in need of protection. Strossen argues forcefully that "[w]omen do not need the government's protection from words and pictures."[6]

Pornography and Violence

One of the major issues related to pornography is whether it incites or encourages individuals to commit acts of violence. Many advocates of censoring pornography believe that it does. There has been considerable research on this topic by psychologists. Civil libertarians believe that there is no convincing evidence of a link between pornography and violence. A related issue is whether media portraying violence, such as video games, lead young people to commit violent acts. The 1999 shooting at Columbine High School in Colorado, in which two students shot and killed thirteen students and teachers and then themselves, brought this issue to the fore, because the two students who did the shooting played a lot of violent video games.[7]

Academic Freedom

The principle of academic freedom encompasses a number of First Amendment issues.[8] First and most important, it protects the free speech rights of faculty and students in colleges and universities. A public university, for example, cannot fire a faculty member or deny recognition to a student group because it does not like the ideas the person or the group has expressed. To do so would involve a content-based restriction of freedom of speech. Academic freedom also includes the freedom to teach, including teaching ideas that are controversial.

The most famous academic freedom case in U.S. history is the 1925 *Scopes* case, which arose after the state of Tennessee outlawed the teaching of evolution.[9] The First Amendment prohibits any restriction on teaching certain subjects because the content of that subject is offensive to some people. At the same time, the government cannot require the teaching of a subject that advances a particular religious point of view. This issue has arisen in the controversy over the teaching of creationism.[10] Academic freedom also involves certain due process rights for both students and teachers. A college or university may dismiss a faculty member or suspend a student for unprofessional conduct but must grant the individual a fair hearing, including the opportunity to rebut the charges.[11]

Scientific Research: Stem Cell Research and Cloning

Another academic freedom issue involves medical advances in stem cell research.[12] Stem cells are derived from embryos at the blastocyst stage. The importance of stem cells is that they can transform into any more developed cell type. Current research focuses on the possibility of treating certain illnesses such as Parkinson's disease by injecting healthy new cells into a patient's body to replace diseased or damaged cells. Some researchers believe that it might be possible to treat spinal cord injuries by injecting healthy spinal cord cells into a patient.

Some people are opposed to stem cell research on religious grounds. In particular, they object to the use of embryos derived from abortions as a source of stem cells. In 2001, President George W. Bush banned the use of federal funds in most stem cell research. Civil libertarians and most scientists oppose religious-based restrictions on stem cell research as a violation of the separation of church and state.

Notes

1. Catherine A. MacKinnon, *Only Words* (Cambridge, MA: Harvard University Press, 1993).

2. Donald A. Downs, *The New Politics of Pornography* (Chicago: University of Chicago Press, 1989).

3. *American Booksellers Association v. Hudnut*, 771 F2d 323 (1985).

4. Nadine Strossen, *Defending Pornography: Free Speech, Sex, and the Fight for Women's Rights* (New York: New York University Press, 1995).

5. Paul Boyer, *Purity in Print: Book Censorship in America from the Gilded Age to the Computer Age* (University of Wisconsin Press, 2002).

6. Strossen, *Defending Pornography*, 14.

7. Majorie Heins, *Violence and the Media: An Exploration of Cause, Effect, and the First Amendment* (Arlington, VA: First Amendment Center, 2001).

8. Stephen H. Aby and James C. Kuhn IV, comps., *Academic Freedom: A Guide to the Literature* (Westport, CT: Greenwood Press, 2000).

9. Ray Ginger, *Six Days or Forever? Tennessee v. John Thomas Scopes* (New York: Oxford University Press, 1974) and Edward J. Larson, *Summer for the Gods: The Scopes Trial and America's Continuing Debate over Science and Religion* (New York: Basic Books, 1997).

10. Larry A. Withman, *Where Darwin Meets the Bible: Creationists and Evolutionists in America* (New York: Oxford University Press, 2002).

11. David Rubin and Steven Greenhouse, *The Rights of Teachers* (New York: Bantam Books, 1984).

12. Bruno Leone, ed., *Cloning* (San Diego, CA: Greenhaven Press, Thompson/Gale, 2003).

4

Freedom of Association: 21st Century Issues

| Robert Bresler

The twenty-first century began with the Supreme Court's deciding a case that indicated a greater interest in protecting freedom of association. This reflected the more conservative perspective of the Rehnquist Court, particularly with the addition of Justices Antonin Scalia and Clarence Thomas. Inasmuch as constitutional protection of associational rights limits the power of the state to regulate the private sphere, a conservative Court found much to value in more fully protecting that right. Whether future Courts will continue to strengthen associational rights will depend upon whether the political consensus becomes more egalitarian or more **libertarian**. The dramatic 2000 presidential election was a reminder that at the beginning of this new century both the country and the Court were closely divided.

James Dale Challenges the Boy Scouts

In 2000 the Supreme Court ruled on a case that tested the capacity of that body to find a balance between the imperatives of associational freedom and antidiscrimination. *Boy Scouts of America v. Dale*[1] involved a clash between an American institution that embodied many traditional values and gay and lesbian groups who wished to be granted the protection of the state against social exclusion.

At the age of eleven, James Dale joined the Monmouth Council in New Jersey, a division of the Boy Scouts of America (BSA). He remained in the Scouts until he was eighteen, during which time he earned twenty-five merit badges, was admitted into the prestigious Order of the Arrow, and earned the rank of Eagle Scout, an award given to only three percent of all Scouts. He applied for adult membership and was approved as an assistant scoutmaster of Troop 73 of the Monmouth Council. During that same time he entered Rutgers University, where he became co-president of the Rutgers University Lesbian/Gay Alliance. In 1990 he attended a seminar about the health needs of lesbian and gay teenagers and was interviewed by a local newspaper about his advocacy of the need of homosexual teenagers for gay role models. The newspaper published the article over a caption identifying Dale as the co-president of the Lesbian/Gay Alliance.

Soon after the article's appearance Dale received a letter from James Kay, the Monmouth Council executive, revoking Dale's membership in the Boy Scouts. When Dale replied asking for an explanation, Kay informed him that membership in the Boy Scouts was a privilege and could be withdrawn "whenever there is a concern that an individual may not meet the high standards of members which BSA seeks to provide for American youth." When Dale sent another letter asking for the specific reason for his dismissal, Kay informed him that the grounds for the decision "are the standards of leadership established by the Boy Scouts of America, which specifically forbid membership to homosexuals."

The New Jersey Courts Respond

In 1992 Dale filed a complaint against the Boy Scouts in New Jersey Superior Court's **chancery** division, alleging that the organization had violated New Jersey's public accommodations law that prohibited, among other things, discrimination on the basis of sexual orientation in places of public accommodation. Upon filing the complaint, Dale gave an interview to the *New York Times* in which he asserted, "I owe it to the organization to point out to them how bad and wrong this policy is . . . Being proud about who I am is something the Boy Scouts taught me." He later stated on television, "Yes, I am gay, and I'm proud of who I am . . . I have pride, I stand up for what I believe in, I mean what you see is what you get. I'm not hiding anything. But the Scouts don't like that."[2]

The chancery court granted summary judgment in favor of the Boy Scouts, ruling that New Jersey's public accommodations law was not applicable because BSA was a distinctly private group and not a place of public accommodation. The court found that "since its inception Scouting has sincerely and unswervingly held to the view that an 'avowed' sexually-active homosexual is engaging in immoral behavior which violates the Scout Oath (in which the person promises to be 'morally straight') and the Scout law (whereby the person promises to be keep himself 'clean')." Thus, the chancery court held that the Boy Scouts' position on active homosexuality was protected by the First Amendment's freedom of expressive association that prevented the government from forcing the Scouts to accept Dale as an adult leader.

The New Jersey Superior Court's appellate division reversed and held that the BSA was a place of public accommodation and not an exclusively private group under the New Jersey Law Against Discrimination (LAD). It rejected the Boy Scouts' federal constitutional claims because Dale was "not asserting a right under LAD to alter the content of the BSA's viewpoint."[3]

The New Jersey Supreme Court affirmed the appellate division's decision, agreeing that the BSA is a place of public accommodation. The New Jersey Supreme Court held that the Boy Scouts was a large organization, engaged in broad public solicitation for members, advertised for members, received a federal charter, maintained relationships with the federal and local governments, and was frequently partners with public schools. The New Jersey Supreme Court ruled that the LAD did not violate the Boy Scouts' federal constitutional rights "to enter into and maintain . . . intimate or private relationships . . . [and] to associate for the purpose of engaging in protected speech."

The court concluded that the expulsion of Dale was based more on prejudice than a unified Boy Scout position and that his reinstatement would not compel the Boy Scouts to express any message. The BSA had argued that the "clean" provision of the Scout law and the "morally straight" provision of the Scout oath were evidence that BSA condemned homosexuality. The New Jersey Supreme Court rejected this argument, claiming, "The words 'morally straight' and 'clean' do not, on their face express anything about sexuality, much less that homosexuality, in particular, is immoral." The court failed to see how Dale's membership in the Boy Scouts would impair "in any significant way" BSA's ability to accomplish its purposes. The Boy Scouts appealed the case to the U.S. Supreme Court and were granted certiorari.

The Boy Scouts Supreme Court Brief

In their legal brief to the Supreme Court, the Boy Scouts challenged the New Jersey Supreme Court ruling on several grounds. They disputed the court's interpretation of what constitutes a public accommodation under the New Jersey statute. In doing so, they pointed out that if any organization that solicits members, uses public facilities, or has any connection to the state could be considered a public accommodation, then numerous organizations would have to change their character and membership. The Boy Scouts would have to admit girls, and the Girl Scouts would have to admit boys. The BSA brief insisted that freedom of association must presuppose the freedom not to associate. Equally important, it must also presuppose the freedom to select leaders who would play an important role in articulating and transmitting the group's values. This would have to include adult leaders of the Scouts.

The BSA brief insisted that the New Jersey court had misread the meaning of the *Roberts* trilogy. The organizations involved in those cases differed markedly from the Boy Scouts. They were quasi-commercial organizations; they did not have a moral code logically related to membership criteria; and they did not have goals exclusively related to personal, moral, and physical development. The Boy Scouts was an inherently expressive organization with a clear moral code, and courts must give deference to an expressive organization's characterization of its own beliefs. For example, accepting a Ku Klux Klan member as a leader would interfere with the Boy Scouts' message of the importance of racial harmony, just as the B'nai B'rith could not be forced to accept an anti-Semite.

At the heart of the BSA brief was the claim that *Hurley*[4] controlled the case and that freedom of expressive association included the right to be silent about issues. As the brief put it, "Boy Scouting does not convey an explicit 'anti-gay' message to the boys under its care; but it does not wish to convey approval of homosexual conduct either . . . Dale cannot force Boy Scouting to grant him a platform upon which to expound those beliefs, or to garb him in the uniform of a Scoutmaster when he does so . . . *Hurley* established that the organization has the right to exclude those who wish to proclaim their sexual identity as a part of the organization's message."[5] The Boy Scouts was claiming that the government cannot decide what a private association's message is or force its own interpretation on any organization's moral message. Should an organization decide to alter its message, it can do so at any time without any involvement of the state.

The BAS brief also argued that the relationship of Scouts to their leaders constituted an intimate association. The characteristics of such an association were defined by Justice Brennan in *Roberts* as "deep attachments and commitments to the necessarily few other individuals with whom one shares not only a special community of thoughts, experiences, and beliefs but also distinctly personal aspects of one's life."[6] The Scouts is a large national organization, but they are organized into troops of typically fifteen to thirty boys and in small patrols that are composed of three to eight boys. The adult leader is to serve as a role model and friend, providing a close personal relationship with an adult outside of the family.[7]

In its amicus brief with the conservative women's group Eagle Forum supporting the Boy Scouts, the libertarian Cato Institute argued that private organizations need to be protected against "government's tendency toward self-aggrandizement . . . and to expand the public sphere in order to enforce the latest prescribed orthodoxy." The state's interest in nondiscriminatory access to publicly offered goods and services, the original purpose of most public accommodation laws, the brief argued, should not extend into unlimited access to noncommercial, private, expressive associations. Such groups should be allowed to define their own messages and their own qualifications for members. Private expressive associations should include "all nonprofit, noncommercial organizations that have some expressive purpose . . . and . . . the burden should be on the state to prove compelling evidence that such entity can be categorized as a public accommodation." The Boy Scouts' expressive purpose was at the heart of its educational mission to inculcate young Scouts with certain values. Should the Boy Scouts be forced to accept James Dale, who had made his sexuality a public matter, they would be placing its imprimatur "on a person who exemplifies particular values and behaviors that the Boy Scouts rejects." It would be similar to *Hurley* in that having Dale as an adult leader suggests a public and explicit position on homosexuality that the Boy Scouts would rather not assert or support.[8]

The *Dale* Supreme Court Brief

The lawyers' brief for James Dale argued that the freedom of expressive association did not grant the BSA an unqualified right to select its leaders in defiance of a state civil rights law. The inclusion of a human being into an organization cannot be translated into speech; otherwise, the Dale brief asserted, "all discriminators could raise a First Amendment shield to any equal opportunity statute."[9] The brief contested the assertion that the Boy Scouts was a private organization, citing its federal charter granted in 1916 and other benefits from the federal government such as tax exemption and supplies and equipment from the Department of Defense. In addition the brief cited the nearly 500 public schools and school-affiliated groups in New Jersey that sponsor scouting units and the benefits the Scouts receive from the state—exemption from state taxes and the waiver of registration fees for motor vehicles owned by local BSA councils.

Thus, the Boy Scouts was different from other private organizations such as a Jewish dating service, an Asian American theater company, or a Croatian Cultural Society and could come within the ambit of a state public accommodation law barring discrimination. Even if one were to grant that the Boy Scouts was a private organization, the Dale brief cited the *Roberts* doctrine: that the freedom of association was not an absolute right, that the government can impose certain limits to serve a compelling state interest not related to the suppression of ideas so long as those interests cannot be achieved through means significantly less restrictive of associational freedoms. The Boy Scouts thus had, according to the Dale brief, no unqualified right to select its leaders in defiance of a civil rights law that served a compelling state interest, namely, New Jersey's interest in eliminating discrimination. "Expressive associations," the Dale brief claimed, "have no unqualified right to select their leaders in defiance of civil rights prohibitions."[10] Relying heavily on *Roberts,* Dale's lawyers asserted the Court should ask if ending the policy of excluding gays would "affect in any significant way the members' ability to carry out their expressive purposes [and] if so whether New Jersey's interest [antidiscrimination] outweighs any such burden."[11] From Dale's perspective, the New Jersey antidiscrimination law did not interfere with the Boy Scouts' core purposes. The Boy Scouts did not associate for the purpose of disseminating the belief that homosexuality was wrong. The Dale brief rejected the BSA claim that condemnation of homosexuality could be inferred from the requirements that Boy Scouts be "clean" and "morally straight." The phrase "morally straight" could not be read as a code word for an antigay policy. The Boy Scout Code allowed its members to have divergent views on a variety of matters, and in fact the Boy Scouts discouraged scoutmasters from disseminating any views on sexual matters.

Both the Dale brief and an amicus brief (filed by the American Civil Liberties Union, the NAACP Legal Defense Fund, the National Organization of Women,

People for the American Way, and other civil liberties groups) argued that *Hurley* was not controlling. In that case the parade was clearly a traditional form of expressive activity and its organizers could control the message they wished to convey. James Dale was excluded simply because of his sexual orientation and not because he wished to alter the Boy Scouts' message. The amicus brief stated, "The Boy Scouts would like to read *Hurley* for the proposition that the state can never enforce its civil rights laws over the opposition of any organization that purports to represent a set of values that conflicts with the states' antidiscrimination goals. But the holding of Hurley clearly does not go so far."[12] The heart of Dale's position was that his inclusion in the Boy Scouts was only an incidental burden on the organization's right of expressive association, since his simple membership could not alone alter the BSA's message. Dale had given no indication that he intended to teach anything about homosexuality and pledged that he would follow the Boy Scouts' guidance to refer to the boys' parents any of their questions about religion or sex. From Dale's perspective the most pressing constitutional claim was New Jersey's compelling interest in ensuring equal opportunity and equal access to goods and services. Gays and lesbians are among those who have been denied equal opportunity to participate in American life. New Jersey's interest in protecting the rights of gay people was a compelling interest placing only a slight burden on the BSA's right of free expression.

A Divided Court Speaks

On June 28, 2000, the U.S. Supreme Court announced its decision in *Boy Scouts of America v. Dale*. By a vote of 5–4, the Court overturned the New Jersey Supreme Court decision and upheld the Boy Scouts' right to expel James Dale. Writing for the majority, Chief Justice William Rehnquist accepted the Boy Scouts' definition of their own message as being in opposition to homosexuality. Rehnquist concluded that no court should impose its own interpretation of an organization's message, which is the business of its leaders. "As we give deference to an association's assertions regarding the nature of its expression," Rehnquist asserted, "we must also give deference to an association's view of what would impair its expression." Rehnquist acknowledged that the rights of expressive association could not be used as a shield to claim that the "mere acceptance of a member from a particular group would impair its message."[13] Dale was not merely gay; he was the co-president of his college gay and lesbian organization and remained a gay rights activist.

In reaching this conclusion, Rehnquist relied strongly on *Hurley*. GLIB, claimed Rehnquist, was not excluded from the St. Patrick's Day parade because its members were gay. Rather, it was because of their insistence on marching behind the GLIB banner and imposing their own message on the parade. Accepting a gay activist as an adult leader would have the same effect and would interfere with the Boy Scouts' message.

Rehnquist took issue with the New Jersey court's claim that Dale could not have interfered with the Scouts' message because Boy Scout members do not "associate for the purpose of disseminating the belief that homosexuality is immoral."[14] Associations are granted First Amendment protections even if their "purpose" is not to disseminate a certain message. Just as the Veterans Council had no wish to speak publicly on the question of sexual orientation, neither did the Boy Scouts have to put their policy on the subject in full public view.

As long as an organization engages in expressive activity that could be impaired, it is granted First Amendment protection. Every member of the Boy Scouts does not have to agree with the group's policy for it to be an expressive association. The fact that the Boy Scouts has an official position is enough, and Dale's presence would burden it. As Rehnquist put it, "The Boy Scouts has a First Amendment right to choose to send one message but not the other. The fact that the organization does not trumpet its views from the housetops, or that it tolerates dissent within its ranks, does not mean that it receives no First Amendment protection."[15]

Rehnquist acknowledged that the Court in *Roberts* and *Duarte*[16] had recognized a state's compelling interest in eliminating discrimination against women. However, in those cases the Court had concluded that the enforcement of antidiscrimination laws did not interfere with the ideas that the organization sought to express. Unlike the presence of women in the Jaycees or the Rotary, Dale's presence as a gay activist in the Boy Scouts would, Rehnquist concluded, interfere with their message or their desire to send a muted one.

Writing for the four dissenters, Justice John Paul Stevens argued the Boy Scouts had to meet a higher standard than the majority had imposed to establish a First Amendment claim. Citing *Roberts* and *Rotary,*[17] Stevens claimed that to prevail on an assertion of expressive association against a state's antidiscrimination claim, an association must not simply engage in "some kind" of expressive activity. It must openly avow an exclusionary membership policy or assert some connection between the group's exclusionary policy and its expressive activities. The question should be, according to Stevens, whether the group was organized for the specific expressive purposes that it could be forced to abandon if its exclusionary policy was voided. The Boy Scouts' policies, as Stevens interpreted them, had never clearly articulated "a single particular religious or moral philosophy when it comes to sexual orientation." Its stated policy excluding homosexuals found in a 1978 statement on "policies and procedures relating to homosexuality and Scouting" was an internal memorandum and not circulated beyond the executive committee. It was written in the expectation that state antidiscrimination laws would someday protect homosexuals, but it also included a statement that it was a Scout's duty to "obey the laws."

The 1978 statement said only that homosexuality was not "appropriate." The memo made no effort, Stevens claimed, to connect homosexuality to "the myriad of publicly declared values and creeds of the BSA." Stevens dismissed other policy statements issued between 1991 and 1993. These were made after the Scouts had revoked Dale's membership and claimed that homosexuals do not provide a role model consistent with the expectations of scouting families. Stevens felt those statements taken together with their statements on tolerance and their view that sexual matters were not the Scouts' proper area made BSA's views on homosexuality "equivocal at best and incoherent at worst." To prevail in asserting the right of expressive association against a charge of violating an antidiscrimination law, "the organization must at least show it has adopted and advocated an unequivocal position inconsistent with a position advocacy or epitomized by the person whom the organization seeks to exclude." Stevens argued that the Court's review of whether an organization's views were sincerely held raised valid concerns. Nonetheless, he insisted, "unless one is prepared to turn the right to associate into a free pass out of antidiscrimination laws, an independent inquiry is a necessity."[18]

Stevens found the case clearly distinguishable from *Hurley:* "Unlike GLIB, Dale did not carry a banner or a sign; he did not distribute any fact sheet; and he expressed no intent to send any message . . . The only apparent explanation for the majority holding, then," Stevens concluded, hinting at an ideological bias, "is that homosexuals are simply so different from the rest of society that their presence alone—unlike any other individual—should be singled out for special First Amendment treatment."[19] In his dissent Justice David Souter pointed out that *Dale* was not a free speech case but an expressive association one. In free speech cases such as *Hurley,* the group's position must be taken at face value. An expressive association case, Souter argued, must be based upon "a clear position to be advocated over time in an unequivocal way." This distinction was far clearer to Souter and the dissenters than it was to Rehnquist and the majority.

The Court's decision in *Dale* was a significant departure from *Roberts.* In *Roberts* the Court took the responsibility of interpreting the Jaycees' message and found no reason why the inclusion of women would impair it; in *Dale* the Court accepted on face value exactly how Boy Scouts interpreted their own message. The influence of *Hurley* was quite apparent in the Rehnquist opinion. Dale's presence in the Boy Scouts had become the equivalent of the GLIB banner in the St. Patrick's Day parade. His very presence as a gay assistant scoutmaster was enough to cloud the Boy Scouts' position on homosexual behavior and to interfere with its desire to avoid discussion of sexual issues between the adult leaders and the young Scouts.

The Court's Critics Speak

Some critics of the Court's decision in *Dale* claimed that the reliance on *Hurley* was misplaced. The parade organizers in Boston did not exclude marchers because they were gay; they excluded them because they insisted upon marching behind their own banner. It was the banner, not the individuals as gay people, that interfered with the parade organizers' right to control their own message. Dale was excluded not because of his insistence on bringing his message into the Scouts but as a consequence of being an openly gay man. The Court did not fully explain why the Scouts would not expel a heterosexual who supported gay rights and opposed the exclusionary policy yet would expel Dale, who had the same views but was gay himself. Thus, Dale was a walking billboard as a result of his homosexuality, and his exclusion was not based upon his message but his sexual identity. This kind of discrimination was exactly what the New Jersey statute was designed to prevent. Consequently, the critics felt that as a result of *Dale* any group professing a particular moral message could exclude gay members under the banner of expressive association. One critic imagined that *Dale* could open the floodgates for all kinds of organizations seeking to protect their discriminatory policies behind the banner of expressive association: "Almost all associations—every business, every apartment complex, every residential neighborhood—that wants to discriminate should now be able to file an action under the First Amendment and to demand strict scrutiny of virtually every discrimination law applied to it . . . Why shouldn't states be obliged to accommodate discrimination—exemptions for, say, small businesses or small neighborhoods genuinely dedicated to expressing the belief that blacks, Jews, or women don't belong in the same places as whites, Christians, or men?"[20]

Some argued that the decision was not merely a misreading of past precedents but a disparagement of gay rights. The Court in *Roberts* found a compelling need to eliminate gender discrimination, whereas in both *Hurley* and *Dale* the same weight was not granted to the claims of homosexuals. If antidiscrimination laws served a compelling state interest against the claims of expressive association, were the rights of women more compelling than the rights of gays?[21] It was not clear from *Dale* if the Court felt that it had only weak interest in protecting discrimination on the basis of anything other than race, gender, national origin, and illegitimacy.

The Defenders of the Court Speak

Defenders of the *Dale* decision saw it as an important victory for freedom of association. They feared that if an organization "as potent as the Boy Scouts can be made to bend to the state's will, how much more likely is it that weak and unpopular groups might be forced to capitulate?"[22] The doctrine of expressive association should allow unpopular and despised groups to bolster their strength and to gain a greater hearing for their message. State antidiscrimination laws could become a means to dampen such messages. A militant gay rights group may want to exclude all heterosexuals; a Black Nationalist group may want to exclude whites; a Muslim group may not invite non-Muslims.

Richard Epstein argues that the *Dale* dissenters' insistence that an expressive association claim must be based upon a clear and unequivocal message "restricts full protection for expressive liberties only to those organizations that adopt extreme social positions." Large mainstream organizations often must take nuanced and equivocal positions to avoid splits and possible disintegration.

Expressive liberties must be afforded such groups, as they serve an important function in maintaining social cohesion. The Boy Scouts may realize the concerns of parents, justified or not, about placing their boys under the close supervision of avowed homosexuals on scouting trips. At the same time the Scouts may wish to avoid taking an unequivocal public position on homosexuality for fear of being seen as bigoted. As Epstein puts it, "In order to hold their complex coalition together, it may make sense for the Boy Scouts to gravitate toward a compromise that proves more stable in practice than coherent in theory. Go soft on the formal and explicit denunciations of gay practices, but nonetheless keep those practices out of the Scout troops to meet these parental demands."[23] Why shouldn't freedom of association include First Amendment law in its suspicion of content-based distinctions? Freedom of association, Epstein says, should not protect only organizations with "more emphatic prejudiced and bigoted views."[24]

Apart from the substantive philosophical and political concerns was the issue of whether *Dale* was consistent with *Roberts*. It is hard to argue that there wasn't an important break between the two cases. The *Dale* Court did shift the definition of what constitutes group expression to gain constitutional protection. Under *Roberts,* expressive association claims received close scrutiny and had to be based upon the views that brought the group together, that is, views that were at the core of the association's tenets. Under *Dale,* constitutional protection could broadly embrace "the ability of the group to express those, and only those, views that it intends to express."[25] The *Dale* definition gives to associations much of the same protection afforded to individual expression under the First Amendment. *Dale* did grant to the leaders of expressive associations greater autonomy over the control of their message than was apparent in *Roberts*. Chief Justice Rehnquist simply accepted the Boy Scouts' assertion that homosexual conduct was inconsistent with its notion of what was "morally straight" and gave "deference to an association's assertions regarding the nature of its expression . . . [and to] an association's view of what would impair its expression." Was it simply Dale's gayness that impaired the Boy Scouts' message? Was Dale's homosexuality "so inherently expressive that admitting him to the Scouts would violate the organization's right against compelled association?"[26] Yet the *Dale* Court did not dispute the finding in *Duarte* that antidiscrimination laws serve a compelling state interest and can apply to a private organization so long as they are unrelated to the suppression of ideas and are the least restrictive means of achieving that compelling interest.

The Legacy of the *Dale* Decision

Did the *Dale* Court develop a theory that balances the freedom of expressive association against the state's interest in antidiscrimination? Although the Court did say that expressive associations may not "erect a shield against antidiscrimination simply by asserting that mere acceptance of a member from a particular group would impair its message," it implied that this case was different because Dale was not simply gay but "openly gay" and a "gay rights activist." As Rehnquist put it, "The presence of an avowed homosexual and gay rights activist in an assistant scoutmaster's uniform sends a distinctly different message from the presence of a heterosexual assistant scoutmaster who is on record as disagreeing with Boy Scouts policy. The Boy Scouts has a First Amendment right to choose to send one message but not the other."

It is not clear from the Court's opinion whether the Scouts would have had the same First Amendment protection were they to exclude a gay who was not an activist. If Dale were merely "openly gay" or an "avowed" homosexual and not a gay activist, would the Boy Scouts have the same First Amendment claim? Despite Dale's statement that he would not use the Boy Scouts to proselytize for gay rights, would his very presence then send a message? Was any openly gay person, regardless of his views about the appropriateness or morality of homosexuality, a walking symbol so that groups that either abhor homosexuality or wish to say nothing about such issues could disassociate from him? The Court felt it did not have to address this question of whether being openly gay was a message in and of itself. Neither did the majority nor the dissenting opinion address the question whether the government had the same compelling interest in eradicating discrimination against homosexuals as it does on the basis of other characteristics such as race and gender.

The *Dale* Court did not present a coherent constitutional theory of expressive association, nor did it shed much light on the status of gay rights. The decision did interpret the right of expressive association more broadly than it had in the *Roberts* trilogy. Under *Dale,* the right is available for an organization that does not associate for the express purpose of disseminating a particular message. An organization can propound that message implicitly; it can tolerate dissenting views and yet continue an exclusionary policy.

The case represented another clash between social equality and free expression when both have claims on the same organization. In *Hurley* and *Dale* the claims for gay equality foundered on the assertion of expressive association. In the *Roberts* trilogy, the Court deferred to the state's compelling interest in general equality. Were the Boy Scouts that different from the Jaycees, the Rotary, or the New York Athletic Club? Or was it Dale's gayness that determined the outcome of his case? The case can be looked at as protection from the long arm of state-enforced orthodoxy or as a barrier to full social recognition of the status of gay people. As Kathleen Sullivan put it, "How one views the decision normatively will turn on how one regards a private sphere that deviates from public constitutional values of toler-ance and equality: as a desirable safeguard against centralized homogenization and orthodoxy like the protection of abstinence from flag salutes in *West Virginia State Board of Education v. Barnette*[27] or as a dangerous backwater likely to undermine the public values that depend upon the alteration of social norms."[28]

During the civil rights battles of the 1950s and 1960s, when public accommo-dation law extended racial integration to restaurants, hotels, theaters, and sports arenas, it was clear that racial minorities and African Americans in particular were to be protected from a hostile white majority in the South. Given, however, the so-cial opprobrium the Boy Scouts have suffered as a consequence of their policy, it is not clear in the twenty-first century who is outside the prevailing orthodoxy, James Dale or the Boy Scouts of America. Neither is it clear what group over time would benefit from the Court's decision. As Sullivan reflects, "There is a good argument that the extension of equal protection to gay men and lesbians need not extend all the way down into every private association in New Jersey to be effective and that the right of expressive gay organizations to exclude homophobes is an important im-plicit corollary of the decision."[29]

The Boy Scouts, for its part, has found *Dale* to be a mixed blessing. According to *Newsweek* magazine, the national membership in the Scouts dropped 4.5 percent in 2000 and by 7.8 percent in the Northeast (August 6, 2001). The organization found itself in the middle of the culture wars. As a consequence of the attention given to their policy of barring gays, several state and local governments have found ways to shun them. Connecticut dropped the Boy Scouts from the State Employee Charitable Campaign because of the group's antigay policy. The Connecticut comp-troller, who oversees the charitable campaigns, took the action to ensure the robust administration of the Connecticut Gay Rights Law, which prohibits the use of state facilities in furtherance of discrimination. In July 2003 a federal appeals court up-held the Connecticut policy. But other funding sources have remained steady or increased. According to the United Way national organization, only thirty-five to forty-five chapters out of 1,400 refused to put the Scouts on their funding list. In Minnesota the Twin Cities United Way chapter donations marked specifically for the Scouts went up $500,000 a year after the *Dale* decision.

The Broward County School Board in Florida, which had a policy forbidding the use of school facilities by any group that discriminated on the basis of sexual orientation, voted to ban the Scouts from using school property. The Boy Scouts successfully challenged the action in federal district court. The district court ruled that for the school board to deny the Scouts the use of their facilities on the same basis as other private groups would violate the First Amendment. Although the school board could express its own view on intolerance on homosexuality, it could not punish the Boy Scouts for a contrary view.[30] New York City school chancellor Harold O. Levy announced in December 2000 that the Boy Scouts could no longer use the public schools as sites for recruiting new members and that the organization was barred from bidding on school contracts; soon after that announcement Boy Scout membership in New York City dropped by half.[31]

Despite the public clamor, the Boy Scouts refused to alter their policy. In February 2002 they issued a public statement that "homosexual conduct is inconsistent with the traditional values espoused in the Scout Oath and Law and an avowed homosexual cannot serve as a role model for the values of the Oath and Law."[32] This statement was also a message to any chapter that might be considering altering its policy, as was the case with local chapters in New York and Rhode Island.

Others came to the Boy Scouts' defense. In June 2001 the Senate approved a bill introduced by Senator Jesse Helms (R–NC) that would withhold federal funds from public schools that denied "equal access" to the Boy Scouts and any other group that expressed its "disapproval of homosexuality." The final bill, the Boy Scouts of America Equal Access Act[33] required schools to allow the Scouts to use facilities on the same terms as other groups. Schools were, however, free to withhold sponsorship of the Scouts.

The treatment of the Scouts after *Dale* is in some ways reminiscent of the treatment of the Communist Party in the 1950s. Many private groups shunned the party and its members. Universities, unions, bar associations, and the entertainment industry refused to hire its members. To be a member of the Communist Party was not necessarily illegal, but anyone so exposed would be treated as a pariah. People and institutions for various reasons did not want to be associated with Communists and asserted their right of nonassociation. Private groups who refuse to assist the Scouts may be asserting their own rights of nonassociation in the same way the entertainment industry refused to hire Communists. . . .

Associational rights have been viewed differently by the Court, however, when an organization is not being denied outright the right to determine its own membership, but is only being denied public benefits because of its exclusionary policy. In 2010, the Supreme Court heard the case of *Christian Legal Society v. Martinez.*[34] The Christian Legal Society at the University of California, Hastings School of Law, filed suit against the university for violating its First Amendment rights. The university had failed to provide any funding to the organization since membership in said organization required members to sign a pledge that they believed in Jesus Christ. The university was following a state law that said that all registered student organizations were required to accept all students regardless of their status or beliefs. The district court dismissed the case. The appellate court [concluded] that the university's conditions did not violate the Christian Legal Society's First Amendment rights.

The Supreme Court upheld the appellate court decision that the university policy did not transgress on the organization's First Amendment freedoms. They believed the law club was seeking preferential exemption from the university's policy.

Conclusion

There is still much to be settled in this area. . . The terrain of the freedom of association has been mapped out only in the broadest strokes. The Court will have to refine this doctrine in the twenty-first century and find the proper balance between society's competing values.

Glossary

Chancery: a court of public record.

Libertarian: individuals who believe in maximizing individual rights and minimizing state rights.

Notes

1. *Boy Scouts of America v. Dale,* 530 U.S. 640 (2000).
2. Ibid.
3. *Dale v. Boy Scouts of* America, 706 A.2d 270, 293 N.J. Super. Ct. App. Div. (1998).
4. *Hurley v. Irish American Gay, Lesbian and Bisexual Group of Boston,* 515 U.S. 557 (1995).
5. Brief for Petitioner, 21.
6. *Roberts v. United States Jaycees,* 468 U.S. 609 (1984).
7. Brief for Petitioner, 39–44.
8. Amicus Brief for Cato Institute and Eagle Forum.
9. Brief for Respondent, 11.
10. Brief for Respondent, 22.
11. Brief for Respondent, 17.
12. ACLU Amicus Brief, section I.B.
13. *Boy Scouts of America v. Dale,* 530 U.S. 640 (2000).
14. *Dale v. Boy Scouts of America,* 706 A.2d 270, 293 N.J. Super. Ct. App. Div. (1998).
15. *Boy Scouts of America v. Dale,* 530 U.S. 640 (2000).
16. *Rotary Club International v. Rotary Club of Duarte,* 481 U.S. 537 (1987).
17. Ibid.
18. *Boy Scouts of America v. Dale,* 530 U.S. 640 (2000).
19. Ibid.

20. Jed Rubenfeld, "The First Amendment's Purpose," *Stanford Law Review* 53 (April 2000): 767–832.

21. Christopher S. Hargis, "*Romer, Hurley,* and *Dale:* How the Supreme Court Languishes with 'Special Rights,'" *Kentucky Law Journal* 89 (Summer 2000): 1189–1225.

22. Dale Carpenter, "Expressive Association and Anti-Discrimination Law After Dale: A Tripartite Approach," *Minnesota Law Review* 85 (June 2001): 1515.

23. Richard A. Epstein, "The Constitutional Perils of Moderation: The Case of the Boy Scouts," *Southern California Law Review* 74 (November 2000): 119–143.

24. Ibid.

25. *Boy Scouts of America v. Dale,* 530 U.S. 640 (2000).

26. David McGowan, "Making Sense of *Dale,*" *Constitutional Commentary* 18 (Spring 2001): 121–175.

27. *West Virginia State Board of Education v. Barnette*, 319 U.S. 624 (1943).

28. Kathleen M. Sullivan, "Sex, Money, and Groups: Free Speech and Association Decisions in the October 1999 Term," *Pepperdine Law Review* 28 (2001): 723–746.

29. Ibid., 741.

30. *Boy Scouts of America v. Till*, 136 Supp. 2d 1308 [S.D. Fla. 2000].

31. Jennifer Gerarda Brown, "Facilitating Boycotts of Discriminatory Organizations through an Informed Association Statute," *Minnesota Law Review* 87 (December 2002): 481–509.

32. Press release, Boy Scouts of America, February 2, 2002.

33. Boy Scouts of America Equal Access Act, 210 U.S.C. 7905 (2000).

34. *Christian Legal Society v. Martinez,* 561 U.S. _ (2010).

5

Freedom of Speech

| Earl Pollock

This chapter deals with one of the key aspects of the First Amendment: Congress shall make no law respecting an establishment of religion, or prohibiting the free exercise thereof; or abridging the freedom of speech, or of the press; or the right of the people peaceably to assemble, and to petition the Government for a redress of grievances. Thus, it focuses on freedom of speech, with other chapters looking at the other aspects of the First Amendment.

Each of the liberties protected by the First Amendment is an essential element of a democratic society. But freedom of speech occupies a unique status because it is the necessary foundation for each of the others (and, indeed, for most other rights protected by the Constitution). As Justice Benjamin Cardozo pointed out: "Freedom of expression is the matrix, the indispensable condition, of nearly every other form of freedom."[1] For example, without freedom of speech, how could there be freedom of religion? Likewise, without freedom of speech, how could there be a meaningful right to assemble or to petition the government to redress grievances?

Historians sharply differ on what the framers of the Bill of Rights viewed as the scope of freedom of speech. Thus, although the question is much disputed, some historians contend that as originally understood the First Amendment only prohibited "prior restraints" on speech and did not bar prosecutions for sedition or libel against the government.[2]

Perhaps relying on that view, the Federalist-dominated Congress adopted the infamous Sedition Act of 1798, prohibiting the publication of false, scandalous, and malicious writing against the Government of the United States, or either House of Congress, or the President, with intent to defame them; or to bring them into contempt or disrepute; or to excite against them the hatred of the good people of the United States, or to stir up sedition within the United States.

Numerous Jeffersonian Republicans (including their leading newspapers) were prosecuted under the act. Although the Supreme Court was never called upon to rule on the act's constitutionality, the act was upheld by several lower federal courts. (The act expired by its own terms in 1801, and all those convicted under it were pardoned by Jefferson upon his taking office as president.)

Whatever may have been its intended scope when the Bill of Rights was adopted, the freedom of speech guarantee has (starting in the World War I period) received an increasingly expansive interpretation by the Supreme Court. These decisions are reviewed in the succeeding portions of this chapter.

The Court's decisions have emphasized the importance of freedom of speech in advancing knowledge and "truth" in the "marketplace of ideas." In the oft-repeated words of Justice Oliver Wendell Holmes dissenting, "the best test of truth is the power of the thought to get itself accepted in the competition of the market . . . That at any rate is the theory of our constitution."[3]

The Court's decisions have also emphasized the function of freedom of speech in facilitating representative democracy and self-government. Thus, in *Buckley v. Valeo*, the Court declared that the First Amendment "affords the broadest protection to such political expression in order to assure [the] unfettered interchange of ideas for the bringing about of political and social changes desired by the people."[4] Although First Amendment protections are not confined to "the exposition of ideas,"[5] "there is practically universal agreement that a major purpose of that Amendment was to protect the free discussion of governmental affairs, . . . of course includ[ing] discussions of candidates. . ."[6] This no more than reflects our "profound national commitment to the principle that debate on public issues should be uninhibited, robust, and wide-open."[7]

But, while "it is no doubt true that a central purpose of the First Amendment 'was to protect the free discussion of governmental affairs' . . . [the Court has] never suggested that expression about philosophical, social, artistic, economic, literary, or ethical matters—to take a nonexclusive list of labels—is not entitled to full First Amendment protection."[8]

Freedom of Speech Overview

Although the wording of the First Amendment ("Congress shall make no law . . . abridging the freedom of speech.") expressly applies only to Congress, the Amendment's guarantees have been held to be "incorporated" in the Due Process Clause of the Fourteenth Amendment and are thus equally applicable to the States. The First Amendment is stated in absolute terms ("shall make no law"), but it has never been construed to bar every regulation that might be said to involve some form of "speech." Examples of speech unprotected by the amendment include perjury, bribery, and obscenity.

Another category of speech traditionally unprotected by the amendment is speech that advocates or incites violence or other illegal action. But in *Brandenburg v. Ohio*, the Court sharply narrowed this category, holding that government cannot "forbid or proscribe advocacy of the use of force or of law violation except where such advocacy is directed to inciting or producing *imminent* lawless action *and is likely to incite or produce such action*."[9] (Italics added.)

The core of freedom of speech, as the Court has frequently declared, is that government cannot regulate speech based on its *content*—its subject matter, its message, its ideas, its viewpoint. Content-based speech restrictions, unlike content-neutral restrictions, are tested under a strict scrutiny standard, are presumptively unconstitutional, and can be sustained only by a demonstration of a "compelling" governmental interest.

The distinction is illustrated in several of the decisions examined in this chapter. Thus, in the *R. A. V.* case,[10] the challenged statute sought to prohibit a particular kind of message (addressed to race, color, creed, religion, or gender) and was therefore content-based and held to be invalid. By contrast, although similarly aimed at the burning of a cross, the statute upheld in *Virginia v. Black* was content-neutral since it focused on the purpose and effect of the cross burning, quite apart from the nature of the message.[11]

Content-neutral speech regulations are tested under a less exacting standard of review than restrictions based on content. A content-neutral regulation can be justified by a showing that it serves a "substantial" or "significant" governmental interest (as distinguished from the "compelling" interest needed to justify a content-based speech regulation).

First Amendment issues frequently arise in connection with government restrictions on the use of public property—streets, sidewalks, and parks. As the Court recognized in *Cantwell v. State of Connecticut*, a state may by general and non-discriminatory legislation regulate the times, the places, and the manner of soliciting upon its streets, and of holding meetings thereon, and may in other respects safeguard the peace, good order, and comfort of the community, without unconstitutionally invading the liberties protected by the Fourteenth Amendment. However, such time, place, and manner restrictions must be reasonable "so [that] that they leave open ample alternative channels for communication of information."[12] Time, place, and manner restrictions must be content-neutral, serve a substantial state interest (for example, control of automobile or pedestrian traffic), and provide objective standards for the granting of licenses or permits. Regulations that allow an administrative authority to grant or deny permits on the basis of the content of the applicant's message, or give the administrative authority untrammeled discretion to grant or deny permits, will almost certainly be found to offend the First Amendment. For example, in *Saia v. New York*, the Court (6–3) declared unconstitutional a city's requirement of a permit to operate a sound truck where the mayor had unlimited discretion whether to grant a permit.[13] But in *Kovacs v. Cooper*, the Court (5–4) upheld an ordinance restricting the decibel level on sound trucks using public streets.[14] The Court emphasized that the law did not prohibit all such devices, but rather was a reasonable time, place, and manner restriction.

Police Department of Chicago v. Mosley, involved an ordinance that barred picketing or demonstrations within 150 feet of a school building while the school was in session, except for peaceful picketing in connection with a labor dispute. The Court (9–0) held that the ordinance, by allowing only labor picketing and not other types of protests, was not content-neutral and was therefore invalid.[15] In contrast, in *Hill v. Colorado*, the Court (6–3) rejected a challenge by antiabortion groups to a law restricting "oral protest, education, or counseling" on public sidewalks. The law made it unlawful, within 100 feet of the entrance to any health care facility, for any person to "knowingly approach" within 8 feet of another person, without that person's consent, "for the purpose of passing a leaflet or handbill to, displaying a sign to, or engaging in oral protest, education, or counseling with such other person." The majority held that the restriction on speech was content-neutral on the ground that the law applied regardless of the subject or viewpoint of the speech. In his dissent, Justice Scalia argued that the language and history of the law showed that it was a content-based restraint aimed at antiabortion speech.[16]

Symbolic Speech

The "speech" protected by the First Amendment typically involves the use of words, whether written or spoken, to communicate a message. But in many instances non-verbal conduct may be employed as a mode of communication. Marches and picketing are examples of expressive conduct recognized as "speech" under the First Amendment (subject, of course, to reasonable time, place, and manner restrictions explained in the previous comment "Freedom of Speech Overview"). Symbolic conduct in a public place or before an audience may also qualify for constitutional protection. As the Court stated in *West Virginia State Board of Education v. Barnette*, "Symbolism is a primitive but effective way of communicating ideas."[17]

Each of the first five cases digested in this chapter deals with the application of the First Amendment to a particular type of symbolic speech—setting a fire to burn an object (a cross, draft card, or flag) to express a point of view.

In *Brandenburg v. Ohio* the defendant had coupled the burning of a cross with verbal advocacy of illegal action. The Court concluded that the violence urged by the defendant was neither imminent nor likely and held unconstitutional a state syndicalism law prohibiting, e.g., advocacy "of crime, sabotage, or unlawful methods of terrorism as a means of accomplishing industrial or political reform."[18] In *United States v. O'Brien*, the defendant was charged with burning his draft card in violation of the selective service statute requiring registrants to maintain such cards in their possession. Although acknowledging that the defendant's conduct included "speech elements," the Court held that enforcement of the draft card requirement was justified because the government had a substantial "non-speech" interest in administering and enforcing the selective service program. The defendant was convicted, the Court said, "[f]or the noncommunicative impact of his conduct, and for nothing else."[19]

By contrast, in the *Texas v. Johnson* flag-burning case, the palpable purpose of the statute (prohibiting flag mistreatment "in a way that the actor knows will seriously offend one or more persons likely to observe or discover his action") was to restrain communication. The statute, it was held, was not justified by a substantial government interest unrelated to the suppression of free expression.[20]

In the other two "burning" cases—*R. A. V. v. St. Paul*[21] and *Virginia v. Black*[22]—the Court (except for Justice Thomas) accepted cross-burning conduct as "speech" presumptively entitled to First Amendment protection. However, the Court reached opposite conclusions in the two cases; the "speech" claim was rejected in *R. A. V.* and upheld in *Virginia v. Black*. In *R. A. V.* the St. Paul ordinance (prohibiting a cross burning when it "arouses anger, alarm or resentment in others *on the basis of race, color, creed, religion, or gender*") was held to be content-based and therefore invalid because it singled out specific disfavored subjects for punishment. On the other hand, unlike the St. Paul ordinance, the statute upheld in *Virginia v. Black* (prohibiting a cross burning "*with the intent of intimidating any person or group of persons*") was content-neutral because it contains no list of taboo subjects. (Italics added.)

Symbolic speech issues frequently arise in the public schools. A leading case is *Tinker v. Des Moines Independent Community School District,* holding it impermissible to bar a student from wearing a black armband to protest the Vietnam War— an action the Court characterized as "closely akin to 'pure speech' ."[23] According to the Court: "it can hardly be argued that either students or teachers shed their constitutional rights to freedom of speech or expression at the schoolhouse gate."[24] Generally student speech in public schools can be restricted only if it is vulgar or profane or if there is serious reason to believe that it is likely to cause material disruption. The decision *in Morse v. Frederick* added that speech (in that case, a banner proclaiming "Bong Hits 4 Jesus" in front of the school during a school-sponsored activity) can also be regulated if it is reasonably perceived by school officials to promote a drug-use message.[25]

Obscene (unlike "offensive" or "indecent") speech is not within the area of constitutionally protected speech or press. To regulate speech as obscene, the government must meet all three of the following tests: (1) "the average person, applying contemporary community standards, would find that the work, taken as a whole, appeals to the prurient interest," *and* (2) "the work depicts or describes, in a patently offensive way, sexual conduct specifically defined by the applicable state law," *and* (3) "the work, taken as a whole, lacks serious literary, artistic political, or scientific value."[26]

Offensive Speech Under the First Amendment

The Court's opinion in *Cohen v. California* goes beyond the protection of political messages and articulates a far broader principle—that the government may not prohibit or punish speech just because others might find it offensive or indecent.[27]

In an exception to that principle, *FCC v. Pacifica Foundation,*[28] the Court (5–4) upheld the authority of the Federal Communications Commission to prohibit and punish indecent language over federally licensed television and radio frequencies. However, in cases involving other communications media—telephones, cable television, and the Internet—the Court has distinguished its *Pacifica* holding on various grounds and has struck down federal regulations prohibiting indecent speech.

Sable Communications v. FCC invalidated (6–3) a federal statute prohibiting indecent as well as obscene telephone calls. The Court declared that "Sexual expression which is indecent but not obscene is protected by the First Amendment" and that the challenged "statute's denial of adult access to such messages far exceeds that which is necessary to serve the compelling interest of preventing minors from being exposed to the messages."[29] In *United States v. Playboy Entertainment Group,* Inc., the Court (5–4) held unconstitutional a provision of the federal Cable Act that required cable television channels "primarily dedicated to sexually-oriented programming" to either "fully scramble or otherwise fully block" those channels or to limit their transmission to hours when children are unlikely to be viewing.[30] This provision, the Court held, is a content-based restriction on speech and therefore can stand only if it satisfies strict scrutiny. On that predicate, the majority concluded that the statute was not "narrowly tailored" because the statute's purpose could be effectively achieved by a far less restrictive alternative provided in the act (the option of subscribers to block adult-oriented channels). In *Ashcroft v. American Civil Liberties Union,* the Court (5–4) held unconstitutional the federal Child Online Protection Act, aimed at protecting children from exposure to sexual material on the Internet.[31] The Court held that the government had failed to meet its burden of showing that less restrictive alternatives (particularly the use of blocking and filtering software) would not be equally effective in achieving Congress's goal.

"Hate Speech"

Offensive speech concerning, for example, race, religion, or gender is sometimes called "hate speech." But calling it "hate speech" does not change the basic constitutional principles or create a category of speech that is more subject to government regulation than other types of offensive speech. Unless it meets the requirements of an established exception to First Amendment protection (e.g., "fighting words," a narrow exception limited to intimidating speech that is directed to a specific individual and tends to cite an immediate breach of the peace), it is entitled to the same protection as other speech.

However, as *Wisconsin v. Mitchell,* illustrates, the First Amendment does not preclude imposing a more severe sentence for violent crimes motivated by bias or "hate" against members of racial minorities and other designated groups.[32]

Speech Codes

Notwithstanding *Cohen* and other Supreme Court decisions protecting "offensive speech" under the First Amendment, hundreds of state universities and colleges have adopted "speech codes" prohibiting and penalizing speech that expresses bias or hate or "insensitivity" toward minorities or women. The University of Michigan, for example, adopted a regulation subjecting individuals to discipline for "[any] behavior, verbal or physical, that stigmatizes or victimizes an individual on the basis of race, ethnicity, religion, sex, sexual orientation, creed, national origin, ancestry, age, marital status, handicap or Viet-Nam era veteran status," which "has the purpose or reasonably foreseeable effect of interfering with an individual's academic efforts, employment, participation in University sponsored extracurricular activities or personal safety." A federal district court held that the regulation was unconstitutional under the First Amendment as overbroad and too vague.[33]

Similarly, a federal district court struck down a University of Wisconsin speech code that prohibited, among other things, "discriminatory comments" directed at an individual that "intentionally . . . demean" the "sex . . . of the individual" and "[c]reate an intimidating, hostile or demeaning environment for education, university related work, or other university-authorized activity."[34] College speech codes have also been struck down by courts in California and Pennsylvania.

Although such speech codes have generally been rejected or withdrawn by public institutions whenever they have been challenged on First Amendment grounds by threat of court action, speech codes in the American workplace are flourishing.

Title VII of the 1964 Civil Rights Act provides that it is an unlawful employment practice for an employer "to discriminate against any individual with respect to his compensation, terms, conditions, or privileges of employment because of such individual's race, color, religion, sex, or national origin." Successful plaintiffs may recover substantial damages; complaints may also be filed with the Equal Employment Opportunities Commission (EEOC). "Discrimination" under Title VII has been defined to include sexual or racial "harassment"—either (1) "*quid pro quo*" sexual harassment (typically involving a claim that a female employee was pressured by the employer to submit to sexual advances) or (2) sexual or racial harassment creating a "hostile work environment." To be actionable under Title VII, the Supreme Court has held, a hostile work environment must be "sufficiently severe or pervasive to alter the conditions of the victim's employment and create an abusive working environment."[35]

Harassment creating a hostile work environment is frequently found on the basis of offensive speech that is not protected by the Amendment, such as sexual demands, threats, obscene propositions, obscene pictures, and "fighting words." But many cases have also found harassment on the basis (in whole or in substantial part) of offensive speech that the First Amendment, outside the workplace, does protect—including content-based comments, jokes, magazines, and cartoons that insult or annoy women or minorities.[36] Indeed, courts have acknowledged that the very purpose of Title VII is to "prevent . . . bigots from expressing their opinions in a way that abuses or offends their co-workers."[37]

The result is to suppress content-based expression that in other contexts is protected by the First Amendment.[38] Moreover, it is not required that the employer himself have uttered the offensive speech. The employer is held responsible if he knew or should have known of the offensive speech contributing to the hostile work environment and failed to take corrective action. The fear of such liability creates a powerful incentive for employers to censor the speech of their employees.[39]

In an effort to justify the regulation of speech otherwise regarded as protected, offensive speech is sometimes characterized as "conduct" rather than speech.[40] But if offensive speech is protected by the First Amendment—i.e., if it does not fall into one of the traditionally unprotected categories such as obscenity or "fighting words"—changing the label to "conduct" does not change its communicative character. As pointed out in the section "Symbolic Speech" in this chapter, nonverbal conduct may in some instances (e.g., flag burning) be recognized as speech; even more clearly, *verbal conduct* (i.e., speech) constitutes speech.

Nor does it lose its protected status because it offends someone; that indeed is the very nature of offensive speech. For example, "Cohen's crudely defaced jacket" no doubt outraged the sensibilities of some who saw it at the courthouse, and the Nazi march in Skokie, Illinois, was no doubt terrifying to many Skokie residents, but in both cases the courts ruled that the offensiveness must be tolerated because of the higher demands of the First Amendment.

Nor does offensive speech, if otherwise protected, lose its protection because the effect of the speech—such as a hostile work environment—is legislatively or administratively declared illegal. By that standard, the freedom of speech guaranteed by the Constitution could readily be made a dead letter.

In *R. A. V. v. St. Paul,* the Court dealt tangentially with the constitutionality of Title VII. At issue was an ordinance prohibiting a form of "fighting words." Although "fighting words" is a class of speech unprotected by the First Amendment, the majority held that the ordinance was nevertheless invalid because the ordinance (applicable only to disfavored subjects of "race, color, creed, religion, or gender") was content-based. Apparently in response to the dissenters' claim that such an interpretation of the First Amendment would also invalidate Title VII, the majority opinion observed that "a *proscribable* class of speech can be swept up incidentally within the reach of a statute directed at conduct, rather than speech. . . . Thus, for example, sexually derogatory 'fighting words,' among other words, may produce a violation of Title VII's general prohibition against sexual discrimination in employment practices."[41] While that may be true of a proscribable (unprotected) class of speech, such as fighting words, the Court's opinion is silent on whether protected speech may be similarly utilized. Although Title VII was enacted more than half a century ago, there still remains an apparent direct conflict between what Title VII forbids in the workplace and what the Constitution otherwise protects.[42]

Federal Hate Crime Laws

"Hate crime" laws of the type challenged in *Wisconsin v. Mitchell* do not criminalize conduct that is not already illegal. Instead of adding new prohibitions, such laws increase the punishment for violating already-existing criminal statutes of general applicability (statutes that prohibit, for example, homicide or other crime regardless of the identity of the victim) if it is proved that the crime was motivated by bias against a member of one of the protected groups.[43]

In addition to such punishment-enhancing laws, some criminal statutes—also characterized as hate crime laws—specifically prohibit conduct that injures members of certain protected groups. A federal statute adopted in 1969[44] provides for prosecution of conduct that "by force or threat of force willfully injures, intimidates or interferes with, or attempts to injure, intimidate or interfere with . . . any person [1] because of his race, color, religion or national origin and [2] because he is or has been" engaging in specified federally protected activities (such as voting, serving on a jury, or traveling in interstate commerce). Penalties for covered offenses involving firearms are prison terms of up to ten years, while offenses involving murder, kidnapping, or sexual assault are subject to life imprisonment or the death penalty.

The 1969 law would have been significantly expanded if it had been amended by a bill known as the Local Law Enforcement Hate Crimes Prevention Act. The bill would have expanded the law in two major respects: First, it would have eliminated the requirement of the 1969 statute that the victim be engaged in federally protected activity. Second, the bill would have expanded the existing prohibition to cover violent crime motivated by the "actual or *perceived* race, color, religion, national origin, *gender, sexual orientation, gender identity or disability of any person*" (additions italicized). The bill was approved in 2007 by both the House and Senate. It was passed by the Senate as part of the proposed Defense Authorization Act, which President Bush indicated he would veto if it included the hate crimes provision. In December 2007, while the proposed Defense Authorization Act was under consideration by a Senate-House conference committee, the hate crimes provision was removed before submittal of the legislation to the President for approval.

Freedom of Expressive Association

The First Amendment has been read as implicitly protecting people's right to associate with each other for expressive purposes. The Court has recognized that "freedom to engage in association for the advancement of beliefs and ideas is an inseparable aspect of the 'liberty' assured by the Due Process Clause of the Fourteenth Amendment, which embraces freedom of speech."[45] In this case, the Court held unconstitutional an Alabama law requiring the NAACP to disclose its membership lists. The Court declared: "Inviolability of privacy in group association may in many circumstances be indispensable to preservation of freedom of association, particularly where a group espouses dissident beliefs."[46]

Issues concerning freedom of association arise in a variety of other contexts. For example, in *Boy Scouts of America v. Dale,* the Court held that New Jersey could not require the Boy Scouts to reinstate an openly gay scoutmaster.[47] On the other hand, in upholding an order under a Minnesota law prohibiting the Jaycees from excluding women from full membership, the Court rejected the claim that the State was violating the members' First Amendment freedom of association.[48] The Court relied on the very large size of the organization, its nearly indiscriminate membership requirements, and the extensive participation of nonmembers in the group's activities. The Court found that the club did not involve the kind of "intimate or private" relation or expressive activity that warrants constitutional protection.

Freedom of association may also be invoked to protect organizations from state interference in the way they express their views. *Hurley v. Irish-American Gay Group of Boston,* which was cited in the *Boy Scouts* majority opinion, concerned the validity of an order under the Massachusetts antidiscrimination law requiring a veterans group that organized the Boston St. Patrick's Day parade to allow an Irish-American gay group to carry a gay rights banner in the parade. The veterans group contended that allowing such participation would introduce a "sexual theme" into a parade that was intended to focus on "traditional religious and social values."[49] The Supreme Court unanimously held that organizing a parade was an inherently expressive activity and that it violated the First Amendment to require the organizers to promote a message that they did not want to promote.

The Aftermath of the *Boy Scouts* Decision

The "FAIR" Case

Because of their opposition to the federal prohibition against gays serving in the armed forces, a large number of colleges and universities prohibited or restricted access on their campuses to military recruiters. In response, Congress enacted a statute known as the Solomon Amendment providing that, as a condition of receiving federal funding, colleges and universities must grant the same access to military recruiters as they do to any other recruiters. Forum for Academic and Institutional Rights, Inc. (FAIR), is an association of law schools and law faculties, whose members have policies opposing discrimination based on, *inter alia,* sexual orientation. When the schools were threatened with a cutoff of federal funding under the Solomon Amendment, FAIR sued claiming that the law violated their First Amendment rights. Relying primarily on the *Boy Scouts* decision, they claimed that their denial of equal access to military recruiters was a constitutionally protected way of expressing their opposition to the federal policy on gays.

The Court of Appeals for the Third Circuit upheld (2–1) the law schools' contention, but the Supreme Court unanimously reversed (8–0, Alito not participating).[50] In an opinion by Chief Justice Roberts, the Court distinguished the *Boy Scouts* decision in rejecting the First Amendment claim. The Court concluded that "The Solomon Amendment neither limits what law schools may say nor requires them to say anything, all the while maintaining eligibility for federal funds. . . ." According to the Court, the schools are not "speaking" when they host interviews and recruiting receptions. They are instead facilitating recruitment to assist their students in obtaining jobs. Thus, a law school's recruiting services lack the expressive quality of, for example, the Boston gay parade held to be protected communication in *Hurley.* The Court held that nothing about recruiting suggests that law schools agree with any speech by recruiters, and that nothing in the Solomon Amendment restricts what they may say about the military's policies. The Court further held that the Solomon Amendment does not violate the law schools' freedom of expressive association. Unlike the order rejected in the *Boy Scouts* case, the Solomon Amendment does not force a law school "to accept members it does not desire." Law schools "associate" with military recruiters only in the sense that they interact with them, but recruiters are not part of the school. They are instead outsiders who come onto campus for the limited purpose of trying to hire students—not to become members of the school's expressive association.

The Boy Scouts of America Equal Access Act

The Supreme Court decision in *Boy Scouts of America v. Dale* sparked efforts in many communities to deny Boy Scouts the use of public facilities for their meetings and activities. Congress responded by passing (as part of the No Child Left Behind Act of 2001) the Boy Scouts of America Equal Access Act. The Act provides that no public school receiving federal financial assistance shall deny equal access or a fair opportunity to meet, or discriminate against, any group officially affiliated with the Boy Scouts of America . . . that wishes to conduct a meeting within that designated open forum or limited public forum, including denying such access or opportunity or discriminating for reasons based on the membership or leadership criteria or oath of allegiance to God and country of the Boy Scouts of America.

Campaign Regulation and the First Amendment

In recent years one of the most important and controversial issues under the First Amendment has been the constitutionality of various types of restrictions imposed on contributions and expenditures in connection with federal elections. The three leading cases are *Buckley v. Valeo*,[51] *McConnell v. Federal Election Commission*,[52] and *Federal Election Commission v. Wisconsin Right to Life, Inc.*[53]

Buckley, involving a challenge to the 1974 amendments to the Federal Election Campaign Act, upheld the principle that contributing or spending money in connection with federal elections is a form of political speech protected by the First Amendment. The Court, however, drew a sharp distinction between contribution limits and the expenditure limits, upholding the former and invalidating the latter. The Court viewed expenditure limits as restricting the nature and quantity of political speech, but saw little direct effect on political speech through limits on contributions and accordingly recognized a broader congressional power to regulate contributions. The Court also emphasized that restrictions on the amount that a person or group could contribute to any particular candidate were justified to prevent "the actuality and appearance of corruption resulting from large individual financial contributions," but that independent expenditures to support a candidate do not have the same risk of corruption or the appearance of corruption.

In 2002, Congress adopted the McCain-Feingold law, known as the Bipartisan Campaign Reform Act (BRCA).[54] A primary purpose of BRCA was to place limits on the use of unregulated "soft money" and to require candidates to finance their campaigns primarily with "hard money"—federally regulated contributions to candidates by individual citizens (not to exceed $2,000 per citizen for each election for each candidate). Toward that end, BRCA established a highly detailed code of restrictions governing the financing of campaigns. Violations of the restrictions were subject to heavy criminal penalties. The two main changes were the following:

1. *Ban on "Soft Money" Contributions:* The amendment prohibits national, state, district or local political party committees from directly or indirectly soliciting funds for, or making or directing contributions to, either a political party or other political organization or a tax-exempt corporation that makes expenditures in connection with an election for federal office (including but not limited to spending money for voter registration, voter identification, or get-out-the-vote activities, promotion of a political party, or advertising that refers to a clearly

identified candidate for federal office and promotes or supports, or attacks or opposes, a candidate for that office).

2. *Ban on "Electioneering Communications":* §203 of the act prohibits all corporations (including nonprofit advocacy groups) and unions from paying for an "electioneering communication," defined a television or radio communication that refers to a clearly identified candidate for federal office, and is made within a "blackout period"—60 days before a general election or 30 days before a primary election.

The only ads that §203 allowed a corporation or union to run during a "blackout" period were "issue ads" that contain no reference to any candidate. In addition, any person (not just corporations and unions) who makes disbursements for the cost of "electioneering communications" in the aggregate amount of $10,000 in any calendar year must within 24 hours file with the Federal Election Commission a statement containing full details of the expenditure. (Excluded from the definition of "electioneering communications" is any "communication appearing in a news story, commentary, or editorial distributed through the facilities of any broadcasting station, unless such facilities are owned or controlled by any political party, political committee, or candidate.")

In 2003 in the *McConnell* case, the Supreme Court by a 5-to-4 decision upheld the constitutionality of these new restrictions "on their face"—i.e., without precluding later challenges to the act as applied in particular circumstances. Because of the complexity of the statute and the variety of views among the justices, the eight opinions in *McConnell* total 298 pages in the official report.[55] While acknowledging that "Money, like water, will always find an outlet," the majority concluded that "In the main we uphold BCRA's two principal, complementary features: the control of soft money and the regulation of electioneering communications."

In sustaining the §203 prohibition on electioneering communications, *McConnell* held that the First Amendment does not bar the regulation of ads that either expressly support or oppose a candidate's election or are their functional equivalent. The decision, however, did not address the question of what criteria should be used in categorizing a specific ad—whether it is a "functional equivalent" of an ad expressly supporting or opposing a candidate's election (and therefore prohibited) or is instead an "issue ad" (and therefore unregulated).

That question was presented in the *Wisconsin Right to Life* case.[56] The ads in question were placed by Wisconsin Right to Life, Inc. (WRTL), a nonprofit corporation engaged in advocacy on political issues. In 2004 WRTL sponsored three radio ads opposing filibusters on federal judicial appointments and urging people to "Contact Senators Feingold and Kohl and tell them to oppose the filibuster." The ads were to be run during a pre-election "blackout" period when Feingold, but not

Kohl, was running for reelection. Emphasizing the content of the ads, WRTL argued (with the support of such diverse advocacy groups as the American Civil Liberties Union and the National Rifle Association) that the ads were constitutionally protected "grassroots lobbying" on the filibuster issue.

In an opinion by Chief Justice Roberts (joined by Scalia, Kennedy, Thomas, and Alito), the Court (5–4) held that an ad can be deemed the "functional equivalent" of a campaign ad "only if the ad is susceptible of no reasonable interpretation other than as an appeal to vote for or against a specific candidate." According to the majority, "Discussion of issues cannot be suppressed simply because the issues may also be pertinent in an election. Where the First Amendment is implicated, the tie goes to the speaker, not the censor."[57] On that basis, the Court concluded that the three WRTL ads could not be constitutionally prohibited.

In light of that conclusion, Roberts and Alito stated that they found it unnecessary to revisit the *McConnell* holding that §203 on its face does not violate the First Amendment. In a concurring opinion, three justices (Scalia, Kennedy, and Thomas) went further, urging that the *McConnell* §203 ruling be explicitly overruled. And the four dissenters (Stevens, Breyer, Souter, and Ginsburg) claimed that the practical effect of the majority decision, despite its disclaimer, was to overrule the *McConnell* §203 ruling without saying so. The prediction of the *McConnell* majority that "Money, like water, will always find an outlet"—despite statutory restraints—has since been amply confirmed.

In the 2004 campaign, notwithstanding the 2002 Act, record amounts of funds were spent on behalf of the presidential and congressional candidates. This was accomplished in part through "soft money" raised through so-called "independent" political committees—known as "527 organizations"—dedicated to supporting certain candidates but ostensibly expending funds without coordination with the favored candidates or their parties. Although obliged to disclose their donors and expenditures, these organizations can raise money from corporations, unions, and wealthy individuals without the limits applicable to campaigns and parties. In the 2004 campaign, 527s spent $550.6 million in support of candidates. At least 46 people contributed $1 million or more to 527s; one of the 46 gave $26 million, and another gave $23 million.[58]

In the 2004 campaign, in addition to the money spent by candidates and 527s, approximately $30 billion ("by conservative estimate") was spent by nonprofit groups—known as "501c organizations"—in promoting voter registration and turnout and in sponsoring political "issue advertising." These 501c organizations are not only tax-exempt but (unlike 527s) are not required to disclose either their expenditures or the sources of their funds.[59]

In the November 2006 midterm election, spending by candidates and 527s reached new records. On advertising alone, more than $2 billion was spent in the campaign—$400 million more than the $1.6 billion spent in the 2004 presidential campaign.[60] The expenditures for the 2008 presidential and congressional elections exceeded $5.3 billion, and the cost of the presidential race exceeded $2.4 billion—50 percent more than the 2004 campaign.[61]

Notes

1. *Palko v. Connecticut*, 302 US 319 at 327 (1937). See also Christopher Wolfe, *The Rise of Modern Judicial Review: From Constitutional Interpretation to Judge-Made Law* (New York: Basic Books, 1986), 182–183; Antonin Scalia, *A Matter of Interpretation and the Law* (Princeton, NJ: Princeton University Press, 1997), 124–125; and Geoffrey Stone, *Perilous Times: Free Speech in Wartime* (New York: Norton, 2004), 42.

2. Stone, *Perilous Times*, 25–26.

3. *Abrams v. United States*, 250 US 616 at 630 (1919).

4. *Roth v. United States*, 354 US 476 at 484 (1957).

5. *Winters v. New York*, 333 US 507 at 510 (1948).

6. *Mills v. Alabama*, 384 US 214 at 218 (1966).

7. *New York Times Co. v. Sullivan*, 376 US 254 at 270 (1964).

8. *Abood v. Detroit Board of Education*, 421 US 209 at 211 (1977).

9. *Brandenburg v. Ohio*, 395 US 444 (1969).

10. *R. A. V. v. St. Paul*, 505 US 377 (1992).

11. *Virginia v. Black*, 538 US 343 (2003).

12. *Heffron v. International Society for Krishna Consciousness, Inc.*, 452 US 640 at 648 (1981).

13. *Saia v. New York*, 334 U.S. 558 (1948).

14. *Kovacs v. Cooper*, 336 U.S. 77 (1949).

15. *Police Department of Chicago v. Mosley*, 408 U.S. 92 (1972).

16. *Hill v. Colorado*, 530 U.S. 703 (2000).

17. *West Virginia State Board of Education v. Barnette*, 319 U.S. 624 at 632 (1943).

18. *Brandenburg v. Ohio*, 395 U.S. 444 (1969).

19. *United States v. O'Brien*, 391 US 367 at 382 (1968).

20. *Texas v. Johnson*, 491 US 397 (1989).

21. *R.A.V. v. St. Paul*, 505 US 377 (1992).

22. *Virginia v. Black*, 538 U.S. 343 (2003).

23. *Tinker v. Des Moines Independent School District*, 393 US 503 at 505 (1969).

24. *Tinker* at 506.

25. *Morse v. Frederick*, 551 U.S. 393, 127 S.Ct. 2618 (2007).

26. *Miller v. California*, 413 US 15 (1971).

27. *Cohen v. California*, 403 U.S. 15 (1971).

28. *FCC v. Pacifica Foundation*, 438 U.S. 726 (1978).

29. *Sable Communications v. FCC*, 492 U.S. 115 (1989).

30. *United States v. Playboy Entertainment Group*, Inc., 529 U.S. 803 (2000).

31. *Ashcroft v. American Civil Liberties Union*, 542 U.S. 656 (2004).

32. *Wisconsin v. Mitchell*, 508 U.S. 476 (1993).

33. *Doe v. University of Michigan*, 721 FSupp 852 (ED Mich 1989).

34. *UMW Post, Inc. v. Board of Regents of University of Wisconsin System*, 774 FSupp 1163 (ED Wis 1991).

35. *Mentor Savings Bank v. Vinson*, 477 US 57 at 67 (1986). In *Harris v. Forklift Systems, Inc.*, 510 US 17 (1993), the Court added the requirement that the challenged conduct must be severe or pervasive enough to create an objectively hostile or abusive work environment that a reasonable person would find hostile or abusive.

36. See, e.g., Eugene Volokh, "What Speech Does 'Hostile Work Environment' Harassment Law Restrict," 85 *Georgetown Law Review*, 627 (1997); Kingsley Browne, "Title VII as Censorship: Hostile-Environment Harassment and the First Amendment," 52 *Ohio State Law Journal*, 481 (1991).

37. *Davis v. Monsanto Chemical Co.*, 858 F2d 345 at 350 (6thCir 1998), certiorari denied, 490 US 1110 (1989); *Andrews v. City of Philadelphia*, 895 F2d 1469 at 1486 (3dCir 1990) (quoting Davis).

38. Compare, e.g., *Hustler Magazine, Inc. v. Falwell*, 485 US 46 at 52–53 (1988) (holding protected a "parody" portraying the plaintiff as engaged in "a drunken incestuous rendezvous with his mother in an outhouse"); *NAACP v. Clairborne Hardware Col*, 458 US 886 at 921 (1982) (reversing a judgment against the NAACP that had been based upon a boycott against certain white-owned businesses and holding that a judgment that rests, or might rest in part, upon protected expression is invalid.

39. Browne, "Title VII as Censorship: Hostile-Environment Harassment and the First Amendment," 483.

40. Barbara Lindemann and David Kadue, *Primer on Sexual Harassment* (Arlington, VA: BNA Books, 1992), 598; John Gould, *Speak No Evil: The Triumph of Hate Speech Regulation* (Chicago: University of Chicago Press, 2005), 133; and Browne, *Title VII as Censorship*.

41. *R. A. V. v. St. Paul*, 505 U.S. 377 at 389 (1992).

42. See Cynthia Estlund, "Freedom of Expression in the Workplace and the Problem of Discriminatory Harassment," *Texas Law Review* 588 (1997); Gould, *Speak No Evil*, 30.

43. *Wisconsin v. Mitchell*, 508 U.S. 476 (1993).

44. 18 US Code, sec 245(b)(2).

45. *NAACP v. Alabama ex rel Patterson*, 357 U.S. 449 at 460 (1958).

46. Ibid.

47. *Boy Scouts of America v. Dale*, 530 U.S. 640 (2000).

48. *Roberts v. United States Jaycees*, 468 U.S. 609 (1984).

49. *Hurley v. Irish-American Gay Group of Boston*, 515 U.S. 557 (1995).

50. *Rumsfeld v. Forum for Academic and Institutional Rights, Inc.*, 574 U.S. 47, 126 S. Ct.1297 (2006).

51. *Buckley v. Valeo*, 424 U.S. 76 (1974).

52. *McConnell v. Federal Election Commission*, 540 U.S. 93 (2003).

53. *Federal Election Commission v. Wisconsin Right to Life, Inc.*, 551 U.S. 449, 127 S. Ct. 2652 (2007).

54. *The Presidential Campaign Reform Act (BCRA)*, U.S. Public Law 107–155, 107th Cong., 2d sess. (27 March 2002).

55. *McConnell v. Federal Election Commission*, 54 US 93 (2003).

56. *Federal Election Commission v. Wisconsin Right to Life, Inc.*, 551 US 449 (2007).

57. Ibid.

58. *New York Times*, 17 December 1994.

59. *Washington Post*, 21 August 2004.

60. *Washington Post*, 3 November 2006.

61. *New York Times*, 2 December 2007; *USA Today*, 23 October 2008.

6

The First Amendment and the SEC

| Revised by Nancy S. Lind and Erik T. Rankin

Recap of the Traditional Legal Doctrine

Until the mid-20th century, in constitutional **jurisprudence**, what has come to be known as **commercial speech** had been excluded from the coverage of the First Amendment. Commercial speech, most narrowly construed, is any speech or publication that advertises a product or service for profit or business purposes.[1] Some authorities, however, assert a considerably broader definition of the concept. **Commercial speech** has been extensively regulated at the state and federal levels. For example, food and drug ads are subject to extensive regulation. The states and the federal government extensively regulate the speech and publications of corporations and other business entities.

Modern commercial speech doctrine began in 1942 with the *Valentine v. Chrestensen* case.[2] In that litigation a businessman in New York City disseminated a leaflet that on one side advertised a business exhibition of a former navy submarine and on the other side contained a purportedly political critique of the municipality's refusal to grant wharfage facilities for the show. The defendant was convicted of violating a statute banning the dissemination of advertisements in the streets. In upholding the conviction the Supreme Court stated:

> This court has unequivocally held that the streets are proper places for the exercise of the freedom of communicating information and disseminating opinion and that though the states and municipalities may appropriately regulate the privilege in the public interest, they may not unduly burden or proscribe its employment in these public thoroughfares. We are equally clear that the Constitution imposes no such restraint on government as respects purely commercial advertising.[3]

This decision was always read to exclude commercial speech (even where incidentally enriched by a political message) from the protections of the First Amendment. In a series of decisions beginning in the mid-1970's, the Court reversed itself and introduced limited First Amendment protection for commercial speech. For example, in *Virginia State Board of Pharmacy v. Virginia Citizens*

Consumer Council, Inc.[4] the Court protected from prior restraint the advertisement of prescription drug prices. In *Linmark Associates, Inc. v. Town of Willingboro*[5] the Court held that a city may not prohibit by ordinance the posting of "For Sale" or "Sold" signs despite the municipality's purpose of discouraging white flight of homeowners from a racially integrated area. The Court always emphasized that because of the supposed robustness of commercial speech, and the assumed relative ease of verification, the First Amendment protection would be far more limited than political or artistic speech. For example, courts have always held that potentially misleading commercial speech could be restrained by governmental regulation.

In *Central Hudson Gas & Electric Corporation v. Public Service Commission*[6] the Court struck down a public utility regulation banning public utility advertising promoting the use of electricity. The state utility commission had maintained that the ads violated the national goal of preserving energy. The Court applied the following four-part test for commercial speech: at the outset, we must determine whether the expression is protected by the First Amendment. For commercial speech to come within that provision, it at least must concern lawful activity and not be misleading. Next, we ask whether the asserted government interest is substantial. If both inquiries yield positive answers, we must determine whether the regulation directly advances the governmental interest asserted, and whether it is not more extensive than is necessary to serve that interest.[7] The Court concluded that the complete ban on the ads was more pervasive regulation than necessary to satisfy the public policy of preserving energy.

In 1989 the Court directly construed the meaning of the fourth part of that test. It rejected the "least restrictive means" interpretation. As the Court put it:

> In sum while we have insisted that "the free flow of commercial information is valuable enough to justify imposing on would-be regulators the costs of distinguishing . . . the harmless from the harmful," quoting *Zauderer* . . . "we have not gone so far as to impose upon them the burden of demonstrating that the distinguishment is 100% complete, or that the manner of restriction is absolutely the least severe that will achieve the desired end. What our decisions require is a 'fit' between the legislature's ends and the means chosen to accomplish those ends," Posadas, 478 U.S. 341—a fit that is not necessarily perfect, but reasonable; that represents not necessarily the single best disposition but one whose scope is in "proportion to the interest served," *In re R.M.J.,* supra, 203; that employs not necessarily the least restrictive means, but, as we have put it in the other contexts discussed above, a means narrowly tailored to achieve the desired objective.[8]

The courts and commentators are far from unanimous in defining the contours of commercial speech.[9] There are some who assert that such speech includes any publication or speech that is primarily, or perhaps solely, related to the economic self-interest of the speaker or his audience and the implementation of a commercial action. They would emphatically not limit the definition to product or service advertisements. Obviously much turns on the exact definition of the doctrine.

Although a completely satisfactory definition of commercial speech may be elusive, everyone agrees that it certainly includes advertising of a product or service for purposes of profit. For example, the salesperson that hypes shaving cream is engaged in commercial speech. However, the political philosopher who hypes socialism in a book for large royalties is uttering protected First Amendment non-commercial speech. The government, under certain circumstances, can lawfully restrain even truthful shaving cream advertisements before they are published or spoken.[10] With respect to truthful speech, the regulatory agency must follow the *Central Hudson* test set forth above.[11] The government can civilly or criminally punish the huckster after the fact if the ad is fraudulent.[12] The political philosopher is in a different league. The government cannot engage in prior restraint of the political message. Further, the government cannot successfully prosecute the political philosopher on the grounds that his statements are false.

The Purposes Served by the First Amendment: Commercial Speech Compared with Fully Protected Speech

One popular rationale for the difference between the limited protections of commercial speech and the greater protection of political speech, or for that matter for a position that would deny any First Amendment protection to commercial speech, is the crucial role political speech, as distinguished from commercial speech, plays in a free democratic society.[13] Political speech is essential for the workings of a free democratic society. Almost by definition democracy entails the conflict and contest among competing political parties and ideas. For that to work, unfettered political expression is necessary.

Some have argued that the only purpose intended to be served by the First Amendment is to aid the democratic political process, sometimes defined as a kind of New England town meeting.[14] Professor Robert Bork, in a well-known article, argued that no speech, including artistic speech, not advancing a political goal, is constitutionally protected.[15] These positions, at least under a narrow construction, that would exclude artistic and scientific speech have been rejected by many commentators and all the courts. They unacceptably deprive us of protection for most speech, except campaign utterances. They certainly appear to rest on dubious and narrow assumptions about the nature of the political process. They disregard the learning, on the right, of interest group theory and, on the left, of Marxist analysis, and in the center the commonsense of journalists and the rest of us, about the inextricable interplay of the economic, artistic, financial, and political.

A second reason, often suggested, is that unfettered competition among differing political ideals, will ultimately lead to the truth. The free market in ideas will finally winnow out falsehood.[16] Truth in politics or art, unlike in the commercial realm, is not easy to achieve. Truth will emerge only after a sometimes lengthy process of debate and intellectual confrontation. The government bureaucrat, by fiat or command, cannot, or out of bias will not, determine the relative truthfulness of contrasting political or artistic ideas. She is able, it is asserted, to perform that function with respect to commercial speech. Therefore, the free competition among ideas, in Justice Oliver Wendell Holmes's famous marketplace of ideas, is a better process for arriving at political truth than is government dictation.

A third reason often advanced is that free speech in the political and artistic worlds (but not the commercial arena) is important for the growth and flowering of the human personality.[17] This argument from the values of self-expression extends to the listener or the disseminator of the speech in this sense, free speech is related to the ideal of privacy or autonomy. Each person should be free to express himself or herself in speech or writing, or to receive without restriction information and opinions and artistic messages.

Commercial speech, particularly in its clearest mode (i.e., the advertisement of services or products), does not, in the opinion of many scholarly commentators, fall within the intendment of one or more of these reasons.

Let us initially take up the third goal, that of self-expression of listener or transmitter. The Supreme Court has emphasized that advertisements impart information and opinion to the consumer. Only if we engage in a kind of invidious content discrimination, and denigrate the content value of advertisements, as compared with the content value of campaign speeches and trivial novels, can we escape the conclusion that ads contribute to the personal edification of the listener.

Take the mundane sale of shampoo and the shampoo advertisement. A shampoo ad is unqualifiedly commercial speech. The shampoo advertisement, however, is an idea or concept as well as a description of a collection of chemicals. It embodies a particular culture's idea of personal hygiene and beauty and the expression of the human personality. The countercultural hippie of the 1960s no doubt would scoff at the idea of beautifying hair shampoo as a bourgeoisie conceit. Conceits of the middle class, however, need protection of the First Amendment, just as do the notions of a (self-described) elite.

Manufacturers of shampoo and hair conditioners sell not just an aggregate of chemicals. They sell a particular concept of beauty and cleanliness. Some may ridicule the intellectual weight of the hair shampoo idea, but that very ridicule represents an artistic and cultural judgment. For example, in another realm of discourse, music, some may advocate heavy metal music and some may deem it garbage, but most would grant the music full First Amendment protection.

Certainly we cannot base a distinction between the advertisement of shampoo and the dissemination of a political or artistic idea on the absence or presence of the profit motive. In that regard, consider the following series of thought experiments. Harold Kasofsky authors a book extolling the merits of ABC shampoo. The XYZ Publishing Company publishes the book. Kasofsky and the publisher both have a clear and direct economic interest in the success of the book. It appears clear, however, that the government cannot engage in prior restraint or censorship of the book, or in criminal prosecution after the publication. (We assume in this example that Kasofsky has no financial interest in the shampoo company.) We would think that if the government could restrain publication of the book on the grounds that the book is false, we would have opened a vast breach in First Amendment protection of political and artistic speech. For example, take a novel in which a much admired hero uses and extols the virtues of ABC shampoo. Should the government be able to restrain, in advance, the publication on the grounds that the shampoo leaves the hair a mess? As we like to say, to ask the question is to answer it.

But consider XYZ Publishing Company ads promoting sales of the book. That appears to fit the definition of commercial speech. Yet if we permit prior restraint of the ad we have in effect almost succeeded in prior restraint of the book in the sense that it will be difficult to sell it by word of mouth.

Remember that the strongest (i.e., least controversial) definition of commercial speech is the advertisement of a product or a service for sale. In modern society, however, it is virtually impossible to promote ideas unless the promoter of the idea can in some way commercially merchandise the concept. Traditional political speech is always an ad for an idea. For example, consider a political science professor who, based on his serious research, wants to extol the virtues of tougher anti-merger laws. He can chat about it at a party given at his house. Obviously that is an absurdly ineffectual method. He can write a widely read book. That is an effective method, but it entails the sale by him of a product (i.e., a book for profit) and the sale of that book by a commercial publisher. He can hit the lecture circuit if he is well known. There he can give speeches for a fee to promote his idea. In all those cases he is selling an idea for a fee. Unless we agree that we can distinguish between advertising ideas and products, his material is nothing more than commercial speech.

Now let us consider the argument that political speech is necessary for the success of the democratic system. Commercial speech, it is asserted, does not meet that noble purpose. Debate on socialism versus capitalism, conservatism versus liberalism, and the like, it is argued, is the warp and woof of democratic discourse and struggle. The selling of shampoo is ignoble trade. Government can ban the advertising of shampoo, where such advertising has the tendency to be fraudulent, without impairing the quality of democracy.

The argument based on democracy succeeds only by a tortured definition of the term. If we define the democratic process as campaign speeches by politicians running for office, and limit unfettered First Amendment protection only to that speech, we reach an unnaturally constrained result. Obviously we have to open up the definition to reach everyone in society who wants to comment on the political debate. Moreover, the debate frequently centers on economic interests of business or labor. Further, we cannot limit comment to the issues raised by the elected politicians. Every member of society must have the freedom to attempt to express his definition of the issues in the political process.

Assume that the ABC Shampoo Company desires a sharp tax break for its shampoo business. Further, it wants a decrease in food and drug regulation of its product. Also, it wants to eliminate government regulation of its product ads. There is no doubt under the current state of the law that the government cannot prevent spokespersons for the company from writing articles and giving speeches (so long as they are not in reality advertisements for a product) promoting the changes.[18] They are self-interested in the proposals, but surely self-interest cannot be a bar. That would limit debate to saints and move the discussion to the realm of religion and theology. We cannot bar or censor speeches and ads because they involve an economic or commercial subject. That would limit free debate to theological issues only.

The courts, however, assert that the shampoo ad itself is commercial speech. How does the ad differ from the corporate campaign to cut shampoo business taxes and eliminate regulation of the product, including the elimination of regulation of the ads? The difference is scarcely obvious. Some have argued that the ad is an element of the contract of sale.[19] A misrepresentation of fact would involve a violation of the contract, and basic contract law is somehow immune from usual First Amendment principle. Of course, that argument assumes the answer. The issue is whether ads (i.e., a kind of speech), even if deemed part of a contract, can be censored or otherwise regulated. At that point we are back to the issue of the policy difference, if any, between ads and so-called political speech.

Justice William J. Brennan, Jr. has forcefully pointed out that economic or commercial speech is an essential part of the political process:

> Speech about commercial or economic matters, even if not directly implicating the central meaning of the First Amendment, . . . is an important part of our public discourse . . . As *Thornhill suggests*, the choices we make when we step into the voting booth may well be the products of what we have learned from the myriad of daily economic and social phenomenon that surround us.[20]

A major rationale for the First Amendment (in the realm of politics and science, albeit fiercely criticized in the scholarly literature)[21] is the free marketplace-of-ideas concept. The free clash of ideas will lead to the truth. Related to that is the rationale that truth in ideas is elusive and not easily ascertainable by the government bureaucrat. Indeed, he may not want the truth if it will harm his selfish bureaucratic interests. In this sense of the First Amendment there is an obvious similarity between the free market of the economist and the Oliver Wendell Holmes sense of the free market in ideas.[22] Both involve a laissez-faire attitude to the world. Indeed, Ronald Coase has pointed out the identity between the two concepts and argued, therefore, for a similarity in treatment between product ads and political ideas.[23] He has asserted that the realm of political and artistic ideas is the business of the intellectual. The latter promotes the First Amendment to protect his business. The intellectual, however, denigrates the usefulness of the world of the businessman, and hence argues for a lesser protection under the First Amendment for product ads and whatever might be deemed merely commercial speech.

Let us evaluate the argument that free speech produces the truth. In certain senses this appears valid. The free pursuit of the scientific method, untrammeled by government censorship, will produce truth in the fields of physics, biology, chemistry, and the like. Even there the process is long, painful, and sometimes quite messy. The process is less obvious in certain artistic and political realms. Popular results may be achieved, but that is merely a definitional statement if we presume the majority vote to be a democratic process. For example, many thinkers believe that the welfare system in modern liberal capitalist societies is a disaster, but the system persists.[24] This does not prove that their view is correct or incorrect. Indeed, each opposition party passionately believes that their election defeat is a grievous blow against the truth as well as other values. Thus Democratic party activists (who admire the welfare system) argue that Republican party victories at the national level are catastrophes for the causes of truth, equality, and justice. Some may argue that in the long run the truth will emerge, but there is no empirical evidence for that point of view. In any event, in the short run, which may last for decades, considerable harm may ensue. A famous example is the electoral victory of the Nazis in Germany in the early 1930s.

It is often argued that the falsity or truth of a product ad is far more easily ascertainable than artistic or political speech. If the shampoo ad asserts that Whiz Shampoo preserves a bouncy look for the entire day, then government chemists can verify the claim or disprove it. (Even there, much may depend on the subjective notion of "bouncy.") Hence, it is argued, censorship of the ad, or punishment for its publication, should be permissible in certain cases and, indeed, this claim has some limited validity. There may be various product claims that can be easily verified or disproved by government bureaucrats. There are many claims, however, that are not easily verifiable. The artificial heart (when introduced into the market) is an example. Scientific dispute about the state-of-the-art is acute and vigorous. The argument approaches, and frequently passes beyond, the border of so-called fact into the realm of delicate judgment and value-balancing. The same is true in the so-called realm of the political.

Some political claims are clearly false. For example, the political argument by some that the Nazi holocaust against the Jews is a fiction is indisputably false. Yet few would argue that the First Amendment does not protect the right of Americans in the United States to advertise or publicize the loathsome lie. The rationale is the slippery slope thesis. If the government is permitted to censor in one area, albeit obvious, it will soon act to censor the truth when it harms the government.

There are other political positions that many experts take to be false. For example, many professional economists would agree about the general evils of protectionism.[25] Nonetheless, they would agree (at least on advice of counsel) that the First Amendment permits fools, as they see it, to make fallacious arguments in favor of protectionism. It is not clear why apparently false product ads, however, should be censored. In many instances false political ideas (e.g., racism) can cause immeasurably greater harm than a false product ad; yet the former are protected by the full strength of the First Amendment.

During the past few decades a voluminous literature has developed about the harmful effects of government economic regulation.[26] Such studies demonstrate that it is not enough to measure a free-market approach against some ideal of government regulation. It is important, rather, to compare the free market, imperfect as it may be, with the costs of imperfect government regulation. In that comparison, government regulation is often found seriously wanting. Further, in many cases it is hardly clear that government regulation actually does improve things. One thing is constant, however; regulation almost always restrains free choice of groups and individuals. Therefore, it is doubtful that product ad regulation will invariably or even usually benefit the consumer or the public. Thus, if there is a growing body of evidence that product ad regulation may be more harmful than previously imagined, the balance in favor of affording such speech full First Amendment protection may shift.[27]

The direct and indirect costs of political censorship are frequently cited. That is, censorship, even though it occasionally will stop a blatantly false and dangerous idea, will cost too much in lost human autonomy and the disasters that might result from mistaken governmental action. Government restraint chills individual freedoms and is fallible. Hence the fundamental decision is made in favor of laissez-faire in political and, likewise, in artistic speech. The same argument would seem to be indicated for commercial speech. Claims are made, for example, that federal restraint of drug advertising and sales has, according to cited research, actually caused more harm than good.[28] It has chilled the development and sale of valuable drugs that would have saved many lives.

The argument is often made that commercial speech (i.e., product ads) is difficult to chill by government censorship. This is the robustness argument of economists.[29] Put simply, the contention is that the commercial interest is great enough to withstand the costs of government restraint. It is further asserted that proponents of political speech are comparatively easy to intimidate by government action. This is an empirical proposition that is debatable. While the relative timidity of businessmen is often noted, the tenacity of committed political activists, on the other hand, is a common phenomenon. It is most plausible indeed to assert the exact opposite. That is, regulation of political speech will tend to chill less than restraint of commercial speech.

Some Concluding Remarks on Commercial Speech

The definition of commercial speech, narrowly construed, includes only product or service advertisements. Some have argued for a broader definition that encompasses speech closely connected to economic self-interest. The latter definition is, as much of the preceding discussion indicates, too broad. Much of political or artistic speech directly or indirectly involves economic interest. Political issues such as protection versus free trade, tax policy, and agricultural programs are debated by groups with a vested interest in the issue. If we barred economic greed, we would exclude much of so-called political speech from the full protection of the First Amendment.

In conclusion, the distinction between commercial and noncommercial speech does not have much of a foundation in policy or logic. We have established, at the very least, that whatever commercial speech may be, it cannot turn on economic self-interest, robustness, ease of verification, or commercial greed. However, even if there is a significant distinction between the most naked of advertisements for a product or a service and political speech, the federal securities laws restrain corporate speech that more closely approaches fully protected speech than traditionally defined commercial speech.

SEC Speech: Preliminary Considerations

SEC Speech—Mandatory Disclosure versus Outright Prohibition

We must, at this point, consider the differences between mandatory disclosure requirements and outright prohibitions on speech. For example, the Investment Advisers Act of 1940, as interpreted by the Securities and Exchange Commission (SEC) for the past few decades (until the Supreme Court disagreed), forbade the dissemination of investment letters unless the investment adviser was first registered with the SEC.[30] The SEC contended that if the investment adviser's registration is rejected or revoked, as is permitted under the Act, because of specified prior misconduct, then no market letter, however truthful, may be disseminated. On the other hand, corporate proxy statements and prospectuses may be published and disseminated (without licensing of the corporation), provided they satisfy certain SEC disclosure mandates.[31] In both instances the government engages in a form of prior restraint.[32] The question is whether the two cases entail the same legal inquiry under the First Amendment. The Supreme Court, to date, has indicated that there are significant differences between disclosure requirements and outright prohibitions on speech. In the *Zauderer vs. Office of Disciplinary* Council case the Court asserted that although it "has not attempted to prescribe what shall be orthodox in politics, nationalism, religion, or other matters of opinion . . . [it has permitted prescription of] what shall be orthodox in commercial advertising."[33] The Supreme Court reasoned that "the extension of First Amendment protection to commercial speech is justified principally by the value to consumers of the information such speech provides."[34] In this regard, the Court asserted that it would not subject mandatory disclosure requirements to the *Central Hudson* strict "least restrictive means" test pursuant to "which they must be struck down if there are other means by which the States' purposes may be served."[35] Hence SEC mandatory disclosure would, under this analysis, be subject to a less rigorous test than the four part *Central Hudson* test.

The attempted distinction between mandatory disclosure and outright prohibition cannot survive analysis. The giveaway is the Court's statement that although the government cannot proscribe orthodoxy in politics, it can do so in commercial advertising. It is indeed true that a regime of mandatory disclosures will create government orthodoxy in whatever field, including commercial advertising, the government invades.

The evils of mandatory disclosure in the political and artistic domains are clear enough. The mischief inherent in the government's power to "correct" disclosures before publication is identical to the mischief inherent in its power to issue a blanket prior bar. Government censors, by the use of disclosure requirements, can gut arguments with which they disagree and tip the dialectical balance irretrievably in the direction they favor. Consider the debate in the summer of 1985 on the White House flat tax proposals.[36] Career bureaucratic government censors, who are hostile to the White House position, could, under an SEC-type disclosure statute, require "disclosure" that the proposal unduly favors the wealthy, gives little comfort to the poor, and harms the middle class. Different government censors, favorable to the proposal, might require their Democratic opponents to "disclose" that the White House tax bill will maximize incentive, assist the poor, and benefit the middle class. These examples can be multiplied endlessly. They simply illustrate that in political or artistic debate, truth is often in the eye of the partisan beholder.

The same obnoxious result can occur in SEC financial disclosures. For decades the SEC required disclosure of historical "hard" data. It forbade the disclosure of so-called soft projection data about predictions of future earnings and budgets.[37] Yet the futuristic "soft" data were crucial to an informed evaluation of investments. This mandatory disclosure structure led to a defective system of disclosure that frustrated investors and distorted the financial truth.[38] The moral here, as in the political area, is clear; in technical-financial disclosures, as in political speech, the government's power to require specific disclosure is the power to mandate the government's version of proper orthodoxy. That power interferes with all of the various values the First Amendment is presumed to advance. It interferes with the free market's pursuit of truth because governments have no monopoly on that precious commodity, and indeed frequently have an interest in suppressing it. Government-mandated disclosure stifles the receipt by investors of information, and hence interferes with personal development and freedom. Government-mandated disclosures also harm the political-democratic process, since it imposes government orthodoxy in important economic and financial areas of a supposedly free society. In short, the government's power to mandate specified disclosure possesses to an identical degree and kind the evils that all of us recognize in outright prohibition.

SEC Speech: Distinguished from Commercial Speech

Commercial speech, as used in the courts, usually is defined as an advertisement of a product or service for business purposes. It may include a wider variety of economically centered speech. But the wider and more inclusive the definition, the greater is the difficulty in distinguishing commercial speech, so liberally defined, from fully protected speech, however the latter is defined.

As we have noted, some economists distinguish commercial speech from political speech by the presence or absence of externalities. Speech in the form of an advertisement for a product or a service seems not to be affected by complexities of external benefits.[39] Most of the "benefits" of advertising particular goods or services are captured by the seller of the products.[40] Hence commercial speech is robust and not easily chilled by regulation. The amount of such speech is not under produced, as a result of the absence of free riders capturing the benefit of the speech. Political speech, however, it is argued, is under produced.[41] Property rights in such speech are diffuse and undeveloped. Therefore, disseminators are less than amply rewarded, and free riders can reproduce the speech without penalty. Accordingly, some argue that the First Amendment is necessary to facilitate some production of that fragile product. But the government cannot require it or censor it or regulate its content, since that would create a government orthodoxy of thought that is repugnant to First Amendment philosophy. Moreover, some argue that the government can more easily distinguish truth from falsity in the area of commercial speech than in the area of political speech.[42] These arguments of economists have been endorsed by the Supreme Court in many opinions. Consequently, all other matters kept equal, there are, it is asserted, good reasons for applying the protections of the First Amendment to political speech in more ample form than to commercial speech.

We shall review these arguments in the SEC context below. These distinctions of economists do not serve to distinguish SEC-regulated speech from political speech, or to conflate it with commercial speech, as traditionally defined in the courts.

In the *SEC v. Wall Street Publishing Institute, Inc.* case, the court declined to apply the definition of commercial speech to speech involving the purchase and sale of securities. Nevertheless, it developed a theory that speech relating to economic transactions, such as sale of securities and taxation, was subject to governmental power on a scale at least as great as is the case with commercial speech. The court, however, recognized that the speech regulated by the commission is obviously different in a significant sense from the advertisement of a product or a service. A toothpaste corporation advertises toothpaste. That is traditional commercial speech. A publicly held toothpaste corporation is the scene of a vigorous battle between contending shareholder groups for power in the organization. The groups disseminate messages to shareholders. That is **proxy speech**. But as we shall demonstrate soon, that is speech about the governance of a corporation, not the advertisement of a product or a service. It is speech that is political in a traditional sense (i.e., speech about who shall govern). It is about complex financial and economic issues that government cannot easily verify as to truth or falsity. It is also speech that in one form or another, corporations will voluntarily supply because of the economic advantages to the corporation in doing so.

The toothpaste corporation may be the subject of a hostile takeover. The commission regulates the disclosure statements of bidder and target corporations. This, like the proxy campaign, is a conflict over control. In that sense it is, like proxy battles, similar to traditional political campaigns. The difference is that the subject of the struggle for power is a corporation, not a political agency or department.

The toothpaste corporation may sell securities to the public to raise capital. The purchasers become "owners" of the organization. Even the purchasers of debt securities become important stakeholders in the organization with rights, frequently, as to direction of the business or financial structure. Corporate speech about the transaction in the form of prospectuses and registration statements is entirely different from the traditional advertisement of toothpaste. It is more akin to the enrollment of members in an organization.

Corporations issue periodic statements about financial and business news. The SEC regulates the content and frequency of such information. For example, corporations are circumscribed with respect to their ability to time the announcements of ending merger negotiations. This speech, again, is not an advertisement for a product or a service. It is information about an organization that is of use to its members (i.e., shareholders and note holders) and of use to prospective shareholders.

All of the speech regulated by the SEC is potentially complex, subject to different interpretations by experts, and essentially difficult to verify because of the financial subtleties involved. All of it is directly or indirectly related to the governance of publicly held corporations. It is speech vastly different from commercial speech as traditionally defined.

Analysis of Varieties of SEC-Regulated Speech

Proxy Speech

Judge Edward A. Tamm, in a famous opinion on proxy regulation stated that "it is obvious to the point of banality to restate the proposition that Congress intended by its enactment of section 14 of the Securities Exchange Act of 1934 to give true vitality to the concept of shareholder democracy . . ."[43]

Fair corporate suffrage is an important right that should attach to every equity security brought on a public exchange. Managements of properties owned by the investing public should not be permitted to perpetuate themselves by the misuse of corporate proxies.[44] The commission has attempted to implement this mandate by developing proxy rules that require detailed disclosure of the matters proposed for action at shareholder meetings. It has also promulgated Rule 14a-8 requiring corporations at corporate expense to include certain shareholder 'proposals in the corporate proxy statement.[45] The commission has, to date, excluded shareholder proposals to nominate candidates for the board of directors from this cost-free privilege.[46] Shareholders, of course, are free to solicit at their own expense proxies for any valid corporate purpose, subject to the proxy regulations on required disclosure."[47]

Proxy Regulation as Control of Corporate Governance

Proxy regulation, then, rests on the notion of maximizing democracy for shareholders in the corporation. Commission regulation covers shareholder policy proposals as well as contested elections of directorial slates. In both instances the basic pattern of regulation is fairly constant. Corporate management, or the insurgent shareholder group, in the case of elections, is required to file detailed disclosure documents with the commission. Many of such filings must be made before transmission to the public shareholders. The staff reviews the materials for purposes of evaluating the truth or falsehood of the materials. If the staff believes the material to be misleading, it may go to a federal district court to enjoin the proxy disclosure or it may proceed administratively against the offending material and the person who wrote it.

Naturally the process would not withstand the usual First Amendment scrutiny in the case of political contests. In fact, no statute that required congressional candidates to clear the content of their speeches in advance (or subsequent to delivery) with the SEC would withstand constitutional attack. Yet the purpose of the commission proxy regulation is to promote democracy in the governance of corporations.

Let us consider if, on proper analysis, this is permissible regulation, even within the orthodox legal concept, and not forbidden restraint of fully protected speech.

Assume that Virtue Inc. is a publicly held publishing corporation. The management and board of directors are currently dominated by Harold Victorian, the chief executive officer, who believes in the moral necessity of publishing ethically uplifting romances. Under his direction the corporation publishes only novels that eschew sexually explicit content and promotes only happy endings for the good guys and gals and bad endings for the evil characters. To date, this concept of morality has resulted in smashing economic success for the shareholders. Recently, however, earnings have begun to trend downward. An insurgent group of shareholders wants to elect a new group of directors who will reverse the aesthetic judgments of Harold Victorian and publish sexually salacious novels. Both groups file proxy materials with the SEC, as they are required to do. The SEC staff evaluates their contrasting aesthetic and economic claims. Perhaps the Victorian group writes that ethically "pure" books are better literature. The SEC staff will, no doubt, request additional proxy material, admitting that many critics deplore the literary values of latter-day Victorian prudery. The reader can imagine other SEC censorious edicts that might ensue. The point is that federal proxy rules permit an intrusion into what appears to be a political and artistic process.

Assume now that Virtue, Inc. publishes a book by Professor So-and-So devoted to the theme that maintaining Harold Victorian's standards of modesty in the novel will be a literary achievement to be devoutly prayed for. Assuredly, no government censor could lawfully require the book to be pre-filed (or post-filed) with the SEC for review and comment. Yet, if distributed as proxy material, it is deemed to be of different constitutional texture.

The usual rationale for SEC regulation (except for the *SEC v. Wall Street Publishing Institute* case) of the proxy materials is that they deal with commercial speech. Shareholders invest in the corporation. They make intelligent governance decisions to hold or sell only if, *inter alia*, proxy regulation provides them with truthful information. Although governance decisions usually may be made for economic investment reasons, there is a difference between ordinary purchase decisions and the process of corporate governance. The latter requires shareholder choices that affect employees, communities, and fellow shareholders. This is governance, not merely a share or product purchase decision.

Shareholder democracy is supposed to facilitate the shareholder control and management of a business in which each shareholder has invested. This is clearly a different process than a product advertisement. The latter is traditionally defined as commercial speech. Yet even such ads are not easily differentiated from fully protected speech. But, governance of a corporation is surely different from an advertisement. It is true that the shareholders' interest in the corporation is primarily economic. However, the citizens' interest in the polity also is, to a considerable extent, economic. Yet the First Amendment protects the citizens' speech. Because much of American life revolves around and is affected by the modern corporation, it would seem that shareholders and management should enjoy the strong version of First Amendment protection in their speech dealing with the governance of that significant element in American life.

The First Amendment also recognizes the freedom of individuals to associate, to govern their own organizations, and to control their memberships, free of interference by the government. This freedom is based on the First Amendment right of free expression. Any governmental interference must prove a compelling state interest for the restriction. The Court has distinguished between organizations that are primarily expressive in nature, and those that are commercial. Hence it maintains the right of the government, for example, to interfere in the internal governance of the business corporation. By now, however, it must be apparent that it is inherently impossible to distinguish between the political and the economic, at least in speech that is not merely an advertisement for a specific product or service. Most political organizations have economic interests that they pursue on behalf of the membership. It appears unduly artificial to distinguish business corporations from bar associations, or real estate trade groups, or chiropodist associations, all of whom, directly or indirectly, lobby legislators for their economic advantage.

The Bellotti and Austin Cases—Corporate External Political Speech

In our further analysis we are going to do the following. First, we explore the Supreme Court doctrine on corporate external political free speech, as distinguished from internal or proxy speech. We demonstrate that the two kinds of speech cannot be meaningfully distinguished. We explore in that regard the rights of minority shareholders to express their opinions. Next, we analyze the complexity of proxy disclosure. In that context we demonstrate the inability of government to easily differentiate truth from falsehood. We explore the government tendency to establish a prevailing orthodoxy on disclosure that is not necessarily married to truth or lack of bias. We discuss the fragility or robustness of proxy speech. We close with an analysis of the role of the free market in gathering and disseminating information.

In *First National Bank of Boston v. Bellotti*[48] a Massachusetts statute prohibited certain corporations from making expenditures "for the purpose of . . . influencing or affecting the vote on any question submitted to the voters, other than one materially affecting any of the property, business or assets of the corporation."[49] The statute specified that "[n]o question submitted to the voters solely concerning the taxation of the income, property or transactions of individuals shall be deemed materially to affect the property, business or assets of the corporation."[50]

The corporate appellants wanted to spend money to state their opinions in opposition to a proposed constitutional amendment to impose a graduated income tax on individuals. The attorney general of Massachusetts stated that he would enforce the statute against them. The corporations brought the action to have the statute declared unconstitutional.

Justice Lewis F. Powell, speaking for the Court, stated that press corporations do "not have a monopoly on either the First Amendment or the ability to enlighten."[51] Further, the prior cases granting First Amendment rights to press corporations (which appellants were not) are based not only on the speakers' rights to self-expression, but also on the public's right to "discussion, debate and the dissemination of information and ideas."[52] This approach differs from the argument of *Baker* that emphasizes the allegedly coercive profit-seeking imperatives of the corporate speaker.[53]

The Court emphasized that its commercial speech cases also are based on the "societal" interest in the "free flow of commercial information,"[54] not the interest of the seller in his business.[55] Ironically, the statute would free up corporate speech directly pertaining to business, but restrict speech of a political nature. Yet the commercial speech doctrine gives less protection to commercial speech than to political speech.

Next, the Court points out that the legislature is prevented from "dictating the subjects about which persons may speak and the speakers who may address a public issue."[56] Hence the government cannot restrict corporations to discuss only their business.[57] This traditional explication of First Amendment doctrine indicates that the Court might take a dim view of Massachusetts efforts in the future to impose disclosure requirements on the speech in question, as distinguished from the flat ban in question in the case.

The Court considered two possible justifications for the ban on corporate speech. One was the alleged overwhelming influence and power of the corporations. The Court distinguished referenda on issues from campaigns for candidates. Hence it was able to distinguish statutes such as the Federal Corrupt Practices Act that banned certain corporate contributions to political candidates.[58] The Court argued that contributions to corporate-sponsored candidates created the possibility of corruption of elected officials through the "creation of political debts."[59]

Further, the Court asserted that there had been no proof that the speech of corporations in Massachusetts had been "overwhelming" in its influence.[60] Moreover, the Court emphasized that the Constitution "protects expression which is eloquent no less than that which is unconvincing."[61] The Court cited at this point *Miami Herald Publishing Co. v. Tornillo*, where it held that the First Amendment "prohibits a State from requiring a newspaper to make space available at no cost for a reply from a candidate whom the newspaper has criticized."[62]

Appellee argued that the state had an interest in protecting the rights of corporate shareholders who might disagree with the positions of the corporate management.[63]

The Court questioned this supposed purpose because of the over inclusiveness and under inclusiveness of the statute.[64] That is, it permitted corporations, for example, to spend funds on speaking out against legislation as distinguished from **referendum**. This suggested that the state was interested in chilling speech on certain topics, not in protecting shareholders. Also, it prohibited corporate action on the latter even if all of the shareholders supported it. But in the final analysis, the Court argued that "shareholders may decide, through the procedures of corporate democracy, whether their corporation should engage in debate on public issues."[65] Further, shareholders have the judicial remedy of a derivative action to challenge improper corporate expenditures. The Court responded to Justice Byron White, dissenting, who argued that union members in closed or agency-shops may not be compelled to make union dues payments for political purposes with which they disagreed. Justice Powell emphasized that "no shareholder has been 'compelled' to contribute anything . . . [T]he shareholder invests in a corporation of his own volition and is free to withdraw his investment at any time and for any reason."[66] Therefore, even assuming that protection of shareholders is a "compelling" interest,[67] the Court found no "substantially relevant correlation between the government interest asserted and the State's effort" to ban the speech.[68]

Although Justice Powell does not discuss the difference between definitions of commercial and political, the difficulty of the distinction in the corporate setting is evident in this case. It is inherently incoherent to distinguish protection of external corporate political speech from internal proxy commercial speech. The corporations argued for the inadvisability of a graduated income for individuals. They believed that the adoption of the tax would "materially affect their business in a variety of ways,"[69] such as "discouraging highly qualified executives . . . from settling . . . in Massachusetts . . . and tending to shrink the disposable income of individuals available for the purchase of the consumer products manufactured by at least one of the plaintiff corporations."[70]

Now assume an internal corporate struggle over the inadvisability or advisability of opposing the tax legislation. The SEC proxy regulations would apply if the corporations' securities involved met the definitions in the proxy statute and the regulations thereunder. The commission would take the position that proxy speech is commercial speech, and hence subject only to the limited protection of the four-prong *Central Hudson* case. That protection is diluted by the *Zauderer* doctrine that liberally permits mandatory disclosure regulation of commercial speech by the government.[71] In this example the speech, when external, is political, but is transmogrified to commercial when internal proxy speech.

Naturally government power over internal proxy speech means government influence over ultimate external corporate speech. If the latter, as in the *Bellotti* case, is fully protected, it appears fairly obvious that the SEC must be appropriately limited when attempting to interfere with that speech in the proxy realm.

The role of minority shareholders must be considered. Perhaps SEC censorship and regulation of proxy speech is justified as a method of protecting their interests. As a distinguished economist has argued, "[a]s owners, dissident shareholders possess the right to present these views together with management's views."[72]

Justice Powell answered that contention. He pointed out that shareholders govern the corporation and are the ultimate arbiters of corporate speech and conduct. In short, the majority controls. In addition, minority shareholders have resource to derivative suits. Also, minority shareholders have greater freedom to move in and out of the corporation than does the citizen who dissents from political policy of a given state and wants to move out. The lazy or imperfect management are subject to the disciplining threat of hostile takeovers.

Consider a member of a congressional district who votes against the incumbent congresswoman. Should she have the right to compel the member of Congress to insert the views of the minority, who voted against her, in all of her important speeches? Should an impartial government arbiter be established to allocate scarce space in her speeches to minority views or views of the weak and uninfluential? This would involve a drastic reordering of constitutional policy. Some elements of that concern, it is true, are evident in the various corrupt practices acts that attempt to lessen the power of rich and powerful constituents. But a constitutional doctrine that went much further along the lines suggested by proxy regulation would constitute an entirely different structure. In the realm of the publicly held corporation the dangers of majority coercion are less than in the political world. Shareholders can sell out, can diversify their portfolios, and can pick and choose their investments. It does appear that the free market in securities is a stronger buffer for minorities than for their equivalents in the world of politics.

On March 27, 1990, the Court handed down an opinion that seemed to undermine the principles of the *Bellotti* opinion.[73] The Court by a 6-to-3 opinion upheld a Michigan statute that prohibited corporations, excluding media corporations, from using general treasury funds for supporting, by way of newspaper advertisement or otherwise, candidates for state elections. PAC contributions were permitted by the statute.

Appellee Michigan State Chamber of Commerce, a nonprofit corporation, desired to place a newspaper advertisement in support of a particular candidate for state office. It brought suit for relief against the statute on First Amendment grounds.[74]

The Court (Justice Thurgood Marshall writing the opinion) concluded that the statute was supported by a compelling state interest. That interest was the prevention of corruption or the appearance of corruption by the use of vast corporate wealth. That evil is compounded by the fact that corporations receive the benefit of special state law, such as limited liability, and have "little or no correlation to the public's support for the corporation's political ideas."[75]

The Court felt that the statute was "sufficiently narrowly tailored to achieve its goal" because it is exactly drafted to achieve its object while at the same time allowing for corporate political activity through the use of PACs. The latter structure permits individual contributors to give to a group whose ideas they share. On the other hand a corporation that makes political expenditures coerces minority shareholders who do not share the political viewpoint of management.[76]

The decision against the Chamber's advertisement would not penalize politically oriented not-for-profit corporations. The Chamber was a business entity. Its members would be like shareholders of a profit corporation: even if they dissent from the political message they will be reluctant to leave because of the economic incentives inducing them to join in the first place.[77]

The Michigan statute is not "under inclusive" because it does not apply to the expenditures for political speech of unincorporated labor unions. Business corporations have a special ability to amass great wealth. Also, union members can forgo contribution to union political activities; stockholders cannot do this in corporations.[78]

Finally, the Court concluded that the statute did not violate the Equal Protection Clause of the Fourteenth Amendment, despite its exclusion of media corporations. The media's crucial role in distributing news and opinions would thereby be preserved.[79]

Justice Antonin Scalia delivered a stinging dissent.[80] He called it an "Orwellian announcement."[81] He pointed out that other groups and individuals are given state advantages ranging from tax breaks to cash subsidies. He argued that it is basic that the state cannot condition such favors on loss of the First Amendment protection.

The other reason for restricting corporate speech on candidates was that corporations are wealthy. Scalia pointed out that this will also bar wealthy individuals from speech, something the Court did not concede it was doing.[82]

He recognized that prior cases conceded that corporate political contributions to candidates could be corrupting.[83] He argued that campaign expenditures were a different matter. He quoted *Buckley v. Valeo* to the effect that independent advocacy "may well provide little assistance to the candidates' campaign and indeed may prove counterproductive."[84] That is, candidates may suffer public disfavor from corporate endorsements. He argued that corporate speech on candidates will be effective only if the public finds it true.[85]

The Court argued that corporate wealth has no bearing on the public support for the ideas it espouses. Justice Scalia countered that this constitutes government interference in the relative power of different advocates. This, he submitted, is foreign to First Amendment doctrine, which leaves it to the marketplace of ideas rather than using government to chill more powerful voices.[86] Scalia further argued that it is impossible to find any so-called neutral principle that distinguishes too much power from just enough power.[87]

Justice Brennan in his concurrence argued that the statute protects minority shareholders. Scalia pointed out that the statute permitted corporate expenditures for political positions not directed at a particular candidate. This distinguished it, in the Court's opinion, from the *Bellotti* statute, which banned corporate general political speech.[88] Shareholders were not uniformly protected, therefore, by the Michigan statute. The Michigan statute seemed to be designed solely to protect political candidates.[89]

Justice Scalia argued that shareholders, when they become members, know that the majority of shareholders or management may make new or different business decisions. This may include investment in South Africa or operation of an abortion clinic. That, as he put it, is the "deal."[90] The shareholder can always sell out if he disagrees.[91] Further, the Brennan concern should extend to dissenting members of groups like the American Civil Liberties Union, not just corporations that are run for profit.[92]

Next, Scalia pointed out that government restrictions on political speech must be "narrowly tailored to serve a compelling governmental interest."[93] He pointed out that all corporations, not just wealthy entities, were covered.[94]

Scalia then addressed the exemption for media corporations. They are exempted because of their crucial role in educating the public. Justice Scalia maintained that giant wealthy media corporations, given the Court concern with the power of corporate wealth, would be more likely to corrupt the political dialogue than business corporations who usually concentrate on economic transactions.[95] Scalia also argued that the majority decision might permit statutes that banned media corporations, on the theory that they too were potentially corrupting due to their amassed wealth.[96]

Finally, Scalia eloquently argued that the First Amendment was premised on the philosophy that the government cannot be trusted to set the parameters of fair debate.[97] He emphasized that the First Amendment was not designed to chill the discrimination of ideas with little public support because of the origin of the ideas. Further, he argued that to eliminate the opinion of powerful corporations with great economic interest in Michigan would impoverish the debate.[98] Also, he asserted that the decision gave unincorporated unions an advantage over large employers.[99]

Justice Anthony Kennedy also wrote a dissenting opinion in which Scalia joined. He argued that the Court decision reduces the amount and diversity of expression and the size of the audience. This follows because in modern society all effective communication requires the payment of money.[100]

This Court opinion undermines the *Bellotti* rationale. By emphasizing the corrupting nature of corporate expenditures for candidates, and legitimating governmental leveling of the political playing field, the court seemed to be moving toward greater and greater restriction on corporate speech. Ironically, Justice Scalia, who wrote the opinion in the *Board of Trustees of the State University of New York* case, narrowing protection of commercial speech, defends corporate political speech in this opinion. Since the Court was restricting corporate political speech, it appeared to be logically easier, in the future, for the Court to further lessen the protection afforded to commercial speech and speech regulated by the SEC. Also ironically, Justice Brennan, who has written stirring defenses of First Amendment protection of commercial speech, concurred in the *Austin* decision.

Rule 14a-8: Brigading of Commercial and Political

Rule 14a-8 of the commission requires the corporation to carry at its cost certain messages of dissident shareholders that it opposes. These proposals are not necessarily limited to commercial issues, but may include political and social messages such as proposals to limit investment in South Africa and resolutions to cease the sale of napalm because of use in the Vietnam War.[101]

In the *Pacific Gas & Electric Co. v. Public Utility Commission* case[102] the Court held that California could not compel the utility to transmit messages of a consumer group with which it disagreed. The plurality opinion of Justice Powell argued that this would burden the utility's expression by chilling its views to avoid disseminating hostile views, and would interfere with editorial judgment.[103]

Justice Stevens, dissenting, cautioned the plurality that the California rule was similar to SEC Rule 14a-8, which "[p]resumably the plurality does not doubt the constitutionality of.[104] The Justice also stated that "[t]his regulation [14a-8] cannot be justified on the basis of the commercial character of the communication, because the Rule can and has been used to propagate purely political proposals."[105] In this passage the justice, while supporting the regulation, inadvertently raises questions about the inherent inability to distinguish the commercial in proxy regulation from the noncommercial.

The plurality opinion, in response, argued that the SEC Rule 14a-8 "allocates shareholder property between management and certain groups of shareholders. Management has no interest in corporate property except such interest as derives from the shareholders; therefore, regulations that limit management's ability to exclude some shareholders' views from corporate communications do not infringe corporate First Amendment rights."[106]

This approach directly conflicts with Justice Powell's earlier views in *Bellotti* on management power to disseminate views despite the objections of a minority shareholder group. It is consistent with the *Austin* opinion. It adopts the impartial arbiter-SEC view. It grants to the SEC power to allocate corporate property, that is, space on proxy statements, as between disparate groups within the corporate organization. It permits the government to impose costs on the majority to benefit a minority view. Thus, in dicta, it moves in the direction of government as impartial speech allocator, despite Court doctrine in the traditional political area (now diluted by *Austin*) that the government cannot equalize speech between contesting groups of unequal power because of the First Amendment. Such governmental power would create the substantial risk that government bureaucrats would distort the internal debate because of their bias, or ignorance, or self-interest, or inability to distinguish truth from falsehood, or from their desire to perpetuate their power. The plurality opinion further distinguishes corporate speech to the external world (the *Bellotti* case) from speech by the corporation "*to itself*."[107] The plurality asserts that such rules on internal governance do not "limit the range of information that the corporation may contribute to the public debate."[108]

The evolution of Rule 14a-8 demonstrates dramatically the difficulty of distinguishing the commercial from the political. In the late 1960s the rule permitted management to exclude a proposal if "it clearly appears that the proposal is submitted by the security holder . . . primarily for the purpose of promoting general economic, political, racial, religious, social or similar causes . . ."[109] In 1968 an organization called the Medical Committee for Human Rights requested Dow Chemical Corporation to include a resolution calling on the board of directors to cease the sale of napalm for use in the Vietnam War. The court, emphasizing the purpose of the proxy rules to facilitate shareholder democracy, doubted that exclusion of proposals motivated by general political concerns would be consistent with congressional intent.[110] The resolution was within the corporate power to implement, since the product was produced and sold by the corporation. Clearly, business and political motives or effects were involved. In the instant case napalm production was a small part of the company's business, but in that era able young executives might not work for a company that produced napalm for the war.

The rule was amended several times subsequent to the litigation.[111] In relevant part it now permits omission of a proposal that relates to operations accounting for less than 5 percent of assets and sales, "and which is not otherwise significantly related to the issuer's business."[112] The reference to social or political motivation as a disqualifier has been dropped. The "significantly related" escape clause may permit proposals of social or political concern that are within the corporate power to accomplish (e.g., cease investment in South Africa) to be included where moral or political issues are deemed material to shareholders under the securities laws, despite being immaterial on a purely financial basis.[113] Thus the rule now recognizes the frequent conflation of the moral, political, and economic in corporate governance.

Truth and Falsehood

We are by now familiar with the argument that government cannot easily distinguish truth from falsehood in the sphere of political speech.[114] A related, but still distinct concept is that government may be biased and may impose an orthodoxy when it can censor, based on the biases, conflicts of interest and stupidities of the government bureaucrat.

Commercial speech is arguably different in these respects. But surely this cannot be so in the area of proxy speech (or SEC speech in general). Corporate financial and business disclosure is a complex and controversial area. Experts continually debate the meaning and accuracy of modes of disclosure. A distinguished testament to such debate and complexity is the book by Homer Kripke in which he discusses a myriad of complex accounting disclosures and financial disputes among SEC experts.[115] One example he discusses was the decades-long disastrous fixation of the commission on so-called hard, or historical, data versus so-called soft, or futuristic, data. Outside experts long argued, in vain, that the SEC chilling of corporate budget and earnings forecasts deprived investors of the most significant information they would need. Kripke remarks, "SEC thinking does change, but slowly."[116] Ultimately the commission liberalized its rules on projections, but not until decades had elapsed under the dominion of the old doctrine.

A prior SEC chairman, the late William J. Casey, once said while chairman: "I am even more unhappy with the content of the contemporary prospectus . . . The disclosure system exists to help investors. Yet as now administered it does so in a strange way by blocking out as obscene—utterly devoid of any redeeming social value—any reference to the matters in which investors are most keenly interested. Projections of future earnings are one example."[117]

The official commission note to SEC antifraud proxy Rule 14a-9 formerly included as samples of potentially misleading statements "predictions as to specific future . . . earnings, or dividends." The prohibition was dropped in July 1979, after the commission was finally convinced of the value of future projections.[118] Until then someone could go to jail for violating that note, which encompassed the commission's belief in the value of hard historical data, as against predictions.

Violations of proxy and other disclosure rules are governed by the commission and court's notions of "materiality."[119] Every fledgling corporate attorney already understands the slippery and indefinable nature of the term. It is fact intensive, and reasonable women and men can and often do disagree about its meaning in a given case or in the abstract. As the Court once put it, the determination of materiality "requires delicate assessments of the inferences a 'reasonable shareholder' would draw from a given set of facts and the significance of those inferences to him."[120] As a distinguished federal district court judge once said, "since no one knows what moves the mythical 'average prudent investor,' it comes down to a question of judgment."[121]

SEC Bias

The commission is hardly free of bias. The interest theory of regulation suggests that interest groups, such as attorneys or investment bankers, may have a powerful influence on the agency. As Henry G. Manne, Dean Emeritus of George Mason

School of Law, has stated, since the development of this theory of regulation, scholars "have been well advised . . . to ask who would be benefitted most by the rule."[122]

The SEC is run by attorneys. The influence of attorneys may be an institutional bias toward more, rather than less, regulation. An attorney staffer who continually resists new regulations (or new enforcement actions) may lose influence within the agency and with the media. An activist attorney, ironically, by securing a great reputation as a regulator, increases his or her market worth when leaving the agency for private practice. This is not based on personal sinister motive, but is the result of impersonal institutional structure and sincere belief in the rightness of regulation and enforcement.

Also, government agencies, as George Benston has argued, "prefer to minimize risk" and "tend to require conservative, uniform procedures that are likely to result in the publication of misleading financial statements."[123] They will tend to demand accounting principles that understate income, future growth and overemphasize contingent liberties. The SEC emphasis on hard historic data, mentioned above, is an example of such bias.

These rather obvious potential distortions of truth, high possibilities of error, biases, conflicts of interest, and drive for power serve to demonstrate that the commission is not some impartial arbiter that can avoid one of the root dangers of government censorship and regulation of speech, to wit, bureaucratically biased and self-interested imposition of orthodoxy.

Fragility or Robustness of Proxy Speech

The next issue turns on the fragility or robustness of the supply of proxy speech in the absence of regulation. The Supreme Court, and scholars in law and economics, such as Richard A. Posner, have used the notion of robustness to justify greater regulation of commercial speech.[124] If proxy speech is indeed fragile (i.e., underproduced absent regulation), it is ironically in the same category as political speech, if we follow the Posner thinking on fragility and robustness. That is, it should be fully protected by the First Amendment to bring greater disclosure.[125] The question is whether proxy speech is indeed fragile. There is good evidence that corporations published ample financial disclosure before passage of the securities legislation in 1933 and 1934.[126] We suspect such corporate voluntary disclosure of financial information in the 1920s provided ample alternative or substitute disclosure in lieu of proxy disclosure of matters taken up at meetings of shareholders.

George J. Benston has provided a theoretical argument for why corporations would voluntarily provide an adequate supply of financial information.[127] He points out that, first, such disclosure assists prospective shareholders and lenders of funds. This will tend to make them pay more for their investment because it is cheaper for the corporation to provide the information than for them to get it on their own.

Second, voluntary supplying of independent CPA-audited reports will reassure such investors, who will then pay more for their investments. Third, provision of the information on a continuous basis signals to investors that the corporation has nothing to hide. This makes potential investors more likely to invest. Benston also provides data for voluntary corporate disclosure of financial information preceding the federal securities acts that is quite impressive in its demonstration of the extent of such voluntary disclosure.

The Benston argument demonstrates that proxy information (as well as all corporate information) may possess a certain real robustness of supply. But, contrary to the Supreme Court argument and the Posner theory, this is an argument against the need for government mandatory disclosure. Because robustness (as Benston demonstrates) leads to an efficient supply of valid information without SEC regulation, and SEC regulation may produce more information than investors need, the argument for mandatory disclosure for robust corporate proxy speech, based on its robustness, is weak.

Many scholars dispute the Benston mode of analysis. They assert that corporations will not voluntarily produce adequate disclosure.[128] If they are correct, that is an argument for the fragility of SEC speech. In the political realm supposed fragility of speech is an argument for the full protection of the First Amendment. That same argument applies to supposedly fragile SEC speech, unless we can agree that, unlike political speech, the government can operate as a safe, unbiased, accurate arbiter of truthful speech.

But that in part turns on the comparative advantage of government to distinguish truth from falsity as compared with the free market. On that issue, as we have already seen, the case for the SEC is hardly free from substantial doubt.

The fragility argument is made to support the need for a First Amendment in the case of political speech. But if we concede that, because of externalities and free-rider effects, not enough political speech is produced, that is an argument for mandatory disclosure of political speech, not merely a passive First Amendment approach. The First Amendment ban against government censorship will not produce nearly as much political speech as a system of mandatory disclosure for fragile political speech. Mandatory disclosure in the case of traditional political speech could be a disaster, but the case for it is ironically stronger than for robust proxy speech (or any speech regulated by the SEC), so long as we make the traditional assumption that the supply of political speech is fragile because of lack of sufficient definition of property rights in it.

Concluding Remarks on Proxy Speech

It is argued that corporate management is too strong in relation to shareholders. Hence proxy restraint of management speech is necessary for the protection of small investors. Until the *Austin* case, this kind of argument had been rejected in the political realms.[129] Surely an incumbent U.S. Senator is more powerful than the ordinary citizen. His or her access to the media is far greater. Both enjoy the same formal freedom, however, under the First Amendment. Shall we limit the senator's speech? Certainly the New York Times corporation is more powerful than the ordinary citizen. Both, however, enjoy the same First Amendment rights to publish on matters of public concern.[130] Shall we limit the corporation's speech? We believe that the costs of limiting free speech by some means test related to power and wealth are, for the reasons expressed in the dissents of Justices Scalia and Kennedy, in the *Austin* Case, too great.

There are considerable arguments against this approach in the realms of art and politics. The dangers of government bias and self-interest outweigh the arguments from disparity of power and influence. Certainly the courts (even after *Austin*) cannot force newspapers and publishers of books to carry the views of individuals, although they often do so by way of letters to the editor and op-ed pages. There is no reason to establish a different policy for proxy material. Indeed, the escape hatches and alternatives for the small shareholder are far greater than in the world of politics. The shareholder can always sell out when the stock price declines. The shareholder can diversify his portfolio and, hence, avoid catastrophic loss. The shareholder can profit from hostile takeovers in which lazy or inefficient incumbent managements are replaced in transactions in which target-company shareholders usually make enormous gains.[131] The free market in the corporate area thus provides safeguards to the small shareholder not present in politics; therefore, the arguments for limiting the free speech attributes of the powerful are less forceful in the corporate realm than the political.

The Supreme Court, in a series of opinions, has ruled that the First Amendment prohibits Congress from limiting political expenditures by candidates or independent groups.[132] That position was qualified by the *Austin* case. Contributions to political candidates can be limited because of the Court's conclusion that there is a potential for corruption in that area.[133] Until the *Austin* case, discussed above, the Supreme Court had recognized that money and speech in modern society are inextricably related. Hence speech that is self-interested or that is disseminated by the use of financial power is not, therefore, stripped of First Amendment protection.

The Court has ruled that newspapers cannot constitutionally be forced to publish the views of individuals or groups that disagree with its editorials.[134] Television networks, on the other hand, were subject to a fairness doctrine because the Court had concluded that they enjoy a special monopoly because of the peculiarities of television broadcast technology.[135] Publicly held corporations are not usually monopolies. Proxy regulation is designed to improve the corporate-political leverage of the shareholder. Yet First Amendment doctrine should not permit a kind of government-controlled egalitarian treatment of speech, including proxy speech.

Furthermore, the shareholder has greater ability and opportunity to opt out of the corporation than the ordinary citizen has to opt out of the polity.

Even after *Austin* the Court agrees that corporations have full First Amendment protection to discuss political issues (as distinguished from expending funds to support specific candidates).[136] The First Amendment is not limited to natural persons. Yet proxy regulation can interfere with corporate political speech. Assume that a corporation speaks out for a tax decrease on products. Full First Amendment protection would appear to be granted. However, an internal dispute over the advisability of such a program, if brought to the point of a proxy contest for differing slates of directors, would be subject to the full range of proxy regulation. That is a policy difference without a good reason.

The modern publicly held corporation is a significant intermediating structure in American life. Like the family, church, and other private groups, it stands between state and individual, preserves the individual from state domination, and enriches the life and diversity of individuals. It is an anomaly that First Amendment principles that apply to so-called political governance should not extend to the governance of the corporation.

Some have argued that the modern corporation should not be analogized to a mini-polity for purposes of justifying increased government regulation.[137] They have maintained that the modern publicly held corporation is a dynamic economic aggregate of interests that is subject to effective discipline from market forces. Hostile takeovers, and the threat of same, may frequently operate to weed out inefficient managements. Such forces operate more effectively than increased government surveillance and interference. This position, however, is not inconsistent with a call for full First Amendment protection of corporate and shareholder proxy speech. To the contrary, it is perfectly consistent with such a philosophy. There is no good reason why economic organizations should enjoy less free-speech protection than other groups.

The economic picture of the corporation emphasizes the powerful competitive forces that serve, even in the absence of free speech, to protect the shareholder. The free markets for control (i.e., hostile takeovers) serve to protect the shareholder from lazy or incompetent managers.[138] As previously stated, shareholders can always sell out and leave a stupid or incompetent management. Shareholders, using modern portfolio theory, can diversify their holdings and avoid catastrophically large investment in one corporation. None of these escape valves are present in state or federal governmental politics. Since shareholders have the escape valves of the free market in shares, the dangers that corporate managements, in proxy communications, may engage in false speech are less threatening than the danger that politicians may lie to their constituents. Yet we protect the politician's speech and regulate the corporate manager's speech. The free market works by way of free individuals seeking out new information and reacting to new demands of consumers and competitors. The free market is basically a process of information-gathering and disseminating. As new events occur, entrepreneurs respond. They seek out new demands and wants of the consumer. They attempt to perceive demands and wants of which the consumer is, as yet, only dimly aware. It is for this reason that the free market is superior to command economies.[139] The government bureaucrat in the socialist state cannot effectively grasp the complexities of society. Thousands of individual businessmen, however, each responding to needs and wants in various communities, can more effectively seek out and transmit information than the government bureaucrat. Price is the key mechanism by which the free-market entrepreneur detects changes in demand and supply. Essential to this, as in the case of the polity, is a free market in speech. Free speech, in business and within the corporation, is essential for the effective functioning of the free market. Proxy speech is part of that process. Shareholders can communicate their demands and wants to management and fellow shareholders. Corporate management is involved in the process. The government censor (i.e., the SEC) is ill-equipped to fulfill that role for much the same reasons as a ministry of culture should not censor novels, and a ministry of politics should not censor politicians.

The constitutional scope of the First Amendment includes a protection of the right of free association.[140] The government cannot prevent a free people from joining private organizations.[141] Neither can the government enjoin the speech people use in connection with their right of free association.[142] It is obvious that the government could not censor the in-house communications of the Democratic or Republican parties. The only distinction, in the case of the corporation, is that it is a commercial organization. However, speech cannot be distinguished based on the presence or lack of economic motive. That would eliminate most speech from First Amendment coverage. Likewise, if one eliminates the right of association from economically interested groups, one would eliminate most groups, with the possible exception of the purest of religious groups.

Hostile Takeover Speech

The Williams Act amendments to the Securities Exchange Act of 1934 require specified disclosure by hostile bidders for the stock of target corporations.[143] The targets' responses are similarly controlled by rules of mandatory disclosure.[144] As in the case of proxy disclosure and the balance of SEC-regulated speech, the government regulation is controlled by the four-prong *Central Hudson* test, and the modification thereof contained in the *Zauderer* and *State University of New York* cases. But as in the case of proxy speech and, again, all SEC-regulated speech, the similarity between traditionally defined commercial speech, and takeover speech is strained. The SEC-regulated takeover speech cannot be rationally distinguished from so-called political speech.

The hostile takeover phenomenon is an alternative method to proxy con tests for the acquisition of control over the target corporation.[145] It replaced the proxy contest route in the 1980s because it proved a much more potent weapon in the hands of the rivals for control. The development of this technique has aroused a national debate.[146] Proponents argue that hostile takeovers discipline indifferent or incompetent incumbent managements, or create synergy benefits in which costs drop as a result of the felicitous combination of different businesses. Opponents of the merger movement argue that it creates unhealthy preoccupation with the short run, makes for a non-competitive economy, displaces competent managements, harms the local communities, and creates unemployment. These are but some of the arguments advanced.[147]

Concern for the target shareholder and for adequate disclosure to them led originally to the Williams Act amendments to the 1934 Act. That Act, as we have indicated, created mandatory disclosure authority for the commission. It also created some substantive interference with the processes of bidders, to protect target shareholders. For example, bidders were prohibited from paying more to selected target shareholders than to others. States have entered the picture. They have created various forms of barriers to hostile takeovers. For example, one form forbids mergers for several years after the bid between target and bidder.[148] Some forms deprive the bidder of voting rights in the target stock acquired unless a disinterested majority of target shareholders approve of the transaction.[149] Some forms forbid the clean-up merger after the bid unless the cash-out merger is made at a specified fair price.[150]

Let us consider the mandatory speech regulation. The arguments made in the proxy section above apply in the case of takeover speech regulation. First, the speech pertains directly to a battle for control. As such, it is speech about corporate governance. Therefore, it is far removed from the traditional advertisement of a product or a service. Second, as in the case of proxy speech, it is impossible to successfully distinguish this speech from all of the kinds of political cum economic speech (e.g., speech about taxes, price supports, and savings and loan policy) that are traditionally fully protected by the First Amendment. Indeed, the takeover movement has been described as one of the major political-economic issues confronting the nation. Moreover, each individual takeover battle creates a potentially significant economic impact on the local community, labor, and suppliers, as well as possible artistic and musical effects on the local culture, depending on the charitable contributions policies of the target and bidder corporations. Bidder and target speech frequently invoke these artistic cum economic, cum social issues. Frequently target managements, in the midst of the battle, will run to Congress or the state legislature and engage in lobbying campaigns to seek legislative support for their battle. The *Bellotti* case (even after the *Austin* case) protects lobbying speech; it should certainly protect takeover speech. Indeed, on traditional grounds, the *Bellotti* case is persuasive. The *Bellotti* case applies to external speech of the corporation. Certainly the takeover speech of the bidder is external; it is directed at the shareholders of the target corporation. Third, the disclosure issues are incredibly complex, elusive, subjective, and partisan, in the sense that competing bidders and target management differ as to the proper disclosure and interpretation. Therefore, it is difficult for government to adequately distinguish truth from falsehood. Fourth, bidders certainly have economic incentives to quickly and adequately disclose their bidding terms, to prevail against competing bidders.

Formal takeover speech should be subject to the full protection of the First Amendment, rather than limited commercial speech protection. State and federal interference with internal corporate governance procedures, to "protect" the target shareholder, should be subject to First Amendment freedom of association scrutiny. For example, some states have prohibited clean-up, or second-stage, mergers for a period of years after the bidder acquires a specified amount of the target corporation stock.[151] Target shareholders may or may not be able to opt out of such restrictions, depending on the nature of the state statute. That restriction constitutes an interference with the internal governance of the target corporation. The regulation, as noted above in the proxy setting, can escape First Amendment scrutiny only if the court concludes that the corporation serves a non-expressive purpose, and hence is not protected by the First Amendment.

Lawrence Tribe has observed that "[c]ritics of the American Constitution as an unacceptably individualistic document . . . will find at least a limited answer in the 'freedom of association' that the Supreme Court has repeatedly described as among the preferred rights derived by implication from the First Amendment's guarantees of speech, press, petition, and assembly."[152] As Tribe points out,[153] Alexis de Tocqueville asserted that the "most natural privilege of man, next to the right of acting for himself, is that of combining his exertions with those of his fellow creatures and of acting in common with them."[154]

Tribe asserts that the cases demonstrate that the government may not interfere in the internal structure of an association, under the First and Fourteenth Amendments, for relatively non-significant reasons.[155] Even when the government interference is supported by an important goal,[156] the government must still demonstrate that a significant *set back* to the goal would result absent the contested interference,[157] and lesser interference would suffice.[158] Further, the right of association includes the right not to associate with others.[159]

These principles should have a direct bearing on government interference in corporate governance provisions designed to chill, or facilitate, changes in control. Again, the only argument against application of these principles is the proposition (discussed above) that organizations formed for purposes of economic gain fall outside their scope.

In the case of *TW Services, Inc. v. SWT Acquisition Corporation*[160] the Delaware Court of Chancery interfered in the internal governance of a corporation against the wishes of a majority of shareholders. SWT sought a preliminary injunction requiring TW to cancel out (redeem) its "poison pill" defense against the hostile takeover effort of SWT. SWT had made a tender offer at 29 dollars a share for all of the shares of TW. Some 88 percent of TW's common stock had accepted the tender. SWT could not close the purchase unless the target management redeemed the "poison pill." The "poison pill" included a flip-in feature that permitted TW shareholders other than SWT to buy additional TW common stock at half price. It also contained a flip-over provision allowing TW shareholders to acquire shares of the bidder at half price in the event the bidder entered into a merger with the target. These provisions would result in a chilling punitive dilution of the target equity at the expense of the bidder.

The issue involved a conflict between the desires of a great majority of the shareholders of the target corporation and the judgment of the management. The latter argued that the long-term interests of the corporation mandated their refusal to permit the takeover to go forward. The 88 percent majority had voted with purses and wallets to go for immediate gain. The management had, in a sense, taken up the cause of future shareholders of the target (similar to the generational issues of political government, the living versus the yet unborn) as well as current shareholders who held for future years. Management also had perhaps taken up the cause, as it saw it, of the future interests of community and labor and suppliers of the corporation.

The Court of Chancery refused to enter an injunction against the target management. The Chancellor asserted that "[q]uestions of this type call upon one to ask, what is our model of corporate governance? 'Shareholder democracy' is an appealing phrase, and the notion of shareholders as the ultimate voting constituency of the board has obvious pertinence, but that phrase would not constitute the only element in a well-articulated model. While corporate democracy is a pertinent concept, "a corporation is not a New England town meeting; directors, not shareholders have responsibilities to manage . . . In all events, resolution of these questions . . . seem inescapably to involve normative questions."[161]

However, the judge admitted that directors should "affirmatively respond" when a "predominating proportion of shares sought a fundamental structural change."[162] He did not in this case, at this juncture, agree that the directors must rescind the poison pill because the bidder also had requested a merger agreement that, under state law, as he saw it, required, even in the case where more than 80 percent of the shareholders wanted to accept the tender offer, directorial initiative and approval.[163]

The Court, as a corollary to the right to associate for lawful ends, has recognized the negative or flipside of the issue. It has endorsed the right not to associate with others in the association. This right must, perforce, include the power of members to end the association. The Delaware court thwarted that right.

State law everywhere grants, over a wide array of circumstances, shareholders the power to veto and sometimes the power to initiate major structural changes. Moreover, state law is largely a kind of enabling clause, pursuant to which shareholders may freely contract among themselves as to the configuration of the corporate governance procedures they desire.[164] The Delaware court appeared to move in a spirit contrary to this structure.

Perhaps the most appropriate method to analyze the Delaware case is in terms of the First Amendment right of free association. Under this philosophical approach the Delaware court appears to have permitted management to interfere with the First Amendment right of the shareholders to determine when and under what circumstances they may terminate the association. The court accomplished that end by denying the right of a majority of shareholders to end the association by selling their stock to the bidder.

Prospectus Speech

In the preceding section we considered proxy and hostile takeover speech. The arguments pertaining to externalities, or fragility of speech, robustness, and ability to distinguish truth from falsity, and bias of the agency apply with equal measure to all SEC regulated speech and need not be repeated. In this section, we will focus on the mandatory disclosure system applied to the sale of securities.

The Securities Act of 1933 regulates the corporate offer and sale of securities.[165] In that Act, Congress established a mandatory system of disclosure. The so-called Truth in Securities Disclosure Act, and regulations passed under authority of the Act, requires corporations to provide specified "news" to potential purchasers of securities. The material must be pre-filed with the SEC before sales may be made.[166] The commission can, by administrative action or with the "assistance" of court injunctive action, engage in prior restraint of prohibited corporate disclosure.[167] The U.S. government can criminally prosecute violators of the disclosure law and regulations.

Section 5(c) of the Act prohibits any offer of a security by mails or in interstate commerce unless a registration statement containing prescribed information has been filed with the commission. Section 5(b)(1) prohibits the use of general written literature for offerings of securities unless in the form of a specified document called a prospectus. There are limited exceptions for written documents called tombstone advertisements and post-effective documents preceded by a statutory prospectus.[168] The contents of the registration statements are specified in complex regulations of the commission, which have evolved over the years.

The justification for this regulation of speech is the commercial speech doctrine. Modern constitutional doctrine, although it gives some protection to that speech, still permits prior restraint of corporate prospectuses and registration statements that offer securities for sale. It also permits criminal prosecution for false or misleading statements. As we have seen, commercial speech has been defined by the Court as advertisements for the sale of services or products.

Corporations sell products or services. The sale of shares of common stock, however, is not the sale of a corporate service or product, since a share of common stock is an ownership interest in an organization. It carries with it certain rights to vote for the election of directors. It represents an interest in a future flow of corporate earnings. The latter carries a present value that is reflected in trading data on the exchanges or the organized over-the-counter markets. The purchase of stock reflects the buyer's judgment that the economic organization, called a corporation, will earn a return that is better than that derived from alternative uses of his cash. The stock purchaser, in the ordinary course of life, also becomes a member of other kinds of organizations. He may join the Democratic Party, a trade union, an environmental group, a trade association, or the American Bar Association, if a lawyer. The government may not censor the published speech of these non-stock corporate entities. It may, however, censor the speech of corporations when that speech promotes the sale of stock.

A share of common stock is an interest in an organization. The organization is called a corporation and is operated for profit purposes. The stock corporation may manufacture steel, sell books or newspapers, or distribute information in the form of computer software. Membership in a publicly held corporation should rest on the same constitutional plateau as membership in other organizations. Consider the American Bar Association. That organization is established and run for the betterment of attorneys. The government could not constitutionally censor the public statements of that group (at least so long as membership is voluntary and not compelled by statute) about, let us say, the need to eliminate tax legislation that harms the membership. More particularly, the government could not censor for content promotional information that it presents to prospective new members. We see no difference between the latter transaction and the sale of common stock in the corporation. Likewise, the government could neither censor promotional public information disseminated by the B'nai B'rith Anti-Defamation League to prospective new members nor the Catholic Church, the Democratic Party, or a local free-trade association.

It will be argued that a stock corporation is primarily an economic entity. Indeed, by law, it must be run with the goal of making, if at all possible, a profit for its shareholders. Hence some will assert that constitutional doctrine can distinguish between that entity and most other associations in the United. States.[169] By now it must be clear that the argument will not sustain rigorous analysis. It is difficult enough to make a credible argument for the distinction between the bare-bones advertisement of a good or service and fully protected speech. The Court, in the case of an advertisement describing the price of prescription drugs, stated that commercial speech is protected to facilitate intelligent private economic decisions and "[t]o this end, the free flow of commercial information is indispensible."[170] That function of commercial speech is more important to most people than most political campaign rhetoric. It is impossible to distinguish in a principled manner between corporations run for economic purposes and all other groups. Indeed, even political parties, such as the Republican and Democratic parties, are organized to further the economic interests of members. The same is true for labor unions. It is true that a stock corporation is operated with the aim of making a cash profit for shareholders in the form of dividends and capital gains. Yet there is a difference from, let us say, the local free-trade association without much meaning. A remarkably huge number of organizations, associations, and groupings in the United States are created and operated to further the narrow economic interests of their members. They attempt to attract membership by publication in the print and television media. If government could censor their books and speeches and other publications, the free-speech process would be severely impaired.

Ironically, modern corporate law reformers seek to emphasize the social and ethical nature of the corporation. For example, the drafts of the American Law Institute Code of Corporate Governance emphasize the ethical, as well as the economic, goals of the publicly held corporation.[171] Even many business leaders, as well as political leaders, are fond of demanding socially responsible action from the large corporation.[172] Modern state statutes all legitimate corporate charitable contributions. Modern courts are more willing than courts in prior years to permit corporate expenditures that do not necessarily maximize the bottom line, as long as ethical and moral purposes are accomplished. In a case often cited in law school casebooks, *Shlensky v. Wrigley*, plaintiff charged the board of directors of the Chicago Cubs with failure to install night lights; hence the shareholders were damaged.[173] The court upheld the director's decision, which was based in part on the desire to preserve the neighborhood, a socially laudable purpose. This is one of many cases in which directors make decisions that are, to some extent, affected by social, as distinct from profit, purposes. This is not the place to debate the wisdom of such judicial doctrine. It is ironic that corporations are urged to moderate their passion for profits on the ground that they are properly more than economic entities, yet constitutional doctrine punishes them because they are deemed to be economic entities. This is not to argue a sort of estoppel assertion against such thinking or to suggest that we should grant First Amendment protection to corporations because they assert the ethical and political function of such organizations. But their concern reflects the inextricable ties, intermingling, and close association of economic organizations with political purposes and the reverse.

It is mistakenly asserted that the arguments made here apply to shares of common stock but not to debt instruments. The former are apparently ownership interests in an organization; the latter are merely indicia of a creditor-debtor relationship.

But that is to emphasize a difference that is not relevant to economic theory or appropriate constitutional doctrine. The public holder of a debt security acquires a series of rights in the corporate organization in the same sense as the holder of common stock. Obviously there are differences. Holders of debt securities receive fixed interest, not a residual share in profits. They usually have no vote for directors. They frequently have rights and powers expressed in the trust indenture, however, that, under certain circumstances (for example, when the debt is not timely paid), in effect grants them more power than the common shareholders. Debt holders have simply struck a different bargain in the organization than have the common share-holders. Some might describe them as more pessimistic investors than the common shareholders. They are, nevertheless, both investors (i.e., participants or members of the corporate organization). They are in a dramatically different relation to the organization than a purchaser of its products or services.

Investment Advice Speech: Licensing Professionals

In June 1985, the Supreme Court struck down a court injunction against Christopher Lowe and his investment newsletters under the Investment Advisers Act of 1940.[174] The SEC had obtained the injunction on the grounds that his publications were illegal because he was neither registered nor exempt from registration as an adviser under the Act. The case is considered here in order to focus on its impact on licensing of professionals.

Lowe was the president and principal shareholder of the Lowe Management Corporation. While registered as an investment adviser, he was convicted of misappropriating funds of clients, of failing to register with New York's Department of Law, of tampering with evidence to hide a fraud of a client, and of converting funds from a bank. The commission, under authority in the Advisers Act and after an appropriate hearing, revoked the license of the Lowe Management Corporation. About a year later the commission sought an injunction in the U.S. District Court for the Eastern District of New York restraining the further distribution of Lowe's investment advisory publications.

As the Supreme Court pointed out, a typical publication "contained general commentary about the securities and bullion markets, reviews of market indicators and investment strategies, and specific recommendations for buying, selling, or holding stock and bullion.[175] The subscribers numbered from 3,000 to 19,000. The Court stated that "it was advertised as a semi-monthly publication, but only eight issues were published in the 15 months after the entry of the 1981 order [revoking registration]."[176] The Court further stated that there was "no adverse evidence concerning the quality of the publications . . . no evidence that Lowe's criminal convictions were related to the publications; no evidence that Lowe had engaged in any trading activity in any securities that were the subject of advice . . . and no contention that any of the information published in the advisory services had been false or materially misleading."[177]

The Supreme Court had consented to hear the case in order to determine the constitutional issue of whether the injunction against publication and distribution of the market letters was forbidden by the First Amendment. However, Justice John Paul Stevens, joined by four of his colleagues, employed a statutory construction to avoid the constitutional issue.[178] He argued that the publications fit within the statutory exemption for *bona fide* publications, and hence were not covered by the Act.[179] Therefore, the commission had no authority to enjoin their publication. The statutory construction knocked out of the regulatory registration requirement box the entire industry of market letters. The Court argued that the legislative history showed that Congress, "sensitive to First Amendment concerns, wanted to make clear that it did not seek to regulate the press through the licensing of non-personalized publishing activities."[180]

Justice Byron White, joined by Chief Justice Warren E. Burger and Justice William Rehnquist, directly bit the constitutional bullet. They concluded that the publications were covered by the Act, but that banning their publication and distribution violated the First Amendment.[181] Justice White stated that the issue "involves a collision between the power of government to license and regulate those who would pursue a profession or vocation and the rights of freedom of speech."[182] He concluded that a person who "takes the affairs of a client personally in hand and purports to exercise judgment on behalf of the client in the light of the client's individual needs and circumstances is properly viewed as engaging in the practice of a profession . . . the professional's speech is *incidental* to the conduct of the profession. If the government enacts generally applicable licensing provisions limiting the class of persons who may practice the profession, it cannot be said to have enacted a limitation on freedom of speech or the press subject to First Amendment scrutiny. Where the personal nexus between professional and client does not exist . . . government regulation ceases to function as legitimate regulation of professional practice with only incidental impact on speech; it becomes regulation of speaking or publishing as such."[183]

Hence the justice concluded that the blanket prohibition of Lowe's investment advisory publications violated the First Amendment. Those publications were addressed to a general audience and no element of personal one-on-one communication or individualized advice was involved. To the extent the Act applied to individualized advice, it was constitutionally sound.

Justice White further asserted that it was not necessary for him to determine whether the newsletters contained fully protected speech or so-called commercial speech. Because the lower-court ban extended to "legitimate, disinterested advice"[184] as well as to "advice that is fraudulent, deceptive or manipulative,"[185] it went too far even if mere commercial speech was involved, since the First Amendment "permits restraints on commercial speech only when they are narrowly tailored to advance a legitimate governmental interest."[186] Although the goal was legitimate—prevention of fraud—less drastic means could have legitimately been used, such as application of anti-fraud concepts and use of reporting provisions. However, in this case, the government would prohibit any newsletter, no matter how accurate. Naturally, if the publications were not mere commercial speech, the ban must fall also. For those reasons Justice White and his colleagues joined in the result but not the opinion of the court majority. The refusal to enjoin seems eminently correct. The opinion of the Court majority, however, is a fairly strained attempt to avoid a constitutional issue.[187]

Regarding an issue avoided by the concurring opinion, it cannot be cogently argued that the Lowe newsletters constitute commercial speech. Commercial speech, in its most commonly accepted meaning, is a product or service advertisement. The Lowe investment letters were not advertisements of Lowe's market services; they were analyses of securities issued by corporations that had absolutely no connection to Lowe or his publications. If Lowe advertised his market letters, those ads would be commercial speech. The court majority emphasized, in the course of its statutory analysis, that "because we have squarely held that the expression of opinion about a commercial product such as a loudspeaker is protected by the First Amendment, *Bose Corp. v. Consumers Union of U.S., Inc.* . . . ., it is difficult to see why the expression of an opinion about a marketable security should not also be protected."[188] Unless we expand the notion of commercial speech to encompass self-interested speech, we do not have commercial speech in Lowe's investment newsletters. The broader interpretation would de-legitimate most of what usually is characterized as political speech.

The concurring opinion, and no doubt all of the other justices, would permit commission regulation of personalized advice. They would permit a complete ban against the rendering of personalized advice by an unregistered investment adviser. They would permit the commission to revoke the registration of an adviser, and thereupon obtain an injunction against his practice of personalized advice. They would permit a statute that required certain standards of education, prior record of honesty, as well as absence of a criminal record as a condition to practice of that profession. Absent such a posture, all state regulation of businesses and professions in the nature of licensing requirements would collapse.

The distinction hangs on dubious assumptions. An investment newsletter that is bought by 300,000 subscribers can do enormous financial harm. For example, if it adheres to a technical or chartist theory, much academic research proves that the advice is worthless.[189] Yet the government could not enjoin its publication. An adviser who personally counsels eighteen persons may be enjoined by a court from rendering such advice (no matter how truthful) if his registration has been denied or revoked.

The justices' definition of harm requires some clarification. Even if we grant that a newsletter may do less harm to one reader than personalized advice to one client, the lesser harm to a reader, multiplied by the total readership, may be greater than the total harm to the limited personal clientele of the adviser.

The justices and the lower courts defended the power of the government to regulate the professions. The states can prevent disbarred attorneys from giving personal advice to an individual. The states can prevent a licensed attorney from soliciting a client in a hospital ward, no matter how truthful his advice. Yet they cannot enjoin in advance the publishing efforts of disbarred attorneys and nonregistered investment advisers.[190] This position is maintained despite the power of the published work to injure its readers, or, indirectly, non-readers who are affected by the dissemination of such opinions.

The courts defend this anomaly on the grounds that professionals engage in a unique and confidential relationship with their clients or patients.[191] Hence they can do great damage to those who depend on them. Further, professionals *qua* professionals hold themselves out as rather special, knowledgeable, and faithful to clients. All of this is no doubt true. It also is true that popular books and newspapers have a powerful influence for good or evil that far transcends the personalized influence of a professional on his relatively few clients.

The distinction, to the extent that it is altruistic in motive, depends on a cynical view of the First Amendment. It appears to assert that where speech can have great influence, as in the case of professional advice, it is subject to greater government control than where it supposedly has less influence, for example, in the form of impersonal newsletters. In a sense, it also is a product of the same mentality that yawns at 50,000 traffic deaths each year, but focuses on the news of an individual murder or death where the victim can be identified and comprehended. Indeed, it is hardly clear that the licensing requirements for professionals are designed to protect the consumer. There is a considerable and compelling literature that demonstrates that licensing is designed to restrict the supply of more professionals, and thus increase the compensation of the groups already within the tent.[192]

The regulatory function in the investment adviser area cannot be considered without some mention being made of the dubious assumptions on which it rests. Modern discoveries of the efficient market and random-walk theories of stock prices have demonstrated that it is impossible, or at least difficult, for any single, gifted analyst to successfully select an individual stock. No one has the ability or power to predict the future earnings of an individual issuer, absent the illegal use of inside information.[193] Therefore, licensing restrictions that condition registration on educational requirements, or past criminal record, or experience have no provable connection with ability to select good investments. The process is largely an exercise in magic and faith. Hence the regulatory effort floats in midair, loose from any rational moorings.

Insider Trading, Scalping, and the Press

The Supreme Court, in its various commercial speech cases, has always endorsed the constitutional ability of the government to prosecute fraudulent statements after the fact of publication. A criminal insider trading case involving a former reporter of the Wall Street Journal aroused some doubts about this practice as it impacted the media. R. Foster Winans wrote the influential journal column titled Heard on the Street for the *Wall Street Journal*. He allegedly engaged in a scalping scheme in which he tipped confederates about future stories. The articles themselves were routine analyses based on publicly available data. They would then buy; the price of the stock would rise on publication of the column. Thereupon his confederates would sell out to the great profit of all of them. His stories were apparently factual and correct. It was the reputation of the column that drove the price of the subject stock up. This practice is commonly called "scalping." The government, in its criminal case, alleged that he had violated his fiduciary duty to his employer not to scalp; hence he had engaged in a federal fraud under Rule 10b-5 in connection with the buying and selling of stock.[194] The government argued that the defendants had unlawfully misappropriated information of the employer in connection with the purchase and sale of securities. The government also alleged violation of the wire and mail fraud statutes.[195] A conviction was obtained in June 1985.[196] The Supreme Court split 4–4 on the SEC Rule 10b-5 insider-trading misappropriation of information theory of the government.[197] It unanimously affirmed the conviction based on the wire and mail fraud counts.[198] In 1988 Congress passed a statute that approved future misappropriation actions under Rule 10b-5.[199]

The media groups bitterly complained that this prosecution would open the doors to government power to mandate the content of news stories.[200] Under the government's theory of action it is in effect instructing the newspaper that advance disclosure of Winan's financial interest (i.e., the scalping scheme) or, alternatively, a decision not to publish the column would cure the offense. That is, the government is mandating news disclosure, or its suppression. The implication is that the government has the power to specify the kinds of financial conflict of interest that a reporter must disclose when discussing the securities markets. The precedent would extend to political matters with a suitable drafted statute. Perhaps a television news anchor could be required to disclose his political biases before reporting on a sensitive news story or risk a government fraud suit.[201]

The issue can be broadened beyond the scalping problem. Assume that Senator X, in running for office, adopts a notoriously and nasty racist position. He advocates the view that blacks and Jews are inferior creatures who should be barred from the political process. It is unlikely that a statute that permitted a government fraud or criminal suit against him could withstand constitutional attack unless he defamed a particular person. If he supports a flat tax and omits qualifiers that would be material in an SEC fraud sense, no government criminal litigation against him could withstand First Amendment protection. When we consider SEC fraud or criminal litigation, however, their validity, or distinction from the senator's example above, must be sustained on some argument that commercial speech is different from political speech. At that point we are back to familiar ground.

Consider the *Wall Street Journal* reporter case.[202] He was commenting on the security of a corporation with respect to which he had no connection. In that respect he is similar to Lowe. The news and comment column he authored was part of a bona fide newspaper of general circulation. He was not offering individualized advice in a professional setting.

It should be eminently clear by now that, particularly in the SEC domain, the differences between so-called political speech and commercial speech are hardly self-evident. The *Wall Street Journal* case is a good reminder that there are many instances in which fraud prosecution will seriously impinge on traditional press media and their control over news content. A tremendous component of legitimate newspaper coverage pertains to economic news and the interests of special interest groups. Extension of SEC fraud and criminal doctrine to the *Wall Street Journal* reporter is dangerous, since it serves as the camel's nose under the tent for legislation regulating considerable areas of newspaper coverage.

Duty to Disclose; Duty to Update

Another disclosure issue of great importance arising under SEC Rule 10b-5 doctrine is the timing of preliminary merger announcements. In the Supreme Court case of *Basic v. Levinson* the Court held that a corporation may not, on pain of violating Rule 10b-5, issue press releases falsely denying materially significant merger talks.[203] The Court did not hold that a corporation (absent insider trading) has an absolute duty to disclose preliminary negotiation talks. The Court asserted that management could safely say "no comment" (i.e., be silent) in response to curious reporters at least so long as the corporation had followed a consistent policy in that regard in the past. That is, a corporation that in the past truthfully denied false rumors of merger talks where there were none, and said "no comment" when the rumors were true, is in an obvious box. The "no comment" is, in that context, a signal of preliminary talks. The signal might be so indistinct as to raise questions of adequacy under antifraud Rule 10b-5. To be safe, a corporation perhaps must say "no comment" in the face of rumors true or false or alternatively, always publicly disclose the exact nature of preliminary negotiations when asked.

The corporate management is in a tight spot. The Court's "no comment" escape hatch is narrow and perilous. Lack of consistency in the past may torpedo the "no comment" response. Management may be required to assert "no comment" in the face of false rumors in order to preserve the ability to keep silent in the face of accurate rumors. But problems under SEC Rule 10b-5 are not solved by an initial, truthful response to a truthful preliminary merger rumor. Assume that the management confirms that XYZ corporation is talking stock for stock merger in the 40-to-45-dollar-per-share range. Negotiations change and proposed terms quickly vary. Must the target corporation in our scenario update the previous confirmation of merger talks? The law on this duty to update is hardly clear. Rule 10b-5 prosecution threatens the management that fails to update when required.[204]

Management is faced with danger if it discloses early stages of the negotiations, but is confronted with grave risk if it keeps silent. In both cases there is the threat of antifraud prosecution. On the purely financial-business front, as distinguished from legal consequences, management may fear that early disclosure of ongoing merger talks will chill the prospects of an efficacious merger. Disclosure may trigger bidding competition. Newspaper publicity may freeze or distort the negotiation posture of the participants around the bargaining table. The disclosure is tricky. Shareholders may not understand the odds against successful completion of the deal.

Whether early disclosure helps or hurts investors is not obvious, or of uniform impact across all deals. Perhaps early disclosure will, by attracting possible bidding competitors, improve the deal for shareholders of one of the two corporations (i.e., the ultimate target corporation). Perhaps early disclosure will chill the prospect of the deal, and hence hurt shareholders. Also, concern about shareholder understanding of disclosure may be totally unfounded.

Corporate law scholars usually will approach this problem in the following manner. Free-market advocates of the view of the corporation as a set of contracts between and among shareholders, management, and other constituencies will argue for a voluntary solution. They will argue that the corporation should be free to voluntarily provide by charter, or charter amendment, for the treatment of the corporate information. This set of scholars will assert that if by charter, shareholders have delegated to senior management the power to determine timing of the preliminary talks, that settles the matter as far as the courts are involved.

Another body of scholars will argue that market failures of various kinds argue against this freedom to contract approach. They will attempt to demonstrate that information and power disparities between shareholders and management require governmental intervention in the process of timing and nature of disclosure. They will point to the asserted ability of management to cheat in the short run without disclosure. They will argue that small shareholders have no rational incentive to take the time necessary to process complex information or to monitor management.

If, however, corporate speech is fully protected by the First Amendment, the nature of the analysis changes. The First Amendment prevents the government from interfering with the right of free association. Therefore, management, given appropriate charter provisions permitting it, should be free to control timing and nature of disclosure about preliminary merger negotiations.

In this regard, a First Amendment distinction can perhaps be made between the case of corporate management flatly lying about the existence of preliminary merger talks (or anything else), and the case where management decides to be silent (i.e., the "no comment" position) about the rumor of talks. In the former the situation is similar to an actionable defamation case in the following respect. There is no information value to the lie. Further, the falsity of the denial is clearly and easily known by management. The First Amendment would clearly protect, however, the right of senior management to determine the timing of the announcement where practice or corporate charter grants that power to the management. The relative cost and benefit of early or later disclosure is difficult to ascertain. Government has no clear advantage over private parties in determining the proper time for disclosure.

A First Amendment analysis should also limit the duty of the management to correct earlier disclosure, particularly where management reserves the right publicly not to correct. Preliminary merger negotiations are complex, move rapidly, and change in a multiplicity of facets. Negotiation positions change so rapidly that there is little information value in repeated efforts to disclose the latest nuance in the bargaining position.

Political lies are, absent clear exceptions such as defamation, protected from government regulation by the First Amendment. Hence a pure absolutist might argue that the corporate lie in the first scenario above should be absolutely protected. In any event, a First Amendment type of analysis in the Basic case would certainly give greater deference to management's determination whether a given stage of negotiation is material. It is obvious that a First Amendment analysis of Basic case kind of issues radically improves the argument in favor of corporate control over the timing and nature of its disclosure.

Remember that a principal argument for the inferior treatment of commercial speech, including SEC speech, is the supposed hardiness of commercial speech, but it is difficult to imagine a more fragile kind of speech than announcements about preliminary merger talks. First Amendment protection of this category of speech would permit management to disclose ongoing talks with less fear of prosecution for failure to update thereafter, while at the same time permitting management to be intelligently silent, when that also is important.

Issues of materiality, timing, and accuracy are incredibly complex and difficult in this area. The argument is frequently made that commercial speech is easily verifiable by the disseminator, and hence should receive less First Amendment protection. Clearly, ease of verifiability, or the E, for error, factor, to recall Judge Richard A. Posner's formula, in preliminary merger cases is similar in difficulty to political speech.

Mandatory Disclosure, Prior Restraint, and the Structure of SEC Regulation

Lawrence Tribe, in his treatise on constitutional law, emphasizes that a major aspect of prior restraint doctrine is what he terms First Amendment due process.[205] This is a shorthand reference, so to speak, to judicial reluctance to permit administrative power, "directly or indirectly to determine *finally* the scope of application of first amendment privileges."[206] Therefore, the Court will frequently strike down overbroad delegation to censors or licensors of the power to restrain publication.[207] Open-ended delegation will be striken even where there is immediate judicial review because of the ability of censors to create "retrospective rationalization" and "contradictory testimony" in the record.[208] In the *Posadas* commercial speech case the administrators were granted the power to censor before publication offending, as they saw it, casino advertisements. The Court majority did not pass on it because it had not been raised by the challengers to the statute.[209] But Justice Stevens, dissenting, stated, "A more obvious form of prior restraint is difficult to imagine."[210]

First Amendment due process also involves the requirement to subject even adequately precise delegation to sufficient judicial review. Tribe summarizes this doctrine of restraint on censorship as follows: (1). The government has the burden of proof to justify the censorship decision; (2) the licensor or censor must act within a specified brief time; (3) the censor must go to court to restrain the unlicensed speech; (4) *ex parte* orders are frowned on; (5) restraints before final judicial determination must be for the shortest possible time; (6) the censorship scheme must assure a rapid final judicial decision; and (7) lower-court orders must be subject to immediate appellate review.[211]

Another aspect to the doctrine of prior restraint (not designated First Amendment due process) implicates the following kinds of issues. For example, certain news is significant only if timely released. Hence prior restraint, let us say, exercised through a lower-court injunction, as distinguished from criminal prosecution after the timely publication, may operate to unduly chill expression. In addition, in certain cases it may be difficult to measure the harm of publication before publication.[212] For example, the argument that publication will harm security may be impossible to measure before the publication. Hence the government has a forbidding burden to justify prior restraint. A publisher cannot disregard a court injunction against publication (as it can with a criminal statute) and then test its constitutionality. The publisher is required to appeal the injunction, and refrain from publication until after the appeal is decided.[213]

Prior restraint is a procedural doctrine. If the speech is protected by the First Amendment, it is protected before or after the fact of publication. If the speech is not covered by the First Amendment it may be prior restrained. The Court has indicated that because of the lower constitutional status of commercial speech, prior restraint doctrine may not apply to it.[214]

Let us consider the policy implications of First Amendment due process and SEC regulation of corporate speech. The SEC regulates through two modes of governance. The first is the system of mandatory disclosure described above. The second is criminal prosecution by the U.S. Justice Department after the fact of publication.

Let us start with a consideration of mandatory disclosure in the context of corporate stock and security offerings. The commission has established an elaborate system of disclosure under Regulation SK and a mass of administrative determinations. The corporation must adhere to this system. As we have observed above, this system amounts to government orthodoxy in corporate disclosure. But there is another aspect to this structure. The proposed registration document is filed in preliminary form with the commission staff. Although there are exceptions in certain cases, the staff reviews the filings and makes comments. As the leading commentator on securities law, in his definitive treatise observes:

> Although in theory the Commission's staff merely "suggests" amendments, the practicalities of financing do not allow any real alternative to complying. The privilege of testing the staff's views by defending a stop-order proceeding is an expensive one in terms of the success of the financing. And although the Commission's final order is subject to judicial review, a court proceeding that may take a year or more is hardly a realistic way to determine whether a company in need of financing is right in insisting that a particular item of information may properly go in the footnote rather than the text of the financial statements.[215]

This analysis captures the process of corporate securities offerings. With modification of detail, it captures the essence of the entire mandatory disclosure structure of the SEC. The corporation is faced with an elaborate structure of pre-publication mandated form and content of expression. The corporation faces enormous cost and time delay in challenging the commission in court, if it wants to vary from the government-imposed orthodoxy. The structure creates evils, all of which are not dissimilar from the evils "due process" prior restraint doctrine, as defined by Tribe, endeavors to prevent.

The essence of SEC mandatory disclosure is administrative (i.e., SEC) primacy in the resolution of First Amendment issues.[216] There is no doubt that the corporation, or corporate employee, will get ultimate judicial resolution of his assertion that a particular SEC disclosure structure violates the commercial speech doctrine, or in general the First Amendment. But the playing field is drastically tilted in favor of the commission. The agency employees, over the years, establish the matrix of appropriate disclosure. Almost every sentence, every paragraph, every financial datum and table is required, or implicated, or implied by the complex detailed nature of the commission's disclosure system. The corporation, as Loss suggests, avoids this at its peril.

Entirely different would be a system devoid of mandatory disclosure requirements and specifications, and limited to after-the-fact criminal prosecution for a fraudulent statement. Without making the empirically debatable statement that prior restraint of a particular alleged fraudulent statement is always more chilling than fear of a long prison term for publication of the same, there is a significant difference between a structure, devoid of mandatory disclosure, in which the Justice Department can initiate criminal prosecution for a lying statement, and the current system of mandatory disclosure.

The latter structure is surely more oppressive, in a First Amendment "due process" sense. The corporation is faced with mandatory administrative requirements as to what it shall publish on descriptions of business, descriptions of property, descriptions of securities, management discussion of financial condition, executive compensation, disagreements with accountants, and much more. The regulation chiefly concerned with this runs for fifty plus printed pages. There are numerous other regulations of the same variety. This creates a disclosure straightjacket, which is, after all, what the commission desires.

As a result, the commission, not the courts, makes all of the initial and decisive decisions in the First Amendment area. It decides what is material disclosure. It decides what is valid or misleading disclosure. It makes the initial, and often final, decisions as to whether the speech is fully protected speech or commercial speech. The corporation can appeal to the courts, but the process is slow and expensive, and, where speed is of the essence, the appeal may not be taken.

On a public policy level, limiting government involvement to the power to criminally prosecute deliberatively lying corporate speech after the fact of publication would present less of an opportunity for the imposition of government orthodoxy in corporate speech. The corporation would have the choice of alternative methods of disclosure untrammeled by the imposed form of mandatory disclosure.

Conclusion

SEC mandatory disclosure regulation of financial statements and business descriptions amounts to a major constraint on corporate and shareholder freedom of expression. The rationale for the supposed constitutionality of such government restraint turns on notions of the difference between commercial speech and political or artistic speech or on some notions of regulation of professionals in the securities industry. On analysis, the distinctions between commercial speech and other forms of expression, and notions of professional regulation do not stand up. Moreover, we have demonstrated that whatever commercial speech is, or stands for, speech regulated by the SEC is not commercial speech as traditionally defined, and is indistinguishable from fully protected speech.

Because the Supreme Court first recognized that commercial speech is constitutionally protected to some extent, it has become more and more difficult to rationally distinguish between commercial speech and other forms of expression. Virtually all of political speech is a dialogue involving economic self-interest. Farmers demand relief against supposedly oppressive bank credit. Their speech is political and protected. Their economic self-interest is obviously not to be denied. Bankers demand more or less regulation, depending on which kinds of banks they represent. Their speech is political. Their interest is selfish and economic. Ministers demand tax breaks for their dwellings. Their vocation is divine; their speech is political; their interest in this regard is economic.

When investment advisers opine on the stocks of corporate issuers (something the financial section of the New York Times does every day), their interest is commercial; their speech, their speech is as political as other varieties of free expression. The Supreme Court majority in the *Lowe v. SEC* case ducked the constitutional issue for reasons that by now should be obvious. Perhaps they were concerned with the possibility that the speech of investment advisers is constitutionally protected, beyond the level now accorded to commercial speech. The same can be said for corporate prospectuses, corporate proxy statements, and perhaps even certain areas of allegedly fraudulent statements involving the media that were invoked in the *Winans* case.

Everybody does agree that product or service advertisements, if nothing else, are commercial speech. As such, the Supreme Court currently affords them limited First Amendment protection. We have demonstrated that even such examples of "pure" commercial speech are difficult to distinguish from political speech.

Even if we accept such distinctions, however, we have demonstrated that corporate proxy and financial statements do not easily fit in with the orthodox definition of commercial speech. Part of the problem is that corporations are organizations. They are owned and managed or involved with various shareholder and management groups. Shares of stock, and even debt instruments, constitute various bundles of rights within such organizations. Therefore, messages by corporate managers, for example, to shareholders, or messages from one shareholder group to another, invoke rights to freedom of expression and freedom of association, all of which should be fully protected by the First Amendment. In addition, corporate speech frequently involves economic and social issues that are indistinguishable from the usual issues that are in the traditional political arena.

Further, such speech is incredibly complex and subjective, and therefore, just as in the case of political speech, difficult for government to verify. Also, the SEC, like any other government agency, is subject to institutional bias, self-interest, and interest group influence, in the fashioning of its disclosure and enforcement policies.

The Court has asserted that commercial speech, unlike political speech, is robust, and hence resistant to regulation. We have demonstrated that there is little, if any, empirical basis for that sweeping conclusion. We have pointed out that commercial speakers will, under threat of regulation and penalty, change their message, if necessary, to get it out to the public. To the extent the argument assumes that commercial speakers will defy regulation and risk punishment, the thesis seems to be that the First Amendment is not needed, since the speakers will get their message out regardless of its absence. This optimistic prediction of commercial bravado is hardly an eloquent argument for removal of First Amendment protection. If the government is an effective verifier of the true and the false in matters commercial, robustness is, therefore, a vice, and more strenuous regulation will make up for the robustness. If, as the evidence indicates, the government is not, then First Amendment protection is called for, rather than speculation about bravado, defined as robustness

The Supreme Court case in *Lowe v. SEC* not only threatens the foundations of SEC financial disclosure regulation, but it and related cases cast a pall on the validity of government regulation of the professions. The judicial distinction rests on personal communication versus publications. The attorney or investment advisers, when dealing one on one with a client, may be constitutionally regulated. When they issue publications to thousands or millions, the First Amendment protection emerges. This great distinction turns on a dubious empirical hypothesis. That hypothesis is that the individual client is more easily fooled by the advisers or lawyer than is a reader of a book or article. Therefore, the harm in the former case is greater than the aggregate harm in the latter. However, it appears far more plausible that a successful, manipulative, and scheming attorney or advisers can do far more harm to society by virtue of successful books and articles than the same individual could when advising a few score clients face to face. At best, therefore, the vast edifice of government regulation of the professions now rests on a dubious empirical assumption.

Glossary

Commercial speech: speech by an individual or corporation intended to make a profit.

Jurisprudence: the study, theory, and philosophy of law.

Proxy speech: speech about the governance of a corporation that is political in nature.

Referendum: a general vote by the electorate on a single political question that has been referred to them for a direct decision.

Notes

1. See John E. Nowak, Ronald D. Rotunda, and J. Nelson Young, *Constitutional Law*, 3d Ed. (St. Paul, MN: West Publishing Co., 1986), 904.

2. *Valentine v. Chrestensen,* 316 U.S. 52 (1942).

3. Ibid., 316 U.S. at 54 (emphasis added).

4. *Virginia State Board of Pharmacy v. Virginia Citizens Consumer Council, Inc.*, 425 U.S. 748 (1976).

5. *Linmark Associates, Inc. v. Town of Willingboro*, 431 U.S. 85 (1977).

6. *Central Hudson Gas & Electric Corporation v. Public Service Commission,* 447 U.S. 557 (1980).

7. Ibid., 447 U.S. at 566. See Michael E. Schoeman, *The First Amendment and Restrictions on Advertising of Securities Under the Securities Act of 1933*, 41 Bus. Law. 377 (1966).

8. *Board of Trustees of State University of New York v. Todd Fox*, 109 S. Ct. 3028 (1989).

9. *See* Contrasting Discussion and Authorities cited in Brief for the SEC, 34–49 and Brief of Petitioners, 29–37 in *Lowe v. SEC*, 472 U.S. 181 (1985).

10. *Central Hudson Gas*, supra note 6.

11. Ibid., 556. The Supreme Court in 1986, using the *Central Hudson* test in a remarkably permissive manner, sustained a ban on advertisements that spoke the truth about a legal product. It ruled 5–4 that Puerto Rico could prevent licensed casinos from soliciting gamblers on the island. Justice Rehnquist, writing for a bare majority, argued that whenever a government is permitted to ban a product, it has the consequential power to chill speech about that product. *Posadas de Puerto Rico Association v. Tourism Co.,* 106 S. Ct. 2968, 2979 (1986).

12. Ibid.

13. As Justices Black and Douglas asserted in their concurring opinion in *New York Times v. Sullivan*, 376 U.S. 254, 296–97 (1964): "[F]reedom to discuss public affairs and public officials is unquestionably, as the Court today holds, the kind of speech the First Amendment was primarily designed to keep within the area of free discussion."

14. See Alexander Meklejohn, *Political Freedom: The Constitutional Powers of the People* (New York: Greenwood Publishing Group, 1965).

15. Robert H. Bork, *Neutral Principles and Some First Amendment Problems*, 47 Ind. L.J. 1 (1971). Judge Bork later renounced his former stance on what speech falls under the protection of the First Amendment. See, e.g., *N.Y. Times*, Sept. 17, 1987, at A1, col. 6.

16. *Abrams v. United States*, 250 U.S. 616, 630 (1919) (Justice Holmes, dissenting).

17. *Whitney v. California*, 274 U.S. 357, 375 (1927) (Justice Brandeis, concurring).

18. See *First National Bank of Boston v. Bellotti*, 435 U.S. 765 (1978). Some troublesome questions can arise as to whether a particular document is an editorial advertisement or an advertisement for a product line. Thus the Federal Trade Commission (FTC) filed a complaint against the R. J. Reynolds Tobacco Company resulting from its publication in the *New York Times* and elsewhere of an editorial advertisement making certain points about a scientific study of risk factor and cigarette smoking. The Reynolds' advertisement did not promote the purchase of any cigarettes and contained no mention of the brand of any of its cigarettes. See Floyd Abrams, "*R. J. Reynolds vs. the Government*: A Chilling Effect on Corporate Speech," *New York Times*, 6 July, 1986, sec. 3, p. 2. The administrative law judge ruled against the FTC on First Amendment grounds. *R. J. Reynolds Tobacco Company, Inc.*108 F.T.C. No. 9206 (Aug. 4, 1986). The FTC and the tobacco company agreed to settle the case in October 1989. Reynolds pledged not to misrepresent scientific studies, but did not acknowledge any wrongdoing or that its materials were advertisements. *New York Times*, Oct. 21, 1989, p. 50.

19. See Daniel A. Farber, "Commercial Speech and First Amendment Theory," *Northwestern University Law Review* 74, 372, 407–8 (1979).

20. *Dun & Bradstreet, Inc. v. Greenmoss Builders, Inc.,* 472 U.S. 749, 787–88 (1985) (Brennan J., dissenting, citing *New York Times v. Sullivan*, 376 U.S. 254, 273 (1964); *Thornhill v. Alabama*, 310 U.S. 88, 102 (1940).

21. See arguments pro and con in Kent Greenwalt, *Free Speech Justifications*, Columbia Law Review 89, 119 (1989).

22. *Abrams v. United States*, 250 U.S. 616, 630 (1919) (Justice Holmes, dissenting).

23. Ronald Coase, "Advertising and Free Speech," in *Advertising and Free Speech*, ed. Allen Hyman and M. Bruce Johnson (Lexington, MA: Lexington Books, 1977). See generally, Bernard H. Siegan, *Economic Liberties and the Constitution* (Chicago: University of Chicago Press, 1980).

24. Charles Murray, *Losing Ground: American Social Policy 1950–1980* (New York: Basic Books, 1984).

25. Milton Friedman and Rose D. Friedman, *Free to Choose* (New York: Harcourt Brace Jovanovich, 1979), 39. [hereinafter Friedman.]

26. See, e.g., George J. Stigler, *The Citizen and the State: Essays on Regulation* (Chicago: University of Chicago Press, 1975); and Friedman, 190–94, 222–27.

27. See, e.g., Richard A. Posner, *Regulation of Advertising by the FTC* (Washington, DC: American Enterprise Institute, 1973), 21.

28. See, e.g., Sam Peltzman, *Regulation of Pharmaceutical Innovation: The 1962 Amendments* (Washington, DC: American Enterprise Institute, 1974).

29. See the discussion of Richard A. Posner in Nicholas Wolfson, *Corporate First Amendment Rights* (Westport, CT: Praeger Press, 1990), ch. 4.

30. *Lowe v. SEC*, 472 U.S. 181 (1985); the Act permits revocation of the advisers' registration because of specified prior misconduct. 15 U.S.C. §80b-3(e) (1982).

31. See Thomas Lee Hazen, *The Law of Securities Regulation 7–8* (St. Paul, MN: West Publishing Co., 1985), 297–310.

32. See *infra*.

33. *Zauderer v. Office of Disciplinary Counsel*, 471 U.S. 626, 651 (1985).

34. Ibid., 652.

35. Ibid., 651, n. 14. In *Zauderer* the court held that the state may not discipline an attorney who seeks clients by using newspaper advertisements that contain truthful illustrations and legal advice. Ibid., 655–56. The attorney had offered in his advertisements to represent women who had been injured by the Dalkan Shield intrauterine device. Ibid., 630. The court, however, permitted the state to discipline the attorney for failure to make required disclosure. He had represented that he would work on a contingent fee basis and, without recovery, would impose no legal fee. Ibid., 652. He failed to disclose that the clients might have to pay litigation costs. The court thus distinguished between mandatory disclosure requirements and outright bans of expression.

36. See, e.g., Schucker, "Reagan Tax Plan is unfair," *New York Times*, 12 June 1985, sec. A, 27 col. 1 (asserting that Reagans's flat tax proposal is unfair and ignorant of social realities).

37. See Louis Loss, *Fundamentals of Securities Regulation* (New York: Little Brown, 1983) 542, n. 81; Robert W. Hamilton, *Cases and Materials on Corporations*, 2d Ed. (St. Paul, MN: West Publishing, 1981), 543.

38. Ibid.

39. Richard A. Posner, "Free Speech in an Economic Perspective," *Suffolk Law Review* 20, 1, 22 (1986).

40. Ibid.

41. Ibid.

42. Ibid., 39–40.

43. *Medical Committee for Human Rights v. SEC*, 432 F.2d 659 (D.C. Cir. 1970), vacated as moot, 404 U.S. 403 (1972).

44. Ibid.

45. Proxy Rule 14a-8. See, generally, Patrick J. Ryan, "Rule 14a-8, Institutional Shareholder Proposals, and Corporate Democracy," *Georgia Law Review* 23, 97 (1988); Susan W. Liebler, "A Proposal to Rescind the Shareholder Proposal Rule," *Georgia Law Review* 18, 425 (1984).

46. Securities Exchange Act of 1934, Public Law 73–291, 79th Cong., 2d sess. (6 June 1934) Rule 14a-8 (c) (8).

47. See Robert W. Hamilton, *Cases and Materials on Corporations*, 3rd ed. (St. Paul, MN: West Publishing, 1986), 571–78.

48. *First National Bank of Boston v. Belloti*, 435 U.S. 765, 98 S. Ct. 1407 (1978).

49. Ibid., 768 (quoting Mass. Gen. Laws. Ann. ch 55, §8 [West Supp. 1977]).

50. Ibid.

51. Ibid., 782 (footnote omitted).

52. Ibid., 783 (footnote omitted).

53. See Wolfson, "The First Amendment and the SEC," ch. 3.

54. *Belloti*, 435 U.S. at 783.

55. Ibid., 783, citing *Virginia State Board of Pharmacy v. Virginia Citizens Consumer Council,* 425 U.S. 748, 764 (1976).

56. Ibid., 785.

57. Ibid.

58. Ibid., 787–88 and n. 26.

59. Ibid., 788 and n. 26.

60. Ibid., 789.

61. Ibid., 790, quoting *Kingsley Int'l Pictures v. Regents*, 360 U.S. at 689 (1959).

62. Ibid., 791, n. 30.

63. Ibid., 792.

64. Ibid., 793–94.

65. Ibid., 794.

66. Ibid., 794, n. 34.

67. Ibid., 795.

68. Id., quoting *Shelton v. Tucker*, 364 U.S. at 485 (1960).

69. Ibid., 770, n. 4.

70. Ibid., quoting court below, 371 Mass. at 777, 359 N.E.2d at 1266).

71. See Wolfson, "Corporate First Amendment Rights and the SEC," ch. 2.

72. George J. Benston, *Government Constraints on Political, Artistic, and Commercial Speech*, Connecticut Law Review 20, 303, 318 (1988).

73. *Austin v. Michigan Chamber of Commerce*, 494 U.S. 652 (1990), 1990 U.S. Lexus 1665 (March 27, 1990).

74. Ibid., 1.

75. Ibid., 12–14.

76. Ibid., 14–15.

77. Ibid., 17–21.

78. Ibid., 22.

79. Ibid., 24–29.

80. Ibid., 45.

81. Ibid., 46.

82. Ibid., 47.

83. Ibid., 52.

84. Ibid., 52 quoting 424 U.S., 45.

85. Ibid., 53.

86. Ibid., 54.

87. Ibid., 53.

88. Ibid., 56.

89. Ibid.

90. Ibid.

91. Ibid.

92. Ibid., 58.

93. Ibid., 59.

94. Ibid.

95. Ibid., 64.

96. Ibid.

97. Ibid., 67–68.

98. Ibid.

99. Ibid., 68.

100. Ibid., 85.

101. Hamilton, *Cases and Materials on Corporations*, 3rd ed. (1986), 610–622.

102. *Pacific Gas & Electric Co. v. Public Utility Commission*, 475 U.S. 1 (1986).

103. Ibid., 10, citing *Miami Herald Publishing Co. v. Tornillo*, 418 U.S. 241 (1974).

104. Ibid., 39.

105. Ibid., 39, n. 8.

106. Ibid., 14, n. 10.

107. Ibid.

108. Ibid.

109. *Medical Committee for Human Rights v. SEC*, 432 F2d 659 (D.C. Cir 1979), vacated as moot, 404 U.S. 403 (1972).

110. Ibid.

111. Hamilton, note 73 supra at 610–22.

112. Securities Exchange Act of 1934, Public Law 73–291, 79th Cong., 2d sess. (6 June 1934) Rule 14a-8 (c) (5).

113. See Ryan, supra note 45; Hamilton, *supra* note 47 at 620.

114. See Wolfson, "The First Amendment and the SEC," chap. 2.

115. Homer Kripke, *The SEC and Corporate Disclosure: Regulation in Search of a Purpose* (New York: Harcourt Brace Jovanovich, 1979).

116. Ibid., 5. See Carl W. Schneider, "Nits, Grits and Soft Information in SEC Filings," *University of Pennsylvania Law Review* 121, 254 (1972).

117. Ibid., 6.

118. Hamilton, 589 (1986).

119. Nicholas Wolfson, *The Modern Corporation, Free Markets vs. Regulation* (New York: Free Press, 1984), 122–24.

120. *TSC Industries Inc. v. Northway, Inc.*, 426 U.S. 438 (1976).

121. *Escott v. Barchris Construction Co.*, 283 F. Supp. 643, 682 (1968).

122. Henry G. Manne, "Insider Trading and Property Rights," in *New Information in Economic Liberties and the Judiciary*, James A. Dorn and Henry G. Manne eds. (Fairfax, VA: George Mason University Press, 1987), 317, 325.

123. George J. Benston, "The Costs and Benefits of Government Required Disclosures: SEC and FTC Requirements, An Appraisal," in *Corporations at the Crossroads: Governance and Reform ed.* Deborah A. DeMott (New York: McGraw-Hill, 1980), 55–57.

124. See Wolfson, *The First Amendment and the SEC*, ch. 4.

125. Ibid.

126. George J. Benston, "Required Periodic Disclosure Under The Securities Acts And the Proposed Federal Securities Code," *University of Miami Law Review* 33, 1471 (1979).

127. Ibid., 1471–84.

128. A. A. Sommer, Jr., Book Review, *Harvard Law Review* 93, 1595 (1980).

129. The First Amendment forbids the favoring of one group over another: "[T]he concept that government may restrict the speech of some elements of our society in order to enhance the relative voice of others is wholly foreign to the First Amendment. . . ." *First Nat'l Bank v. Bellotti*, 765, 790–91 (1978), quoting *Buckely v. Valeo*, 424 U.S. 1, 48–49 (1976). This argument, however, was questioned by the *Austin* case.

130. Ibid.

131. Wolfson, *The Modern Corporation, Free Markets vs. Regulation,* 46–50, 106–7.

132. See *Buckley v. Valeo*, 424 U.S. at 19–23.

133. Ibid., 23–38.

134. *Miami Herald Publishing Co. v. Tornillo,* 418 U.S. 241258 (1974). In *Pacific Gas & Elec. Co. v. Public Utilities Commission of California*, 106 S. Ct. 903, 910–12 (1981) the Court held that a utility commission order requiring a privately owned utility to include in its billing envelopes speech of a third party with which the corporation does not agree unlawfully impairs its First Amendment rights. This opinion put into doubt SEC Regulation 14a-8, which required the board of directors to send out proposals of shareholders that it opposed. See Securities Exchange Act of 1934, Public Law 73–291, 79th Cong., 2d sess. (6 June 1934) sec. 17 C.F.R. & 240. 14a-8 (1985).

135. See Nowak, Rotunda, and Young, supra n. 1 at 874–85. The FCC announced in 1985 that it would no longer enforce the fairness doctrine, finding that it is a violation of the First Amendment rights of broadcasters.

136. Bellotti, supra note 18 at 77.

137. Wolfson, supra note 131 at 41, 54–55.

138. Frank H. Easterbrook, *Manager's Discretion and Investors' Welfare: Theories and Evidence*, 9 Del. J. Corp. L. 540, 564–68 (1984); Henry G. Manne, "Mergers and the Market for Corporate Control," *Journal of Political Economy* 73, 110 (1965).

139. See Thomas Sowell, *Knowledge and Decisions* (New York: Basic Books, 1980), 200.

140. See Nowak, supra note 1 at 947–52.

141. *NAACP v. Alabama*, 357 U.S. 449, 460 (1958).

142. See n. 169, *infra*.

143. Securities Exchange Act of 1934, secs. 13(d) and 14(d), 15 U.S.C.A. Sections 78m(d) and 78n(d).

144. Securities Exchange Act of 1934, sec. 14(d) (4), 15 U.S.C.A. Section 78n(d) (4).

145. For a sampling of significant articles on the market for control, see Henry G. Manne, "Mergers and the Market for Corporate Control," *Journal of Political Economy* 73, 110 (1965); Frank H. Easterbrook and Daniel R. Fischel, "The Proper Role of a Target's Management in Responding to a Tender Offer," *Harvard Law Review* 94, 1161 (1981); Michael C. Jensen, "Takeovers: Their Causes and Consequences," *Journal of Economic Perspectives* 2, 21 (1988); Bernard S. Black, "Bidder Overpayment in Takeovers," *Stanford Law Review* 41, 597 (1989).

146. See, e.g., Larry E. Ribstein, "Takeover Defenses and the Corporate Contract," *Georgetown Law Review* 78, 71 (1989); John C. Coffee, Jr., "The Uncertain Case for Takeover Reform: An Essay on Stockholders, Stakeholders and Bustups," *Wisconsin Law Review*, 435 (1988); John C. Coffee, Jr., "Regulating the Market for Corporate Control: A Critical Assessment of the Tender Offer's Role in Corporate Governance," *Columbia Law Review* 84, 1145 (1984).

147. Ibid.

148. See *An Act Concerning Approval of Certain Business Combinations*, Connecticut Public Act 88–350 (7 June 1988).

149. Henry N. Butler and Larry E. Ribstein, "The Contract Clause and The Corporation," *Brooklyn Law Review* 55, 767, 795 (1989).

150. See Connecticut Public Act 84–431.

151. See supra note 148.

152. Lawrence Tribe, *American Constitutional Law*, 2d ed. (Mineola, NY: The Foundation Press, 1988) 1010.

153. Ibid., 1011.

154. Alexis de Tocqueville, *Democracy in America*, 1st ed., ed. Phillips Bradley (New York: Vintage Books, 1945), 196.

155. Tribe, 1016.

156. Ibid.

157. Ibid.

158. Ibid., 1017.

159. Ibid., 1014.

160. *TW Services v. SWT Acquisition Corp.*, 1989 WL 2090, Del. Ch., (1989) 334.

161. Ibid., 92, 180 n. 14.

162. Ibid.

163. Ibid., 92, 181.

164. Butler and Ribstein, "The Contract Clause and the Corporation," *Brooklyn Law Review* 55, 767 (1989).

165. Securities Act of 1933, sec. 5, 15 U.S.C. 77e (1982).

166. See generally Carl W. Schneider, Joseph M. Manko, and Robert S. Kant, "Going Public: Practice, Procedure and Consequences," *Villanova Law Review* 27, 1 (1981).

167. See Martin L. Budd and Nicholas Wolfson, *Securities Regulation: Cases and Materials* (Charlottesville, VA: Michie Co., 1984), 7, 125.

168. Ibid., 37–50.

169. Justice Sandra Day O'Connor emphasizes this distinction in her concurrence in the Roberts decision. *Roberts v. United States Jaycees*, 468 U.S. 609, 631–33 (1984). She would grant full First Amendment protection to the internal workings of so-called expressive (i.e. noncommercial) associations. *Ibid.,* 633–35. She would grant limited First Amendment protection to the internal workings of non-expressive (i.e., commercial) associations. Ibid., 634–35. Other justices, in the majority opinion, applying a sliding scale, ad hoc approach, would grant full First Amendment coverage to associational activity where appropriate to protect the expressive element of an association. Ibid., 622. All justices agreed that the right of association is not absolute and is subject to compelling state interests (e.g., prevention of gender discrimination).

170. *Virginia State Board of Pharmacy*, 765.

171. *Principles of Corporate Governance: Analysis and Recommendations*, § 2.01 (Tent. Draft No. 2, 1981).

172. Wolfson, supra note 131 at 147–58.

173. *Shlensky v. Wrigley*, 95 I11. App.2d 173, 175; 237 N.E.2d. (1968) 776, 777.

174. *Lowe, v. SEC*, 472 U.S. 181 (1985).

175. Ibid., 185.

176. Ibid.

177. Ibid., 185–86 (footnote omitted).

178. Ibid., 203–11.

179. Ibid., 208.

180. Ibid., 204.

181. Ibid., 235–36 (Justice White, concurring).

182. Ibid., 228.

183. Ibid., 232 (emphasis added and footnote omitted).

184. Ibid., 234.

185. Ibid.

186. Ibid.

187. The concurring opinion states: "One does not have to read the Court's opinion very closely to realize that its interpretation of the Act is in fact based on a thinly disguised conviction that the Act is unconstitutional as applied to prohibit publication of newsletters by unregistered advisers." Ibid., 226 (Justice White, concurring).

188. Ibid., 210, n. 58 (citation omitted).

189. See, e.g., *Economics of Corporation Law and Securities Regulation*, edited by Richard A. Posner and Kenneth E. Scott (Boston: Little Brown, 1980), 155–194.

190. See Nowak, Rotunda, and Young, *supra* n. 1 at 870.

191. 472 U.S. 181, 232 (1985) (Justice White, concurring).

192. See Sowell, supra n. 139, 200.

193. See Note, "The Efficient Capital Market Hypothesis, Economic Theory and the Regulation of the Securities Industry," *Stanford Law Review* 29, 1031 (1977).

194. See Arthur F. Matthews and Theodore A. Levine, "First Amendment Problems Complicate SEC Enforcement," *New York Law Journal* 33, 44 (10 December 1984).

195. *United States v. Winans*, 612 F.Supp. 827 (S.D.N.Y. 1985), aff'd in *part,* rev'd in part, sub. nom. *United States v. Carpenter*, 791 F.2d 1024 (2d Cir. 1986), aff'd 484 U.S. 19 (1987).

196. Ibid.

197. 484 U.S. at 24.

198. Ibid. The justices split 4–4 on the Rule 10b-5 misappropriation count. Hence the convictions on this theory were sustained. The justices unanimously upheld the wire and mail fraud convictions. For an analysis of misappropriation doctrine as a form of protection of property rights in information and, more particularly, as a form of trade secrets law. See Nicholas Wolfson, "Trade Secrets and Secret Trading," *San Diego Law Review* 25, 95 (1988). The doctrine governing insider trading can be summarized as follows:

Corporate insiders, such as officers, directors, and control shareholders, have an affirmative duty either to disclose material information about their corporation before trading or must refrain from trading. See, e.g., *Dirks v. SEC*, 463 U.S. 646 (1983): *Chiarella v. United States*, 445 U.S. 222 (1980). However, R. Foster Winans was a "stranger" to the corporations about which he wrote. He, therefore, had no fiduciary duties to buyer or sellers of their stock. However, the courts have developed the "misappropriation" doctrine. See, e.g., *Newman v. United States*, 464 U.S. 863

(1983); *SEC v. Materia*, 745 F.2d 197 (2d Cir. 1984), *cert. denied*, 471 U.S. 1053 (1985). Anyone, such as Winans, who misappropriates information or wrongfully abuses a special relationship with an employer (here the *Wall Street Journal*) or another, in connection with the purchase or sale of stock, violates SEC Rule 10b-5. Since the *Wall Street Journal* had a policy forbidding scalping and Winans knew of it, he misappropriated his special relationship with the *Journal* when he traded. That is, he misappropriated the *Journal*'s confidential schedule of forthcoming publications in connection with his stock trading. It may be argued that Winans violated the journalist's special relationship of trust with his readership (and not only his employer) in connection with his purchase, and for that reason also violated Rule 10b-5. The latter interpretation, however, would create a relatively radical judicial doctrine, since it would impose Rule 10b-5 responsibilities on all journalists over a wide scope of behavior. In the SEC civil case against him (and at an earlier point in connection with the criminal case), the government asserted the more radical theory that he had violated a fiduciary duty to his readership in not disclosing the scheme, and hence had committed an actionable fraud in connection with the purchase or sale of stock. See Matthews and Levine, supra note, 44.

199. Insider Trading and Securities Fraud Enforcement Act of 1988, Public Law 100–704, 100th Cong., 2d sess. (19 November 1988).

200. Federal District Court Judge Stewart, in his opinion finding *Winans et al.* guilty, had the following to say on the media's objections to the indictment:

On January 21, 1985, the Reporters' Committee for Freedom of the Press, the National Association of Broadcasters, the Newsletters Association, the New York Financial Writers Association, the Media Institute, the Newspaper Guild, the Radio-Television News Directors Association, the American Society of Magazine Editors, the National Newspaper Association, and the Associated Press Managing Editors filed a motion for leave to file a brief as amici curiae in support of defendants' Rule 29 motion to dismiss various counts of the indictment. They filed another motion for leave to file a supplemental memorandum on April 23, 1985. Because of the timing of the latter motion, we did not require the government to respond to the points raised. However, we hereby grant both motions.

The arguments made by the amici with respect to the proper construction of the securities laws are adequately addressed in the text. Amici make a more narrow argument that states in essence that the government's theory rests on ill-defined duties for reporters and editors; criminalization of breaches of those duties will interfere with the editorial process and will create a threat to the amici's First Amendment freedoms. We are not persuaded that the government's theory does create any new duties; as the government stated in their reply brief, "this prosecution under the 'misappropriation' theory creates no obligations, but merely enforces pre-existing obligations as it finds them." Nor does the theory impose any duties at all on publishers and editors as to what they must do if a reporter does disclose trading or tipping. Editors must make decisions about whether or not to run articles all the time, and this theory does not affect that choice at all. If Winans were to have disclosed to his editors prior to publication the fact that he was trading in the stock slated to be the subject of a Heard column the following day, the editors had several choices open to them, including running the column and taking disciplinary action against Winans for his misconduct, as well as seeking criminal penalties. *United States v. Winans*, 612 F.Supp. 827, 843, n. 10 (S.D.N.Y. 1985).

201. See Henry G. Manne, "Insider Trading and Property Rights in New Information," in *Economic Liberties and the Judiciary*, James A. Dunn and Henry G. Manne, eds. (Fairfax, VA: George Mason University Press, 1987) 317; Nicholas Wolfson, "Comment: Civil Liberties and Regulation of Insider Trading," *Economic Liberties*, 339.

202. See supra, n. 194 and accompanying text.

203. *Basic Inc. v. Levinson*, 108 S. Ct. 978 (1988).

204. See Carl W. Schneider, Insights: Corp. & Sec. *Legal Advisor* (February 1989) 3.

205. Tribe, *American Constitutional Law*, 2d Ed. (1988). 1054.

206. Ibid., 1055.

207. Ibid., 1056.

208. Ibid., 1057.

209. Ibid.

210. Ibid., 1057, n. 10.

211. Ibid., 1060–1061.

212. Ibid., 1048.

213. Ibid., 1042.

214. Ibid., 1057, n. 10. Tribe has written: "One difficulty with this approach is that it permits non-judicial determinations of what is commercial. As § 12–18 made apparent, the dividing line between the 'economical' and the 'political' is hazy at best." Ibid.

215. Loss, supra note 37, 129–130 (footnote omitted).

216. Tribe, 1054.

7

Freedom of the Press

| Nancy Cornwell

Introduction

In the early morning hours of March 20, 2003, explosions rocked the city of Baghdad, Iraq. U.S. missiles struck government buildings and the palace of Iraqi president Saddam Hussein, among other strategic targets. That morning marked the beginning of the U.S. "shock and awe" campaign and the beginning of U.S. and coalition troop movement from southern Iraq toward the capital. The events that unfolded on each of the following twenty-one days, as well as during the months of occupation that followed, were reported in excruciating detail by more than 500 journalists "embedded" among U.S. and coalition military units. Many more journalists reported from Kuwait, Bahrain, and other locales on the periphery of the war zone. American television, radio, newspapers, magazines, and Internet news sources were flooded with continuous coverage. When live images were not available, the analysts took over. Media and political analysts compared U.S. press coverage—in principle protected by the U.S. Constitution and free from government influence—and other media, such as the Qatar-based Al Jazeera satellite network, whose information was analyzed skeptically because it was considered tainted by an Arab political agenda and sympathetic to the Iraqi perspective. American media sources were saturated with war coverage.[1] Information overload seemed more a problem than concerns about censorship or disinformation.

In the aftermath of the war, with more time for reflection as the media covered the continuing military occupation, questions emerged about the press's objectivity and freedom in its war coverage. Did the practice of embedding journalists in the war zone serve the principles of a free press? Were the American people, or the world for that matter, watching freedom of the press functioning at its best, or were they witnessing a press subjected to government restrictions in a way that distorted the reality of war? Of even greater concern: Did the process of embedding journalists create the illusion of a free press when, in fact, information and images were restricted and manipulated by the government to shape public opinion about the war? How does this scenario fit into a worldview in which the American press is "free"? To answer this question it is necessary to understand what freedom of the press actually means. There is no simple answer.

The First Amendment to the U.S. Constitution reads as follows: "Congress shall make no law respecting an establishment of religion, or prohibiting the free exercise thereof; or abridging the freedom of speech, or of the press; or the right of the people peaceably to assemble, and to petition the government for a redress of grievances." These forty-five words specify six specific freedoms and guarantee them under the Constitution. So important are these guarantees, so central to our tradition of individual freedom and democratic participation, that this entire chapter is devoted to just one of them: freedom of the press. The United States is the only nation that provides constitutional protection to the press, and the U.S. press is the only private business whose activities receive direct protection under the U.S. Constitution. The American tradition of protecting the press from governmental influence and pressure is unmatched anywhere in the world.

Freedom of the press is not an absolute freedom, even though the language of the First Amendment might imply otherwise. The statement "Congress shall make no law . . . abridging the freedom of . . . the press" sounds comprehensive and clear. In 1960, U.S. Supreme Court Justice Hugo Black stated, "It is my belief that there *are* 'absolutes' in our Bill of Rights and that they were put there on purpose by men who knew what words meant and meant their prohibitions to be 'absolutes.'"[2] His words suggest that all speech is protected and that the First Amendment protects the news media from any censorship or punishment after publication. That, of course, means no libel or invasion of privacy lawsuits and no restrictions in the name of copyright or national security.

Justice Black held the view that any speech involving public matters would be enfolded within the protection of the First Amendment. It has been noted that for Justice Black, this meant that obscenity, libel, and slander are protected expression. Even today's Supreme Court does not go that far. The constraints placed on the press during the war in Iraq, as in many other military conflicts, make it clear that freedom of the press is tempered, in part, by other competing needs and rights, national security being just one example. Thus, in some ways, freedom of the press is not so clear. It can be fluid and subject to external pressures and competing interests and rights. What constitutes freedom of the press, and what it meant when the authors of the Bill of Rights wrote the words "Congress shall make no law abridging . . . freedom of . . . the press," remains a remarkably complex issue.

Justifications for Protecting Expression

It may seem self-evident, but it is worthwhile to discuss why a society would seek to protect expression. There are plenty of cultures and nation-states that restrict expression for all sorts of reasons, ranging from the political to the cultural to the religious. Yet we have chosen to broadly and fundamentally protect expression freedoms. That choice is based on a belief that freedom of expression has some value.

The question is, then, what values justify protecting expression? And do these values hold any connection to why we protect the press?

First Amendment scholar Thomas Emerson reviewed the body of First Amendment **jurisprudence** up to the mid-1960s and culled four values supporting the principle of free and unfettered expression.[3] The first value echoed the words and ideas of the classical liberal theorists. Emerson suggested that a central value of free and open debate is the discovery of truth and knowledge through the free trade of ideas. In language that is reminiscent of John Milton's *Areopagitica* and John Stuart Mill's *On Liberty*, Emerson stated that,

> an individual who seeks knowledge and truth must hear all sides of the question, consider all alternatives, test his judgment by exposing it to opposition, and make full use of different minds. Discussion must be kept open no matter how certainly true an accepted opinion may be; many of the most widely acknowledged truths have turned out to be erroneous.[4]

The idea that free expression is central to discovering truth is not just discussed in philosophical tomes of the seventeenth and eighteenth centuries. It appears in Supreme Court Justice Oliver Wendell Holmes's 1919 dissent in Abrams, in which he passionately stated, "[T]he ultimate good desired is better reached by free trade in ideas—that the best test of truth is the power of the thought to get itself accepted in the competition of the marketplace."[5] It also appears in Justice Louis D. Brandeis's 1927 concurring opinion in Whitney, in which he referred to the Founding Fathers and how "they believed that freedom to think as you will and to speak as you think are means indispensable to the discovery and spread of political truth."[6] Brandeis added,

> If there be time to expose through discussion the falsehood and fallacies, to avert the evil by the processes of education, the remedy to be applied is more speech, not enforced silence.[7]

The idea of protecting the press nests quite nicely with the effort to discover truth or knowledge. In spite of the growth of tabloid journalism and cynicism about the press, there is a general belief that part of the function of the press in a democratic society is to inform citizens about events that interest or affect them.[8]

Emerson suggested that there is a fundamental need in human nature to express oneself as part of the **process of self-actualization.** To restrict freedom of expression is "a negation of man's essential nature."[9] Emerson believed that part of the need for self-fulfillment is realized in one's right to participate in decisions that affect one's life.[10] Given the role the press plays in providing information that may form the basis of such decision-making, the importance of protecting the press as part of the value of individual self-fulfillment is evident. These first two values—discovery of truth and individual self-fulfillment—connect most closely with the individual value of protecting expression. But protecting freedom of the press facilitates those individualistic values.

Emerson's next two values extend beyond the individual value of protecting expression and consider the larger social values associated with a system of free expression. He suggested that protecting expression provides an important safety valve for a society as it changes over time. Society demands, at some level, a certain amount of cohesion, yet it must also adapt and change with new ideas. The free exchange of ideas plays an essential role in revealing and diffusing the tensions built up while oscillating between what Emerson called a "healthy cleavage and necessary consensus."[11] This delicate balance is facilitated by open discussion of the issues and concerns that face the citizenry. As Emerson stated, "[P]eople are more ready to accept decisions that go against them if they have a part in the decision-making process."[12] When most public information is disseminated through the mass media, access to those forms of communication is increasingly essential. It was suggested, for example, in the aftermath of the 2000 national election campaign that fringe candidates such as Ralph Nader would have performed better in the polls if they had as much access to the mass media and the televised presidential debates as the mainstream candidates.

Emerson's fourth value for protecting expression was presented with an eye toward the ideal of **participatory democracy**. The ability to contribute to the democratic process is a value of free expression that extends from the right to share in common decisions. Even if scholars differ on the extent of protection the authors of the Bill of Rights intended with First Amendment protections of expression, they agree that the intent was to protect political expression from government censorship. For Emerson, this right of participation moves far beyond political expression and "embraces the right to participate in the building of the whole culture, and includes freedom of expression in religion, literature, art, science, and all areas of human learning and knowledge."[13]

These values offer a broad justification for protecting expression in a democratic society. The role of a free press is central to facilitating both the individualistic and the social values presented by Emerson.

Theories of the Press

The press operates differently in different societies. It has different ranges of freedom, it is funded differently, and its relationship with the government ranges from being government owned and operated to operating as a "watchdog" of government. In contemporary society, the press falls into five loosely constructed theoretical frameworks or models. The lines between them are diffuse, and some media systems, including our own, straddle different models.

The authoritarian model describes how the press operated in sixteenth- and seventeenth-century England before the abolition of **prior restraint**.[14] It is still the model for the press in some parts of the world. Press operating under this model would be completely controlled by and operate for the benefit of the power controlling it—the government, the monarchy, the dictator, or the like. The government determines who operates the press, including whether the press operates itself. It doesn't necessarily have to be government owned, but control of the press tends to be absolute, so there is little media criticism of the government.

Closely related is the socialist/communist model of the press.[15] The best example of this model was the press in the Soviet Union before its dissolution. The press operating under this model would clearly be state owned and controlled. Information is controlled and filtered to facilitate and further the goals of the state. There is some overlap between this model and the authoritarian model, but in the socialist model the press would never be privately owned and state control reflects a "public ownership," whereas in the authoritarian model the press may be privately owned, but only at the grace of a dictator, a monarch, or a governing elite.

As concerns about media in developing nations came to the fore, another model of the press emerged.[16] Drawn from ideas debated in the United Nations Educational, Scientific and Cultural Organization (UNESCO) in the early 1980s, this new model countered the traditional kinds of press, which did not fit the particular technological, economic, or political conditions or needs of developing nations. Under the "development theory," the press may or may not be owned by the state, and the degree of state control varies. But the press is seen less as a watchdog of government and more as an advocate of the government's efforts to develop the country. That advocacy can bump up against freedom of the press when the publication of material might be harmful to the government's development efforts.

The next two models help describe the American press. The libertarian model explains the press as it functioned after the press licensing system was abolished in England.[17] It is the model that best describes the traditions we inherited in the United States. In this model the press is privately owned by anyone who has the money to start a newspaper or other media outlet. Its objective is not to further the agenda of the state or those in power but instead to inform, to entertain, and to sell. There is little control of the press, aside from the controls imposed by certain court decisions (e.g., those related to libel, obscenity, invasion of privacy, and national security) and the free market. Internal guidelines, ethics, and professional standards of behavior, more than any kind of formal requirements, drive the press to serve larger social goals.

The social responsibility model of the press emerged in the United States in the twentieth century.[18] It rose as a result of concerns about whether the press was acting in a socially responsible manner. The press under this model has detailed codes of conduct and some mechanism to encourage discussion, feedback, or responses within its forum. The potential exists for the government to step in and correct those in media who fail to meet their responsibility to society. Such intervention could range from regulatory requirements to the taking over of the media company.

In the United States the press operates with a blending of the libertarian and social responsibility models. Where the press falls along the continuum between the two models depends on the nature of the media (television versus print; tabloid versus *New York Times*). The American press enjoys tremendous protection in a manner consistent with the libertarian model. For example, it is almost inconceivable to imagine extensive content regulation of the American press by the state. Additionally, the American press embraces a sense of mission to serve as the watchdog of government and to inform the public on important issues of the day. Although the media's success in meeting this mission varies, for a multitude of reasons, it remains a guiding ethic for much of the press and provides a strong connection to the social responsibility model.

Organization of the Discussion

It is with this general understanding of the justification for free expression and this theoretical framework for understanding the role of the press in the United States that we investigate the development and meaning of press liberties in the United States.

Because of the unique role of historical circumstances, technological innovations, court decisions, and precedence in shaping the contemporary meaning of a free press, the material is organized chronologically. This format also provides a context for the historical, political, and social realities of decisive moments in the history of press freedoms. Generally, the development and clarification of press freedoms were not smooth, nor consistent, but the development of contemporary press freedoms is a remarkable story, and it is unique to the United States.

The story does not begin in the United States, however. The roots of contemporary press freedoms stretch back to the writings of John Milton, John Locke, and Thomas Hobbes—English Libertarians who wrote passionately about the importance of individual rights and the problems associated with licensing the press in seventeenth-century England.[19] Related French Enlightenment thinkers such as Montesquieu, Voltaire, and Rousseau looked at ideas of democratic principles and social responsibility—values that manifest themselves in the American press's role as a watchdog of government. The contribution of these varied philosophical principles to journalism is evident in their repeated appearance in American judicial decisions attempting to clarify the scope and meaning of a free press.

A discussion of these intellectual roots of American press freedoms forms the beginning of the next chapter. These principles, emerging as part of the larger Enlightenment movement, played a role in the political debates and struggles in seventeenth- and eighteenth-century England. For example, challenges to the English licensing system and the Crown's practice of controlling publishing through the Stationers' Company (chartered in 1557) were wrapped up in a larger struggle over the monarch's authority to rule Britain. After the authority of the parliamentary system was established in the late seventeenth century, ubiquitous control of printing in England became administratively unmanageable. As a result, more than a century of licensing printers ended in 1694 as the last licensing law expired, and English **common law** subsequently recognized that there could be no prior restraint imposed on the press. In other words, the government could not prevent the press from publishing. There continued to be mechanisms for punishing the press after it published something "improper, mischievous, or illegal."[20] Likewise, varied forms of common law prosecution for libel were fundamentally altered in the colonies after the trial of John Peter Zenger for seditious libel in 1744. Before the Zenger trial, truth was no defense against a charge of libel. In fact, in the case of seditious libel, it was thought that truthful criticism of British authority was worse, as it might stir up dissent among the Crown's subjects. The decision in the Zenger trial, initially informally and ultimately formally, established truth as a defense against any libel charge.

The philosophical influences on the Founding Fathers, English common law protections for press, and growing resistance to the British decision to tax newsprint under the Stamp Act of 1765 all helped shape the development of the Bill of Rights in 1791. The common law protection against prior restraint and the early developments in libel law were already part of the framework in which the authors of the Bill of Rights worked. However, the road to the freedom of press clause in the Bill of Rights was neither simple nor smooth. There was resistance generally to a Bill of Rights among the **Federalists**, and even while the Bill of Rights was being penned, the freedom of press clause was not unanimously supported by the thirteen states.

It is generally agreed that one of the intentions of the authors of the Bill of Rights was to prevent government from intruding on the right of the press to publish by preventing publication, licensing publishers, levying taxes, or controlling the sources of newsprint. Even after the Bill of Rights was ratified in 1791, the meaning of a free press remained unclear. Thus, we will discuss attempts to undermine, limit, challenge, interpret, and reinterpret the meaning of a free press during the eighteenth and nineteenth centuries.

The 1800s are noted for the judicial activity undertaken to regulate speech and the press at the state level.[21] During that century, it was thought that the Bill of Rights prevented only Congress, the federal legislature, from passing laws abridging the freedom of the press. Few cases addressing press freedoms came before the U.S. Supreme Court during the nineteenth century.

The twentieth century was the most judicially active century for the press. Two world wars, perceived threats of fascism and communism, national security concerns arising out of those fears, and the rise of electronic media all formed the impetus for judicial attempts to clarify the meaning of a free press. Journalists developed substantial protection against libel lawsuits, especially concerning public figures. As surveillance technology developed, concerns about invasion of privacy increased. While the press became vulnerable to potential invasion of privacy suits, protections developed that recognized the value of news.

The numerous military conflicts involving the United States during the twentieth century and beyond—the two world wars, the Korean War, the Vietnam War, the invasions of Grenada and Panama in the 1980s, and the Gulf War in 1990, and then the invasion of Afghanistan in 2001 and the invasion of Iraq in 2003—all invite an effort to understand the role and limitation of the press during times of war. Furthermore, national security concerns, including the publication of classified documents by the press, were hot spots of judicial activity during the 1900s. Throughout most of the 1900s, the courts reflected back on the early philosophical principles embraced as part of the rationale for protecting the press. The courts attempted to remain true to those principles within a contemporary context complicated by the development of electronic media, shifts in media ownership patterns, and accelerating technological innovation.

We will extend discussion of major press themes to the twenty-first century, which looks to be one of the most fascinating with regard to press freedoms. The past century provided us with a relatively clear understanding of governmental limits on censoring the press and the conditions under which the press is protected from libel and privacy lawsuits. But the twenty-first century has already introduced new challenges to press freedoms. It is here that we will see the enormous role technological innovation has played in reshaping the practice of the press in the United States. Satellite and videophone technologies have confounded government efforts to control the press in the name of national security. Enhanced surveillance technology increases the complexity of balancing privacy with freedom of the press. More and more invasion of privacy lawsuits are targeting paparazzi and other celebrity journalists who aggressively photograph, videotape, and document every possible movement of movie stars and television personalities. New distribution technologies, in combination with the relaxation of media ownership rules, have facilitated the streamlining of news operations, ultimately reducing the number of journalists.

As we look forward into the century ahead, an interesting conundrum emerges. There is, at times, a divergence between a free press in principle and a free press in practice. There are wide-ranging protections for journalistic endeavors, yet there are increasing criticisms of the quality of journalism, the range of views journalists present, and the narrowing of news sources at the very time in history that the variety of news outlets has burgeoned to unprecedented numbers. In an age when Americans may get news and information from radio, television, magazines, newspapers, and the Internet, limits on media ownership—justified on the principle of spectrum scarcity for the broadcast media and of media outlet scarcity within a market—are ringing hollow in the halls of the Federal Communications Commission. Over the past twenty-five years, the number of broadcast radio and television stations a corporation can own has increased. Restrictions on the number and kinds of media a corporation can own within a single market are disappearing or are under increasing scrutiny on First Amendment grounds. Critics of the relaxed ownership rules argue, however, that media concentration does not serve the larger ideals that justify freedom of speech or freedom of the press. They argue that to preserve the democratic principles justifying those freedoms, the government must in fact set limits on ownership across markets and on cross-ownership within markets.

At issue are competing interpretations of the freedom of press clause. Does the clause articulate a negative liberty, meaning that it prohibits any regulatory or legislative agenda? Or can it be read more broadly, as a positive liberty? Can the government take an activist role and encourage the widest range and dissemination of information and ideas to the public? Regulations and legislation that limit the range of ideas are expressly prohibited, but policies that enhance freedom of expression serve the larger principles behind the First Amendment's freedom of speech and press clauses.[22]

Judicial precedent leans in the favor of the freedom of press clause reflecting a negative liberty. In other words, the government is restricted from infringing on the liberty of the press without showing that the restriction serves a more important interest. Still, there are examples in the history of electronic media regulation: the public interest requirement of broadcasters, the old Fairness Doctrine, and the now-diluted Federal Communications Commission restrictions on ownership. The rationale behind these electronic media policies is the belief that balanced presentations of wide-ranging ideas serve the public and the democratic process. In the end, any analysis of what freedom of the press means in this country will recognize that much of the development and refinement of the freedom of press clause is more about fine-tuning the balance between competing rights, needs, and responsibilities than believing that the tension may ever be resolved.

Glossary

Common law: the system of law used by Britain and the United States that is based on custom and court decisions.

Federalists: supporters of the U.S. Constitution who valued separation of powers.

Jurisprudence: philosophy of law.

Participatory democracy: participation by citizens in political decisions.

Prior restraint: when government prohibits speech prior to its publication.

Process of self-actualization: the process of trying to maximize one's abilities and achieve one's potential.

Notes

1. Jacqueline Sharkey, "The Rise of Arab TV," *American Journalism Review* (May 2003): 26–27.

2. Hugo L. Black, "The Bill of Rights," *New York University Law Review* 35 (1960): 865–881, 867.

3. Thomas Emerson, *Toward a General Theory of the First Amendment* (New York: Random House, 1966).

4. Thomas Emerson, *The System of Freedom of Expression* (New York: Random House, 1970), 6–7.

5. *Abrams v. United States*, 250 U.S. 616 at 630 (1919).

6. *Whitney v. California*, 274 U.S. 357 at 375 (1927).

7. *Whitney v. California,* 274 U.S. 357 at 377 (1927).

8. Bruce W. Sanford, *Don't Shoot the Messenger: How Our Growing Hatred of the Media Threatens Free Speech for All of Us* (Lanham, MD: Rowman and Littlefield, 1999).

9. Emerson, *Freedom of Expression.*

10. Emerson, *Freedom of Expression.*

11. Emerson, *Freedom of Expression.*

12. Emerson, *Freedom of Expression.*

13. Emerson, *Freedom of Expression.*

14. Frederick Seaton Siebert, Theodore Peterson, and Wilbur Schramm, *Four Theories of the Press* (Urbana, IL: University of Illinois Press, 1956).

15. Siebert, *Four Theories of the Press.*

16. Denis McQuail, *Mass Communication Theory,* 2nd ed. (Beverly Hills, CA: Sage, 1987).

17. Siebert, *Four Theories of the Press.*

18. Siebert, *Four Theories of the Press.*

19. J. Herbert Altschull, *From Milton to McLuhan: The Ideas Behind American Journalism* (New York: Longman Press, 1990).

20. Sir William Blackstone, *Commentaries on the Laws of England,* Vol. 4 (Boston: T.B. Wait and Sons, 1818), 15.

21. Donna Dickerson, *The Course of Tolerance: Freedom of Press in Nineteenth-Century America* (Westport, CT: Greenwood Press, 1990).

22. Owen M. Fiss, *Liberalism Divided: Freedom of Speech and the Many Uses of State Power* (Boulder, CO: Westview Press, 1996).

8

Twenty-First Century Issues

| Nancy Cornwell

When reviewing the progress and evolution of the First Amendment's protection of press freedoms, one has an impulse to suggest that the twenty-first century is an extraordinary time to be a journalist. There is some truth to such a statement. There are more ways to "be" a journalist than ever before. Technological options for news delivery systems continue to multiply. Technology has reshaped the face of news in exciting if also problematic ways.

However, some fascinating trends in press freedoms have already emerged. Technological advances continue to send surges through the practice of journalism, altering, for example, the power dynamic between the public, political or military organizations, and the press. New forms of information control are emerging on the heels of literally instantaneous transmission of front-line political or war news. No longer are obstacles such as geographical distance or remoteness a barrier to timely transmission of news.

Technological innovation is changing the very definition of journalist as the Internet provides the means for anyone to practice "the trade" as well as the definition of "news" itself. There is no cyberspace editor scrutinizing content or ensuring that professional standards of journalism are maintained. Journalists themselves are using cyberspace to explore new forms of expression through the use of Web logs ("blogs"), a virtual space that allows journalists to break free of traditional notions of the journalistic writing structure (the inverted pyramid) and create something on the order of a journalist's "journal."

In an age when any cell phone or personal digital assistant (PDA) may have the capability of functioning as a camera and technology allows virtually continuous access to the Internet, powerful tools now exist to allow the spreading of news and information, suggesting a shifting balance between those who would share information and those who would restrict it.

In addition, technological convergence, in combination with two decades of deregulation, is reshaping the ownership and business structures of the media. Large corporations are swallowing smaller media outlets. Local new operations are consolidating, regionalizing, and networking. A single company may own virtually all of the media within a single market. Cities fortunate enough to host two daily newspapers increasingly found the papers merging non-editorial operations under joint operating agreements.

These patterns suggest that two significant forces are driving twenty-first-century press freedoms: technological innovation and shifts in media regulation. For example, some technological innovations are promoting new regulatory frameworks, undermining the rationale for other regulatory structures and ultimately outpacing most regulatory efforts. Likewise, existing regulatory traditions are shaping the use of new technologies.

The New Libels: Product Disparagement, Business Defamation, and SLAPP Lawsuits

Following the onrush of news stories about mad cow disease and safe food supplies, after the initial appearance of the disease, also known as bovine spongiform encephalopathy (BSE), in 1996, farmers and ranchers quickly learned what bad publicity could do to the health of their industries. The media have a unique ability to inflate the level of public attention to and concern about issues that have a relatively minor impact through intensive coverage. Communication theorists refer to this as the **agenda-setting** effect of news coverage.[1] Although the press is not necessarily effective at directly telling the public what to think, it seems particularly good at telling the public what to think *about*. In other words, intense coverage of a topic raises its relative importance in the public's mind. Intensive coverage is the modus operandi of the highly competitive modern media industry, which has an insatiable appetite for content. This hunger is heightened by the presence of multiple 24-hour cable news networks, hours of daily local news broadcasts, prime-time network news programs, and Internet versions of all of these media as well as most print news.

The surge of public concern about the risk of mad cow disease is a good example of agenda setting. In early 2004, there was one documented case of mad cow disease in the United States, traced to a cow imported from Canada. That single case prompted calls to test every cow for the disease (not realistically possible) and resulted in the destruction of hundreds of cattle out of concern that other cows from the Canadian herd (imported to the United States but never clearly identified) might also be infected. The media fascination with the story may well lead to improvements in the handling of meat products, but that is an outcome unrelated to the importance the news attached to an isolated instance of mad cow disease. Similar effects arose from the severe acute respiratory syndrome (SARS) scare in late 2003. And there continues to be an excessive media-fed fear that children will be abducted by strangers when, in fact, the overwhelming majority of abductions are committed by acquaintances or family members.

The economic fallout from these news-constructed crises can be significant. Toronto, for example, with numerous reported cases of SARS, lost substantial tourist revenue. So it may not seem surprising that some states have passed laws that make journalists increasingly vulnerable to product disparagement lawsuits. These trade libel or "veggie" libel laws exist in about thirteen states, mainly states with big investments in food production. One of the first notable lawsuits of this kind occurred in the mid-1990s, when CBS was sued for a *60 Minutes* segment on apple producers' use of a chemical called Alar (daminozide). The *60 Minutes* report suggested that consumption of Alar, typically sprayed on apples as a preservative, was linked with cancer. Not surprisingly, apple consumption declined, costing growers an estimated $130 million. Washington apple growers sued under Washington's food disparagement law, claiming the CBS report was false or greatly exaggerated. The appellate court dismissed the case because the apple growers faced the impossible task of proving that CBS's claim was false.[2]

On the heels of the Alar case, product disparagement laws were modified to better protect the agricultural industry, allowing food producers to sue the media when false information (that is, information that is not based on reliable scientific data) was published suggesting the product was unsafe. In other words, any news report suggesting a food product was unsafe had better be supported by reliable scientific data. This requirement has increased the press's exposure to trade libel suits. Even if the media are likely to prevail in such a lawsuit, they have to expend money and resources on a defense.

Returning to the example of mad cow disease, it first appeared on the U.S. media's radar in 1996, when British researchers announced a connection between mad cow disease and a fatal human brain disorder. The researcher thought the most likely source of infection was consumption of infected beef. The sequence of the media events that followed is described in the opinion of a U.S. district court in Texas:

> The British Health Minister's announcement generated numerous reports in the United States. Print media reports included: A March 21, 1996, *New York Times* article announced "Britain Ties Deadly Brain Disease to Cow Ailment." On March 28, 1996, *The Wall Street Journal* ran an article entitled "Agriculture Officials Say Mad-Cow Risk Is Small in U.S. but Don't Rule It Out." An April 5, 1996, *New York Times* article quoted an expert estimating that "a teaspoonful of highly infective cattle feed is enough to cause mad-cow disease." An April 8, 1996, *Newsweek* headline read, "Mad Cow Disease in the U.S.? Don't panic, but one version's already here." Television reports included: A March 14, 1996, *Dateline* report on Mad Cow Disease which included video of a CJD [Creutzfeldt-Jakob disease] victim hospitalized in New York. On March 22, 1996, CNBC's *America's Talking* aired a segment on Mad Cow Disease that featured a debate between Dr. Gary Weber and Howard Lyman. The CNBC program attracted the attention of staffers on *The Oprah Winfrey Show* to Weber and Lyman as prospective guests for the "Dangerous Foods" program.[3]

During the discussion of mad cow disease on the *Oprah* show, Oprah Winfrey commented, "It has just stopped me cold from eating another burger." As a testimony to the power of the *Oprah* show, cattle prices dropped. Texas ranchers sued Winfrey, putting to the test the state's False Disparagement of Perishable Food Products Act. Winfrey prevailed, but not because of her free press or free speech rights (although she may ultimately have prevailed on First Amendment grounds) but because the Texas judge determined that beef in the form of live cattle was not a perishable agricultural product.

As with traditional libel law, the constitutional protection provided to the press requires that the plaintiff bear the burden of proof. Thus, in the *Winfrey* case, ranchers faced the burden of proving that Winfrey intended to harm the industry by knowingly making false statements. Likewise, in October 2003, Sharper Image filed a product disparagement lawsuit against Consumers Union over a report criticizing the effectiveness of its Ionic Breeze Quadra air cleaner. Consumers Union brought a "special motion to strike" to force Sharper Image "to show that its claims have legal and factual merit, thus placing a heavy burden of proof on the plaintiff."[4]

Another defamation tort permits businesses to sue if false defamatory statements harm the company's reputation. The business defamation tort has been used more than once to target Consumers Union, which publishes *Consumer Reports,* a product testing and review magazine. In the mid-1980s, the Bose Corporation unsuccessfully sued Consumers Union over a critical review of the company's speakers.[5] In another trade libel lawsuit, Suzuki Motor Corporation sued Consumers Union over a poor safety rating for its Samurai SUV. Suzuki requested $60 million in damages but had to show that Consumers Union acted with **actual malice**. The initial efforts on the part of Consumers Union to have the case dismissed were unsuccessful, but a jury trial scheduled for late 2004 was avoided when the parties reached a settlement. However, in a severely divided Ninth Circuit Court en banc hearing, Judge Alex Kozinski articulated the key concern about trade libel lawsuits:

I find it incomprehensible that a review truthfully disclosing all this information could be deemed malicious under *New York Times Co. v. Sullivan,* 376 U.S. 254 (1964).[6] If CU can be forced to go to trial after this thorough and candid disclosure of its methods, this is the death of consumer ratings: It will be impossible to issue a meaningful consumer review that a band of determined lawyers can't pick apart in front of a jury. The ultimate losers will be American consumers denied access to independent information about the safety and usefulness of products they buy with their hard-earned dollars.[7]

Kozinski's language is reminiscent of earlier court justifications for the protection of commercial speech. Although commercial speech does not enjoy the same level of vigorous protection that other forms of speech do, the courts recognize the importance of protecting a company's right to advertise because of the importance of providing customers with the information necessary to make informed choices. Consumers Union clearly enjoys the full protection provided to the press, but its legal problems represent the kind of risks the press runs into when criticizing the products and activities of major corporations.

Businesses have yet another means by which to sue critics of the company, products, policies, or practices. A company, especially a large one, has far more resources for the financial expense of a lawsuit than most individuals or small-scale media companies. Thus, a lawsuit or the threat of a lawsuit may provide sufficient pressure to squelch further criticism. These suits, known disparagingly as strategic lawsuits against public participation (SLAPP), are a relatively new legal strategy. The term SLAPP was coined by two University of Denver faculty members in a 1988 article outlining the implications such suits have for political participation.[8]

Some states have created anti-SLAPP statutes to serve as a deterrent to the use of SLAPP suits. In recent years, the California Supreme Court, for example, has broadly interpreted the reach of the state's anti-SLAPP statute. In three decisions, the court strengthened "the protection for expressive activities by confirming that the statute applies to any lawsuit arising from a defendant's exercise of First Amendment rights—even where the plaintiff did not subjectively intend to chill the defendant's expression, and even where the defendant's expression is alleged to be a breach of confidentiality or otherwise unlawful."[9] Toward the end of 2003, the California legislature passed an amendment to the bill to address the growing number of businesses that were, ironically, using the anti-SLAPP statute against consumers.[10] The amendment focused on stopping what Governor Gray Davis called the "corporate abuse" of the statute and refocused its purpose of protecting the First Amendment rights of California citizens.[11]

In spite of the growing number of business and trade libel suits and product disparagement suits, determining when the press has acted with actual malice is extremely difficult, because it is a much higher standard than the simple making of a mistake. The plaintiff must show that the press knowingly published false information or was reckless in addressing its responsibility to verify the story's truthfulness before publishing. Additionally, the courts often recognize that the press must have the First Amendment "space" to make a mistake. The "single mistake rule" protects the press from lawsuits resulting from a single error by requiring that plaintiffs prove that the statements in question reflect a pattern of journalistic incompetence or recklessness.

As new areas of libel develop, some of them, such as product disparagement and business or trade libel, demand serious judicial scrutiny. The press has a well-established constitutional and common law protection against libel charges. Unless the plaintiff is a private individual and the defamation is an issue of private concern, the plaintiff generally bears the entire burden of proof. That protection, in combination with the requirement that the plaintiff bears the difficult challenge of proving that the defamatory statement was false, provides a wide mantle of protection for the press.

Where's the Gatekeeper? The Challenge of the Internet

Not too long ago, a television advertisement for high-speed DSL Internet service aired that began with a man sitting off in a room surfing the Internet. He hears his computer say in a computer-like voice, "You have reached the end of the Internet. Please go back." He gets up and walks into the next room; his wife asks why he is not still surfing the 'Net, to which he responds that he is finished. In reality, of course, there is no end of the Internet, because there are no real boundaries. It is a seemingly endless collection of everything from high-quality research to news to junk to commerce to pornography. This expanse of virtual space poses all sorts of interesting challenges and opportunities for the press. It is also making a mess of the established, comparatively tidy categories of media law. The Internet does not face spectrum limitations, as broadcasting does, yet it delivers content to the user in a way that is visually similar to broadcasting. Children and youths use the Internet readily, and arguably young people are using the Internet more often than they do other informational media, such as newspapers. Today's youths, if they read news, are likely to read it online.

The Internet consists of a vast array of linked networks comprising innumerable documents, home pages, images, and so on. The relationship between the Internet and users makes it different from other media. The current regulatory environment for the Internet, shaped by several court decisions, appears to mimic that of print media more than those of broadcasting and cable television. Still, concerns remain about the Internet because of the availability of inappropriate material to minors (such as sexually explicit images and unmonitored "chat rooms") as well as privacy, security, and fraud. The continuing problem facing any regulatory effort is, simply, the slow-moving machinery of government, which leaves regulators struggling to keep pace with a class of technology that is developing in rapid and unexpected ways.

Along with the explosion of information on the Internet, there is plenty of "journalism" in cyberspace, which makes freedom of the press an important consideration. Most newspapers have online editions, for example, and most broadcast news networks and stations have highly developed Web sites. Search portals, such as those of Google and yahoo, use news services in an effort to hold users at the portal site longer while ad banners appear. Most traditional news outlets, including the *New York Times*—"the newspaper of record"—offer customized news delivery, which one legal scholar, concerned about the civic repercussions of selective exposure to customized information, calls the "Daily Me."[12] How, then, do traditional free press issues translate to the virtual world?

Appropriation and the Internet

One of the new forms of misappropriation involves the plethora of unauthorized images of celebrities appearing on the Web. Generally, this is not a pressing issue for journalists (unless they maintain private Web sites), because use of celebrity images on a Web site as part of a news story is not subject to **appropriation lawsuits**. But the line between news and non-news Web sites is hazy, and thus it is not completely clear when use of a "likeness" is newsworthy and when it may constitute unauthorized appropriation.

There are more visual cues associated with traditional forms of news—newspapers, news magazines, television news—that help to discern when the news exemption applies. The Web can be less clear. The visual norms of the Web are still emerging and are not always distinct. A Web site for the NBC *Today* show and a fan site for the *Today* show may not look significantly different. One may have to look at other clues, such as the URL or copyright information to determine the nature and ownership of the site.

Also, although appropriation is not a concern with news, copyright is a different story. If a news organization publishes someone else's photograph of a celebrity on its Web site, the organization may be in violation of copyright.

Finally, a critical factor in regulation of the Web is that the Internet is not confined by the geopolitical boundaries of the nation-state. This means that the ability to sue for content on Web sites based outside the United States is dramatically limited. It also means that, because a Web site based in Oklahoma can be viewed anywhere, a celebrity seeking to sue for appropriation can go jurisdiction shopping to find a sympathetic court or favorable state laws.

Libel and the Internet

Who is liable when a defamatory statement is posted on the Internet? One of the new areas of libel law involves determining the extent of liability for Internet service providers (ISPs), Web sites hosting listservs, bulletin boards, or discussion groups. The Telecommunications Act of 1996 and the parts of the Communications Decency Act that survived constitutional challenge provide a protective shell for ISPs. Internet service providers may screen out obscene material and interact with content in other ways in an effort to manage services such as bulletin boards. In such cases, a federal appellate court has ruled that ISPs are not liable for content posted by a third party.[13] This protection does not apply to the producers of content. Journalists or media firms that maintain their own Web sites are liable for the content of their sites. E-mail messages are also subject to libel suits if they contain defamatory material and are widely disseminated and otherwise meet the standards of proof for libel.

The number of Internet libel cases is growing. One notable Internet defamation case involved the cyber-gossip of Matt Drudge on his Web site, the *Drudge Report.* The *Drudge Report* garnered public attention when it broke the story of the President Clinton–Monica Lewinsky affair. But it was Drudge's later story in which he suggested that President Clinton's aide, Sidney Blumenthal, had a history of spousal abuse that triggered the first high-profile libel case involving a "news" Web site. Drudge retracted his story the next day, but Blumenthal filed a $30 million lawsuit against Drudge and AOL, the ISP that carried some of Drudge's content. The suit against AOL was dropped because of the *Zeran* ruling,[14] but the case against Drudge proceeded. At one point, Drudge tried to get the case dismissed by arguing that it was a SLAPP suit. The court denied the petition.[15] Ultimately, Blumenthal dropped the suit and paid a small fee to Drudge's legal counsel, with the condition that Drudge not countersue.[16] One notable outcome of the case was that in one of the rulings the court determined that Drudge was not a journalist. If the case had proceeded to trial, that determination may have affected the level of fault that Blumenthal would have needed to prove.

Blogs: Random Acts of Journalism?

The practice of journalism has found a home in most forms of media, including the Internet. Moreover, what it takes to be called a journalist is relatively loosely defined. It is easy to conclude that the content reported in daily newspapers is journalism, even if it is not always good journalism. Most magazine writing falls under the umbrella of journalism, whether it is a lengthy *New Yorker* magazine piece or a brief description of European fashion trends in *Vanity Fair.* We might categorize the stories differently—hard news, soft news, features, and so on—but they are still recognized as journalism. The work of the New Journalists—defined by a kind of creative nonfiction and emblematized by Hunter S. Thompson, Tom Wolfe, and Truman Capote in the 1960s and 1970s—found legitimacy as a journalistic enterprise over time. In short, journalism encompasses many forms of writing that diverge markedly from the traditional inverted pyramid story structure and explore different narrative storytelling styles.

The Internet is yet another medium for practicing journalism. Although the colonization of the Web by the traditional media was initially an extension of the local, regional, and national news outlets, a new form of Internet journalism that goes beyond news media Web sites has emerged. Journalists themselves have created and maintain official and personal Web logs, or "blogs." Blogs are continuously updated Web-based postings. They tend to be more personal and opinionated, and, depending on their purpose, they may contain additional or breaking news that didn't fit into the confines of newspaper or news broadcast formats. This new phenomenon comes with its own vocabulary. People who post blogs are bloggers. The practice of posting blogs is called blogging.

In one form or another, blogs have been around as long as the World Wide Web. The first Web log is generally attributed to Dave Winer, who remains an active voice in the debates surrounding the use of blogs in journalism.[17] It was the development of blogger-friendly software (the first being Pitas.com in July 1999) that dramatically expanded the growth of these "diaries" on the Web.

The first newspaper blog is credited to the Charlotte *Observer* in North Carolina, which provided ongoing Web postings during Hurricane Bonnie in 1998.[18] It was an innovative way to provide up-to-the-minute coverage of a major regional event. The content was like that of traditional news; it was the way it was delivered that was new. But simply posting print versions of stories or providing breaking news updates is not the only way journalists use blogs. Technology journalist and blogger J. D. Lasica refers to Web logs as the "anti-newspaper," meaning that they have some characteristics that are distinctly different from traditional news media.

Where the editorial process can filter out errors and polish a piece of copy to a fine sheen, too often the machinery renders even fine prose limp, lifeless, sterile, and homogenized. A huge part of blogs' appeal lies in their unmediated quality. Blogs tend to be impressionistic, telegraphic, raw, honest, individualistic, highly opinionated, and passionate, often striking an emotional chord.[19]

Blog content may range from tedious accounts of daily life to political rants to commentary and reporting that is equal to any print product. Blogs often include a mechanism for readers to provide feedback, which creates a more interactive relationship between journalists and readers than exists with newspapers or broadcast news. Dan Gillmor, a *San Jose Mercury News* columnist and author of one of the longest continuously published blogs, finds that the most interesting quality of his blog is the interactive, participatory nature of his entries. Readers respond, comment, and correct postings in what amounts to an ongoing conversation.[20]

Breaking news lends itself well to the blog format. *Florida Today* posted continual updates on the *Columbia* shuttle explosion. KFOR-TV reporter Sarah Stewart blogged the developments of a high-profile murder trial using a laptop and an Internet connection through a cell phone. David Abrams, of the Virginia *Gazette,* blogged the trial of Washington, D.C., sniper John Allen Muhammad. Using wireless technology, he filed minute-by-minute updates that mimicked live reporting. It is a comparatively effective alternative to live continuous coverage when courtrooms do not allow the use of cameras.[21]

Blogs sometimes function as a supplement to a reporter's print or broadcast news story. A reporter might use a blog to provide additional news or background facts and Web links, or to develop personal reflections or opinions that would not be appropriate as part of an objective news story. This type of reflective, opinion-based blogging, however, raises a host of questions about the practice of journalism. For blogs associated with an existing media outlet, such as a newspaper, how opinionated may a reporter or columnist be in an online forum? What are the editorial obligations of a newspaper to ensure credibility and accuracy in a blog? Some newspapers require that blogs pass through an editor before posting. The *Sacramento Bee* instituted such a policy after readers complained about the postings of Daniel Weintraub during the California gubernatorial recall election. However, passing material through the editorial process may increase the media outlet's liability for its content.

Many new media outlets do not edit their blogs. Gregg Easterbrook, a senior editor at the *New Republic,* maintained an unedited blog on the magazine's Web site. In one posting he made ethnic slurs about the heads of Disney and Miramax studios as part of an entry about the Quentin Tarantino movie *Kill Bill Vol. 1.* His remarks prompted him to issue an apology, which was also posted on JewishFilm. com. The incident provides real insight into the pitfalls associated with the immediacy of blogs:

> I'm ready to defend all the thoughts in that paragraph. But how could I have done such a poor job of expressing them? Maybe this is an object lesson in the new blog reality. I worked on this alone and posted the piece—what you see above comes at the end of a 1,017-word column that's otherwise about why movies should not glorify violence. Twenty minutes after I pressed "send," the entire world had read it. When I reread my own words and beheld how I'd written things that could be misunderstood, I felt awful. To anyone who was offended I offer my apology, because offense was not my intent. But it was 20 minutes later, and already the whole world had seen it.[22]

In this case, the recognition of the mistake seemed sufficient to end the matter. That has not always been the case. At least one journalist has been fired for content on his blog. Steve Olafson, a reporter for the *Houston Chronicle,* maintained a personal blog under the pseudonym Banjo Jones. In his blog, he criticized some of the public officials he covered as a reporter. He also criticized the *Chronicle.* When his identity was revealed, he was fired because his boss believed he had "compromised his ability to do his job."[23]

Another type of blog emerged in concert with the 2004 elections. "Watchblogs" are dedicated to tracking election coverage in various media. Watchblogs are typically maintained by regular citizens, not by journalists or media outlets. Watchblogs, an entirely new spin on the letter to the editor, reader feedback, and media criticism, are designed to monitor press coverage of the election. In short, it is a watchdog for the watchdog. Most watchblogs operate with a political or ideological agenda. Some do a comprehensive job of monitoring the record of reporting on candidates, and others remain anonymous and lack credibility.

The wide range of blogs illustrates the ongoing debate over the way blogs reinvent journalism on the Internet. As with much Web content, notions of objectivity and editorial gatekeeping are not presumed. Professional training and adherence to a set of professional norms are not a prerequisite to "doing" journalism.

The fluidity of blogging practices has generated plenty of skeptics about the role of blogs in newsgathering. Instead of exercising editorial oversight, some media outlets pressured their journalists to shut down their blogs. CNN asked correspondent Kevin Sites, who was covering the war in Iraq, to shut down the blog he started in early March 2003. After a six-month hiatus, Sites's blog was back, and he was a freelance journalist on assignment for NBC News. His Web site, *www.kevinsites.net,* carried a disclaimer that the space was a personal site and was not affiliated with NBC.

The *New York Times* started a blog called *"Times* on the Trail" to cover the 2004 political campaign. The *Times* exercises editorial control over the blog, but intends to use the site in a different way. According to Len Apcar, editor in chief of *NYTimes.com,*

> We thought there were a lot of blogs out there, but we didn't necessarily think that the quality was very good. We thought that there was a lot of rumor out there, a lot of wild opinion being bandied about, but we also thought there was a vehicle here for short-form information, continuous updating, some development observations, insights, that might not rise to a full article but are worthy of reporting.[24]

Apcar called the debates over editing and over whether a newspaper should blog a "red herring." He refers to the *New York Times* experiment not as a blog but as an updated news service. The *Times* may be breaking new ground in its particular approach to managing blog content, but it is by no means at the forefront of media blogs. The official, ongoing news media blogs tend to be less controversial journalistically than the independent journalists' Web logs.[25] These blogs, like that of Kevin Sites, mentioned above, contain the personal reflections of journalists and remain formally distinct from the media outlet for which the journalists work, or they are the blogs of journalists unaffiliated with any other media outlet.

An interesting emerging phenomenon seen with independent journalists is "blograising." Several journalists have placed appeals for financial contributions on their blogs. Most requests are for funding to cover costs associated with a specific story. For example, Christopher Allbritton, a former AP reporter, posted a request for funds to allow him to travel to Iraq as an independent reporter. His appeal brought in about $13,000.[26] Independent journalists and blograising are presenting interesting questions about the practice of journalism, the editorial function, the notion of interested readers paying for a specific story, and, ultimately, whether blogging is a legitimate form of journalism.

Some online journalists believe blogging is the best form of journalism, free of constraints on expression and outside a system that is "inherently compromised by the business interests and skewed editorial policies of their publications."[27] As one freelance journalist and blogger suggests, "blogging [is] neither superior nor inferior to traditional journalism—just infinitely fascinating."[28] Blogging may be the "purest form of journalism."[29] The jury is still out on blogging as a form of journalism, but blogs are common on the Web and continue to have an impact on traditional forms and structures of news delivery. However, blogs may be pushed aside by the even greater immediacy offered by social media as a means to spread and gather information.

In the end, more questions than answers about blogging remain. Are bloggers journalists? Mickey Kaus, who operates the Web log, *kausfiles.com*, believes they are journalists, but a different kind of journalist operating in an environment with different standards.[30] Yet the issue remains unsettled. The judge in Blumenthal's libel suit against Matt Drudge, for example, concluded that Drudge was not a journalist.

If we are to assume that bloggers are journalists, should they enjoy the same press protections that traditional media journalists enjoy? Will the traditional rules of libel and invasion of privacy apply to bloggers? Will plaintiffs filing lawsuits against bloggers have to show actual malice? Will various codes of professional practice emerge to mitigate the kinds of journalism that generate lawsuits? Would such codes stifle the freewheeling form of blogs?

Should professional norms and structures be established for blogs so that it is easier to distinguish objective news coverage from opinion? Should blogs be considered valid or reliable news sources? Should media outlets edit blogs and risk liability? Would it violate reporters' First Amendment rights for a media employer to require its journalists not to file Web logs?

Is the growth of Web logs a reaction to the diminishing credibility of mainstream media? Is blogging a possible solution to the growing concentration of ownership in the media and the potential narrowing of ideas that accompanies it? Will blogging democratize the Web, opening new venues for diverse expression, or go mainstream as more media start their own blogs? Is the incorporation of blogs into traditional media outlets a way to create a more interactive interface with the audience and perhaps reverse the exodus of viewers and readers to other media?

Blogging is not going to disappear, but it may be supplanted or surpassed by wireless social media.

The Business of the Media: Twentieth-Century Ownership Issues

The exodus of television viewers mentioned above and broadcast audience fragmentation are growing concerns among broadcast news media, which historically have counted on large audience numbers to generate revenue for their advertiser-supported industry. Much of the attrition is due to the growth of cable and satellite television, but there is some evidence that news consumers are migrating to alternative news sources for information, including those available through the Internet.[31] The attrition to the Internet is still minimal compared with the impact of major media news sources, and it has not reached a point where it is replacing current sources of news. For example, in a 2003 study of news coverage of the war in Iraq, respondents were asked to choose the source(s) they used most often for news. Eighty-seven percent of Americans with Internet access still turn to the television for their news. Even more reassuring for mainstream news organizations is evidence that their own Web sites are a main source of information even for Internet users. For example, of those who went online for news:

• 32 percent used television network news Web sites
• 29 percent used newspaper Web sites
• 15 percent used government sponsored sites
• 10 percent used foreign news sites
• 8 percent used alternative news sites
• 4 percent used blogs[32]

Still, the Internet is a player in the media environment, as evidenced by the almost universal presence of Internet sites for commercial media and news outlets. That presence adds additional punch to the deregulatory argument that there are sufficient media choices to reconsider whether limits on media ownership remain justified. Not surprisingly, the FCC continues to loosen ownership limitations that have been in place since the mid–twentieth century. The deregulatory trend gained momentum in the 1980s, but it is a key twenty-first century issue for the press. Although ownership patterns are not an express limit on freedom of the press in the classic sense of direct government restrictions, there is an argument that non-regulatory structural changes to the media industry, like a growing concentration of ownership, have an impact on the philosophical justifications used for protecting the press, namely, the importance of preserving the "marketplace of ideas."

Thus, it is not surprising that the changing ownership patterns of the mass media have become a source of increasing concern among media critics, analysts, and scholars specifically because of a belief that it exacerbates economic pressure on the news-gathering operations of the media and further limits the range of ideas.

The trend in ownership concentration is remarkable. Media companies were, at one time, limited to owning seven television stations, seven AM radio stations, and seven FM radio stations (with no more than one television station in the same market). Today, a media company may own as many radio stations as it can afford (as exemplified by Clear Channel's inventory of over 1,200 radio stations—an average of 5.7 stations per market). Additionally, the number of television stations is structured on the audience "reach" of a single company. Under the original 7/7/7 rule, in addition to limiting the number of stations a single company could own, the total reach of one company could not exceed 25 percent of the national audience. This effectively meant that the big media companies of the late 1970s (primarily ABC, NBC, and CBS) owned and operated stations in the largest urban markets. Other network-affiliated stations were owned by numerous companies and simply contracted to carry a particular network's programming during certain parts of the day. However, the ownership "cap" increased to 35 percent as part of the late-twentieth-century deregulatory trend.

In June 2003, the FCC proposed raising the cap to 45 percent. While the proposal for the new cap was under consideration, Viacom and Fox purchased stations that pushed their companies' reach to 39 percent each. At the culmination of contentious public debate over what would happen to the Fox and Viacom stations if the cap did not expand to 45 percent—a debate that reached its peak during the parallel criticism of Viacom's CBS network's refusal to air a political ad during the 2004 Superbowl (discussed below)—Congress attached a **rider** to an appropriations bill reducing the cap to 39 percent, backing off the FCC's proposed 45 percent cap. This congressional move saved Viacom and Fox from having to divest some media holdings, but it is still opposed by media watch groups as well as by small broadcasters who are afraid of being swallowed up by larger companies.

Ownership caps are not the only ownership issue shaping the early twenty-first century. In June 2003, the FCC eliminated the newspaper/broadcast cross-ownership ban. Before this ruling, a media company could not own a newspaper and a broadcast outlet in the same market. The Third Circuit Court of Appeals ordered a stay of the new rule pending judicial review. Civic groups argue that the conglomeration of ownership reduces the diversity of views in broadcasting and reduces localism in news and public affairs. Small broadcasters also joined the request to restrict ownership of newspapers and broadcast outlets in the same market. Newspaper companies are complaining about being singled out, noting that the FCC already allows a company to own both a cable system and a broadcast outlet within a given market.

On a larger scale, conglomeration of the media continues. For example, below is a listing of the top nine television companies, based on 2002 revenue (note that some of these companies have other media holdings, such as radio stations, cable television, and newspapers):

- News Corporation (Fox TV) owns 35 stations in 26 markets ($2.3 billion)
- Viacom owns 35 stations in 28 markets ($1.8 billion)
- General Electric (NBC-TV) owns 14 stations in 14 markets ($1.7 billion)

- Tribune Co. owns 26 stations in 22 markets ($1.2 billion)
- Disney (ABC-TV) owns 10 stations in 10 markets ($1.2 billion)
- Gannett owns 21 stations in 19 markets ($880 million)
- Hearst-Argyle owns 27 stations in 24 markets ($780 million)
- Sinclair owns 62 stations in 39 markets ($756 million)
- Belo owns 19 stations in 15 markets ($700 million)[33]

The mom-and-pop cable businesses, common until the early 1980s, have largely disappeared. In their place are several large companies, such as Comcast, Time Warner, and Cox. Major broadcast networks are owned by larger parent corporations. General Electric has owned the NBC network for decades. CBS, once owned by Westinghouse, is now part of Viacom (also one of the largest television station groups). ABC was purchased by Capital Cities, which was purchased by the Walt Disney Corporation. In February 2004, Comcast, the largest cable company, announced a $54.1 billion bid for Disney, but the bid was rejected.

There was a time when media companies were not permitted to be vertically integrated and own the means of producing, distributing, and transmitting media content. Those restrictions dissipated with the deregulatory fervor of the 1980s and 1990s. Now media corporations commonly own production studios, distribution companies, and the broadcast or cable outlets to air their products. The Comcast bid for Disney is a reflection of its need for high-quality programming to complement its extensive cable delivery system as the largest cable provider in the country. The purchase of Disney would position Comcast to remain competitive with other vertically integrated media corporations, such as the News Corporation (owner of Fox News Channel, Fox Sports Network, FX, Fox Broadcasting Network, television stations, DIRECTV, and 20th Century Fox production studios as well as significant newspaper and publishing holdings).

The Jessica Lynch story illustrates the way in which vertical integration may affect news content. As part of the intense bidding for an interview with Lynch, who had been a prisoner of war in Iraq, CBS made her an offer that outlined a multifaceted package of possible media products involving MTV, Simon and Schuster Publishers, CBS entertainment, and CBS News.[34] Critics have raised questions about whether these kinds of offers indicate that news operations are not distinctly separate from other entertainment and publication divisions of large media corporations.

Content-based regulations have always been most restrictive for broadcasters and the broadcast medium. For example, the broadcasting editorial rule prevented broadcasters from taking editorial positions on the air. The rule was rationalized on the spectrum scarcity principle: Not everyone could have a license to broadcast, so broadcasters could not use their unique and special position to editorialize. In the fall of 2000, shortly before the national elections, the FCC eliminated the broadcast editorial rule. Now broadcasters have the same First Amendment freedom to editorialize that newspapers have long enjoyed. Given the wide-ranging media options available to the public, the scarcity principle no longer seemed persuasive as a justification for restricting the First Amendment freedoms of broadcasters.

This change, combined with the increasing concentration of media ownership, set in motion another trend in media news. Note that among the top nine station group owners listed above, most have more stations listed than markets listed. In other words, many group owners own or operate more than one station in a market, either through duopoly or local marketing agreements. This ownership structure allows the consolidation of news services. In some markets television group owners are cutting costs by combining news operations and providing a regional news service from a central location. As pointed out by NewsLab, a nonprofit training and research resource for television newsrooms, the Seattle market provides a good example of television news consolidations. "Viacom-owned KSTW airs a 10 p.m. a newscast produced by Cox-owned KIRO across town, using KIRO reporters and anchors. It's easy enough to see what KSTW gets out of the arrangement—a local newscast where it had none. But what does the audience get? Basically, the same homogenized news, at a different time on a different channel."[35] At the very least, studies suggest that the quality and quantity of local news have declined in recent years. [36]

The pattern is already entrenched in radio news. There are more radio stations on the air than ever, but hardly any provide local news outside of drive time weather and traffic reports. Concern about news coverage seems to be supported by the comments of Lowry Mays, founder and CEO of Clear Channel: "If anyone said we were in the radio business, it wouldn't be someone from our company . . . We're not in the business of providing news and information. We're not in the business of providing well-researched music. We're simply in the business of selling our customers products."[37]

Newspapers are not immune to the trends apparent in broadcasting, although the trends are manifested quite differently. Newspapers have not had to face the regulatory hand of the FCC, in part because they face no physical scarcity, nor do they use the public airwaves. Ironically, though, the majority of cities in the United States have only one daily newspaper, but many have four or more television stations and ten or more radio stations. Such figures raise interesting questions about where the *real* scarcity lies. In fact, newspaper scarcity is driven by economic factors, not physical limitations or regulatory oversight. Over the past decade or so, cities have seen competing daily newspapers suffer severe economic losses. In many of the cities that long had two competing daily newspapers, one has been driven out of business. To avoid the growing trend toward single-newspaper towns, the federal government permits two newspapers to join non-editorial functions if one of the papers is clearly on the brink of financial failure. Joint operating agreements

(JOAs) under the Newspaper Preservation Act provide a limited antitrust exemption and are intended to maintain the diversity of editorial content that would be lost if one of the newspapers went out of business.

One example of a JOA occurred in Denver, Colorado. Until January 5, 2001, the *Denver Post,* owned by MediaNews Corp., and the *Denver Rocky Mountain News,* owned by the E. W. Scripps Howard Company, competed vigorously in the Denver market. Both papers suffered economically, in part because the competition suppressed advertising rates. U.S. Attorney General Janet Reno agreed with the Department of Justice's Antitrust Division that the *Denver Rocky Mountain News* was in danger of financial failure. A third entity was jointly created to handle printing and commercial operations for both papers. The news and editorial departments remained separate. The papers continue to publish separate issues during the week. The *Denver Rocky Mountain News* publishes the Saturday paper, and the *Denver Post* publishes the Sunday paper.[38]

There is some concern that JOAs are entered into too quickly. In the Denver case, questions were raised about whether the *Denver Post* was sufficiently open with its financial data, and some criticism was leveled at the *Denver Rocky Mountain News* because it apparently still had the advertising base to survive. With any JOA, a larger concern is whether the editorial positions of the papers will soften or whether the news staff may be less competitive. One interesting aside in the Denver case is that while the two newspapers competed, advertising rates were kept artificially low for the Denver market—so low, in fact, that the nearby city of Aurora was unable to launch an economically viable daily newspaper. As a result, Aurora was one of the largest cities in the country without a daily newspaper.

In the end, JOAs are likely to remain at least a temporary solution for the few remaining cities that have struggling competing daily newspapers.

War and the New Journalist

The history of press censorship has often been presented as a struggle between the press and the government over the question of prior restraint. Many aspects of this press/government relationship were clarified during the twentieth century. It remains extremely difficult for the government to justifiably censor the press, but national security has remained a well-established exception since first articulated by the Supreme Court in the 1931 *Near* decision.[39] The press/government dance around national security concerns continues into the twenty-first century with new challenges driven in part by technological innovation. The court never addressed the constitutionality of the press pool system because the Gulf War ended and the court concluded the issue was moot, in spite of plaintiff pleadings that resolution was necessary for future military/press relations. Still, the government recognized the shortcomings of the press pool system during the Gulf War. From a military public relations or propaganda perspective, the front-line successes were never effectively covered by the press under the pool system.

Thus, with both sides dissatisfied with aspects of the pool system, an alternative system of using "embedded" reporters was tested during the war in Iraq. The embed system had enormous public relations appeal because it provided independent documentation of the military front-line effort with the credibility that accompanies such coverage. As a subtle form of control, the embed system placed reporters in close contact with individual soldiers and successfully played on the power of the personal relationships between reporters and soldiers that inevitably developed over time. Reporters had ample opportunity to tell the human stories of individual military personnel—the same people who were protecting them from injury during military action.

The enormous impact of live video imagery of intense combat pulled audiences into the emotion and power of the fighting. Without question, this new arrangement served the interests of both the military and the media well. Never did the military look so good, and never did the media come away with such rich visual material and compelling personal stories.

At the same time, the embed system raises serious questions about journalists' objectivity. Might it have been difficult for journalists to be objective about the troops who actively protected their lives? Sharing hardships, dangers, exhaustion, and loss of life put journalists in a complicated relationship with the people they were covering. Journalists are still reflecting, with hindsight, on whether the embed system might have at times jeopardized journalistic objectivity.

The embed system was not without challenges from the media. Larry Flynt, publisher of *Hustler* magazine, questioned the constitutionality of placing any limits on the number of journalists traveling with the troops after his reporter was barred from accompanying the first wave of troops entering Afghanistan in late 2001. All press coverage was dramatically limited initially and limited to covering maneuvers such as food drops and air strikes. By May 2002, *Hustler* had an embedded journalist in Afghanistan. Still, Flynt pursued the constitutional question in court. The U.S. Court of Appeals for the D.C. Circuit ruled in early 2004 that reporters do not have a constitutional right to be embedded with troops, although they are free to cover the war on their own.[40] This is not a surprising ruling given that the courts have supported military decisions to deny press access to military bases where the remains of soldiers were returned from overseas.

In addition to the public relations advantages of the embed system, the new arrangement was also prompted by another technologically driven shift in military/press relations. Communication technology innovations over time have generally served to limit the military's ability to control the dissemination of information simply by controlling journalists' mobility. During the invasion of Afghanistan, improved technology allowed journalists to be remarkably mobile while still providing live reports from the field. Dispatches that formerly required a mobile van full of transmission equipment and a satellite link could be made with equipment no larger than a small suitcase. The refinement of videophone technology makes it possible to transmit low-quality video images from anywhere a journalist can make the satellite link. This development makes live remote reporting highly portable. Journalists moved into Afghanistan on their own to gather stories from small bands of Afghan fighters and local villagers. Similar video technology drove much of the visual coverage during the war in Iraq.

The rules governing the press under the embed system allowed for live broadcasts (when troops were not engaged in combat), and the material was not censored, but the guidelines prohibited the transmission of any information on military planning or the location of military units. Geraldo Rivera, reporting for Fox News, lost his embed slot when, during one of his live reports, he drew a map in the sand describing the general location of his unit. Eight days after his expulsion from Iraq, Rivera reappeared on Fox News reporting from Kuwait as an independent journalist. Peter Arnett was fired from MSNBC/NBC for giving an interview to Iraqi television in which he stated, "It is clear that within the United States there is growing challenge to President Bush about the conduct of the war and also opposition to the war." Five days later his stories started appearing in the *London Daily Mirror.*

What are the concerns about the embed process for the audience? One prevailing criticism of the embed system is that no one embedded journalist had much insight into the larger patterns, issues, and context of the war.[41] Like ethnographers, journalists were looking deep, talking about the minute details, telling personal stories of soldiers, and bringing to the audience a narrow slice of the picture. The big picture was harder to see. Reports were also provided by non-embedded or "unilateral" journalists, although they struggled to gain access to the heart of military action.

The long-term impact of the new reporter embed system will play out over the next few years. One thing is clear already: The implications of the embed system for press freedoms are critical. Any restriction on the press comes at a cost to First Amendment rights. The issues raised by the pool system, the embed system, and any other effort to use national security as a justification for restricting the press chips away at the ideal of a free and unencumbered press. The ability to report independently on the activities of the government goes to the heart of the First Amendment.

Climate of Secrecy

The heightened security resulting from the terrorist attacks of September 11, 2001, and the subsequent invasion of Afghanistan and the war in Iraq have changed the degree of press access to governmental activities related to terrorism. The USA

PATRIOT Act, for example, weakens privacy protections for electronic communications, allowing the government to monitor communications more easily. Immigration and Naturalization Service (INS) hearings, previously open to the public, have become closed for security reasons, and INS records have been sealed. The Courts of Appeals in the Third and Sixth Circuits have split on whether closing deportation hearings to the press violates the First Amendment. The Sixth Circuit held the rules unconstitutional. Judge Damon Keith quoted Justice Hugo Black's dissent in the Pentagon Papers case, saying, "The word 'security' is a broad, vague generality whose contours should not be invoked to abrogate the fundamental law embodied in the First Amendment. The guarding of military and diplomatic secrets at the expense of informed representative government provides no real security for our Republic."[42] The judge added that the executive branch, empowered by the USA PATRIOT Act,

seeks to uproot people's lives, outside the public eye, and behind a closed door. Democracies die behind closed doors. The First Amendment, through a free press, protects the people's right to know that their government acts fairly, lawfully, and accurately in deportation proceedings. When government begins closing doors, it selectively controls information rightfully belonging to the people. Selective information is misinformation. The Framers of the First Amendment 'did not trust any government to separate the true from the false for us. They protected the people against secret government.[43]

A couple of months later, the Third Circuit Court of Appeals ruled that INS proceedings were not the same as criminal and civil trials and therefore did not require the same degree of openness to the press. The security concerns at stake thus overrode the right of a free press.[44] The U.S. Supreme Court declined to review the Third Circuit decision. The Department of Justice has not appealed the Sixth Circuit decision. With the split in these two circuit decisions, the issue remains largely unresolved.

There are other areas where the press has faced diminished access to government information. The Justice Department, under the direction of Attorney General John Ashcroft, and empowered by the 2002 Homeland Security Act adopted "a more conservative approach toward interpreting the federal Freedom of Information Act."[45] As a result, the government released less information to the press. The act also removed some government advisory committees from open meeting laws.[46] Possibly the most damaging part of the Homeland Security Act for journalists is the provision that "criminalizes disclosure of information" that is not (and should not be) classified.[47] The risk of criminal prosecution may have a chilling effect on journalists' coverage of the government's activities with regard to domestic and international terrorism.

As part of the USA PATRIOT Act, the government began to identify foreign terrorist organizations (FTOs). An organization labeled as such may have its assets frozen; no one in the United States may provide any material support to the organization; and noncitizens associated with the organization can be prevented from entering the United States. One of the questions raised under the laws guiding designated FTOs is whether official or unofficial Web sites may be censored, sanctioned, or regulated in some manner. Many of the targeted Web sites, such as "The Road to Jihad" and the official sites of Hezbollah and the Islamic Resistance Movement (HAMAS), regularly change URLs to thwart hackers, so it is difficult to locate them even if there are legitimate means of imposing sanctions on them. Furthermore, many are hosted outside the United States and thus outside the reach of U.S. law. Nevertheless, given the traditionally high level of protection for publishers under the First Amendment's free press rights, questions arise about the protection available to those publishing on the Web, information that is not legally obscene, is not a violation of national security, and does not advocate likely and imminent lawless action. Highly provocative publications, *The Anarchist Cookbook* (a recipe book for building explosives) or *Hit Man: A Technical Manual for Independent Contractors* (a how-to manual on killing people), have not been censored by the government. However, the Fourth Circuit Court of Appeals did suggest that the publisher of *Hit Man* could be liable for the death of three people.[48] Ironically, although the publisher agreed to stop publishing *Hit Man,* he forfeited his copyright and the text of the book is now available in its entirety on the Web. So far, no one has sued the Web site owner. The courts ruled that an anti-abortion Web site called "The Nuremberg Files," which posted publicly available personal information (home address, phone number, license plate information, etc.) about physicians who perform abortions, could be censored. Initially, the Ninth Circuit Court of Appeals recognized that the information on the site might increase the likelihood of harm to these doctors, but it was not clear that the information would produce imminent lawless action. Later, in an en banc rehearing, the court concluded that elements of the site posed a threat to the named doctors and had to be removed.[49] The anti-abortion site is occasionally available via the Internet without the offending content of the original Nuremberg Files site. However, the original site is "mirrored" at times, on a Web server in the Netherlands—beyond the reach of U.S. law. Clearly, the twenty-first century will remain a battleground over where to draw the line, with Web site publishers posting highly offensive or provocative content that stretches the limits of a free press.

The Oldest Profession Meets the Newest Technology

The Internet presents a hornet's nest of First Amendment issues, from copyright to incitement to illegal activity. Nowhere have the courts struggled more than with publication of sexually explicit material on the Internet. This twenty-first-century issue brings to a crossroads historically protected sexual material in a medium that is arguably more accessible and even more intrusive than other pornographic media. The most heated debate related to Internet pornography is generated when the question of children enters the mix. The courts have determined that sexually explicit material cannot all be banned solely on the grounds that it may be inappropriate for children. Adults have a constitutionally protected right to view pornographic material, as long as it is not legally obscene and does not involve children. The press also has a constitutional right to publish sexually explicit material that is not legally obscene.

Thus, the question becomes that of how to protect an adult's constitutional right to pornography and a publisher's right to a free press while protecting the welfare of minors. With print, video, or film pornography, the answer has been not to censor but to control access to the material by minors. The problem became more complicated with the advent of the Internet for a variety of reasons. First, young users of the Internet are often more adept at navigating, searching, and circumventing barriers to Web site access than adults, who did not grow up with Internet technology. Stories abound of kids beating filtering software. Second, Web sites have an ability to get around filters with deceptive meta-tags, shifting URLs, and other techniques similar to those used to baffle search engines and to undermine spam filters. Some adult Web sites provide warnings about the material they contain beyond their home page and require visitors to check a box stating that they are at least eighteen years old. This tactic may provide some liability protection for the content providers but is not likely to be an effective deterrent to a motivated minor. Some Web sites attempt to screen out minors by requiring that a credit card number be provided before a user can enter the site, under the assumption that minors do not have access to credit cards. Thus, although sexually explicit Web sites may include "barriers" to entry, they do not provide the same level of protection as the requirement of proof of age before a person can buy *Hustler* magazine or enter an adult store.

In grappling with this issue, Congress has passed several laws designed to control access to sexually explicit material on the Internet. However, initial attempts to control pornography did not withstand First Amendment scrutiny. In 1997, the Communications Decency Act of 1996 was struck down by the Supreme Court.[50] The Court unanimously ruled that the law was overbroad because it encompassed speech that was constitutionally protected for adults.

Subsequent legislative efforts to narrow the language of bills restricting pornography focused on protecting children. The first result was the Children's Online Protection Act of 1998 (COPA). However, COPA was challenged and ruled overbroad in federal district court, and then at the appellate level it was ruled too reliant on "community standards" to determine what is harmful to minors. In 2002, the Supreme Court heard the appeal and remanded the case to the lower court, reversing the appellate decision and asking the lower court to further consider the law as a whole.[51] The case then worked its way back to the Supreme Court after being ruled unconstitutional at the appellate court level for a second time. Oral arguments before the Court occurred in March 2004 and a narrowly divided Court decided four months later that the Child Online Protection Act violated the First Amendment because there were less restrictive means to limit minors' access to pornography.[52]

Some free press and free speech advocates argue that the least restrictive means of controlling children's access to Internet pornography is the use of filtering software or the creation of a controlled domain that is safe for children. Requiring use of a credit card—a component of the COPA—goes too far in the minds of civil libertarians, because for privacy reasons, adults may not want to provide credit card information to view material that otherwise would be freely accessible. According to the American Civil Liberties Union (ACLU), which challenged the law before the Supreme Court, the law criminalizes expression involving "sexual advice and education, Web-based chat rooms and discussion boards involving sexual topics, and Web sites for bookstores, art galleries, and the news media."[53]

In 2002 the Supreme Court struck down the Child Pornography Protection Act of 1996 (CPPA), which criminalized computer-generated images of child pornography. In an affirmation of the free expression rights of Internet publishers, the Court ruled that digital imagery of "virtual" minors engaged in sexual activity is not the same as pornography using actual minors (which is not protected expression). The banning of child pornography has long been based on the harm it causes children. Such harm is difficult to demonstrate in the case of virtual, computer-generated images. Justice Kennedy noted that the law, if upheld, might have banned artistic or literary expression that portrayed minors engaging in sexual activity. Movies such as *American Beauty* (which won an Academy Award) and *Traffic* would have been at risk of falling within the reach of the CPPA.[54]

Other Internet protection laws have been more successful, in part because they have not infringed on publishers' right to a free press. Instead they focus on providing mechanisms to prevent access to sexually explicit material by children. The Children's Internet Protection Act requires that all libraries receiving federal funding for Internet access must provide filtering software on their Internet computers. The Supreme Court upheld the law when it was challenged by the American Library Association.[55] However, there was no majority opinion; instead the decision was made up of numerous concurring opinions. Thus, the specific law was upheld and is now in effect, but the precedential power of the Court's opinion is less clear.

The Children's Online Privacy Protection Act of 1998 (COPPA) requires that Web site operators targeting children under thirteen years old seek verifiable consent from a parent before collecting personal information about a child Web user (including Web activity tracked with "cookies"). Furthermore, the law provides measures for the protection of children's privacy and safety online. One element of COPPA that raises First Amendment concerns is that without being able to collect certain information about children, Internet services have a more difficult time determining the age of users for some free Web services such as chat or e-mail.

The intersection of children's welfare and key Internet issues such as privacy and control of pornography remains unsettled in the early twenty-first century. Navigating the government's special interest in the welfare of children and the competing right of a free press will make the Internet a contentious arena for articulating future press freedoms in the virtual world.

Media, Politics, and Cultural Norms

The Radio Act of 1927 introduced the requirement that broadcasters operate in the "public interest, convenience, and necessity." Over the years, the media and the press seem to have degraded in the eyes of the public. Newton Minow, an FCC chair appointed by President Kennedy, set the stage for public dialogue about television in a 1961 address to the National Association of Broadcasters in which he famously referred to television as a "vast wasteland."[56] His statement was in response to the failure of broadcasters to meet their obligation to serve the public as well as their private interests.

Minow's words fell hard on an industry recently rocked by the quiz show and payola scandals. During his two-year service on the FCC, Minow became a household name and brought to a larger audience the idea that television could be something more than it was. In subsequent years the debate about the state and quality of broadcasting ebbed in and out of public discussion. Sometimes public pressure produced change, if only temporarily. In the 1970s, public pressure pushed the networks to introduce after-school programming such as *Schoolhouse Rock* and ABC's *Afterschool Specials*. In the 1980s, the deregulation of broadcasting, which included a shift in the very meaning of the public interest, seemed to go unchallenged, possibly overshadowed by the growth in cable television.

Peggy Charren, a homemaker disillusioned with the quality of television programming for children, started Action for Children's Television in 1968. Her efforts reintroduced a strong public interest obligation to children's programming with the passage of the Children's Television Act of 1990 (CTA). The law established multifaceted limits on advertising during children's programming, set minimum numbers of hours of educational programming, and required broadcasters to report their educational programming as part of their license obligation. In principle, failure to meet the requirements of the CTA could result in a challenge to the broadcaster's license renewal. However, leaving it up to broadcasters to define what programming is educational resulted in a show such as *Mighty Morphin' Power Rangers* being reported as educational programming because it taught the triumph of good over evil.

Although much of this history reflects a struggle over regulation of content and does not have a direct impact on freedom of the press, these kinds of concerns speak to the underlying justifications of why we as a country are committed to protecting the press. At this point in the early twenty-first century, we see juries increasingly willing to punish reporters who use provocative or even outrageous methods to gather information (thus the growth of news-gathering torts and intentional infliction of emotional distress lawsuits). The public appears to be responding to the increasing propensity of broadcast television, in its competition with cable television and other media, to push the edge of cultural norms or abandon any obligation to higher-quality programming or issues of public concern.

Nowhere was this tendency more evident than in the events involving CBS and Super Bowl XXXVIII. On January 25, 2004, a significant percentage of Americans turned on their televisions to watch Super Bowl XXXVIII. Although most remember the controversy generated by the football game's half-time show featuring singers Janet Jackson and Justin Timberlake, many were unaware of a controversy associated with the Super Bowl broadcast in the weeks preceding the game. CBS, a subsidiary of Viacom, refused to air a political ad submitted by the nonprofit advocacy organization *MoveOn.org*. The organization had spent months building a grassroots campaign to challenge the policies of the Bush administration, and its ad was the winning entry in a contest in which over 1,100 such ads were created and submitted by the general public. Fund-raising efforts collected the $2.25 million needed to air the thirty-second ad once during the Super Bowl. However, CBS held firm on its network policy of not airing advocacy ads. Controversy erupted when it was discovered that CBS nevertheless intended to air an advocacy ad paid for by the White House Drug Policy Office—among the barrage of Super Bowl ads about beer, flatulent horses, and erectile dysfunction. CBS's justification was that the MoveOn.org ad was an advocacy ad, whereas the White House ad was a public service announcement. Nevertheless, the network was accused quite openly of truckling to the current administration, which was poised to affirm new ownership limits highly favorable to CBS (and Fox Broadcasting).

Then, during the Super Bowl's halftime show (produced by MTV, which is also owned by Viacom), Justin Timberlake, in a choreographed dance sequence, ripped off part of Janet Jackson's bustier, exposing her breast. CBS already had a brief delay on the signal and was able to cut away to a wide camera shot almost immediately. Nevertheless, the fallout from the event quickly took on a life of its own.

For example, the producers of the NBC network show *E.R.* were compelled by network executives to remove a brief shot of an elderly woman receiving emergency care, because the shot involved ripping opening her shirt, briefly exposing her breast. The network-level decision was prompted by NBC affiliate stations' nervousness over carrying the scene on the heels of the Super Bowl flurry. The NBC affiliates were afraid it could expose them to FCC indecency fines. Never mind that on a previous episode of *E.R.* there had been a similar emergency room shot in which a patient's breast was briefly exposed. Katie Couric, during a February 5, 2004, *Today* show interview with Noah Wyle, one of the actors on *E.R.,* made an offhand, half-joking, but revealing comment about being careful to not overly criticize NBC for the decision to edit *E.R.* because she didn't want to get fired.

The 2004 Grammy Awards program, airing two weeks after the Super Bowl, prompted an apology from CBS, when the hip-hop group Outkast's performance of *Hey Ya,* in stereotypical Native American costume, elicited from the Native American Cultural Center a public condemnation, a formal complaint with the FCC, and a call for a boycott of CBS, Arista Records (Outkast's label), and the National Academy of Recording Arts and Sciences (a Grammy sponsor).

But it didn't end there as the FCC began to reevaluate its indecency fine structure, hoping to increase the fine tenfold, from $27,500 per incident to $275,000. However, Congress moved more quickly, and the House voted to raise fines for broadcasters and entertainers from $27,500 and $11,000, respectively, to $500,000 each.[57] The House also introduced the Clean Airwaves Act (H.R. 3687). Although historically the FCC has defined indecent material as patently offensive sexual content and has considered the context in which the language or imagery was used, this bill, which did not pass, specifically identified eight words that, regardless of context, would have been reason for FCC fines.

Three television networks and Clear Channel Communications agreed with the proposed new law on indecency. In the midst of this, Clear Channel (which has over 1,200 radio stations) and Infinity Broadcasting (owned by Viacom) adopted zero-tolerance policies for indecency. Thus, Clear Channel canceled *The Howard Stern Show* (the most common target for FCC fines) and the controversial *Bubba the Love Sponge* (WXTB-FM, Atlanta) and developed a policy of making radio disc jockeys pay a portion of any future indecency fines.[58] Additionally, both radio and television outlets implemented a delay in broadcasting live events and programs to allow them to deal with "slips."

The industry trade publication, *Broadcasting and Cable* magazine, lambasted the willingness of broadcasters to capitulate to the groundswell of interest in re-regulating media content: "From expunging Bubba to stifling Stern, broadcasters are sacrificing control over content on the altar of political expedience . . . [T]his universal knee-jerk reaction—emphasis on the jerk—is a shameful chapter in broadcasting history. At a time electronic media should be fighting for their rights, they are happily giving them away."[59]

These shifts raise the question of whether the press remains insulated from content pressures facing the media in general. In a time of reactive concern about offending people and in a time with increased concentration of ownership of media interests, can the press act autonomously? One example that raises concern about press autonomy is MSNBC's decision to cancel *Donahue,* Phil Donahue's talk show. Donahue's show, like several other talk shows, was considered news pro-gramming for regulatory purposes. Donahue's ratings were lower than desired and his show was expensive to produce, but from early on there had been some com-plaints from viewers that Donahue's opinions were too liberal. There was pressure from NBC and its parent company, General Electric, to change the tone of Dona-hue's delivery after focus groups indicated that Donahue seemed "unpatriotic."

Rick Ellis, co-owner of a Web site dedicated to daytime television, noted:

While it's unclear just when the decision was made to cancel Donahue, nearly everyone interviewed for this piece believe that the reasons are more complex than just liberal vs. conservative. 'This is a ratings-driven business, and it's im-portant not to lose track of that in this discussion,' one CNN executive told me on Monday. 'But I won't lie and tell you that your public beliefs and persona don't matter to viewers . . . There are a lot of people out there who believe that the press is inherently liberal. And I would be an idiot if I did anything to en-courage that conversation.' One journalist who works at a competing network says that in the end, the most important lesson to come out of this story is the increasing use of focus groups and polling to determine news programming. While Donahue isn't claiming to be Edward R. Murrow—he is a talk show host—he's talking about the news, with newsmakers. It's a distinction that es-capes most viewers anyway. And if we're moving towards a future where net-work wonks are testing everything before they let us report it . . . Well, frankly, that scares the hell out of me. [60]

Cable and satellite programming have managed to slip under the radar of an angry Congress and FCC. Only those members of Congress who opposed the vote to increase indecency fines have articulated a concern over the First Amendment issues raised by punishing the content of media. With the dilution of any public interest burden on broadcasters, all that is left is reactive regulation. Many issues regarding the current trend in indecency laws remain a concern. Small broadcast-ers, including community radio stations and college stations, would be unable to pay the new fines. And yet it is the small, volunteer-run or student-run stations—typically with minimal professionally trained staff—that have the greatest chance of running afoul of FCC guidelines.[61]

The New Media and the First Amendment

A new social media platform, twitter, developed in 2006 when Jack Dorsey intro-duced the ability of individuals to send short ten to twenty word "tweets" to describe what they were doing or thinking at a particular time. The twitter blogging service was compared to bulletin boards of earlier eras stated a federal court judge in *United*

States v. Cassidy.[62] The court made this analogy in a lawsuit where a leader of a Buddhist sect claimed he was harassed by numerous posts placed on twitter. The court assumed for purposes of First Amendment analysis that these twitter publications are not within one of the categories of speech that fall outside of First Amendment protection: "obscenity, fraud, defamation, true threats, incitement or speech integral to criminal conduct."

In 2011 the U.S. Supreme Court reaffirmed that the First Amendment protects free speech in a digital age. The California state legislature passed a law in 2005 that restricted the sale of violent video games from minors. The 7–2 decision in *Brown v. EMA* protected digital content under the First Amendment.[63] The upshot was that video games indeed qualify for First Amendment protections. In writing for the Court, Justice Scalia stated that minors are entitled to a significant measure of First Amendment protections. The Court compared children's books, full of violence and not forbidden to sell to minors, were no different than video games full of gore. Thus, they contended that the California statute could not withstand **strict scrutiny**.

Additionally, old issues like cameras in the courtroom are getting a new life in the era of social networking and new media. For example, the Quincy, Massachusetts district court has begun an experiment to allow cameras, tweets and blogs directly into the courtroom. The Quincy court experiment will provide continuous unedited live streaming of a day in the courtroom. A special wi fi setting will be established and live blogs will be allowed. The experiment will not be restricted to any particular type of case either. Thus, starting on May 2, 2011, the Quincy courtroom would allow "citizen journalists" to watch and hear everything from traffic disputes to murder arraignments.

Yet another albeit similar issue enters the courtroom when judges instruct jurors to refrain from visiting Internet chatrooms, twitter blogs, or social networking sites during the course of a trial. Given the massive influence of Web sites such as facebook, a question arises as to whether restrictions preventing interactions with that site during the course of a trial violate First Amendment rights.

Conclusion

The twenty-first century will host more complex challenges to freedom of the press than have been faced in previous centuries. Many of the traditional concerns about press freedoms have been hashed out over the past 100 years to a certain level of clarity. The continuing struggles related to libel, invasion of privacy, and prior restraint are in the details. For example, it is just plain hard for the government to levy a prior restraint on the press. The government faces an enormous burden in attempting to justify such an action. However, technological innovations have opened new areas of legal exploration for libel, invasion of privacy, and prior restraint. Determining how traditional legal protections translate to the new media environment is a twenty-first-century challenge.

Non-legal constraints on freedom of the press will play a major role in the twenty-first century. Increasing concentration of media ownership and new forms of journalism adapting to new technologies are just two examples of what the press will navigate in the future. The Project for Excellence in Journalism's *State of the News Media 2004,* released in March 2004, is designed to be an annual assessment of the news media in print, broadcasting, cable television, and on the Internet. It intends to evaluate content, audience composition and attitudes, economic shifts, ownership patterns, and journalistic norms. The 2004 report lists eight trends in journalism that succinctly set the stage for future concerns and raise important questions about the future of press freedoms outside the legal arena:

- A growing number of news outlets are chasing relatively static or even shrinking audiences for new

- Much of the new investment in journalism today—much of the information revolution generally—is disseminating the news, not collecting it.

- In many parts of the news media, we are increasingly getting the raw elements of the news as the end product.

- Journalistic standards now vary even inside a single news organization.

- Without investing in building news audiences, the long-term outlook for many traditional news outlets seems problematic.

- Convergence seems more inevitable and potentially less threatening to journalists than it may have seemed a few years ago.

- The biggest question [concern for the future of quality journalism] may not be technological but economic.

- Those who would manipulate the press and public appear to be gaining leverage over the journalists who cover them.[64]

These trends will contribute to the shape of journalism in the coming years. Although they do not raise explicit concerns about *government* control of the press, the shifts in ownership, technological innovation, economic priorities and pressures, and professional norms of the profession will be some of the indicators of the future health of a free and unfettered press in the United States.

Glossary

Actual malice: knowingly publishing false information intended to cause harm.

Agenda-setting: news media have the ability to increase the salience of public issues.

Appropriation lawsuits: the use of the work of another that is portrayed as their own.

Rider: an additional provision added to a legislative bill.

Strict scrutiny: the most stringent form of judicial review.

Notes

1. Maxwell McCombs and Donald Shaw, "The Agenda Setting Function of Mass Media," *Public Opinion Quarterly* 36, no. 2 (1972): 176–187.

2. *Auvil v. CBS "60 Minutes,"* F3d 75 (9th Cir 1955).

3. *Texas Beef Group v. Winfre,* 11 FSupp2d 858 (ND Texas 1998).

4. Consumers Union, "Consumers Union Files Motion to Strike Sharper Image Lawsuit Under California Anti-SLAPP Statute," *Consumers Union* (3 November 2003).

5. *Bose Corporation v. Consumers Union,* 486 US 485 (1994).

6. *New York Times v. Sullivan,* 376 US 254 (1964).

7. *Suzuki Motor Corporation v. Consumers Union of the United States,* 330 F3d at 11100–1113 (2003).

8. Penelope Canan and George W. Ping, "Strategic Lawsuits Against Public Participation," *Social Problems*, no. 5 (1988): 506–519.

9. Kelli Sager and Rochelle Wilcox, "California Supreme Court Affirms Expansive of Anti-SLAPP Statute," *Findlaw* (2003). Available at http://library. lp.findlaw.com.

10. *California Code of Civill Procedures,* sec. 425.17 (2004).

11. Office of the Governor of California, "Governor Davis Signs Legislation Protecting First Amendment Rights/Ending Frivolous Lawsuits," *Office of the Governor* (2003).

12. Cass Sunstein, *Republic.com* (Princeton, NJ: Princeton University Press, 2001).

13. *Zeran v. America Online,* 129 F3d 327 (4th Cir 1997).

14. *Blumenthal v. Drudge,* 26 Media LRep 1717 (1998).

15. *Blumenthal v. Drudge,* 29 Media LRep 1347 (2001).

16. Howard Kurtz, "Clinton Aide Settles Libel Suit Against Matt Drudge—at a Cost," *Washington Post*, 2 May 2001, p. C01.

17. J. D. Lasica, "Weblogs: A New Source of News," Available at http://www. jdlasica.com/2001/05/24/weblogs-a-new-source-of-news.

18. Chip Scanlan, "Blogging Bonnie," *Poynter Online* (18 September 2003). Available at www.poynter.org.author/chipscan/page/18.

19. Lasica, "Weblogs."

20. Lasica, "Weblogs."

21. American Press Institute, "The Cyber Journalist List" (2004). Available at http://www.cyberjournalist.net/cyberjournalistnet-in-the-news-2004.

22. Greg Easterbrook, "An Apology from Greg Easterbrook Re: New Republic, Jews, Kill Bill Film Violence," *Jewish Film.com* (16 October 2003). Available at http://web.archive.org/web/20040214084048/http://www.tnr.com/easterbrook.mhtml?pid = 868.

23. David Gallagher, "Reporters Find New Outlet, and Concerns, in Web Logs," *New York Times,* 23 September 2002, p. C9.

24. Jonathan Dube, "Q&A With NYTime.com Editor on blogs," *Cyborjournalist* (12 February 2004). Available at http://www.cyberjournalist.net/new/000935.php.

25. American Press Institute, "The Cyber Journalist List."

26. Liz Cox, "Blograising Begins," *Columbia Journalism Review* 42, no. 2 (2003): 9.

27. Lasica, "Weblogs."

28. J. D. Lasica, "Blogging as a Form of Journalism," Available at http://www.jdlasica.com/2001/05/31/blooging-as-a-new-form-of-journalism.

29. Kelly Heyboer and Jill Rosen, "Blogging in the Newsroom," *American Journalism Review* 25, no. 8 (2004): 10–11.

30. Jim Rutenberg, "In Politics the Web Is a Parallel World With Its Own Rules," *NYTimes.com* (22 February 2004). Available at http://www.freerepublic.com/focus/f-news/1082985/posts.

31. Project for Excellence in Journalism, "State of the News Media 2004," *Journalism.org* (15 March 2004). Available at http://state of the media.org/2004.

32. Terrance Smith, "The Real-Time War," *Columbia Journalism Review*, May-June (2003): 26–28.

33. "Cable System's: Top 100," *Broadcast and Cable* (23 February 2004), p. 2A.

34. Ibid.

35. Deborah Potter, "The Big Get Bigger," *Newslab* (6 March 2003). Available at www.ajr.org/article.asp?id = 3098.

36. "Who Owns Your News," *USCLaw,* Spring (2003). Available at www.weblaw.usc.edu/news/assets/docs/Spring2003Magazine.pdf.

37. Christine Chen, "Clear Channel: Not the Bad Boys of Radio," *Fortune.com* (18 February 2003). Available at www://money.cnn.com/magazines/fortune/fortune_archive/2003/03/03338343/index.htm.

38. Andy Vuong, "New Script for Weekend Readers," *DenverPost.com* (31 March 2001). Available at http://extras.denverpost.com/business/joa0331a.htm.

39. *Near v. Minnesota*, 283 US 697 (1931).

40. *Flynt v. Rumsfeld*, US App LEXIS (2004) 1561.

41. Smith (2003) and Jennifer LaFleur, "Embed Program Worked, Broader War Coverage Lagged," *News Media and the Law* 27, no. 2 (2003).

42. *Detriot Free Press v. Ashcroft*, 303 F3d 681 (9th Cir 1997), 693.

43. *Detriot Free Press*, 683 footnotes omitted.

44. *New Jersey Media Group v. Ashcroft*, 308 F3d 198 (3d Cir 2002).

45. Lucy Dalglish, "The Ups and Downs of Homeland Security," *News Media and the Law* 27, no 1 (2003): 3.

46. Gail Russell Craddock, "Security Act to Pervade Daily Lives," *CSMonitor.com* (21 November 2002). Available at http://csmonitor.com/2002/1121/p01s03 -usju.html.

47. Rebecca Daugherty, "Homeland Security Act Blocks Unclassified Information from Public, Protects Companies That Provide It," *News Media and the Law* 27, no. 1 (2003): 9.

48. *Rice v. Paladin Enterprises*, 128 F3d 233 (4th Cir 1997).

49. *Planned Parenthood at Columbia/Williamette, Inc. v. American Coalition of Life Activists*, 290 F3d 1058 (9th Cir 2002).

50. *Reno v. ACLU*, 521 US 844 (1997).

51. *Ashcroft v. ACLU*, 535 US 564 (2002).

52. *Ashcroft v. ACLU*, 124 SCt 2783 (2004).

53. *Ashcroft v. ACLU*, 2004.

54. *Ashcroft v. Free Speech Coalition,* 535 US 234 (2002).

55. *United States v. American Library Association*, 539 US 194 (2003).

56. Newton Minow, *How Vast the Wasteland Now* (New York: Gannet Foundation Media Center, 1991).

57. Carl Hulse, "House votes, 391–22, to Raise Broadcasters' Fines for Indecency," *NYTimes.com* (12 March 2004). Available at http://www.nytimes.com/ 2004/03/12/politics/12INDE.html.

58. John Eggerton, "Assume the Position," *Broadcasting and Cable* 1 March (2004): 2–3.

59. *Broadcasting and Cable* 1 March (2004): 34.

60. Rick Ellis, "Battling for the Soul of Donahue," *AllYourTV.com* (5 March 2003). Available at http://www.commondreams.org/views03/0226–11.htm.

61. Jeff Kosseff, "Small Broadcasters Fear Vote May Spell Disproportionate Fines Over Content," *Oregonian* 11 March (2004): B1, B4.

62. *United States v. Cassidy*, No. TWT 11–091 (D. Md. Dec. 15, 2011).

63. *Brown v. EMA*, 564 U.S. _____ (2011).

64. Project for Excellence in Journalism, "State of the News Media 2004," *Journalism.org* (15 March 2004). Available at http://www. state of the news media. org/2004.

9

The Establishment Clause

| Earl Pollock

The First Amendment, in addition to protecting freedom of speech and the press, provides that "Congress shall make no law respecting an establishment of religion, or prohibiting the free exercise thereof." As already noted, even though the First Amendment expressly refers only to Congress, it has been interpreted to apply also to the States, and not just the federal government.

The Amendment's two religion clauses, the Establishment Clause and the Free Exercise Clause, normally complement each other. To a great extent, they are two sides of a single coin; both are designed to protect religious freedom. Thus, any government action that violates the Establishment Clause (by, for example, discriminating in favor of one religion) probably also violates the Free Exercise Clause.

However, the two clauses may sometimes conflict with each other because of their somewhat different functions. The Court has noted the difficulty of finding "a neutral course between the two Religion Clauses, both of which are cast in absolute terms, and either of which, if expanded to a logical extreme, would tend to clash with the other."[1]

The Establishment Clause seeks government neutrality, not only between religions but also between religion and a lack of religion; but the Free Exercise Clause, by its terms, gives special protection to religion—the very opposite of neutrality. Thus, any government action that supports free exercise (for example, an income tax deduction for contributions to churches) can arguably also be characterized as aiding religion. Because of this tension between the two clauses, neither clause can be read entirely in isolation or as an absolute command, nor must each be interpreted in conjunction with the other to enable them to coexist.

Everson v. Board of Education[2] is a landmark in church-state constitutional law. The case also illustrates the challenge of reconciling the two religion clauses. The Court held that "the clause against establishment of religion by law was intended to erect 'a **wall of separation** between church and State.'" Yet the Court then proceeded to hold that the challenged law did not violate the Establishment Clause, relying in part on the ground that the Free Exercise Clause "commands that New Jersey cannot hamper its citizens in the free exercise of their own religion."[3]

Early Conceptions of the Establishment of Religion

In the *Everson* majority opinion, Justice Black quotes Thomas Jefferson's statement that the Establishment Clause was intended to erect "a wall of separation between church and state."[4] The statement appeared in a letter Jefferson wrote in 1802 in response to a letter from Danbury, Connecticut, Baptist ministers complaining of the Connecticut state government's favoritism to the Congregationalist church.

Since the First Amendment at that time applied only to the federal government, the ministers' letter acknowledged "that the national government cannot destroy the laws of each State" but expressed the hope "that the sentiments of our beloved President . . . will shine & prevail through all these States and all the world till Hierarchy and tyranny be destroyed from the Earth." In his response to the ministers, Jefferson did not address their concerns about problems with state establishment of religion, but confined his comment to the national level. Jefferson's letter stated in part:

> I contemplate with sovereign reverence that act of the whole American people which declared that *their* legislature should make no law respecting an establishment of religion, or prohibiting the free exercise thereof, thus building a wall of separation between church and state. (Underscoring Jefferson's.)[5]

For the next half century there was apparently no further reference to the "wall of separation" until the Supreme Court's opinion in *Reynolds v. United States* upholding a federal law against polygamy in the territories.[6]

At the time the nation was founded, the term "establishment of religion" referred to a legal affiliation between a State and a particular church that received benefits from the state—in particular, financial support through public taxation. "The classic establishment of religion denoted a legal union between a state and a particular church that benefited from numerous privileges not shared by other churches or unbelievers."[7]

In some States religious tests admitted only Christians or even only Protestants to public office. "More troubling to most dissenters, the constitutions of some states allowed establishment ministers to collect salaries raised by state taxes and permitted laws that gave the established clergy the exclusive right to conduct marriages."[8]

Before the American Revolution, either the Anglican or Congregationalist church was established by law in 9 of the original 13 colonies. By the end of the Revolution, both the nature and number of state establishments of religion had substantially changed. The term "establishment" acquired an additional meaning to reflect the development of "multiple or general" establishments, not limited to a single church.[9] In that sense, established churches continued in six States—Massachusetts, Connecticut, New Hampshire, Maryland, Georgia, and South Carolina.[10]

The Anglican Church was everywhere disestablished because of its close relationship to the British Crown. But Congregationalism remained established in Massachusetts, Connecticut, and New Hampshire until the 1830s—nearly half a century after adoption of the Constitution. And until 1877 only Protestants could be members of the New Hampshire state legislature, and until 1876 only Christians could hold public office in North Carolina. The adoption of the First Amendment had no effect on these state restrictions since the Amendment expressly applied only to the national government. The Establishment Clause was added to the Bill of Rights because of concern that Congress might follow the example of the colonies and create a national establishment of religion.[11]

The First Amendment became applicable to the States only under the "incorporation" interpretation of the Fourteenth Amendment. In 1925, in *Gitlow v. New York*, the Supreme Court ruled that the Fourteenth Amendment incorporated the free-speech and free-press guarantees of the First Amendment.[12] In 1940, in *Cantwell v. Connecticut,* this doctrine was extended to the religion clauses of the First Amendment.[13]

Government Aid to Religious Schools

The Court's church-state decisions since *Everson* are difficult to reconcile. But the overall trend has been to enlarge the kinds of aid that government can give to religious schools. In *Board of Education v. Allen*, the Court held that a State could *lend books on secular subjects* to parochial school students.[14] But three years later, the Court rejected reimbursement of religious schools for the *cost of teachers' salaries, textbooks, and instructional materials,* because of excessive "entanglement" between government and religion, even for the teaching of secular subjects.[15]

Subsequent decisions, however, held it was permissible to provide *sign interpreters* for parochial students[16] and to allow *remedial education instructors* in parochial schools.[17] And in *Mitchell v. Helms,*[18] the Court (6–3) held that the federal government could loan equipment and software to parochial schools as part of a broad program as long as the equipment is not used for religious instruction.

Even more important than the Court's specific holding in *Mitchell* is the rationale of Justice Thomas's plurality opinion, joined by Rehnquist, Scalia, and Kennedy. Under their approach, government aid to religious schools would be unrestricted—whether direct or indirect—regardless of how it might be used (even if the aid is "divertible" for religious uses), provided that the aid is allocated on the basis of criteria that neither favor nor disfavor religion and is made available to both public and nonpublic schools (including religious schools) on a nondiscriminatory basis.

Two Justices (O'Connor and Breyer) concurred in the result in *Mitchell* but objected to the test advanced by the plurality opinion. In their view, that opinion "foreshadows the approval of direct monetary subsidies to religious organizations, even when they use the money to advance their religious objectives."

The three other Justices (Stevens, Souter, Ginsburg) dissented, contending that government aid to religious schools should be allowed only if it is of a type (unlike, for example, cash or buildings) that cannot be "diverted" for religious uses.

Prayer in Public Schools

Except for the infamous 1857 *Dred Scott* decision,[19] probably no decision in the history of the Supreme Court (even *Brown v. Board of Education*[20]) has sparked the same national uproar as *Engel v. Vitale*.[21]

At issue in the *Engel* case was the constitutionality of a school board's direction that each class at the beginning of each school day should recite a brief prayer composed by the New York State Board of Regents: "Almighty God, we acknowledge our dependence upon Thee, and we beg Thy blessings upon us, our parents, our teachers, and our Country." Although the prayer was nondenominational in nature, and although students who wished to do so could remain silent or be excused from the room while the prayer was being recited, the Court (6–1, Frankfurter and White not participating) held that the policy violated the Establishment Clause.

In an opinion by Justice Black (who had also authored the *Everson* opinion), the Court stated:

> [B]y using its public school system to encourage recitation of the Regents' prayer, the State of New York has adopted a practice wholly inconsistent with the Establishment Clause. . . .
>
> [T]he constitutional prohibition against laws respecting an establishment of religion must at least mean that in this country it is no part of the business of government to compose official prayers for any group of the American people to recite as a part of a religious program carried on by government.
>
> . . . There can be no doubt that New York's state prayer program officially establishes the religious beliefs embodied in the Regents' prayer. . . . Neither the fact that the prayer may be denominationally neutral nor the fact that its observance on the part of the students is voluntary can serve to free it from the limitations of the Establishment Clause. . . .
>
> It is neither sacrilegious nor antireligious to say that each separate government in this country should stay out of the business of writing or sanctioning official prayers and leave that purely religious function to the people themselves and to those the people choose to look to for religious guidance.[22]

Justice Potter Stewart dissented, denying that "an 'official religion' is established by letting those who want to say a prayer say it" and contending "that to deny the wish of these school children to join in reciting this prayer is to deny them the opportunity of sharing in the spiritual heritage of our Nation."[23]

Two years later, in *School District of Abington v. Schempp,* the Court (8–1) declared unconstitutional state-sponsored Bible readings and recitation of the Lord's Prayer in public schools. The Court emphasized that these religious exercises were prescribed as part of the curricular activities of students, conducted in school buildings, and supervised by teachers. Distinguishing the study of the Bible in a literature or comparative religion course, the Court said that "the exercises here do not fall into those categories. They are religious exercises, required by the States in violation of the command of the First Amendment that the Government maintain strict neutrality, neither aiding nor opposing religion."[24]

In *Wallace v. Jaffree,* the Court (6–3) declared unconstitutional an Alabama law that authorized a moment of silence in public schools for "meditation or voluntary prayer."[25] In the Court's view, the legislative history of the law was clear that its purpose was to reintroduce prayer into the public schools.

The dissenting opinion of Chief Justice Burger in *Wallace* relied heavily on his opinion for the Court two years earlier in *Marsh v. Chambers,* sustaining (6–3) the Nebraska Legislature's practice of beginning each of its sessions with a prayer by a chaplain paid by the State.[26] In *Marsh* (without even any reference to *Engel*) the Court held:

> The opening of sessions of legislative and other deliberative public bodies with prayer is deeply embedded in the history and tradition of this country. From colonial times through the founding of the Republic and ever since, the practice of legislative prayer has coexisted with the principles of disestablishment and religious freedom. In the very courtrooms in which the United States District Judge and later three Circuit Judges heard and decided this case, the proceedings opened with an announcement that concluded, "God save the United States and this Honorable Court." The same invocation occurs at all sessions of this Court.
>
> . . .[T]he Continental Congress, beginning in 1774, adopted the traditional procedure of opening its sessions with a prayer offered by a paid chaplain. . . . [T]he First Congress, as one of its early items of business, adopted the policy of selecting a chaplain to open each session with prayer. . . .
>
> Clearly the men who wrote the First Amendment Religion Clauses did not view paid legislative chaplains and opening prayers as a violation of that Amendment, for the practice of opening sessions with prayer has continued without interruption ever since that early session of Congress. It has also been followed consistently in most of the states. . . .
>
> This unique history leads us to accept the interpretation of the First Amendment draftsmen who saw no real threat to the Establishment Clause arising from

a practice of prayer similar to that now challenged. We conclude that legislative prayer presents no more potential for establishment than the provision of school transportation, *Everson v. Board of Education*, 330 U.S. 1 (1947), beneficial grants for higher education, *Tilton v. Richardson*, 403 U.S. 672 (1971), or tax exemptions for religious organizations, *Walz v. Tax Comm'n of New York City*, 397 U.S. 664 (1970).

. . .In light of the unambiguous and unbroken history of more than 200 years, there can be no doubt that the practice of opening legislative sessions with prayer has become part of the fabric of our society. To invoke Divine guidance on a public body entrusted with making the laws is not, in these circumstances, an "establishment" of religion or a step toward establishment; it is simply a tolerable acknowledgment of beliefs widely held among the people of this country.[27]

The Court further rejected the objections "first, that a clergyman of only one denomination—Presbyterian—has been selected for 16 years; second, that the chaplain is paid at public expense; and third, that the prayers are in the Judeo-Christian tradition."[28]

Against this background, the Court was confronted with the issue of whether its school prayer decisions should also bar prayers at public school functions *outside* the classroom—graduation ceremonies (*Lee v. Weisman*[29]) and school football games (*Santa Fe Independent School District v. Doe*[30]) and determined in both cases that the prayers violated the Establishment Clause.

Adding "Under God" to the Pledge of Allegiance

In 1942, in the midst of World War II, Congress adopted a joint resolution officially recognizing the Pledge of Allegiance to the Flag of the United States of America. The pledge then stated: "I pledge allegiance to the flag of the United States of America and to the Republic for which it stands, one Nation indivisible, with liberty and justice for all." In 1954 Congress amended the wording to insert "under God" after "one Nation."

In *Elk Grove Unified School District v. Newdow*, 542 U.S. 1 (2004), the Supreme Court was asked to consider the applicability of the *Lee* and *Santa Fe* decisions to the "under God" addition.[31] The case, however, ended inconclusively when the Court dismissed the case on the ground that the plaintiff lacked standing to bring the lawsuit.

At issue in the case was a school district's requirement that teachers lead a recitation of the pledge every day in class. California law provides that every public elementary school must begin each day with "appropriate patriotic exercises" and that this requirement may be satisfied by recitation of the pledge. The Elk Grove Unified School District implemented the state law by requiring that "[e]ach elementary school class recite the pledge of allegiance to the flag once each day." Students who objected on religious grounds could abstain.

The plaintiff, an atheist, claimed that the recitation of the pledge in his daughter's elementary school classroom violated the First Amendment. The District Court dismissed the claim, but the Ninth Circuit (2–1) reversed. The court majority held that, although the plaintiff's daughter was not required to recite the pledge, she was unconstitutionally coerced to listen to a religious message during the daily recitation of the pledge by others. The dissenting judge argued that the inclusion of the two words in the pledge was *de minimis* and insufficient to constitute coercion.

After granting review, the Supreme Court (5–3) declined to pass on the constitutional issue, holding that the girl's father lacked the requisite standing because of his lack of legal custody of his daughter and the mother's desire to have her continue reciting the pledge. Stevens's opinion for the majority was joined by Souter, Kennedy, Ginsburg, and Breyer. Rehnquist, Thomas, and O'Connor wrote separate opinions addressing the merits and rejecting the constitutional challenge. (Scalia recused himself because he had previously made a speech in which he had stated his view that inclusion of "under God" in the pledge did not violate the Constitution.)

Religious Symbols on Public Property

Religious symbols on public property are frequently challenged under the Establishment Clause. Determining their constitutionality is likely to be fact-specific and turn on the particular context and history of the display.

For example, in *Capitol Square Review and Advisory Board v. Pinette*,[32] the issue was whether the Ku Klux Klan (KKK) should be prevented from erecting a large cross in a public park across from the Ohio statehouse. The park, under Ohio law, is designated as a forum for discussion of public questions. In light of the park's designation, seven Justices (although without any opinion joined by a majority) agreed that allowing the cross could not be deemed a governmental endorsement of religion and, furthermore, that excluding the cross would violate KKK's free speech rights.

Another case, *Allegheny County v. Greater Pittsburgh ACLU*, involved two different religious displays: a nativity scene in a display case in a county courthouse, and a menorah next to a large Christmas tree in front of a city building (with a sign saying that the city supports "liberty").[33] The Court held that the nativity scene violated the Establishment Clause (5–4) because it was inherently a religious symbol implying endorsement of Christianity. On the other hand, the display combining the menorah and the Christmas tree was found permissible (6–3) because it did not endorse any particular religion and was instead a neutral reflection of the holiday season.

In *Stone v. Graham*, the Court (6–3) struck down a Kentucky statute requiring that a copy of the Ten Commandments be posted in every public school classroom in the state.[34] The Court stated:

> The pre-eminent purpose for posting the Ten Commandments on schoolroom walls is plainly religious in nature. The Ten Commandments are undeniably a sacred text in the Jewish and Christian faiths, and no legislative recitation of a supposed secular purpose can blind us to that fact.[35]

In 2005, 25 years later, the Court decided two new cases involving displays of the Ten Commandments. Both cases were decided 5 to 4. In one case, the Court upheld a six-foot-high Ten Commandments monument on the grounds of the Texas Capitol, while ruling in the other case that framed copies of the Commandments on the walls of two Kentucky county courthouses were unconstitutional. The ten individual opinions in the two cases total 136 pages and reflect a wide variety of views—leading one Court of Appeals to describe this area of the law as "Establishment Clause purgatory."[36]

In the Kentucky case, *McCreary County v. ACLU*,[37] the Ten Commandments displays were originally placed in the courthouses for the express purpose of demonstrating "America's Christian heritage." After an initial challenge, local officials added copies of the Declaration of Independence, the Mayflower Compact, the Bill of Rights, and other historic documents; the officials called the expanded group of documents the "foundations of American law and government."

In his opinion for the majority holding the displays unconstitutional, Justice Souter emphasized the history of the courthouse displays. The claim that the displays had a secular purpose, he said, "was an apparent sham."[38] In her concurring opinion in the Kentucky case, Justice O'Connor said, "It is true that many Americans find the Commandments in accord with their personal beliefs. . . . But we do not count heads before enforcing the First Amendment." She said that the country had worked well, when compared with nations gripped by religious violence, by keeping religion "a matter for the individual conscience, not for the prosecutor or bureaucrat."[39]

Dissenting in the Kentucky case, Justice Scalia (joined by Rehnquist and Thomas) accused the majority of demonstrating hostility to religion and departing from the intent of the Constitution's framers:

> How can the Court *possibly* assert that "the First Amendment mandates governmental neutrality between religion and nonreligion," and that "[m]anifesting a purpose to favor adherence to religion generally" is unconstitutional? Who says so? Surely not the words of the Constitution. Surely not the history and traditions that reflect our society's constant understanding of those words. . . .

Nothing stands behind the Court's assertion that governmental affirmation of the society's belief in God is unconstitutional except the Court's own say-so, citing as support only the unsubstantiated say-so of earlier Courts going back no farther than the mid-20th century. And it is, moreover, a thoroughly discredited say-so. It is discredited, to begin with, because a majority of the Justices on the current Court (including at least one Member of today's majority [Justice O'Connor]) have, in separate opinions, repudiated the supposed principle of neutrality between religion and irreligion. And it is discredited because the Court has not had the courage (or the foolhardiness) to apply the neutrality principle consistently.[40]

What distinguishes the rule of law from the dictatorship of a shifting Supreme Court majority is the absolutely indispensable requirement that judicial opinions be grounded in consistently applied principle. That is what prevents judges from ruling now this way, now that—thumbs up or thumbs down—as their personal preferences dictate.

The display upheld in the Texas case, *Van Orden v. Perry*,[41] is one of hundreds of granite monuments that were erected in public places around the country by the Fraternal Order of Eagles in the 1950s and 1960s. The monument is one of 17 monuments and 21 historical markers in the 22-acre park and includes (in addition to the Ten Commandments) an American eagle, two Stars of David, and a symbol of Christ.

In sustaining the constitutionality of the Texas monument, Chief Justice Rehnquist's plurality opinion (joined by Scalia, Kennedy, and Thomas) acknowledged that "Of course, the Ten Commandments are religious" but stated that in addition "the Ten Commandments have an undeniable historical meaning" and that "Simply having religious content or promoting a message consistent with a religious doctrine does not run afoul of the Establishment Clause." Rehnquist pointed to "an unbroken history of official acknowledgment by all three branches of government of the role of religion in American life from at least 1789." He further stated:

We need only look within our own Courtroom. Since 1935, Moses has stood, holding two tablets that reveal portions of the Ten Commandments written in Hebrew, among other lawgivers in the south frieze. Representations of the Ten Commandments adorn the metal gates lining the north and south sides of the Courtroom as well as the doors leading into the Courtroom. Moses also sits on the exterior east facade of the building holding the Ten Commandments tablets. Similar acknowledgments can be seen throughout a visitor's tour of our Nation's Capital.[42]

Rehnquist distinguished *Stone v. Graham,* which struck down the posting of the Commandments in school classrooms, on the ground that the Court has been particularly vigilant in monitoring compliance with the Establishment Clause in public schools.

Justice Breyer (who had voted with the majority in the Kentucky case to invalidate the postings in the courthouses) provided the fifth vote in the Texas case to uphold the validity of the monument. In his opinion concurring in the judgment, Breyer stated that the Texas monument presented a "borderline case" that depended not on any single formula but on context and judgment. Although acknowledging that the text of the Ten Commandments "undeniably has a religious message," he stated that the text itself is not determinative because the Court must examine "the message that the text . . . conveys . . . [in] the context of the display." The monument's physical setting, he said, "suggests little or nothing of the sacred," and the passing of 40 years without any previous dispute about the monument suggested that the public had understood the monument not as a religious object but as part of a "broader moral and historical message reflective of a cultural heritage." Further, he said, a contrary decision would lead to the removal of many long-standing depictions of the Ten Commandments in public places, and "it could thereby create the very kind of religiously based divisiveness that the Establishment Clause seeks to avoid."[43]

In his dissenting opinion (joined by Ginsburg), Justice Stevens agreed that

> The wall that separates the church from the State does not prohibit the government from acknowledging the religious beliefs and practices of the American people, nor does it require governments to hide works of art or historic memorabilia from public view just because they also have religious significance.[44]

But he contended that,

> Viewed on its face, Texas' display has no purported connection to God's role in the formation of Texas or the founding of our Nation; nor does it provide the reasonable observer with any basis to guess that it was erected to honor any individual or organization.[45]

Instead, "The message transmitted by Texas' chosen display is quite plain: This State endorses the divine code of the 'Judeo-Christian' God." Rejecting Rehnquist's analysis, Stevens stated: "This Nation's resolute commitment to neutrality with respect to religion is flatly inconsistent with the plurality's wholehearted validation of an official state endorsement of the message that there is one, and only one, God."[46]

O'Connor and Souter (joined by Stevens and Ginsburg) also filed dissenting opinions in the Texas monument case. The four dissenters were the four Justices who, along with Breyer, found the Kentucky courthouse displays invalid. Only Breyer voted for the result in both decisions.

Glossary

De minimus: Latin term for "the law cares not for small things."

Wall of separation: belief espoused by Thomas Jefferson that government should not be involved in the business of religion.

Notes

1. *Walz v. Commissioner*, 397 US 664 at 668–669 (1970).
2. *Everson v. Board of Education*, 330 US 1 (1947).
3. *Everson.*
4. *Everson.*
5. Philip Hamburger, *Separation of Church and State* (Cambridge, MA: Harvard University Press, 2002), 161.
6. *Reynolds v. United States*, 98 US 145 at 164 (1878).
7. Leonard W. Levy, *Original Intent and the Founders' Constitution* (New York: Macmillan, 1988), 174.
8. Hamburger, *Separation of Church and State*, 90.
9. Levy, *Original Intent and the Founder's Constitution*, 185, 190.
10. Levy, 189.
11. Levy, 175.
12. *Gitlow v. New York*, 268 US 652 at 666 (1925).
13. *Cantwell v. Connecticut*, 310 US 296 (1940).
14. *Board of Education v. Allen*, 392 US 236 (1968).
15. *Lemon v. Kurtzman*, 403 US 602 (1971).
16. *Zobrest v. Catalina Foothills School District*, 509 US 1 (1993).
17. *Agostini v. Felton*, 521 US 203 (1997).
18. *Mitchell v. Helms*, 530 US 793 (2000).
19. *Dred Scott v. Sandford*, 60 US 393 (1857).
20. *Brown v. Board of Education of Topeka*, 347 US 383 (1954).
21. *Engel v. Vitale*, 370 US 421 (1961). See Bruce Dierenfield, *The Battle over School Prayer* (Lawrence, KS: University Press of Kansas, 2007) concerning the controversy.
22. *Engel.*
23. *Engel.*
24. *School District of Abington v. Schempp*, 374 US 203 (1963).
25. *Wallace v. Jaffree*, 472 US 38 (1985).
26. *Marsh v. Chambers*, 463 US 783 (1983).
27. *Marsh.*
28. *Marsh.*
29. *Lee v. Weisman*, 505, US 577 (1992).

30. *Santa Fe Independent School District v. Doe*, 530 US 290 (2000).

31. *Elk Grove Unified School District v. Newdow*, 542 US 1 (2004).

32. *Advisory Board v. Pinette*, 515 US 753 (1995).

33. *Allegheny County v. Greater Pittsburgh ACLU*, 492 US 573 (1989).

34. *Stone v. Graham*, 449 US 39 (1980) (per curiam).

35. *Stone.*

36. *ACLU v. Mercer County*, 432 F23d 624 at 626 (6th Cir 2005).

37. *McCreary county v. ACLU*, 545 US 844 (2005).

38. *McCreary County.*

39. *McCreary County.*

40. *McCreary County.*

41. *Van Orden v. Perry*, 545 US 677 (2005).

42. *Van Orden.*

43. *Van Orden.*

44. *Van Orden.*

45. *Van Orden.*

46. *Van Orden.*

10

The Free Exercise Clause

| Earl Pollock

Compelled Exemptions

Under the Constitution people may think and believe anything that they want. In *Reynolds v. United States*,[1] the first case to construe the Free Exercise Clause, the Court recognized that "Congress was deprived of all legislative power over mere opinion, but was left free to reach actions." Similarly, in *Cantwell v. Connecticut*,[2] the Court pointed out that the Free Exercise Clause "embraces two concepts—freedom to believe and freedom to act. The first is absolute but, in the nature of things, the second cannot be."

As those decisions emphasize, one of the key functions of the Free Exercise Clause is to protect the expression of religious beliefs and views. But the more difficult issues involving the Clause arise in connection with the validity of religious *exemptions* from statutes. These exemptions are of two types: (1) exemptions that the government *may* choose to grant (*permitted* exemptions) and (2) exemptions that the government *must* grant (*compelled* exemptions).

When a legislature enacts a statute such as a tax law, the legislature has broad discretion in choosing whether to grant an exemption that benefits churches and religious groups, *provided* that the exemption is not limited to religion and also includes other educational or cultural organizations. But if the exemption discriminates in favor of religion, a significant question is presented under the Establishment Clause. Thus, as the *Texas Monthly* decision[3] recognized, a tax exemption exclusively for religion is essentially a government subsidy for religion and is therefore invalid.

On the other hand, if the legislature enacts a statute that contains no exemption for religion and either requires or forbids certain conduct (for example, prohibiting polygamy), and if a member of a particular religion claims that complying with the statute would interfere with his or her exercise of the religion, a significant question is presented under the Free Exercise Clause: Does the Clause require the State to accept the claim and refrain from enforcing the statute in that situation—thereby in effect imposing on the State an exemption that its legislature had never granted—or does the statute trump the religious claim?

Early Supreme Court decisions resolved that issue in favor of legislative authority. In *Reynolds v. United States*,[4] the Court held that the Free Exercise Clause

283

did not exempt Mormons from complying with a federal law prohibiting polygamy law in the territories.

In later decisions such as *Sherbert v. Verner*,[5] which held that a State could not deny unemployment benefits to individuals who left their jobs for religious reasons, the Court interpreted the Free Exercise Clause more broadly to impose a heavy burden on government to justify denial of a religious exemption from a generally applicable statute. Under those decisions, the statute was subject to "**strict scrutiny**" and the government was obliged to carry the burden of demonstrating a compelling governmental interest for refusing to grant the exemption.

But in its 1990 *Smith* decision,[6] the Supreme Court again changed course and instead placed the burden on the person or group seeking the exemption. The decision, involving the eating of peyote as an act of worship and communion, upheld an Oregon law that prohibited the use of peyote for sacramental purposed and ignited a national controversy.

In 1993, in response to the *Smith* decision and expressly for the purpose of overruling the decision, Congress enacted the **Religious Freedom Restoration Act** (RFRA). Four years later, in *City of Boerne v. Flores*,[7] the Supreme Court held that Congress exceeded its powers in subjecting States to the requirements of RFRA.

Prior to the *Smith* decision, in addition to the *Reynolds, Yoder*,[8] and *Sherbert* cases cited in the opinions, the Court had considered exemption claims under the Free Exercise Clause in numerous cases, including, e.g., *United States v. Lee*[9] (rejecting an Amish challenge that their freedom of religion was violated by the requirement that they obtain Social Security numbers and pay Social Security taxes); *Goldman v. Weinberger*[10] (rejecting a claim by a Jewish army psychologist to wear a yarmulke while on duty); *Braunfeld v. Brown*[11] (rejecting a challenge to Sunday closing laws); *Jimmy Swaggart Ministries v. Board of Equalization of California*[12] (rejecting a free exercise challenge to the payment of sales and use taxes for the sale of goods and literature by religious groups); and *Gillette v. United States*[13] (denying a conscientious objector exemption to a draft registrant who objected only to a particular war on religious grounds).

Justice Kennedy's opinion that Congress did not have authority under the Fourteenth Amendment to enact RFRA, is premised on the **doctrine of judicial supremacy** and the twentieth-century conflation of *Marbury v. Madison*.[14] Chief Justice Marshall's opinion in *Marbury* held only that the Court was not precluded from considering the Constitution in cases before it. But the case is invoked in *City of Boerne* as authority to preclude Congress from implementing the Fourteenth Amendment—notwithstanding an express constitutional grant of power to Congress to "enforce" the Amendment.

The Aftermath of the *City of Boerne* Decision

In response to the *City of Boerne* decision, holding that §5 of the Fourteenth Amendment did not authorize Congress to enact RFRA as applied to the States, a dozen

States enacted so-called "little RFRAs." These statutes restored in their jurisdictions the pre-*Smith* test, requiring proof of a compelling interest to overcome the assertion of a religious free exercise claim in those States.

Congress also responded to the *City of Boerne* decision by enacting in 2000 the **Religious Land Use and Institutionalized Persons Act** (RLUIPA)—this time invoking (instead of the Fourteenth Amendment) Congress's authority under its spending and commerce powers. Section 3 of the RLUIPA prohibits federally funded programs (including state prisons and mental hospitals) from burdening the religious exercise of prisoners without a "compelling government interest." In *Cutter v. Wilkinson*,[15] five Ohio prison inmates, adherents of "non-mainstream" religions such as Wicca and Asatru, invoked §3 to protest denial of access to ceremonial items and opportunities for group worship. The State contended that enforcement of §3 would compromise prison security and violates the Establishment Clause. Rejecting that contention, the Court unanimously held that §3 on its face is compatible with the Establishment Clause because it alleviates exceptional government-created burdens on private religious exercise. In addition, the Court held that religious accommodations need not "come packaged with benefits to secular entities"; if it were otherwise, all manner of religious accommodations would fall (such as, for example, providing chaplains and allowing worship services).

While the *City of Boerne* decision precludes application of the federal RFRA to the States, it did not affect the validity of RFRA as applied to free exercise claims asserted against the federal government. In *Gonzales v. O Centro Espirita Beneficiente Uniao,*[16] it was contended that RFRA requires an exception to the Controlled Substances Act for the use of a hallucinogenic tea (hoasca) by a small church in its religious ceremonies. After the government had seized a shipment of hoasca and threatened prosecution, the church obtained a preliminary injunction prohibiting enforcement of the act against the church. In a unanimous decision, the Supreme Court sustained the preliminary injunction, holding that under RFRA the government had failed to demonstrate, at the preliminary injunction stage, a compelling interest that outweighed the church's religious exercise claim.

In *Locke v. Davey,*[17] the Court ruled (7–2) that the state of Washington could prohibit the use of its Promise Scholarship Program to pursue a degree in devotional theology. Interestingly, the *Church of Lukumi Babalu Aye* case[18] was cited in the majority and dissenting opinions. That case concerned ordinances enacted by the City of Hialeah, Florida, that criminalized ritualistic animal sacrifices, which were struck down by the Court (9–0) as unconstitutional because the texts and operation of the ordinances demonstrated that they were specifically designed to suppress a particular religious practice of the Santeria religion.[19]

In *Cantwell v. State of Connecticut,*[20] a man and his two sons, Newton Cantwell and sons Jesse and Russell, Jehovah's Witnesses who claimed to be ordained ministers, had been convicted of violating a Connecticut statute requiring that any religious, charitable, or philanthropic cause have prior approval by county authority before any solicitation could be made. In *Cantwell* no approval existed. Jessie Cantwell was also convicted of inciting a breach of the peace. The convictions had been sustained by the Connecticut Supreme Court.[21] The U.S. Supreme Court overturned the convictions (9–0), ruling that the defendants' conduct was protected by the Constitution.

Post-*Cantwell* decisions protecting religious solicitation have similarly relied on both the Free Exercise and Freedom of Speech Clauses of the First Amendment. In *Murdock v. Pennsylvania*,[22] and *Follett v. Town of McCormick*,[23] the Court struck down the application of license taxes to Jehovah's Witnesses engaged in door-to-door solicitation. *In Watchtower Bible & Tract Society v. Village of Stratton*,[24] the Court invalidated an ordinance prohibiting door-to-door solicitation without first registering with the mayor and receiving a permit, to the extent the ordinance applied to religious proselytizing, anonymous political speech, and the distribution of handbills.

Glossary

Doctrine of Judicial Supremacy: refers to the right of courts to strike down legislative statutes.

Religious Freedom Restoration Act: law enacted by the U.S. Congress in 1993 to provide a defense for persons whose free exercise of religion is burdened by government.

Religious Land Use and Institutionalized Persons Act: a federal statute passed in 2000 to provide greater protection for religious freedom, particularly in land-use and prison settings.

Strict scrutiny: the most strict standard of judicial review used by the courts.

Notes

1. *Reynolds v. United States*, 98 US 145 at 164 (1878).
2. *Reynolds v. United States*, 98 US 145 at 164 (1878).
3. *Texas Monthly, Inc. v. Bullock*, 489 US 1 (1989).
4. *Reynolds.*
5. *Sherbert v. Verner*, 374 US 398 (1963).
6. *Employment Division, Department of Human Resources of Oregon v. Smith*, 494 US 872 (1990).
7. *City of Boerne v. Flores*, 521 US 507 (1997).
8. *Wisconsin v. Yoder*, 406 US 205 (1972).
9. *United States v. Lee*, 455 US 252 (1982).
10. *Goldman v. Weinberger*, 475 US 503 (1986).

11. *Braunfeld v. Brown*, 366 US 599 (1986).

12. *Jimmy Swaggart Ministries v. Board of Equalization of California*, 493 US 378 (1990).

13. *Gillette v. United States*, 401 US 437 (1971).

14. *Marbury v. Madison*, 5 US (1 Cranch) 137 (1803).

15. *Cutter v. Wilkinson*, 544 US 709 (2005).

16. *Gonzales v. O Centro Espirita Beneficiente Uniao*, 546 US 418 (2006).

17. *Locke v. Davey*, 540 US 712 (2004).

18. *Church of Lukumi Babalu Aye*, 508 US 520 (1993).

19. *Church of Lukumi Babalu Aye.*

20. *Cantwell v. State of Connecticut*, 310 US 296 (1940).

21. *Cantwell.*

22. *Murdock v. Pennsylvania*, 319 US 105 (1943).

23. *Follett v. Town of McCormick*, 321 US 573 (1944).

24. *Watchtower Bible & Tract Society v. Village of Stratton*, 536 US 150 (2002).

Appendix: Pre-2008 Cases

Abrams v. United States, 250 U.S. 616 (1919)

Facts of the Case

The defendants were convicted on the basis of two leaflets they printed and threw from windows of a building. One leaflet signed "revolutionists" denounced the sending of American troops to Russia. The second leaflet, written in Yiddish, denounced the war and U.S. efforts to impede the Russian Revolution. The defendants were charged and convicted for inciting resistance to the war effort and for urging curtailment of production of essential war material. They were sentenced to 20 years in prison.

Question

Do the amendments to the Espionage Act or the application of those amendments in this case violate the Free Speech Clause of the First Amendment?

Legal Provision: Amendment 1

No and no. The act's amendments are constitutional and the defendants' convictions are affirmed. In Clarke's majority opinion, the leaflets are an appeal to violent revolution, a call for a general strike, and an attempt to curtail production of munitions. The leaflets had a tendency to encourage war resistance and to curtail war production. Holmes and Brandeis dissented on narrow ground: the necessary intent had not been shown. These views were to become a classic libertarian pronouncement.[1]

Ashcroft, Attorney General, et al. v. Free Speech Coalition et al., 535 U.S. 234, 122 S.Ct. 1389, 152 L.Ed.2d 403 (2002)

Facts of the Case

The Child Pornography Prevention Act of 1996 (CPPA) prohibits "any visual depiction, including any photograph, film, video, picture, or computer or computer-generated image or picture" that "is, or appears to be, of a minor engaging in sexually explicit conduct," and any sexually explicit image that is "advertised, promoted, presented, described, or distributed in such a manner that conveys the impression" it depicts "a minor engaging in sexually explicit conduct."

The Free Speech Coalition, an adult-entertainment trade association, and others filed suit, alleging that the "appears to be" and "conveys the impression" provisions are overbroad and vague and, thus, restrain works otherwise protected by the First Amendment. Reversing the District Court, the Court of Appeals held the CPPA invalid on its face, finding it to be substantially overbroad because it bans materials that are neither obscene under *Miller v. California*, 413 U.S. 15, nor produced by the exploitation of real children as in *New York v. Ferber*, 458 U.S. 747.

Question

Does the Child Pornography Prevention Act of 1996 abridge freedom of speech where it where it proscribes a significant universe of speech that is neither obscene under *Miller v. California* nor child pornography under *New York v. Ferber*?

Decision

Six votes for Free Speech Coalition, three vote(s) against.

Legal Provision: 18 U.S.C. 2252

Yes. In a 6–3 opinion delivered by Justice Anthony M. Kennedy, the Court held that the two prohibitions described here are overbroad and unconstitutional. The Court found the CPPA to be inconsistent with *Miller* insofar as the CPPA cannot be read to prohibit obscenity, because it lacks the required link between its prohibitions and the affront to community standards prohibited by the obscenity definition. Moreover, the Court found the CPPA to have no support in *Ferber* since the CPPA prohibits speech that records no crime and creates no victims by its production. Provisions of the CPPA cover "materials beyond the categories recognized in *Ferber* and *Miller*, and the reasons the Government offers in support of limiting the freedom of speech have no justification in our precedents or in the law of the First Amendment" and abridge "the freedom to engage in a substantial amount of lawful speech," wrote Justice Kennedy.[2]

Boy Scouts of America v. Dale (99–699) 530 U.S. 640 (2000)

Facts of the Case

The Boy Scouts of America revoked former Eagle Scout and assistant scoutmaster James Dale's adult membership when the organization discovered that Dale was a homosexual and a gay rights activist. In 1992 Dale filed suit against the Boy Scouts, alleging that the Boy Scouts had violated the New Jersey statute prohibiting discrimination on the basis of sexual orientation in places of public accommodation. The Boy Scouts, a private, not-for-profit organization, asserted that homosexual conduct was inconsistent with the values it was attempting to instill in young people. The New Jersey Superior Court held that New Jersey's public accommodations law was inapplicable because the Boy Scouts was not a place of public accommodation. The court also concluded that the Boy Scouts' First Amendment freedom of expressive association prevented the government from forcing the Boy Scouts to accept Dale as an adult leader. The court's Appellate Division held that New Jersey's public accommodations law applied to the Boy Scouts because of its broad-based membership solicitation and its connections with various public entities, and that the Boy Scouts violated it by revoking Dale's membership based on his homosexuality. The court rejected the Boy Scouts' federal constitutional claims. The New Jersey Supreme Court affirmed. The court held that application of New Jersey's public accommodations law did not violate the Boy Scouts' First Amendment right of expressive association because Dale's inclusion would not significantly affect members' abilities to carry out their purpose. Furthermore, the court concluded that reinstating Dale did not compel the Boy Scouts to express any message.

Question

Does the application of New Jersey's public accommodations law violate the Boy Scouts' First Amendment right of expressive association to bar homosexuals from serving as troop leaders?

Decision

Five votes for Boy Scouts of America, four vote(s) against.

Legal Provision: Amendment 1: Speech, Press, and Assembly

Yes. In a 5–4 opinion delivered by Chief Justice William H. Rehnquist, the Court held that "applying New Jersey's public accommodations law to require the Boy Scouts to admit Dale violates the Boy Scouts' First Amendment right of expressive association." In effect, the ruling gives the Boy Scouts of America a constitutional right to bar homosexuals from serving as troop leaders. Chief Justice Rehnquist wrote for the Court that, "[t]he Boy Scouts asserts that homosexual conduct is inconsistent with the values it seeks to instill," and that a gay troop leader's presence "would, at the very least, force the organization to send a message, both to the young members and the world, that the Boy Scouts accepts homosexual conduct as a legitimate form of behavior."[3]

Brandenburg v. Ohio, 395 U.S. 444, 89 S.Ct. 1827, 23 L.Ed.2d. 430 (1969)

Facts of the Case

Brandenburg, a leader in the Ku Klux Klan, made a speech at a Klan rally and was later convicted under an Ohio criminal syndicalism law. The law made illegal advocating "crime, sabotage, violence, or unlawful methods of terrorism as a means of accomplishing industrial or political reform," as well as assembling "with any society, group, or assemblage of persons formed to teach or advocate the doctrines of criminal syndicalism."

Question

Did Ohio's criminal syndicalism law, prohibiting public speech that advocates various illegal activities, violate Brandenburg's right to free speech as protected by the First and Fourteenth Amendments?

Decision

Eight votes for Brandenburg, zero vote(s) against.

Legal Provision: Amendment 1: Speech, Press, and Assembly

The Court's per curiam opinion held that the Ohio law violated Brandenburg's right to free speech. The Court used a two-pronged test to evaluate speech acts: (1) speech can be prohibited if it is "directed at inciting or producing imminent lawless action" and (2) it is "likely to incite or produce such action." The criminal syndicalism act made illegal the advocacy and teaching of doctrines while ignoring whether that advocacy and teaching would actually incite imminent lawless action. The failure to make this distinction rendered the law overly broad and in violation of the Constitution.[4]

Joseph Burstyn, Inc. v. Wilson, 343 U.S. 495 (1952)

Facts of the Case

"In a series of decisions beginning with *Gitlow v. New York* this Court held that the liberty of speech and of the press which the First Amendment guarantees against abridgment by the federal government is within the liberty safeguarded by the Due Process Clause of the Fourteenth Amendment from invasion by state action. That principle has been followed and reaffirmed to the present day. . . . [T]he present case is the first to present squarely to us the question whether motion pictures are within the ambit of protection which the First Amendment, through the Fourteenth, secures to any form of 'speech' or 'the press.'"

Question

Are motion pictures protected under the First Amendment?

Legal Provision: Amendment 1

"It is urged that motion pictures do not fall within the First Amendment's aegis because their production, distribution, and exhibition is a large-scale business conducted for private profit. We cannot agree. That books, newspapers, and magazines are published and sold for profit does not prevent them from being a form of expression whose liberty is safeguarded by the First Amendment. We fail to see why operation for profit should have any different effect in the case of motion pictures. . . For the foregoing reasons, we conclude that expression by means of motion pictures is included within the free speech and free press guaranty of the First and Fourteenth Amendments."[5]

Cantwell v. Connecticut, 310 U.S. 296 (1940)

Facts of the Case

Jesse Cantwell and his son were Jehovah's Witnesses; they were proselytizing a predominantly Catholic neighborhood in Connecticut. The Cantwells distributed religious materials by traveling door-to-door and by approaching people on the street. After voluntarily hearing an anti-Roman Catholic message on the Cantwells' portable phonograph, two pedestrians reacted angrily. The Cantwells were subsequently arrested for violating a local ordinance requiring a permit for solicitation and for inciting a breach of the peace.

Question

Did the solicitation statute or the "breach of the peace" ordinance violate the Cantwells' First Amendment free speech or free exercise rights?

Legal Provision: Amendment 1

Yes. In a unanimous decision, the Court held that while general regulations on solicitation were legitimate, restrictions based on religious grounds were not. Because the statute allowed local officials to determine which causes were religious and which ones were not, it violated the First and Fourteenth Amendments. The Court also held that while the maintenance of public order was a valid state interest, it could not be used to justify the suppression of "free communication of views." The Cantwells' message, while offensive to many, did not entail any threat of "bodily harm" and was protected religious speech.[6]

Chaplinsky v. New Hampshire, 315 U.S. 568 (1942)

Facts of the Case

Chaplinsky, a Jehovah's Witness, called a city marshal a "God-damned racketeer" and "a damned fascist" in a public place. He was arrested and convicted under a state law for violating a breach of the peace.

Question

Does the application of the statute violate Chaplinsky's freedom of speech protected by the First Amendment?

Legal Provision: Amendment 1

No. Some forms of expression—among them obscenity and fighting words—do not convey ideas and thus are not subject to First Amendment protection. In this case, Chaplinsky uttered fighting words; that is, words that "inflict injury or tend to incite an immediate breach of the peace."[7]

Cohen v. California, 403 U.S. 15 (1971)

Facts of the Case

A 19-year-old department store worker expressed his opposition to the Vietnam War by wearing a jacket emblazoned with "FUCK THE DRAFT. STOP THE WAR." The young man, Paul Cohen, was charged under a California statute that prohibits "maliciously and willfully disturb[ing] the peace and quiet of any neighborhood or person [by] offensive conduct." Cohen was found guilty and sentenced to 30 days in jail.

Question

Did California's statute, prohibiting the display of offensive messages such as "Fuck the Draft," violate freedom of expression as protected by the First Amendment?

Decision

Five votes for Cohen, four vote(s) against.

Legal Provision: Amendment 1: Speech, Press, and Assembly

Yes. In an opinion by Justice John Marshall Harlan, the Court reasoned that the expletive, while provocative, was not directed toward anyone; besides, there was no evidence that people in substantial numbers would be provoked into some kind of physical action by the words on his jacket. Harlan recognized that "one man's vulgarity is another's lyric." In doing so, the Court protected two elements of speech: the emotive (the expression of emotion) and the cognitive (the expression of ideas).[8]

Dennis v. United States, 341 U.S. 494 (1951)

Facts of the Case

In 1948 the leaders of the Communist Part of America were arrested and charged with violating provisions of the Smith Act. The Act made it unlawful to knowingly conspire to teach and advocate the overthrow or destruction of the U.S. government. Party leaders were found guilty and lower courts upheld the conviction.

Question

Did the Smith Act's restrictions on speech violate the First Amendment?

Decision

Six votes for United States, two vote(s) against.

Legal Provision: US Const Amend 1; 18 U.S.C. §§ 10, 11

In a 6–2 decision, the Court upheld the convictions of the Communist Party leaders and found that the Smith Act did not "inherently" violate the First Amendment. In the plurality opinion, the Court held that there was a distinction between the mere teaching of communist philosophies and active advocacy of those ideas. Such advocacy created a "clear and present danger" that threatened the government. Given the gravity of the consequences of an attempted putsch, the Court held that success or probability of success was not necessary to justify restrictions on the freedom of speech.[9]

Engel v. Vitale, 370 U.S. 421 (1962)

Facts of the Case

The Board of Regents for the State of New York authorized a short, voluntary prayer for recitation at the start of each school day. This was an attempt to defuse the politically potent issue by taking it out of the hands of local communities. The blandest of invocations read as follows: "Almighty God, we acknowledge our dependence upon Thee, and beg Thy blessings upon us, our teachers, and our country."

Question

Does the reading of a nondenominational prayer at the start of the school day violate the Establishment Clause of the First Amendment?

Decision

Six votes for Engel, one vote(s) against.

Legal Provision: Establishment of Religion

Yes. Neither the prayer's nondenominational character nor its voluntary character saves it from unconstitutionality. By providing the prayer, New York officially approved religion. This was the first in a series of cases in which the Court used the establishment clause to eliminate religious activities of all sorts, which had traditionally been a part of public ceremonies. Despite the passage of time, the decision is still unpopular with a majority of Americans.[10]

FCC v. Pacifica Foundation, 438 U.S. 726, 57 L. Ed. 2d 1073, 98 S. Ct. 3026 (1978)

Facts of the Case

During a mid-afternoon weekly broadcast, a New York radio station aired George Carlin's monologue, "Filthy Words." Carlin spoke of the words that could not be said on the public airwaves. His list included shit, piss, fuck, cunt, cocksucker, motherfucker, and tits. The station warned listeners that the monologue included "sensitive language which might be regarded as offensive to some." The FCC received a complaint from a man who stated that he had heard the broadcast while driving with his young son.

Question

Does the First Amendment deny government any power to restrict the public broadcast of indecent language under any circumstances?

Decision

Five votes for FCC, four vote(s) against.

Legal Provision: Amendment 1: Speech, Press, and Assembly

No. The Court held that limited civil sanctions could constitutionally be invoked against a radio broadcast of patently offensive words dealing with sex and execration. The words need not be obscene to warrant sanctions. Audience, medium, time of day, and method of transmission are relevant factors in determining whether to invoke sanctions. "[W]hen the Commission finds that a pig has entered the parlor, the exercise of its regulatory power does not depend on proof that the pig is obscene."[11]

Gertz v. Robert Welch, Inc., 418 U.S. 323 (1974)

Facts of the Case

Gertz was an attorney hired by a family to sue a police officer who had killed the family's son. In a magazine called *American Opinion*, the John Birch Society accused Gertz of being a "Leninist" and a "Communist-fronter" because he chose to represent clients who were suing a law enforcement officer. Gertz lost his libel suit because a lower court found that the magazine had not violated the actual malice test for libel which the Supreme Court had established in *New York Times v. Sullivan* (1964).

Question

Does the First Amendment allow a newspaper or broadcaster to assert defamatory falsehoods about an individual who is neither a public official nor a public figure?

Decision

Five votes for Gertz, four vote(s) against.

Legal Provision: Amendment 1: Speech, Press, and Assembly

The Court reversed the lower court decision and held that Gertz's rights had been violated. Justice Powell argued that the application of the *New York Times v. Sullivan* standard in this case was inappropriate because Gertz was neither a public official nor a public figure. In the context of the opinion, Powell advanced many lines of reasoning to establish that ordinary citizens should be allowed more protection from libelous statements than individuals in the public eye. However, continued Powell, "the actual malice standard did not lose all significance in cases involving ordinary citizens as he advised states to use it in assessing claims for punitive damages by citizens suing for libel."[12]

Ginsberg v. New York, 390 U.S. 629 (1968)

Facts of the Case

The appellant and his wife operate "Sam's Stationery and Luncheonette" in Bellmore, Long Island. They have a lunch counter, and, among other things, also sell magazines including some so-called girlie magazines. The appellant was prosecuted under two informations, each in two counts, which charged that he personally sold a 16-year-old boy two girlie magazines on each of two dates in October 1965, in violation of 484-h of the New York Penal Law.

Question

This case presents the question of the constitutionality on its face of a New York criminal obscenity statute, which prohibits the sale to minors under 17 years of age of material defined to be obscene on the basis of its appeal to them whether it would be obscene to adults.

Legal Provision: Amendment 1: Freedom of Speech

It is the state's duty and right to protect minors from pornographic material meant for adults.[13]

Hazelwood School Dist. v. Kuhlmeier, 484 U.S. 260 (1988)

Facts of the Case

The Spectrum, the school-sponsored newspaper of Hazelwood East High School, was written and edited by students. In May 1983 Robert E. Reynolds, the school principal, received the page proofs for the May 13 issue. Reynolds found two of the articles in the issue to be inappropriate, and ordered that the pages on which the articles appeared be withheld from publication. Cathy Kuhlmeier and two other former Hazelwood East students brought the case to court.

Question

Did the principal's deletion of the articles violate the students' rights under the First Amendment?

Decision

Five votes for Hazelwood School District, three vote(s) against.

Legal Provision: Amendment 1: Speech, Press, and Assembly

No. In a 5–3 decision, the Court held that the First Amendment did not require schools to affirmatively promote particular types of student speech. The Court held that schools must be able to set high standards for student speech disseminated under their auspices, and that schools retained the right to refuse to sponsor speech that was "inconsistent with 'the shared values of a civilized social order.'" Educators did not offend the First Amendment by exercising editorial control over the content of student speech so long as their actions were "reasonably related to legitimate pedagogical concerns." The actions of Principal Reynolds, the Court held, met this test.[14]

Heffron v. International Society for Krishna Consciousness, 452 U.S. 640 (1981)

Facts of the Case

A Minnesota law allowed the Minnesota Agricultural Society to devise rules to regulate the annual state fair in St. Paul. Minnesota State Fair Rule 6.05 required organizations wishing to sell or distribute goods and written material to do so from an assigned location on the fairgrounds. In other words, walking vendors and solicitors were not allowed. The International Society for Krishna Consciousness challenged the rule, arguing that it restricted the ability of its followers to freely exercise their religious beliefs at the state fair.

Question

May a state, consistent with the First and Fourteenth Amendments, confine religious organizations wishing to sell and distribute religious literature at a state fair to an assigned location within the fairgrounds?

Decision

Five votes for Heffron, four vote(s) against.

Legal Provision: Free Exercise of Religion

Using the "valid time, manner, and place" criteria which the Court employs to assess government restrictions of First Amendment activities, the Court held that Rule 6.05 did not violate the Constitution. Since the rule was applied equally to all groups wanting to solicit at the fairgrounds, not making restrictions based on the content of a group's message, and because the state had an important interest in "protecting the safety and convenience" of the fair's patrons, Justice White argued that the rule's restrictions were legitimate. Allowing all religious, nonreligious, and commercial groups to move about the grounds distributing literature and soliciting funds would result in "widespread disorder" which would be potentially danger-ous to the fair's visitors.[15]

Miller v. California, 413 U.S. 15, 93 S.Ct. 2607, 37 L.Ed.2d. 419 (1973)

Facts of the Case

Miller, after conducting a mass mailing campaign to advertise the sale of "adult" material, was convicted of violating a California statute prohibiting the distribution of obscene material. Some unwilling recipients of Miller's brochures complained to the police, initiating the legal proceedings.

Question

Is the sale and distribution of obscene materials by mail protected under the First Amendment's freedom of speech guarantee?

Decision

Five votes for Miller, four vote(s) against.

Legal Provision: Amendment 1: Speech, Press, and Assembly

In a 5–4 decision, the Court held that obscene materials did not enjoy First Amend-ment protection. The Court modified the test for obscenity established in *Roth v. United States* and *Memoirs v. Massachusetts*, holding that "[t]he basic guidelines for the trier of fact must be: (a) whether 'the average person, applying contemporary community standards' would find that the work, taken as a whole, appeals to the prurient inter-est . . . (b) whether the work depicts or describes, in a patently offensive way, sexual conduct specifically defined by the applicable state law; and (c) whether the work, taken as a whole, lacks serious literary, artistic, political, or scientific value." The Court rejected the "utterly without redeeming social value" test of the *Memoirs* decision.[16]

Morse et al. v. Frederick, 551 U.S. 393 (2007)

Facts of the Case

At a school-supervised event, Joseph Frederick held up a banner with the message "Bong Hits 4 Jesus," a slang reference to marijuana smoking. Principal Deborah

Morse took away the banner and suspended Frederick for 10 days. She justified her actions by citing the school's policy against the display of material that promotes the use of illegal drugs. Frederick sued under 42 U.S.C. 1983, the federal civil rights statute, alleging a violation of his First Amendment right to freedom of speech. The District Court found no constitutional violation and ruled in favor of Morse. The court held that even if there were a violation, the principal had qualified immunity from lawsuit. The U.S. Court of Appeals for the Ninth Circuit reversed. The Ninth Circuit cited *Tinker v. Des Moines Independent Community School District*, which extended First Amendment protection to student speech except where the speech would cause a disturbance. Because Frederick was punished for his message rather than for any disturbance, the Circuit Court ruled, the punishment was unconstitutional. Furthermore, the principal had no qualified immunity, because any reasonable principal would have known that Morse's actions were unlawful.

Questions

1. Does the First Amendment allow public schools to prohibit students from displaying messages promoting the use of illegal drugs at school-supervised events?

2. Does a school official have qualified immunity from a damages lawsuit under 42 U.S.C. 1983 when, in accordance with school policy, she disciplines a student for displaying a banner with a drug reference at a school-supervised event?

Decision

Five votes for Morse, four vote(s) against.

Legal Provision: Amendment 1: Speech, Press, and Assembly

Yes and not reached. The Court reversed the Ninth Circuit by a 5–4 vote, ruling that school officials can prohibit students from displaying messages that promote illegal drug use. Chief Justice John Roberts's majority opinion held that although students do have some right to political speech even while in school, this right does not extend to pro-drug messages that may undermine the school's important mission to discourage drug use. The majority held that Frederick's message, though "cryptic," was reasonably interpreted as promoting marijuana use—equivalent to "[Take] bong hits" or "bong hits [are a good thing]." In ruling for Morse, the Court affirmed that the speech rights of public school students are not as extensive as those adults normally enjoy, and that the highly protective standard set by *Tinker* would not always be applied. In concurring opinions,

Justice Thomas expressed his view that the right to free speech does not apply to students and his wish to see *Tinker* overturned altogether, while Justice Alito stressed that the decision applied only to pro-drug messages and not to broader political speech. The dissent conceded that the principal should have had immunity from the lawsuit, but argued that the majority opinion was "deaf to the constitutional imperative to permit unfettered debate, even among high-school students."[17]

New York Times Co. v. Sullivan, 376 U.S. 254 (1964)

Facts of the Case

Decided together with *Abernathy v. Sullivan*, this case concerns a full-page ad in the *New York Times*, which alleged that the arrest of the Rev. Martin Luther King Jr. for perjury in Alabama was part of a campaign to destroy King's efforts to integrate public facilities and encourage blacks to vote. L. B. Sullivan, the Montgomery city commissioner, filed a libel action against the newspaper and four black ministers who were listed as endorsers of the ad, claiming that the allegations against the Montgomery police defamed him personally. Under Alabama law, Sullivan did not have to prove that he had been harmed; and a defense claiming that the ad was truthful was unavailable since the ad contained factual errors. Sullivan won a $500,000 judgment.

Question

Did Alabama's libel law, by not requiring Sullivan to prove that an advertisement personally harmed him and dismissing the same as untruthful due to factual errors, unconstitutionally infringe on the First Amendment's freedom of speech and freedom of press protections?

Decision

Nine votes for *New York Times*, zero vote(s) against.

Legal Provision: Amendment 1: Speech, Press, and Assembly

The Court held that the First Amendment protects the publication of all statements, even false ones, about the conduct of public officials except when statements are made with actual malice (with knowledge that they are false or in reckless disregard of their truth or falsity). Under this new standard, Sullivan's case collapsed.[18]

New York Times Company v. United States, 403 U.S. 713, 91 S.Ct. 2140, 29 L.Ed.2d. 822 (1971)

Facts of the Case

In what became known as the "Pentagon Papers Case," the Nixon Administration attempted to prevent the *New York Times* and *Washington Post* from publishing materials belonging to a classified Defense Department study regarding the history of United States activities in Vietnam. The President argued that prior restraint was necessary to protect national security. This case was decided together with *United States v. Washington Post Co.*

Question

Did the Nixon Administration's efforts to prevent the publication of what it termed "classified information" violate the First Amendment?

Decision

Six votes for *New York Times*, three vote(s) against.

Legal Provision: Amendment 1: Speech, Press, and Assembly

Yes. In its per curiam opinion the Court held that the government did not overcome the "heavy presumption against" prior restraint of the press in this case. Justices Black and Douglas argued that the vague word "security" should not be used "to abrogate the fundamental law embodied in the First Amendment." Justice Brennan reasoned that since publication would not cause an inevitable, direct, and immediate event imperiling the safety of American forces, prior restraint was unjustified.[19]

R.A.V. v. St. Paul, 505 U.S. 377, 112 S.Ct. 2538, 120 L.Ed.2d. 305 (1992)

Facts of the Case

Several teenagers allegedly burned a crudely fashioned cross on a black family's lawn. The police charged one of the teens under a local bias-motivated criminal ordinance that prohibits the display of a symbol that "arouses anger, alarm or resentment in others on the basis of race, color, creed, religion or gender." The trial court dismissed this charge. The state supreme court reversed. R.A.V. appealed to the U.S. Supreme Court.

Question

Is the ordinance overly broad and impermissibly content-based in violation of the First Amendment Free Speech Clause?

Decision

Nine votes for R.A.V., zero vote(s) against.

Legal Provision: Amendment 1: Speech, Press, and Assembly

Yes. In a 9–0 vote, the justices held the ordinance invalid on its face because "it prohibits otherwise permitted speech solely on the basis of the subjects the speech addresses." The First Amendment prevents government from punishing speech and expressive conduct because it disapproves of the ideas expressed. Under the ordinance, for example, one could hold up a sign declaring all anti-Semites are bastards but not that all Jews are bastards. Government has no authority "to license one side of a debate to fight freestyle, while requiring the other to follow the Marquis of Queensbury Rules."[20]

Roberts v. U.S. Jaycees, 468 U.S. 609 (1984)

Facts of the Case

According to its bylaws, membership in the U.S. Jaycees was limited to males between the ages of 18 and 35. Females and older males were limited to associate membership in which they were prevented from voting or holding local or national office. Two chapters of the Jaycees in Minnesota, contrary to the bylaws, admitted women as full members. When the national organization revoked the chapters' licenses, they filed a discrimination claim under a Minnesota antidiscrimination law. The national organization brought a lawsuit against Kathryn Roberts of the Minnesota Department of Human Rights, who was responsible for the enforcement of the antidiscrimination law.

Question

Did Minnesota's attempts to enforce the antidiscrimination law violate the Jaycees' right to free association under the First Amendment?

Decision

Seven votes for Roberts, zero vote(s) against.

Legal Provision: Association

In a unanimous decision, the Court held that the Jaycees chapters lacked "the distinctive characteristics that might afford constitutional protection to the decision of its members to exclude women." The Court reasoned that making women full members would not impose any serious burdens on the male members' freedom of expressive association. The Court thus held that Minnesota's compelling interest in eradicating discrimination against women justified enforcement of the state anti-discrimination law. The Court found that the Minnesota law was not aimed at the suppression of speech and did not discriminate on the basis of viewpoint.[21]

Santa Fe Independent School Dist. v. Doe, 530 U.S. 290 (2000)

Facts of the Case

Prior to 1995, a student elected as Santa Fe High School's student council chaplain delivered a prayer, described as overtly Christian, over the public address system before each home varsity football game. One Mormon and one Catholic family filed suit challenging this practice and others under the Establishment Clause of the First Amendment. The District Court enjoined the public Santa Fe Independent School District (the District) from implementing its policy as it stood. While the suit was pending, the District adopted a new policy, which permitted, but did not require, student-initiated and student-led prayer at all the home games and authorized two student elections, the first to determine whether "invocations" should be delivered at games, and the second to select the spokesperson to deliver them. After the students authorized such prayers and selected a spokesperson, the District Court entered an order modifying the policy to permit only nonsectarian, nonproselytizing prayer. The Court of Appeals held that, even as modified by the District Court, the football prayer policy was invalid. The District petitioned for a writ of certiorari, claiming its policy did not violate the Establishment Clause because the football game messages were private student speech, not public speech.

Question

Does the Santa Fe Independent School District's policy permitting student-led, student-initiated prayer at football games violate the Establishment Clause of the First Amendment?

Decision

Six votes for Doe, three vote(s) against.

Legal Provision: Establishment of Religion

Yes. In a 6–3 opinion delivered by Justice John Paul Stevens, the Court held that the District's policy permitting student-led, student-initiated prayer at football games violates the Establishment Clause. The Court concluded that the football game prayers were public speech authorized by a government policy and taking place on government property at government-sponsored school-related events and that the District's policy involved both perceived and actual government endorsement of the delivery of prayer at important school events. Such speech is not properly characterized as "private," wrote Justice Stevens for the majority. In dissent, Chief Justice William H. Rehnquist, joined by Justices Antonin Scalia and Clarence Thomas, noted the "disturbing" tone of the Court's opinion that "bristle[d] with hostility to all things religious in public life."[22]

Stanley v. Georgia, 394 U.S. 55, 22 L. Ed. 2d 542, 89 S. Ct. 1243 (1969)

Facts of the Case

Law enforcement officers, under the authority of a warrant, searched Stanley's home pursuant to an investigation of his alleged bookmaking activities. During the search, the officers found three reels of eight-millimeter film. The officers viewed the films, concluded they were obscene, and seized them. Stanley was then tried and convicted under a Georgia law prohibiting the possession of obscene materials.

Question

Did the Georgia statute infringe upon the freedom of expression protected by the First Amendment?

Decision

Nine votes for Stanley, zero vote(s) against.

Legal Provision: Amendment 1: Speech, Press, and Assembly

The Court held that the First and Fourteenth Amendments prohibited making private possession of obscene materials a crime. In his majority opinion, Justice Marshall noted that the rights to receive information and to personal privacy were fundamental to a free society. Marshall then found that "[i]f the First Amendment means anything, it means that a State has no business telling a man, sitting alone in his own house, what books he may read or what films he may watch. Our whole constitutional heritage rebels at the thought of giving government the power to control men's minds." The Court distinguished between the mere private posses-sion of obscene materials and the production and distribution of such materials. The latter, the Court held, could be regulated by the states.[23]

United States v. O'Brien, 391 U.S. 367 (1968)

Facts of the Case

David O'Brien burned his draft card at a Boston courthouse. He said he was ex-pressing his opposition to war. He was convicted under a federal law that made the destruction or mutilation of drafts card a crime.

Question

Was the law an unconstitutional infringement of O'Brien's freedom of speech?

Decision

Seven votes for United States, one vote(s) against.

Legal Provision: Selective Service, Military Selective Service, or Universal Military Service and Training Acts

No. The 7–1 majority, speaking through Chief Justice Earl Warren, established a test to determine whether governmental regulation involving symbolic speech was justified. The formula examines whether the regulation is unrelated to con-tent and narrowly tailored to achieve the government's interest. "[W]e think it clear," wrote Warren," that a government regulation is sufficiently justified if it is within the constitutional power of the Government; if it furthers an important or substantial governmental interest; if the governmental interest is unrelated to the suppression of free expression; and if the incidental restriction on alleged First Amendment freedoms is not greater than is essential to the furtherance of that interest."[24]

Texas v. Johnson, 491 U.S. 397, 109 S.Ct. 2533, 105 L.Ed.2d 342 (1989)

Facts of the Case

In 1984, in front of the Dallas City Hall, Gregory Lee Johnson burned an Ameri-can flag as a means of protest against Reagan Administration policies. Johnson was tried and convicted under a Texas law outlawing flag desecration. He was sentenced to one year in jail and assessed a $2,000 fine. After the Texas Court of Criminal Ap-peals reversed the conviction, the case went to the Supreme Court.

Question

Is the desecration of an American flag, by burning or otherwise, a form of speech that is protected under the First Amendment?

Decision

Five votes for Johnson, four vote(s) against.

Legal Provision: Amendment 1: Speech, Press, and Assembly

In a 5–4 decision, the Court held that Johnson's burning of a flag was protected expression under the First Amendment. The Court found that Johnson's actions fell into the category of expressive conduct and had a distinctively political nature. The fact that an audience takes offense to certain ideas or expression, the Court found, does not justify prohibitions of speech. The Court also held that state officials did not have the authority to designate symbols to be used to communicate only limited sets of messages, noting that "[i]f there is a bedrock principle underlying the First Amendment, it is that the Government may not prohibit the expression of an idea simply because society finds the idea itself offensive or disagreeable."[25]

Tinker v. Des Moines Independent Community School Dist., 393 U.S. 503 (1969)

Facts of the Case

John Tinker, 15 years old, his sister Mary Beth Tinker, 13 years old, and Christopher Echardt, 16 years old, decided along with their parents to protest the Vietnam War by wearing black armbands to their Des Moines schools during the Christmas holiday season. Upon learning of their intentions, and fearing that the armbands would provoke disturbances, the principals of the Des Moines School District resolved that all students wearing armbands be asked to remove them or face suspension. When the Tinker siblings and Christopher wore their armbands to school, they were asked to remove them. When they refused, they were suspended until after New Year's Day.

Question

Does a prohibition against the wearing of armbands in public school, as a form of symbolic protest, violate the First Amendment's freedom of speech protections?

Decision

Seven votes for Tinker, two vote(s) against.

Legal Provision: Amendment 1: Speech, Press, and Assembly

The wearing of armbands was "closely akin to 'pure speech'" and protected by the First Amendment. School environments imply limitations on free expression, but here the principals lacked justification for imposing any such limits. The principals had failed to show that the forbidden conduct would substantially interfere with appropriate school discipline.[26]

West Virginia State Board of Education v. Barnette, 319 U.S. 624 (1943)

Facts of the Case

The West Virginia Board of Education required that the flag salute be part of the program of activities in all public schools. All teachers and pupils were required to honor the Flag; refusal to salute was treated as "insubordination" and was punishable by expulsion and charges of delinquency.

Question

Did the compulsory flag-salute for public schoolchildren violate the First Amendment?

Decision

Six votes for Barnette, three vote(s) against.

Legal Provision: US Const. Amend 1; W. Va. Code § 1734

In a 6–3 decision, the Court overruled its decision in *Minersville School District v. Gobitis* and held that compelling public schoolchildren to salute the flag was unconstitutional. The Court found that such a salute was a form of utterance and was a means of communicating ideas. "Compulsory unification of opinion," the Court held, was doomed to failure and was antithetical to First Amendment values. Writing for the majority, Justice Jackson argued that "[i]f there is any fixed star in our constitutional constellation, it is that no official, high or petty, can prescribe what shall be orthodox in politics, nationalism, religion, or other matters of opinion or force citizens to confess by word or act their faith therein."[27]

Whitney v. California, 274 U.S. 357 (1927)

Facts of the Case

Charlotte Anita Whitney, a member of the Communist Labor Party of California, was prosecuted under that state's Criminal Syndicalism Act. The Act prohibited advocating, teaching, or aiding the commission of a crime, including "terrorism as a means of accomplishing a change in industrial ownership . . . or effecting any political change."

Question

Did the Criminal Syndicalism Act violate the First or Fourteenth Amendments?

Legal Provision: First Amendment

In a unanimous decision, the Court sustained Whitney's conviction and held that the Act did not violate the Constitution. The Court found that the Act violated neither the Due Process Clause nor the Equal Protection Clause, and that freedom of speech guaranteed by the First Amendment was not an absolute right. The Court argued "that a State . . . may punish those who abuse this freedom by utterances . . . tending to . . . endanger the foundations of organized government and threaten its overthrow by unlawful means" and was not open to question. The decision is most notable for the concurring opinion written by Justice Brandeis, in which he argued that only clear, present, and imminent threats of "serious evils" could justify suppression of speech.[28]

Wisconsin v. Yoder, 406 U.S. 208 (1972)

Facts of the Case

Jonas Yoder and Wallace Miller, both members of the Old Order Amish religion, and Adin Yutzy, a member of the Conservative Amish Mennonite Church, were prosecuted under a Wisconsin law that required all children to attend public schools until age 16. The three parents refused to send their children to such schools after the eighth grade, arguing that high school attendance was contrary to their religious beliefs.

Question

Did Wisconsin's requirement that all parents send their children to school at least until age 16 violate the First Amendment by criminalizing the conduct of parents who refused to send their children to school for religious reasons?

Decision

Seven votes for Yoder, zero vote(s) against.

Legal Provision: Free Exercise of Religion

In a unanimous decision, the Court held that individual's interests in the free exercise of religion under the First Amendment outweighed the State's interests in compelling school attendance beyond the eighth grade. In the majority opinion by Chief Justice Warren E. Burger, the Court found that the values and programs of secondary school were "in sharp conflict with the fundamental mode of life mandated by the Amish religion," and that an additional one or two years of high school would not produce the benefits of public education cited by Wisconsin to justify the law. Justice William O. Douglas filed a partial dissent but joined with the majority regarding Yoder.[29]

Yates v. United States, 354 U.S. 298 (1957)

Facts of the Case

Fourteen leaders of the Communist Party in the state of California were tried and convicted under the Smith Act. That Act prohibited willfully and knowingly conspiring to teach and advocate the overthrow of the government by force. This case was decided in conjunction with *Richmond v. United States* and *Schneiderman v. United States*.

Question

Did the Smith Act violate the First Amendment?

Decision

Six votes for Yates, one vote(s) against.

Legal Provision: Smith, Subversive Activities Control, Communist Control, or Other Similar Federal Legislation Except the Internal Security Act (qv.)

In a 6–1 decision, the Court reversed the convictions and remanded the cases to a District Court for retrial. The Court interpreted the Smith Act in the following manner: First, the term "organize" was construed to mean the creation of a new organization, making the Act inapplicable to subsequent organizational acts. Second, the Court drew a distinction between the "advocacy and teaching of forcible overthrow as an abstract principle" and the "advocacy and teaching of concrete action for the forcible overthrow of the Government." The Court recognized that instances of speech that amounted to "advocacy of action" were "few and far between."[30]

Notes

1. "*Schenck v. U.S.*," The Oyez Project at IIT Chicago-Kent College of Law, accessed February 26, 2012, http://www.oyez.org/cases/1901–1939/1919/1919_316.

2. "*Ashcroft v. Free Speech Coalition*," The Oyez Project at IIT Chicago-Kent College of Law, accessed February 26, 2012, http://www.oyez.org/cases/2000–2009/2001/2001_00_795.

3. "*Boy Scouts of America v. Dale*," The Oyez Project at IIT Chicago-Kent College of Law, accessed February 26, 2012, http://www.oyez.org/cases/1990–1999/1999/1999_99_699.

4. "*Brandenburg v. Ohio*," The Oyez Project at IIT Chicago-Kent College of Law, accessed February 26, 2012, http://www.oyez.org/cases/1960–1969/1968/1968_492.

5. "*Joseph Burstyn, Inc. v. Wilson*," ACLU ProCon.org, accessed February 26, 2011, http://aclu.procon.org/view.resource.php?resourceID = 380.

6. "*Cantwell v. Connecticut*," The Oyez Project at IIT Chicago-Kent College of Law, accessed February 26, 2012, http://www.oyez.org/cases/1901–1939/1939/1939_632.

7. "*Chaplinsky v. New Hampshire*," The Oyez Project at IIT Chicago-Kent College of Law, accessed February 26, 2012, http://www.oyez.org/cases/1940–1949/1941/1941_255.

8. "*Cohen v. California*," The Oyez Project at IIT Chicago-Kent College of Law, accessed February 26, 2012, http://www.oyez.org/cases/1970–1979/1970/1970_299.

9. "*Dennis v. United States*," The Oyez Project at IIT Chicago-Kent College of Law, accessed February 26, 2012, http://www.oyez.org/cases/1950–1959/1950/1950_336.

10. "*Engel v. Vitale*," The Oyez Project at IIT Chicago-Kent College of Law, accessed February 26, 2012, http://www.oyez.org/cases/1960–1969/1961/1961_468.

11. "*FCC v. Pacifica Foundation*," The Oyez Project at IIT Chicago-Kent College of Law, accessed February 26, 2012, http://www.oyez.org/cases/1970–1979/1977/1977_77_528.

12. "*Gertz v. Robert Welch, Inc.*," The Oyez Project at IIT Chicago-Kent College of Law, accessed February 26, 2012, http://www.oyez.org/cases/1970–1979/1973/1973_72_617.

13. "*Ginsberg v. New York*," California State University Stanislaus, accessed February 26, 2012, http://www.csustan.edu/cj/jjustice/CaseFiles/Ginsberg-v-New-York.pdf.

14. *"Hazelwood School District v. Kuhlmeier,"* The Oyez Project at IIT Chicago-Kent College of Law, accessed February 26, 2012, http://www.oyez.org/cases/1980-1989/1987/1987_86_836.

15. *"Heffron v. International Society For Krishna Consciousness,"* The Oyez Project at IIT Chicago-Kent College of Law, accessed February 26, 2012, http://www.oyez.org/cases/1980–1989/1980/1980_80_795.

16. *"Miller v. California,"* The Oyez Project at IIT Chicago-Kent College of Law, accessed February 26, 2012, http://www.oyez.org/cases/1970–1979/1971/1971_70_73.

17. *"Morse v. Frederick,"* The Oyez Project at IIT Chicago-Kent College of Law, accessed February 26, 2012, http://www.oyez.org/cases/2000–2009/2006/2006_06_278.

18. *"New York Times v. Sullivan,"* The Oyez Project at IIT Chicago-Kent College of Law, accessed February 26, 2012, http://www.oyez.org/cases/1960–1969/1963/1963_39.

19. *"New York Times v. United States,"* The Oyez Project at IIT Chicago-Kent College of Law, accessed February 26, 2012, http://www.oyez.org/cases/1970-1979/1970/1970_1873.

20. *"R.A.V. v. St. Paul,"* The Oyez Project at IIT Chicago-Kent College of Law, accessed February 26, 2012, http://www.oyez.org/cases/1990–1999/1991/1991_90_7675.

21. *"Roberts v. U.S. Jaycees,"* The Oyez Project at IIT Chicago-Kent College of Law, accessed February 26, 2012, http://www.oyez.org/cases/1980–1989/1983/1983_83_724.

22. *"Santa Fe Independent School District v. Doe,"* The Oyez Project at IIT Chicago-Kent College of Law, accessed February 26, 2012, http://www.oyez.org/cases/1990-1999/1999/1999_99_62.

23. *"Stanley v. Georgia,"* The Oyez Project at IIT Chicago-Kent College of Law, accessed February 26, 2012, http://www.oyez.org/cases/1960–1969/1968/1968_293.

24. *"United States v. O'Brien,"* The Oyez Project at IIT Chicago-Kent College of Law, accessed February 26, 2012, http://www.oyez.org/cases/1960–1969/1967/1967_232.

25. *"Texas v. Johnson,"* The Oyez Project at IIT Chicago-Kent College of Law, accessed February 26, 2012, http://www.oyez.org/cases/1980–1989/1988/1988_88_155.

26. *"Tinker v. Des Moines Independent Community School District,"* The Oyez Project at IIT Chicago-Kent College of Law, accessed February 26, 2012, http://www.oyez.org/cases/1960–1969/1968/1968_21.

27. *"West Virginia State Board of Education v. Barnette,"* The Oyez Project at IIT Chicago-Kent College of Law, accessed February 26, 2012, http://www.oyez.org/cases/1940-1949/1942/1942_591.

28. *"Whitney v. California,"* The Oyez Project at IIT Chicago-Kent College of Law, accessed February 26, 2012, http://www.oyez.org/cases/1901–1939/1925/1925_3.

29. *"Wisconsin v. Yoder,"* The Oyez Project at IIT Chicago-Kent College of Law, accessed February 26, 2012, http://www.oyez.org/cases/1970–1979/1971/1971_70_110.

30. *"Yates v. United States,"* The Oyez Project at IIT Chicago-Kent College of Law, accessed February 26, 2012, http://www.oyez.org/cases/1950–1959/1956/1956_6.